BETWEEN VIRTUE AND POWER

JOHN KANE

Between
Virtue and Power

THE PERSISTENT MORAL DILEMMA OF U.S. FOREIGN POLICY

YALE UNIVERSITY PRESS   NEW HAVEN & LONDON

Set in Scala and Scala Sans by Duke & Company, Devon, Pennsylvania.
Printed in the United States of America by Vail-Ballou Press, Binghamton, New York.

Library of Congress Cataloging-in-Publication Data

Kane, John, 1945 Apr. 18–
Between virtue and power : the persistent moral dilemma of U.S. foreign policy /
John Kane.
p.   cm.
Includes bibliographical references and index.

ISBN 978-0-300-13712-5 (cloth : alk. paper) 1. United States—Foreign relations. 2. United States—
Foreign relations—Moral and ethical aspects. 3. United States—Foreign relations—Philosophy.
4. United States—Territorial expansion. 5. Imperialism—History. 6. Virtue—Political aspects—
United States—History. 7. Power (Social sciences)—United States—History. I. Title.
E183.7.K343 2008
327.73—dc22   2008010955

A catalogue record for this book is available from the British Library.

The paper in this book meets the guidelines for permanence and durability of the Committee
on Production Guidelines for Book Longevity of the Council on Library Resources.

10 9 8 7 6 5 4 3 2 1

For Matt, who will one day have a book of his own.

CONTENTS

Preface   ix

1 Introduction   1

2 Origins and Significance of the American Mythology   18

3 Founding a Virtuous Republic   32

4 Problems of Virtue and Power   50

5 Nonentanglement: The Economic Dimension   66

6 Nonentanglement: The Political Dimension   81

7 Innocent Virtue and the Conquest of a Continent   98

8 From Imperialism to World Peace   123

9 Woodrow Wilson and the Reign of Virtue   144

10 Disillusionment and Hope   165

11 American Isolation 181

12 American Virtue and the Soviet Challenge 200

13 Anticommunism and American Virtue 222

14 Cold War Ironies 238

15 Vietnam: Virtue Stained, Power Humbled 261

16 Putting Humpty Together Again 278

17 Offended Innocence, Righteous Wrath 303

Epilogue 330

Notes 337

Index 393

PREFACE

THIS BOOK BEGAN, in a proximate sense, with a thesis on the American presidency that I pursued in a previous work, *The Politics of Moral Capital* (Cambridge University Press, 2001), and later extended in an article that incorporated the geostrategic plans of the Bush administration (*Presidential Studies Quarterly* 33 [4], 2003: 772–800). An anonymous reviewer of that article presumed and hoped it was the prelude to a book, which got me thinking along that track.

Yet, in a deeper sense, the present volume is the long-ripening fruit of the puzzlement and pain felt by a youth in Australia long ago, during the heyday of the Vietnam War. I vividly remember the moment, reading *Time* magazine, when my eye fell on a small monochrome photo of a truckload of troops passing through the Vietnamese countryside, a soldier at the rear aiming his rifle outward. The caption read something like "U.S. soldier takes a potshot at peasant working his field." This casual atrocity struck me more deeply with horror than any ordinary act of inhumanity because it was committed by *an American.* Until then, it had been an article of faith with me—someone raised on a diet of American books, comics, music, television, and movies—that Americans were always and inevitably *the good guys.*

Many years later, researching that era, it occurred to me that the division and confusion I had experienced mirrored the deep divisions and confusions that afflicted the United States itself during that worst of American wars. The cause was the same: a dismaying dissonance between fact-on-the-ground and mythological expectation. The more I read on America, the more I realized that my painful loss of innocence was a recurring theme in the history of a nation that believed profoundly in the myth of its own innocence and the cosmic importance of maintaining it, especially against the constant threat represented by the profligate use of military power. It was, indeed, a tribute to the resonant success and reach of the American mythology that I, an Australian, should have imbibed it so thoroughly as to feel the same shock at its betrayal.

I could not help but recall my own distant dismay when, in July 2007, I read *New York Times* columnist Bob Herbert's reaction to reports of the maltreatment and murder of Iraqi men, women, and children by U.S. troops. He noted that soldiers who dehumanized the people they were supposed to be fighting for often found, on returning home, that they had dehumanized themselves. "There is no upside to this war," he concluded. "It has been a plague since the beginning. But it's one thing to lose a war. It's much worse for a nation to lose its soul." It was the latest, plaintive expression of the American dilemma of virtue and power that provides the theme for this book, a theme that has seemed to me worthy of extended exploration.

It is conventional to attribute any virtues in a work to people who have advised and commented on it along the way while accepting all faults as one's own. The present book has, however, been such a lonesome endeavor that I fear any plaudits as well as all brickbats are due mainly to myself. An exception must be made for Michael Wesley, who generously read and helpfully commented on the manuscript, and to several anonymous referees, whose input was instructive. Thanks for general encouragement goes to Ian Shapiro, George Edwards III, and Haig Patapan, and to my ever-patient wife, Kay, and daughter, Philippa. Special acknowledgment is due to my son Matt, who faithfully read the whole thing and helped in the editing.

My deepest debt, however, is to the legion of historians whose rich and varied output across the whole sweep of American history has provided the essential foundation upon which this edifice of interpretation has been raised. I profoundly hope that my attempt to contribute to a nation's understanding of itself will not be judged wholly unworthy of their immensely fruitful labors.

CHAPTER ONE

Introduction

WHEN GEORGE W. BUSH came to office in 2001, he offered America an apparently bizarre conjunction of qualities to encapsulate his administration's perspective on foreign policy: "strength and humility." "Strength" signaled a Reaganite determination that the United States would "stand tall" in the world and not allow itself to be pushed around. The question was, to what purposes would American strength be put? In his inaugural address, Bush, speaking in the manner of Woodrow Wilson, expressed an intention to defend freedom, democracy, and peace, but not through direct action abroad. Rather, on a traditional assumption that what is good for America is good for the world, these goals would be secured as a second-order effect of a concerted pursuit of "enduring American interests."[1] Bush's understanding of these interests was deeply ideological, and his actions in the months before September 11 revealed a nation prepared to use its strength to pursue them whether the world liked it or not—as often it did not. Many therefore thought his administration more devoted to obstinate pride than to humility.

On a generous reading, however, the promise of humility seemed to signal that America had finally learned the "humbling" lesson of the Vietnam War—namely, that it had no God-given right to shape other nations in its own image as it might choose.[2] Bush's general stance toward the wider world was strictly "hands-off," even when (as in the case of

Israel) this seemed a plain abrogation of responsibility. There would be no "nation-building" on his watch, nor any of that well-intentioned but often bumbling intermediation in the affairs of other nations that had characterized the Clinton era, and which had occasionally, as in Somalia, ended in humiliation and a loss of American prestige.

The phrase "strength and humility" undoubtedly indicated, most immediately, a repudiation of the Clinton administration's attitude to the deployment of American power, but its historical resonance went far deeper. The slogan revealed, in fact, the persistence of a venerable American dilemma over the proper alignment of virtue and power: "strength" was equated obviously with power and pride, and "humility" with virtue in its most Christian form—virtue as "clean hands" or innocence. An enduring article of American faith prescribes both that power be used only for virtuous ends and that American virtue not be sullied in the exercise of power. Only thus can innocence be preserved without offense to honorable pride. Yet an irresolvable tension has marked the relationship between American power and American virtue from the very beginning, causing recurrent uncertainty about the justice of American actions abroad and rendering the national psyche peculiarly vulnerable to doubtful exercises of power. During the Vietnam era, especially, power and virtue seemed radically sundered and woundingly undermined, causing serious injury to both America's pride and its sense of innocence. The Bush formula thus represented the latest rhetorical attempt—a particularly conservative one—to redeem the difficult marriage of power and virtue that America's traditional self-image demanded.

In this book I analyze the problem of aligning American virtue with American power in order to cast light on what many see as the disconcerting tendency of U.S. foreign policy to oscillate between idealism and realism, or idealism and self-interest. Commentators have, according to their predilections, interpreted American professions of idealism as evidence of either rank hypocrisy or incurable naiveté, yet Americans have generally found it impossible to abandon idealism in the conduct of international relations. Some have preferred rather to abandon realism by retreating altogether from the wider world, producing that other familiar American oscillation between "isolationism and engagement." Many others would agree with President Jimmy Carter that idealism and realism must be maintained in careful balance if America is to be true to itself. The deep popular roots of such attitudes have made them the bane of out-and-out realists, for whom U.S. foreign policy presents a perpetual, insoluble conundrum.[3]

Many previous works have tried to explicate the peculiarities of U.S. foreign policy using a variety of conceptual approaches. Some have employed political or ideological categories (liberalism, economism, racism); others have examined different foreign policy "logics" (hegemonism, realism, isolationism, liberal internationalism, anti-imperialism); still others have identified various specifically American foreign policy "traditions" (Hamiltonian, Jeffersonian, Jacksonian, or Wilsonian). In focusing on the central problem of virtue and power, my aim is to gain a better appreciation of how such disparate logics and traditions relate to one another, and to explain why they jostle so interminably and inconclusively in the practice of U.S. foreign policy. It is a problem that arises, I argue, out of a perceived need to maintain the familiar American myth of destiny and mission and to solve the enduring problem of power and virtue that the myth set for American political leaders.[4]

AMERICAN MYTHOLOGY

The distinctive American myth was grounded in British history and Enlightenment hope, affirmed by the nation's founding elites, carefully elaborated by its historians, instilled in its schoolchildren over succeeding generations, attractively portrayed in its popular culture, embraced by its citizens, promulgated to and eagerly accepted by masses well beyond its shores. In this myth, eighteenth-century optimism about human progress was transformed into a national epic that gave America and Americans a transcendent purpose. It was an inspiring narrative of a people selected by Providence from the Old World to found a New World of liberty and hope, not just for themselves but for the entire human race.

James Madison, trying to persuade the states to accept the new federal Constitution in 1787, stressed the universal significance of the American people's creation of a new form of government that gave full rein to human liberty rather than crushing it. He wrote, "posterity will be indebted for the possession, and the world for the example, of the numerous innovations displayed on the American theatre, in favour of private rights and public happiness. . . . Happily for America, happily, we trust, for the whole human race, [Americans] . . . accomplished a revolution which has no parallel in the annals of human society."[5]

An essential premise of the story was that this American experiment in free government was made possible by the fact that American virtue was relatively uncorrupted by the luxuries and rank subordinations that had supposedly degraded Europeans. The United States therefore had the opportunity to demonstrate that a peaceful, popular republic could maintain itself in existence without infringing on the liberties of its citizens. It would do so by designing institutional arrangements that constrained power and by avoiding the endless dynastic wars that had led Europe into militarism and tyranny. By maintaining its virtue and freedom, democratic America would stand as an example to all the world of what any self-governing, self-reliant, industrious individual might achieve in conditions of political liberty and economic opportunity. Abraham Lincoln, who made preservation of the American mission central to his fight in a bitter civil war, put it thus in a eulogy to his political hero, Henry Clay: "Feeling, as he did, and as the truth surely is, that the world's best hope depended on the continued Union of these States . . . he burned with a zeal for its advancement, prosperity and glory, because he saw in such, the advancement, prosperity and glory, of human liberty, human right, and human nature."[6]

Individual Americans thus found themselves flatteringly cast as the dramatis personae in a grand unfolding story that ennobled even their most ordinary endeavors. It followed that the typical American must always be more than just an American; a true American represented the peaceful and prosperous future that was potentially in store for all humankind. To properly portray that future, however, Americans must preserve the distinctive virtue that made their brave experiment possible. This would always prove problematical, especially because the reality of American virtue was questioned even at the founding, and doubts were expressed about its theoretical possibility in a vast commercial republic. Even those who assumed the truth of American virtue, like Thomas Jefferson, harbored excessive fear about its vulnerability to corruption or contamination. Preserving virtue, whatever virtue was understood to be, would present a perpetual problem in relation to both economic development at home and political entanglement abroad.

The fact that belief in superior American virtue survived and persisted was less the result of the determinations of political theory or the lessons of experience than the successful inculcation of the mythology of mission, of which the assumption of virtue was a part. The myth encouraged the view that the American identity, though particular to Americans, was also universal in its revelation of a virtuous human nature liberated from the constraints of custom, superstition, social artifice, and tyranny. It was an understanding that would sometimes make it difficult for Americans to distinguish their own interests and opinions from the differing ones of other peoples.

The myth, being mythical, never accurately described American realities, for the function of myth is not to reflect and report the superficial realities of this or any other moment. The domain of myth is not empirical reality but imagination, and the source of its sustenance is not reason but faith. One of the functions of myth is to provide people with a deeper story, a narrative that can encompass their own individual stories and give them meaning, worth, and hope. In accepting this story, many different individuals feel themselves to be one people, connected by something larger than mere contingency. The American myth was well adapted to a people who, despite commonalities of history and outlook, were divided by class, by multiple creeds, by sectional interests, by provincial and state jealousies, and by an instinct for independence and liberty that often raised the fearful specter of anarchy.[7] It placed the heroically successful revolutionaries in the vanguard of humanity's struggle for individual liberty while simultaneously tying that liberty to the success and longevity of ordered republican government, thus encouraging them toward their more perfect political union. The motto *e pluribus unum* expressed the intention; the myth helped foster the reality. The American mission to defend and extend human liberty was thus coupled to the success of the American union, and the success of the American union identified with the best interests of the whole world.

Such a grandiose claim was not simply a matter of unilateral arrogation on the part of Americans, for they did not alone invent their flattering myth. It had been largely the creation of enlightened Europeans looking hopefully to the New World to descry the possible future of humanity. Americans gratefully adopted it both to help justify their own rebellion and to provide a thread of common meaning for their new nation. But as a consequence of the initial exchange, Europeans, whether in hope or loathing, would ever after have some spiritual-psychological stake in the domestic politics of the United States, a stake the rest of the world would in time come to share. And Americans, by virtue of their mythology, would never be able to disconnect their own progress from that of the world's. Even their frequent insistence on the need for isolation betrayed, paradoxically, this mythical connectedness. America was, at its foundation, deeply implicated in the world and the world in it.

But the practical question was how the nation must act in the world if it was to fulfill its mythical promise. It was a question that had a parallel in that of how best to spread the Protestant gospel (and even overlapped it, for many Americans would hold that spreading Christianity formed an essential part of the national mission). A good Christian could be a witness to the saving grace of Christ simply by living an upright, blamelessly pious life, but militant Protestantism would transform America into an army of God ready to proselytize the whole world. Similar options presented themselves to leaders as they contemplated the national mission. America might either go about its business blamelessly as an exemplary nation or become a crusader for liberty. It was a choice that was never to be finally settled, though for a long time the main preference was for the stance championed by Thomas Jefferson and most famously expressed by John Quincy Adams, who asserted that America did not go looking "for monsters to destroy." Once the United States became a world power, however, example tended to give way to crusade, though never without protest from those who believed that ruin would follow. What was seldom seriously questioned, though, was belief in the myth itself and in America's universal significance.

The much-discussed national peculiarity of America—its resistance to a politics founded on an ideology of class, its ambivalence toward authority, its lack of European-style discourse of the state—was closely connected to the success of this myth. Many writers have, to be sure, explained America's so-called exceptionalism by pointing to its enduring devotion to a "liberal creed" traceable to the seventeenth-century English philosopher John Locke, the elements of which have been named as "liberty, egalitarianism, individualism, populism, and laissez-faire." American liberalism, it has been said, was so ingrained and unchallenged as to be almost unconscious of itself. It constituted an article of faith rather than of rational assent, turning "Americanism" into a quasi-religious doctrine and "un-Americanism" into a national sin. Louis Hartz, indeed, expressed exasperation over what he perceived to be the irrational attachment of

Americans to a rational theory, a blindness that he claimed had certain unfortunate consequences. Hartz argued that the explanation lay in the fact that American liberals, unlike those of Europe, had not had to contend for power with an entrenched aristocratic class and therefore had never been forced to defend their ideology in a way that would have made them acutely conscious of it.[8]

That may be so, but it was also true that Locke's rational theory had, during the revolutionary upheaval, become firmly embedded in the structure of the American myth. The acceptance of this myth did not depend on rational appraisal, but rather on a faith in the path that the founders had marked out and the story that had been adopted to justify it. Belief in American difference was maintained across time because America, to be truly American, had to show what all the world could or must become. "[I]n the beginning," Locke had written, referring to the alleged "natural state" of American Indians, "all the world was America, and more so than it is now."[9] The American myth proclaimed that one day all the world would once again be America, and even more so than it is now.

AMERICAN REALITIES

In this book I take seriously the pervasiveness of this mythology in American political life and its particular influence on U.S. foreign policy. It is important to note at the start, however, that the myth, though enduring, was neither uncontested nor wholly accepted by all sections of the United States. The slave-based, plantation-dominated culture of the Old South (despite the fact that some of its members helped propagate the myth) inevitably developed an alternate, aristocratic mythology founded on an assumption of natural human inequality.[10] It would take a civil war and, a century later, a civil rights movement to vanquish this opponent, and even then not completely. Nor were the shrewd Yankee merchants and manufacturers of New England particularly enamored of a war-averse myth that venerated human equality. They were more sympathetic to Alexander Hamilton's vision of a muscular United States dominated by an economic elite that would act energetically in the defense of international markets.

In the backwoods, meanwhile, egalitarian and democratically inclined Scots-Irish settlers, forever pressing westward, preserved dourly pessimistic cultural and religious attitudes about human nature, as well as more hard-nosed attitudes to the uses of power than were countenanced by the benignly liberal myth (though the myth might be conveniently deployed to justify their expansive ambitions). This group often chafed at the idealistic restrictions imposed by the central mythology and were capable of deforming it into a bitterly parochial Americanism that was reactionary rather than liberal.[11]

The attitudes and actions of these and many other groups combined in historically complex ways to create the actuality of modern America and its values. The defeat of the South, for example, did not extinguish, and indeed inflamed, a belief in human inequality that would underpin southern segregation and find vitriolic expression in movements like the Ku Klux Klan, Citizens' Councils, and the Liberty Lobby. Nor did the Civil War terminate southern traditions of military valor and honor that, during and after the Spanish-American War of 1898, became relocated in the U.S. military establishment, giving rise to "a regional ethos of military service and combative patriotism" that sat in some tension with the pacific American myth. Such an ethos nevertheless could be usefully summoned at times when the nation, its interests, or its pride needed defending. The western settlers, for their part, were the main progenitors of that powerful folk culture whose pride, pragmatism, individualism, tetchiness, and insularity largely defined the character of an authentic American folk-nation.[12] The stubborn parochialism of this American nation chimed poorly with the universalistic premises of the central myth, and the adherence of many of its members to a millenarian expectation of the world's end and final judgment of sinners ran counter to the myth's optimistic account of human progress. Nevertheless, it was in the bosom of such ordinary, salt-of-the-earth folk that Jefferson had discerned, and hoped to see preserved, the essential American virtue.

As for New England, Hamilton might have lost to Jefferson in the battle for the nation's mythological soul, but the Hamiltonian vision was surely fulfilled in the great industrial-commercial state that the United States became. If this represented the triumph of powerful corporations over powerless individuals, and of bureaucratic organization over personal relations, the myth nonetheless served corporate capitalism by sustaining a fundamental belief in freedom, opportunity, and reward for virtuous industry. Americans would always, in the end, prefer to believe that they were their own masters, and that their individual successes and failures were ultimately their own responsibility. It was a part of the myth that would be severely shaken at times, particularly during the Great Depression, but never destroyed.

Adding to this mix were the successive tides of new immigrants, many of them non-Protestants, who adapted to and in various ways modified the character of the United States. Instead of an egalitarian melting pot, they encountered on arrival a nation that was resolutely white, Protestant, and hierarchical in matters of race, religion, and gender (and only mildly ambivalent about matters of class). Though the immigrants were liable to be treated as unwelcome aliens and second- or third-class citizens, their journey to America and their struggles to gain a foothold were an authentic testament to the attractive power of the "American dream" (which is merely the myth under a different name). Woodrow Wilson said, indeed, that these people, by harboring the ideal in their hearts, had kept it alive at times when Americans themselves had forgotten it, and were thus a source of continuous renewal.[13] More problematical was that portion of the population that had been undeniably American for generations and whose massive cultural influence turned American music and dance into globally popular forms. With respect to the myth, the situation of black Americans represented the greatest, most glaring anomaly both before and after the Civil War, and even after the civil rights movement of the 1960s had promised to end the long road up from slavery. The determined resistance of white America to genuine black assimilation produced a reactive hostility that would see blacks becoming *African* Americans, and many of them disciples of Islam proclaiming the existence of a separate black nation.

The discriminations that mar U.S. history may seem to invite cynicism about a myth that valorizes equality and the advancement of people of whatever gender, creed, color, or class. And indeed, continued allegiance to the myth has often exposed Americans to the charge of sheer bad faith. From early in the nineteenth century, when visitors from Europe came curious to observe firsthand the brave American experiment, they often expressed shock at the blatant hypocrisy of Anglo-Americans with regard to their own ideals. Mrs. Fanny Trollope, for instance, declared that she might have respected Americans despite their rough manners and peculiar customs but "it is impossible for any mind of common honesty not to be revolted by the contradictions in their principles and practice.

. . . You will see them with one hand hoisting the cap of liberty and with the other flogging the slaves. You will see them one hour lecturing . . . on the indefeasible rights of man, and the next driving from their homes the children of the soil [Indians], whom they have bound themselves to protect by the most solemn promises."[14]

The American myth often functioned better for ideological self-deception than as a spur to moral progress. More disturbing than hypocrisy or self-deception, however, was the conscious deformation of the myth to accommodate Anglo-American prejudices. During the nineteenth century, under the impulse of Darwinian sociology and "scientific" racism in an era of renascent imperialism, some Americans recast the myth as the doctrine of Manifest Destiny that excluded whole categories of people from its purview while only imperfectly including others. Teddy Roosevelt's robust racism, expressed with his customary candor, underpinned his virile, imperialistic view of the national destiny, but even the anti-imperialistic Christian humanitarianism of Woodrow Wilson frankly excluded American Indians and blacks from the exemplary American nation. Such groups could have no role in the grand narrative other than that of either impediments to or burdens on its progress.

The tendency of the myth on those whom it definitely embraced, meanwhile, was to induce complacency about their own superior virtue. Virtue was accepted as something one had, not by dint of any effort, but simply by being a "true" American. The American character might be supposed universal, but Anglo-Americans had a natural tendency to see their virtue as inherent and unique and their "chosenness" as something other than the result of historical accident. The popular refrain that Americans were God's own people in God's own country smacked unavoidably of Calvinistic election. Anglo-Americans were sometimes inclined to see themselves not simply as the exemplary bearers of universal civic and political values and thus as witnesses to the world of their validity, but as a people uniquely qualified to embody and fulfill them.

These partial and particularistic versions of the American myth and of American virtue confused but never annihilated the universalistic conception—nor could they, without undercutting the essential American world mission that was the myth's core. Despite institutional oppression and stubborn prejudice, despite exclusivist interpretations, the original myth survived to constitute a permanent remonstration and a perennial promise to which all Americans could make effective ideological appeal when political conditions allowed—from Elizabeth Cady Stanton for women in 1848 to Martin Luther King for black Americans in 1963.[15] It was significant that arguments and contests over labor, gender, and racial relations in the United States were not, as elsewhere, structured in purely moral or ideological terms but more typically as arguments over the real meaning of the central mythology or, as the Progressive Herbert Croly put it, *The Promise of American Life*. "An America which is not the Land of Promise," Croly wrote, "which was not informed by a prophetic outlook and a more or less constructive ideal, would not be the America bequeathed to us by our forefathers." Samuel Huntington said: "America is not a lie: it is a disappointment. But it can be a disappointment only because it is also a hope." Huntington, following Hartz, located that hope in Americans' singular adherence to their "liberal creed," but the myth of America was the vehicle that conveyed that creed across time. And the mythical narrative was after all a progressive one, marking out a destiny to be achieved rather than denoting a timeless state of being. It was capacious enough at its foundations to allow the hope that current prejudices would be overcome at last and that excluded groups could make good on a premise of equality, liberty, and the right to happiness that, in itself, admitted no exceptions. Lincoln gave all honor to Thomas Jefferson for basing the Declaration of Independence on an "abstract truth, applicable to all men of all times, and so to embalm it there, that today, and in all coming days, it shall be a rebuke and a stumbling block to the very harbingers of reappearing tyranny and oppression."[16]

This was one reason why, despite cynicism, the original myth survived, apparently indestructible. Huntington argued that it is precisely the persistent gap between ideal and reality that made the United States different, and made its political history one of "repetition of new beginnings and flawed outcomes, promise and disillusion, reform and reaction."[17] So if at times America's myth seemed to disappear from view, sunk under a sordid weight of discrimination, violence, meanness, corruption, self-absorption, materialism, and political pettiness, it nevertheless proved its resilience by its capacity for revival at moments of crisis, when it could be employed to recall the nation to its true nature and destiny.

It also, however, presented perennial challenges to American leaders who had perforce to keep the mythical faith alive by preserving some semblance of innocent virtue. American innocence has been declared lost on numerous occasions—during the War of 1812, the Mexican War of 1845, the Civil War; during the period of U.S. imperialism; in the fields of Flanders during World War I; above Hiroshima and Nagasaki during World War II; with the assassination of John F. Kennedy in 1963; in the paddy fields of Vietnam and the cell blocks of Abu Ghraib prison in Iraq. But American innocence, being a mythical quality, could be many times lost and just as frequently regained as long as faith was constantly renewed.

But if faith betrayed may summon renewal, faith shattered induces grief, confusion, and despair. I contend in this book that America's mythological faith suffered a severe blow in the mid-twentieth century from which it has never fully recovered. Much of U.S. history since then had been marked by explicit or tacit attempts to either restore that faith or deny it was ever really damaged. It is to elucidate this moral crisis that I have chosen the mythological theme of virtue and power as a vehicle for exploring U.S. foreign policy from its inception to the present day.

THE ARGUMENT OF THE BOOK IN SUMMARY

This book argues that the distinctive American mythology incorporated certain tensions and contradictions that produced a persistent and consequential moral dilemma for U.S. foreign policy that continues to the present. At the heart of this dilemma was a tangle of attitudes concerning power and virtue that formed part of America's intellectual and emotional inheritance. Americans nursed a grave suspicion of power because power threatened individual liberty and endangered virtue, yet simultaneously they maintained that the growth of American power was a natural product of American virtue, the just desert of industrious labor in an abundant land. If virtue led to great power, how was that power to be used so as not to destroy virtue? This question seemed so bedeviling because the American conception of virtue was itself mixed and contradictory.

Much has been written about the significance of civic republican virtue to the American founders, but as important for the argument of this book is the idea of *virtue as innocence* that the American mythology also fostered. This idea, highly influential on Jeffersonian thought, derived from an Enlightenment attitude that combined Christian benevolence with Rousseau's notion of natural innocence. Such virtue aligned readily with a transcendent American nationalism founded on a providential myth of mission that benevolently embraced all humanity, and which required the United States to show qualities of selflessness and humility in its relations with the world. Such innocent virtue stood in considerable tension, however, with a virile republicanism that dignified stern martial virtues. Republican virtue aligned more readily with a fiercely parochial nationalism that exalted the particular nation at the expense of the universal, emphasizing qualities of self-assertion and patriotic pride.

Yet both forms of virtue (for different reasons that were seldom clearly distinguished in American minds) fostered distrust of military power. Civic republicanism, though resolute in defense of country, harbored the fear that armies and navies raised to defend the nation might quickly turn into instruments of domestic tyranny, causing a fatal forfeit of liberty. Transcendent nationalism, on the other hand, regarded any exercise of military power, even in justified defense, as inherently brutalizing and thus destructive of innocent virtue. Since the corruption of virtue in either case appeared to threaten the American mission—through either loss of liberty or loss of innocence—policies of nonmilitarization and non-entanglement with foreign nations (endlessly embroiled in brutal wars and corrupting power politics) had a wide and enduring appeal.

Such fears led, in the nineteenth century, to a policy of "isolationism" that was really one of political nonentanglement with other nations, meaning the avoidance of formal treaty alliances that might drag the new nation into foreign wars that could only damage it. This was, at least in part, a way of avoiding the corrupting influence of Old Europe and thus keeping the American mission alive. But isolationism was always a misnomer because isolation was compromised from the start by a commitment to economic engagement. Trade was the nation's lifeblood and one aspect of its genius, and trade had to be defended. In an effort to secure its trade from the depredations of warring trading partners without reliance on a large standing navy, the United States very early adopted a policy of neutrality among combatants, which proved hopelessly unrealistic whenever seriously tested. During the nineteenth century, Americans found that protection of trade routes (as well as the penetration of new markets once capitalist production burgeoned) necessitated repeated deployments of U.S. forces and thus a steady growth of military power. Indeed, economic expansion and integration turned the United States into a potential world power, confronting it with the moral problem of how to dispose of its newfound might in ways that seemed compatible with its benevolent mission.

This choice was usually presented in stark terms that pictured power and virtue as antithetical: *either* power *or* virtue. Reflecting this supposed antithesis, Americans tended to divide into two broad camps on matters of foreign policy (these would become known as the conservative and liberal positions, respectively). The first preferred, when the chips were down, to emphasize power in the defense of U.S. interests, prestige, and pride; the second was more tenderly concerned to maintain clean hands for the sake of innocent virtue. Yet both groups remained opposed to entangling alliances with other nations for fear of contamination and corruption, though each understood the danger differently. Conservatives claimed they just wanted the world to leave America alone; liberals wanted to play an enlightened leadership role without compromising nonentanglement. Neither could be reasonably described as "realist," such was the pervasive spell of the mythology. Even an allegedly rare American realist like Teddy Roosevelt could not dispense with the myth, though he tried to recast it on the model of late-nineteenth-century imperialisms—national aggrandizement covered by the moral fig leaf of a "civilizing mission." This never succeeded long or well with an anti-imperialist public too deeply imbued with the idea of a more selfless and exemplary mission. Moreover, when U.S. military actions abroad stained innocent virtue, especially in a cause that seemed less than wholly just, policy makers at home came under serious critical fire. This was a recurring pattern from the time of the American takeover of the Philippines in 1898 to the invasion of Iraq in 2003.

These highly conflicted feelings explained why it seemed urgent and necessary at the start of the twentieth century to reconcile burgeoning American power, with all its responsibilities and opportunities, with American virtue, whose maintenance was central to the nation's raison d'être. Yet reconciliation proved difficult. The failure of Woodrow Wilson's anguished response to the problem—that American power might be properly deployed for selfless ends like securing world peace, defending democracy, and safeguarding human rights—produced profound disillusionment. After the political battle over the League of Nations had been lost, it seemed on reflection that the United States had put itself at hazard in a great European conflict merely to prove the old truth that involvement in war was incompatible with the maintenance of virtue.

Americans fell back on their traditional isolationism (still, in reality, political nonentanglement, since isolation was tempered before the Great Depression with economic internationalism).

Isolationism was, however, discredited by America's failure to halt the rise of fascism in Europe and Japan and thus to prevent another destructive world war. It seemed vanquished once and for all when a victorious America emerged from that war as the most powerful nation on earth. After World War II, a so-called liberal consensus developed around a willingness to use American power to resist evil and to underwrite multilateral organizations designed to preserve world peace and order. Fascism had proved that the power of evildoers could be countered only by the power of good people, who must be prepared permanently to mobilize their power to ensure general security and universal prosperity. The power-virtue dilemma seemed at last resolved: the power of American virtue ensured the virtuousness of American power.

This happy resolution was, however, soon derailed by the onset of the Cold War. In this ideological conflict, American virtue became dangerously identified with a rigid anticommunism that had searing consequences at home. Meanwhile, the nation became deeply embroiled in balance of great power politics that necessitated actions and engagements seemingly incompatible with innocent virtue. The dilemma reasserted itself most bitterly and consequentially in Vietnam, where the war wounded pride by undermining the credibility of American power and sapped confidence in virtue by staining American innocence. U.S. foreign policy after Vietnam became, in important part, a struggle by both Democratic and Republican administrations to repair this moral injury by restoring confidence in American virtue while trying to allay the deep uncertainty that Vietnam had bequeathed concerning the proper disposition of still-preponderant American power.

This disabling uncertainty caused great resentment among conservatives of the old school. Though very few of them were any longer genuine isolationists, the spirit of isolationism survived among them but in altered form. The main issue was no longer isolation-versus-entanglement but rather unilateralism-versus-multilateralism (along lines established by the 1919 debate over the League of Nations). Conservatives preferred unilateralism, which was merely the old nonentanglement doctrine come to terms at last with the opportunities presented by America's great power. A proud America with the capacity to act decisively in the world must not let itself be contaminated by entangling alliances, even with friendly nations, but must remain free to choose the terms and occasions of its engagement. Since America was by mythological definition good, so would be the results of its uses of power, even hegemonic power. This developing conservative view was reinforced by the Manichean circumstances of the Cold War (communism must not be simply "contained" but "rolled back") and by hostility toward a United Nations critical of America's segregated social arrangements. It would be further strengthened by formerly leftist neoconservatives whose anticommunism caused them to migrate to the Right, bringing with them a missionary zeal lacking in old conservatism. The result was a new style of conservatism that urged unilateral engagement, that repudiated defensive inwardness and aimed at reconfiguring the whole world so as to consolidate forever the benign dominance of U.S. power.

In the early twenty-first century, a fortuitous confluence of neoconservative idealists, old-style conservatives resentful of the shackling of U.S. military might post-Vietnam, and an insular president whose mind was made receptive by the stunning attacks of September 11, 2001, gave the engaged unilateralists their chance. The eventual result was the war in Iraq.

The trumped-up reasons given for a war of preemption would have mattered little had a peacefully democratic Iraq been established after a brief, victorious conflict that toppled the dictator. This was never in the cards. The administration's willingness to intervene with force did not imply abandonment of the principle of nonentanglement, either in the conduct of the invasion (which disparaged the U.N. and even old allies, relying only on a decidedly subservient "coalition of the willing") or, more disastrously, in its aftermath. The American lack of postwar planning and consequent failure to assert authority—leaving a vacuum that allowed the drift toward insurgency—were not accidental but purposely willed by top members of the administration, according to whose ideological lights American responsibility was limited to delivering Iraqis their freedom from tyranny. The United States might indulge in "regime change" but was emphatically not into "nation-building." The dominant view was that U.S. power could be deployed without cost to benefit a nation, thereafter a region, and ultimately the world, all without the necessity of America becoming entangled in prolonged occupation and government of a foreign state. When contaminating entanglement was the actual outcome, Americans renewed their reputation as imperialists, albeit bizarrely incompetent ones. The administration's hubristic confidence in American power had run aground on its own failure to comprehend the dimensions and complexities of the task it had undertaken or to provide the means necessary to accomplish it.

Compounding this failure in the deployment of power, a self-consciously tough administration revealed an almost preternatural blindness to the damage done to innocent virtue by repudiation of the Geneva Conventions, use of torture, extraordinary rendition, Guantánamo detainment, and so on. America's moral stock plummeted as it had not since Vietnam. Anti-Americanism grew apace. If the Cold War and Vietnam had shattered the post–World War II conjunction of virtue and power that underpinned the liberal consensus, Iraq had more swiftly smashed the too-easy conservative assurance of the virtuous efficacy of American power. Once again, power had been discredited and virtue sullied. The ancient dilemma remained unresolved, the American mission was again in grave doubt, and U.S. foreign policy was plunged once more into deep uncertainty.

CHAPTER TWO

Origins and Significance of the American Mythology

THE IDEA OF AMERICA'S justificatory mission is an historically embedded article of national faith. Like all faiths, it can be expected to impose certain constraints upon the faithful even as it opens to them certain possibilities. Faith may be a malleable constraint, but it is a constraint nevertheless, conditioning what actions may be deemed acceptable or otherwise. Contrarily, it may also, when it has an enduring hold on masses of people, be wielded by political leaders as a powerful political instrument. If the American faith was originally adopted and promulgated by elites (not necessarily in *bad* faith) for the sake of fostering political unity and conformity, it has ever since acted as a constraint upon governing elites and the actions they may safely take. Keepers of the true flame, whose number has included many of America's most prominent leaders, have guarded and nurtured the faith across the generations. Less idealistic politicians have had no choice but to accommodate it by rationalizing their actions in the light of it. If it has often been manipulatively or ritualistically deployed by politicians for their own purposes, it has also had to be carefully negotiated to avoid backlash. Its persistent refrain can be heard both in America's unchanging rhetoric of hope and in the inevitable dismay that many of its citizens express when the nation seems to betray its own mission.

In pursuing the effects of the exalted but problematic national ideal across succeeding generations, this book assumes, quite obviously, that culture and ideas are causally important in history.[1] While seeking to avoid oversimplifying the complex intentions, understandings, and political motives of U.S. leaders over two hundred years—and while certainly not pretending to provide exhaustive explanations of U.S. foreign policy over such a period—it nevertheless wishes to show that a dilemma centered on virtue and power played a real and recurrent role, especially in the field of foreign policy. I begin by examining more closely the nature and origins of the American mythology and its relationship to ideological thought.

TRADITIONS, IDEOLOGIES, AND MYTHOLOGIES

Most scholars who have explored ideas in U.S. history have made "traditions" their main objects of study. Many have naturally stressed the dominance of the liberal, or liberal democratic, tradition; others have asserted a rival republican tradition; Rogers Smith, on the other hand, has delineated a tradition he calls "American ascriptivism" whose tenets of cultural, racial, and sexual inequality contradict liberalism.[2] At the core of each of these traditions is a particular set of specifically *ideological* beliefs and values. In liberalism, it is an assumption of human equality, the rule of law, limited government, individual rights, and a free market; in republicanism, it is civic virtue, popular sovereignty, and government regulation for a definable public good; in ascriptivism, it is the presumption of the natural inequality of human beings and the consequent need for various hierarchical discriminations in society. Though each ideology indicates certain basic political and economic roles and the rights of people eligible to fill them, to become traditions each must be embodied in functioning social, legal, and political institutions. In Smith's view, sexism, racism, and ethnocentrism constitute genuine American traditions (rather than merely the residual prejudices of imperfectly enlightened people) precisely because they have been systematically embedded in numerous political, legislative, and judicial decisions over historical time.

If specifically ideological beliefs gain practical effect by becoming thus embedded in living traditions, what can be said of the ideas that constitute myths? Smith argued that the myth of mission during the Progressive era comforted an electorate composed largely of middle-class white men who "found reassuring the fact that this mission justified keeping the poorer classes, the nonwhite races, and women in subordinate places for the foreseeable future, even if it promised more freedom and equality eventually to those who proved worthy." But this is to say that the myth worked *ideologically* to sustain particular sociopolitical relations, even if ideology is here conceived as "false consciousness." Indeed, anthropologists inform us that myths generally function in just this political manner, though they do so through narratives that foster a sense of collective meaning and identity rather than by expounding a rationally argued political philosophy. Myth might indeed be conceived as an ancient, narrative, and nonrationalistic form of ideology. Equally, however, ideology might be seen as a modern, highly rationalized form of myth, for ideologies are typically deeply impregnated with narrative meaning (consider the liberal story of freely contracting agents in a state of nature, or the Marxist vision of humanity's progress from primitive communism via the travail of history to higher communism, surely a secularized version of the Christian millennial narrative).[3]

It may be that faith in some form of narrative myth is necessary to sustain meaning among purposively intelligent creatures for whom no meaning is unequivocally given. Thomas Heilke puts it thus: "Because we are contingent beings who are temporally constituted, we need narrative to make sense of our existence. Indeed, our temporal existence means that our lives are at root narratively formed, so that the narratives we render to make sense of our existence are but reflections of the deeper narrative—elusive as *that* may be—that *is* our existence."[4]

The greatest illusion of all is, perhaps, that held by certain Enlightenment philosophers that we might live solely according to "reason."[5] The Enlightenment elevation of reason itself constituted a faith, one most conspicuously embodied in the idea of progress. Robert Palmer has written: "A sense of progress was both a 'cause' of the French Revolution, as Condorcet held, and also a rationalization and excuse for its violence. It has been an intellectual concept and an optimistic emotion. It has been a thought and a form of energy; it has operated both at a conscious level and in an unconscious zone in which attitudes of confidence in the future are formed."[6] Does this describe an ideology or a mythology? Obviously, it is both simultaneously. The idea of progress had empirical foundations in the astonishing advances made in the new sciences and the invention of new products and techniques promoting economic growth and affording greater material comfort. These fostered confidence in the human capacity for continuous social and self-improvement, even toward perfection, and supplied the arguments that Enlightenment philosophers forged into an ideological weapon with which to assault the repressive obscurantism of the Old Regime. Progress was a liberating idea that radically energized European civilization, drawing its force from the faith that ever-larger numbers of people put in its new, hopeful narrative. That the idea of progress was indeed a faith (and not simply a fact to be acknowledged) became clear when that faith was challenged and seriously shaken by later philosophical critiques on the limits of human reason and by some of the more disturbing consequences of technological advancement.

Since the American mythology was a product of the European Enlightenment, it is hardly surprising that this same faith lay at its core. Universal progress, both moral and material, was central to the liberalism that so deeply penetrated American political thought, and central also to America's understanding of itself as a distinctive nation with an exemplary role in furthering human progress. In the cauldron of ideas stirred by the American Revolution, rational political argument of a very high order and mythological belief became inseparably mixed. It seemed less true, in the aftermath, to describe the American political faith as an ideology supported by myth than as a powerful myth built around a rational ideology.

Having a national myth that embodied a universalistic ideology gave a peculiar cast to American nationalism. Americans were encouraged to believe that their own nationalism was quite distinct from the ethnocultural nationalism coming into fashion in Europe at the time of the American founding. It is for this reason that many Americans still believe themselves impervious to modern critiques that label ethnocultural nationalism a form of irrationalism.[7] The distinguishing feature of American nationalism allegedly lies in its rejection of parochial attachments to blood and soil in favor of attachment to an ideology that promised the liberation of all humanity. If it can be called nationalism at all, it is a peculiarly *transcendent* nationalism. The United States, it has been repeatedly and sincerely claimed, is exceptional in being founded on an *idea* of universal significance.

This claim, rather than being accepted as simply true, must itself be regarded as part of America's mythological self-understanding. This is not to say it has been inconsequential, for defining the particular American nation in universalistic terms has had profound effects, especially when that idea clashed with America's more prosaic and parochial form of nationalism. The amalgamation of myth and ideology that the "Idea of America" represents is indeed absolutely crucial to the theme of virtue and power that I pursue in this book.

THE NATURE AND ORIGINS OF THE AMERICAN MYTH

All nations have their cherished myths, but the United States has been a particularly fruitful generator of them. It has produced versions of most of the myths recognized as common among nations: of foundation, of election, of military valor, of rebirth and renewal, of territory, of redemption and suffering, of kinship and shared descent.[8]

The central myth, however, was that of America as the proving ground for political values believed universally applicable. The main thrust of this myth was to prove the ability of a virtuous people to constitutionally establish and defensively maintain a free government on the earth. Such a government would be dedicated to the development of a new kind of independent, self-choosing human being, one defined by individual effort and personal capacity rather than by an accident of birth. America's unique role was to demonstrate to a weary world what human individuals could achieve when freed from the power of despotic government and the weight of inherited privilege. The "virgin" wilderness of North America, uncontaminated by the prejudices and oppressions of ancient Europe, was believed to be the ideal natural setting for this noble experiment.

Abraham Lincoln declared that one of his reasons for hating slavery, besides its monstrous injustice, was that it "deprives our republican example of its just influence in the world." His satisfaction at the removal of the anomaly grew from a profound hope that the now unconstrained American example would show that, under conditions of political and economic freedom, every person with average practical sense and a normal desire to improve his or her lot could achieve prosperity and happiness. Indeed, this highly individualistic belief gave birth to yet another pervasive and distinctively American myth valorizing the "self-made man": the *myth of success*, and of deserved success at that. The faith that people could create their own destinies by dint of individual effort and determination retained a powerful hold on the minds of ordinary Americans even when, in an industrial age, their actual thralldom to gigantic enterprises seemed to contradict it.[9]

It is important to recognize that this Idea of America predates the birth of the United States and was in fact a theme of Voltaire and the French philosophes from the 1730s onward. In the period between 1767 (when colonial Americans rose up against the Stamp Act imposed on them by the British government) and 1775, Americans, according to one historian, came to symbolize "the dream of a new order, in which men would escape from poverty, injustice, and corruption and dwell together in universal liberty, equality, and fraternity."[10] For several crucial decades, every development in American politics was closely scrutinized for the meaning it held for France and Europe. The significance of this attention for America itself, as both benefit and burden, can hardly be underestimated. There was huge diplomatic value in a hopeful image that encouraged Europeans to give the financial and material assistance so necessary for the success of the Revolution. Benjamin Franklin, an immensely popular ambassador to France, understood and exploited this well. Yet to be entrusted with creating a model society and turning philosophical dreams into reality was a heavy responsibility indeed.

Americans nevertheless laid hold of that responsibility, turning the European dream into a founding myth of their new republic. The result was that Americans would never be able to disconnect their own domestic progress from the fate of the whole world, and the world would, to a remarkable extent, return the compliment. Such a choice was influenced partly by the fact that influential members of the American elite were members of the Enlightenment fraternity, imbued with its philosophical optimism; Thomas Jefferson's commitments could be seen plainly in the Declaration of Independence. Yet the thirteen colonies had not rebelled in order to realize a philosophical ideal but to defend their own specific interests and their ancient rights and liberties as Britons under custom, law, and charter against a tyrannous British parliament. This perspective inevitably altered, however, as rebellion took a more radical turn and the decision was made to assert independence. Independence made the appeal to English constitutional rights vain, and resort to the rhetoric of natural rights expedient (a transition made easier by the assumption that such natural rights anyway formed the "fundamental law" underlying the British constitution).[11] But America's bold proclamation of Enlightenment ideals further encouraged already sympathetic Europeans to view the rebellion as a noble experiment in republican government, the inauguration of an age of universal liberty. Americans in their turn were increasingly encouraged to see themselves as they were refracted through the hopeful European gaze.

Reinforcing this westward projection of European dreams was the colonists' inheritance of English political traditions. In fact, the two strands were intertwined, for Montesquieu and Voltaire had long ago made it a convention of Enlightenment thought that England was the great exemplar of civil and political liberty. During the 1760s, however, the constitutional balance that supposedly preserved this liberty seemed threatened by encroachments of the crown under George III. English jeremiads, for which the colonists had a hearty appetite, instructed them on the increasing corruption and immorality of English social and political life, reinforcing the impression that the mother country had lost the virtue needed to sustain her own and her subjects' liberties. Even more alarmingly, English corruption seemed to be spreading like a cancer to the colonies themselves. The self-sacrificing emotions and actions provoked by revolution raised the hope that a moral reformation might nevertheless be possible and that republican virtue might be reclaimed in America. The colonists could imagine themselves picking up the torch of liberty that was falling from the corrupt English grasp. English émigré Thomas Paine declared in *Common Sense,* the pamphlet that galvanized popular revolutionary opinion in America, that Americans had it in their power to begin the world over again, freedom having been generally "hunted from the globe": "Europe regards her like a stranger, and England hath given her warning to depart. O! receive the fugitive and prepare in time an asylum for mankind." It was but a short imaginative step for the rebel colonists to move from the defense of their own particular liberties to the defense of Liberty as such.[12]

The fact that even the admired English system could lend itself to tyranny implied that progress toward true liberty in the world had yet some way to go. America, by accepting the burden of establishing it more securely, assumed a new and glorious role in a grand historical narrative of Liberty's progress. Americans found support for this role in English radical Whig and Dissenting traditions of political thought to which, before the Revolution, they had often turned. Prominent English Dissenters encouraged the colonists to see their own struggles and constitutional endeavors in millennial terms. The opinions of Richard Price, a friend of

Franklin's, were both representative and influential, for he was widely read in America. Price argued that, next to the introduction of Christianity, the American Revolution might be the most important step in the progressive course of human improvement. It is worth quoting his words of rejoicing at the victorious conclusion of the Revolution, for they express the essential features of the American myth of mission: "[I]n its termination, the war has done still greater good . . . by providing, in a sequestered continent possessed of many singular advantages, a place of refuge for opprest [sic] men in every region of the world, and by laying the foundation there of an empire which may be the seat of liberty, science and virtue, and from whence there is reason to hope these sacred blessings will spread till they become universal and the time arrives when kings and priests shall have no more power to oppress, and that ignominious slavery which has hitherto debased the world exterminated. I therefore think I see the hand of Providence in the late war working for the general good."[13]

The convergence between the apocalyptic religious views of a man like Price and those of secular Frenchmen like A.-R.-J. Turgot and the Marquis de Condorcet (the great prophet of human progress who was averse to all religion, but especially Christianity) meant that Americans, whether conventionally religious or not, could find intellectual support for a singular, appealing image of the national mission. In 1782, St. John de Crèvecoeur, a Frenchman who had farmed in New York State, drew an idealized picture of the American "new man" as an amalgam of all the hopes of the European Enlightenment: simplicity, virtue, equality, naturalness, tolerance, liberty, humanitarianism, a desire for political reform, and a symbol of unlimited individual opportunity. In 1786, Condorcet emphasized the promise of material progress, the inevitable result as he saw it of the enlightenment, equality, and liberty that Americans enjoyed. "It is not enough," he wrote, "that the rights of man be written in the books of philosophers and inscribed in the hearts of virtuous men; the weak and ignorant must be able to read them in the example of a great nation. America has given us this example."[14]

French praise of America was sometimes so extravagant as to embarrass the Americans themselves and draw appeals for moderation from Franklin, Paine, and Jefferson. Nevertheless, the hopeful and flattering French projection inevitably made a deep impression on the American heart and soul. As Americans suffered the deprivations and injuries of revolutionary warfare, they could take comfort from Europeans who believed that the colonists had acted on pure principle and not from motives of self-interest. As Gordon Wood concluded: "[Americans] could only be flattered by the portrait, 'so very flattering to us,' that the Enlightenment had painted of them. Whatever the social reality may have been—and on examination it did not seem inconsistent—they could not help believing that America was what Europe said it was. Everywhere they looked there was confirmation of what the Enlightenment and the English radicals had said about them."[15]

Once the common struggle had ended, however, there was more to divide newly independent states fearful of the domination of a central power than to bring them together in an ideal republic. The principal worry that plagued European sympathizers during these early years was that such a loose federation would descend swiftly into anarchy, creating conditions conducive to the rise of dictatorship. Even after the Philadelphia delegates of 1787 had achieved their "more perfect union," the new United States remained a state with no "natural" sense of popular nationhood. When Jefferson referred to "my country," even as president, he meant Virginia. Moreover, some of the revolutionists, like Paine and Joel Barlow, positively disavowed the romantic nationalism then coming into fashion in Europe as contemptibly parochial. They identified themselves as "citizens of the world," the compatriots of anyone who believed in the principles of freedom, equality, reason, and human perfectibility.

It was this attitude, ironically, that provided the answer to how a disparate and quarrelsome people, divided on sectional and ideological lines, could foster a popular national identity. The European Enlightenment Idea of America would be adopted as the nation's own. The concept of nationalism was blended with the idea of individual rights to produce a different kind of national identity, one that achieved unity, not through cultural homogeneity, but rather through the embrace of individual difference and belief in the possibility of individual advancement. Americans would fulfill their exemplary world mission simply by being themselves.

The issue was not uncontested—during the presidencies of George Washington and John Adams, members of the elite were deeply divided among themselves as to what sort of nation America would be—but the universalistic conception ultimately triumphed. It was no accident that veterans of the American Revolutionary War produced, during this period, a series of histories and memoirs that began to weave the diffuse strands of colonial history into a compelling narrative, one that emphasized an American destiny underwritten by Providence. The histories of the separate colonies were rewritten as stages of a single story leading from Jamestown and Plymouth Rock to an inevitable conclusion: the Declaration of Independence and the birth of a new nation, finally confirmed in the Constitution of 1789.[16] The revolutionary upheavals in France after 1793 also allowed Americans to revise their views of the significance of their own revolution, which could now be seen as a precursor to the French Revolution, the first stage in the progressive emancipation of all civilized humanity from the tyranny of rank, custom, and prejudice. The popular influence and political ascendancy of Thomas Jefferson and his followers after 1800 would confirm this mythology and make it an ineradicable part of America's self-understanding. The presidency of Andrew Jackson, from 1829 to 1837, would complete it by adding a definite stamp of *democracy* that had been merely nascent at the founding.

From its inception, the mythology of mission asserted the unique importance of the American experiment, giving rise to belief in what became known as "American exceptionalism." Whether America was, in an empirical sense, exceptional or not, and if so in what ways and whether for good or ill, was not the point. Having staked a national identity on the proposition that the United States represented the future of free humanity, having defended that idea of nationhood against competing versions, having triumphantly if tragically affirmed it through a devastating civil war, Americans came to have a deeply vested interest in *believing* in the exceptional nature of their own polity. The exceptionalist tradition was, in other words, nothing more than a repository of that mythology which was an indispensable part of the national heritage. Exceptionalism became an article of political faith that, like all articles of faith, was perennially liable to doubt and in need of periodic renewal and reaffirmation, but one that somehow survived the disillusionments occasioned by often-bitter experience. In troubled times, when faith seemed to dim, someone was always sure to proclaim the need to "remythologize" America.[17] Americans proved unwilling or unable to discard their most prominent myth, even if sometimes it seemed in their best interests that they should.

And there was a sense in which America proved indeed exceptional, namely, in the global success of a myth aimed as much at foreigners as at Americans. If Americans were chosen, their chosenness was different from that of most other self-identified chosen peoples. An elect is usually exclusive, regarding itself as separate from and perhaps superior to the bulk of humankind. An American, however, was an American not by virtue of membership in an exclusive class or group but because he or she represented the potentiality of common humanity to attain to the individualistic ideal. The moral meaning of America necessarily extended beyond the confines of the American state. True, the United States was not the only nation to conceive of its particularity in this universalistic way—revolutionary France, nineteenth-century Germany, and the Soviet Union did likewise—but it was by far the most successful. Its international success came partly from its role as a destination for hopeful immigrants and partly from the genius it proved to have for popularizing its own mythology. It is doubtful, in fact, whether the exceptionalist myth could have lasted so well had not the rest of the world come to have a vested interest in believing it also.

THE MYTHOLOGY AND THE PROBLEM OF AMERICAN NATIONALISM

Yet the very success of the mythology of mission created permanent tensions between *actual* America and *ideal* America. It has been said that every nation has its characteristic vice, and that that of the United States is hypocrisy. If this is true, it is very largely a consequence of the enduring gap between the actual and the ideal, or between the factual and the mythological. Consider the following.

America is: a nation dedicated to liberty and equality, large sections of which were long addicted to slavery and segregation; an anti-imperialist nation that mythologized and glorified its conquest of an entire continent and the destruction of its original inhabitants; a nation that believed power inevitably corrupted virtue but also that American virtue would inevitably lead to wealth and power; a nation that valorized agrarian, republican simplicity while developing the world's most complex industrial civilization; a nation that strove to isolate itself politically from a wicked world while pursuing ever-deeper economic entanglement; a nation with an abiding puritanical streak but one that produced a profane culture based on pleasure and consumption; a nation that regarded its citizens as non-nationalistic examples of universal humanity but that fostered a proudly parochial and loudly assertive patriotism; a nation founded in the secular values of the Enlightenment that remains one of the most religious of all developed countries; an optimistic nation dedicated to success and progress that yet harbors millenarian expectations of Armageddon and the End of Days; a nation that combines a firm conviction of its own innocence with an abiding belief in original sin; a nation that led the democratic Free World but supported and maintained vicious dictatorial regimes around the globe; an antimilitarist nation that developed the most powerful military machine the world has seen.

Of special interest to the theme of this book is the way that the tension between actual and ideal revealed itself in an American nationalism that was rather schizophrenic in nature—aggressively assertive on the one hand, in denial of its own existence on the other. A genuinely developing ethnocultural nationalism was countered by the universalistic myth, giving rise to opposing attitudes that eventually settled into conservative and liberal camps. These tended to regard one another with mutual contempt. Conservative nationalists wrapped themselves in the flag and despised liberal internationalists whose patriotism seemed to them lukewarm or treacherously defective; liberals appealed to universal norms of peace and benevolence and scorned the patriots for their backwardness, parochialism, and dangerous bellicosity. Such antagonistic attitudes were naturally most sharply revealed in matters of foreign policy. Parochial nationalists stressed American pride and the righteous exercise of American power; transcendent nationalists emphasized universalistic virtue and the maintenance of American innocence. A certain regionalism was associated with this division, with parochial nationalism more prevalent in the South, West, and Midwest and transcendent nationalism on the eastern and western seaboards.

It would be a mistake, however, to regard this distinction as simply defining two warring Americas—a "blue" nation versus a "red" one—or to think that the nationalistic pole represented realism, the other idealism. The mythology has been too pervasive for that. Whether one stressed national pride or national innocence, one had to come to terms with the other pole in some accommodating manner. The American republic was obliged to be *for* something other than itself. U.S. foreign policy had to include *but be more than* a simple defense of U.S. interests. Patriotic virtue (which is after all the same in all nations, differing only in the particularity of its object) also had to be uniquely representative virtue in the American case. Though conservative patriots emphasized American power, they were seldom unaffected by the appeal to transcendent virtue and proved generally unable or unwilling to relinquish the idea of an American mission with a universal purpose. In other words, they were seldom pure "realists." Liberal Americans, on the other hand, even at their most idealistic, were never able to avoid the consequences of America's existence as an individual nation with particular interests to defend. They have, in other words, been forced to come to terms with exigencies of power that often seriously compromise their moral ideals. It is within these persistent crosscurrents of myth-informed American nationalism that the dilemma of virtue and power arises in foreign policy.

CONCLUSION

The question of how to fulfill the historic mission generated oppositions beyond just idealism/realism or universalism/particularism. One also had to decide between engagement and isolation, between national expansion and consolidation, between internationalism and nationalism, between multilateralism and unilateralism. Moving among these, one could arrive at numerous permutations and combinations of foreign policy while arguably remaining within the parameters of the dominant American mythology. The oppositions did not line up neatly in two columns so that one set or the other could be chosen as defining a distinctive position, but rather interwove in complex fashion. If one chose engagement with the world rather than isolation, for instance, the question still had to be answered whether engagement implied national expansion or national consolidation. It also remained to be decided whether engagement would be pursued for purely national goals or for international ones (notably the creation and maintenance of a world order) and whether, in the latter case, these would be pursued unilaterally or multilaterally.

The controversies over such questions usually revolved, either implicitly or explicitly, around the problem of American power and how best to dispose it so as to preserve virtue. Since the crux of the myth of mission was an assumption of special virtue whose possession allowed America to be the harbinger of universal human liberation, it followed logically that loss of virtue would doom the mission and destroy the world's best hope. Yet the matter was complicated because Americans held contradictory views on both power and virtue. Before exploring how the issue evolved in historical circumstances, therefore, we must look more closely at the complexities and confusions surrounding these concepts. I begin by examining what Americans thought they were doing when they attempted to found a *virtuous* republic.

CHAPTER THREE

Founding a Virtuous Republic

THE FOUNDERS WERE INSISTENT on the need for virtue yet uncertain whether Americans really possessed it, or, even if they did, how long they could sustain it in a large commercial republic devoted to the pursuit of self-interest. There was considerable irony in the fact that, just as Americans were settling on a myth that asserted the reality of their virtue, they were designing institutions on the assumption that widespread virtue could not be expected. Self-interested human beings were eminently corruptible, most especially by power, either by possessing it or by being made subject to it. Power was the antithesis of virtue, its nemesis; only power could resist power. Yet, in another common view, power was the product of virtue. The enterprising virtue of Americans in an abundant land was sure to be rewarded by prosperity, leading to national wealth and national power. How was such power to be disposed so that it would not destroy the virtue that had produced it?

To understand how such a conundrum came to be formulated, we must examine the questions of virtue and power with which Americans wrestled in the first days of the republic. Of especial importance to this book is the Christian-Enlightenment idea of *virtue as innocence,* which I explore in the next chapter. Before approaching that, however, I first address the much-discussed issue of American republicanism, since the concept of civic virtue sat at the core of the republican ideal.

A VIRTUOUS REPUBLIC?

One cannot speak of American republicanism without adverting to the long-running, often heated dispute over the relative significance to be accorded different intellectual traditions in the American founding. The debate was ignited by scholars challenging the accepted view, most firmly established by Louis Hartz in the 1950s, that U.S. politics are characterized by a monolithic consensus on a liberalist ideology. The intellectual core of American liberalism was taken to be John Locke's view of government as resulting from a contract among free individuals for the sake of protecting their equal natural rights to liberty and property. In the 1960s and 1970s, certain historians convincingly demonstrated that the American revolutionists had in fact appealed explicitly to a more ancient tradition of republicanism. The waters were further stirred by followers of the political theorist Leo Strauss, who, for their own neoconservative purposes, wished to argue either for or against the existence of premodern elements in the American founding.[1]

The main problem was that ancient republicanism appeared to be incompatible with modern liberalism. Republicanism's central theme was not individual natural right, but the ideal of a virtuous, independent, armed citizenry dedicated to the preservation of a common good that included, centrally, the survival of the republic itself. As well as being prepared to defend the republic against external enemies, republican citizens had to be ever vigilant to preserve their liberty from the encroachments of a powerful executive, and to defend their austere, self-denying virtue against the corrupting influence of luxury, self-interest, and faction (which was merely private interest writ large). Such virtue seemed antithetical to the "possessive individualism" allegedly encouraged by liberalism.[2]

When the flurry of research that this debate provoked had more or less settled, it was possible to conclude with some confidence that the rhetorical and ideological resources available to the revolutionists in their argument with Great Britain had been both manifold and complex; the choice could not be reduced to one of *either* this *or* that internally coherent and therefore exclusive tradition. Hartz's liberal consensus thesis was qualified but by no means overturned. It was nevertheless true, as Gordon Wood's work made clear, that the revolutionists themselves, entranced by a nostalgic image of the Roman republic, had initially conceived the question of virtue very much in terms of a pure republican ideal. They accepted the view, influentially expressed by Montesquieu, that a stern, self-renouncing virtue was essential in a democratic republic. Democratic citizens must learn to love the laws and love their country and to prefer public goods above their own private ones. Since loving the democracy meant loving equality, frugal citizens must eschew the accumulation of riches that would destroy equality and limit their desires to securing necessities. The preservation of virtue required laws that ensured frugality and equality—for instance, laws requiring the equal division of land into small portions and strict limitations on inheritance.[3]

Public documents of the time and several state constitutions listed the essential virtues as justice, moderation, temperance, industry, frugality, and honesty. A sermon from 1778 by Phillips Payson argued that the virtues necessary for a free people were love of country, knowledge and learning, a spirit of liberty, the absence of exorbitant wealth, and the relative absence of the lust for power and "other evil passions."[4] Most generally accepted, however, was the view that what marked citizens and their representatives as virtuous was their capacity—by a combination of character, deliberation, and wise reflection—to care for, correctly discern, and act decisively for the common good. How was such virtue possible in a commercial republic dominated by the pursuit of self-interest?

Montesquieu, to be sure, had allowed that a commercial republic could also be virtuous, for the qualities of frugality, economy, intelligence, and foresight were also those required of successful merchants. But Montesquieu assumed that commercial wealth should accumulate to the benefit of the state, not the individual. He took from Machiavelli the thought that virtue was preserved by keeping the state rich and the citizens poor, and equally poor at that, so that private passions turned into zeal for the public good. But Americans framed the debate in such a way that they seemed forced to choose either commercial wealth (implying the rule of self-interest) or agrarian subsistence (implying Spartan republican virtue). Certainly, the debate sparked by Tom Paine's pamphlet among the colonists in 1776 was conducted very much in this mode of either/or: either devotion to the private interest or to the public; either commerce and wealth or agrarianism and frugality; either pride and ambition or humility and self-abnegation; either art and sophistication or rustic simplicity; either the maintenance of civic virtue or the encouragement of private vice. The argument continued after the Revolution had been won, with some observers lamenting the increasing refinement, opulence, and luxury of society that was a result of Americans' obsession with individual happiness. Many Federalists, including George Washington, attributed the evident weaknesses exhibited by the Confederation during the 1780s to a lack of virtue among Americans. Leaders like Madison were profoundly disillusioned by what they perceived as the states' persistent evasion of, or indifference to, federal authority and the way that self-interested state majorities trampled the rights of minorities and individuals. Many attributed the fault, not to state constitutions, which were in general deemed excellent, but to the failure of a natural aristocracy of talent and virtue to emerge to occupy positions of leadership.[5]

In these circumstances, some Americans began to argue that a well-functioning democratic republic need not be based on the self-abnegating virtue of its citizens. The example of the ancient republics, probably itself mythical, was anyway out-of-date in the light of American innovations. Montesquieu himself, despite his profound influence on the American federation, was out-of-date. His view of republican virtue was in the end explicitly rejected. The very system of government to which Montesquieu's thought had contributed seemed to render strict republican virtue unnecessary. Americans, as Madison avowed, had advanced the science of politics beyond Montesquieu's imagining. Historical republics had tried, vainly, to ensure their own preservation by deforming self-interested human nature, mercilessly inclining citizens to the common interest by enforcing self-denial and frugality. Indeed, the deliberate primitivism of ancient republics seemed to equate virtue with semibarbarity. American republics, however, had solved the republican problem of corruption and degeneration over time by providing a power of constitutional amendment, allowing constant adaptation through a periodic return to founding principles. More importantly, the constitutions of the American states had institutionalized popular sovereignty through a new principle of representation and also introduced divisions and separations of power, thus creating conditions that could give free play to the natural energies of human beings without endangering the stability of the republic. Traditional republicanism had tried to ensure stability through the balancing of different orders of society (the One; the Few and the Many; or Monarchy, Aristocracy, and Democracy), but in America there were no legal or hereditary orders, and the hoped-for natural aristocracy had failed to emerge. Nevertheless, a different kind of dynamic balance could be achieved among variegated and often conflicting interests, to the general safety of the state.[6]

Increasing the strength of the federal government added an authoritative layer capable of checking and moderating the excesses of the states while nevertheless avoiding central tyranny (always interpreted as the exercise of *arbitrary* power). The internal differentiation caused by the division of power among state and federal governments, reinforced by the increasing differentiation of economic interests that naturally arose in a rapidly expanding commercial republic, created a complex system whose overall dynamic worked to the general good. Pitting interest against interest and power against power seemed a surer bet than relying on individual virtue, assumed always to be in scarce supply. Legislation under these circumstances could not be an expression of some transcendent and unitary common interest, but rather a means of aggregating and reconciling a host of irreducibly particular interests. Nor was there any necessary limit to how many new interests thus could be incorporated and mediated, which meant that the ancient republican problem of size had been solved. It had hitherto been assumed that only small republics could maintain citizen liberty and therefore virtue. The tragedy was that republics had to grow larger to ensure effective defense against external enemies. The fate of a successful republic was thus, ironically, empire. Since the control of empires required centralized, despotic government, liberty was inevitably destroyed. Extending the federative principle, however, solved this problem (as Montesquieu had suggested in Book IX of *The Spirit of the Laws*). It allowed the creation of a political entity large enough to provide security from external threat but internally differentiated enough to prevent corruption and despotism.

The success of such arguments meant that the American republic would be an indisputably *liberal* republic. Its central features—the subordination of military to civilian authority, representative government, an extended franchise, a federal system, separation of powers, and the rule of law—were all put to the service of preserving the presumed natural liberty of individuals to pursue their interests without let or hindrance from either too-powerful government or too-powerful organized interests. Moreover, American institutional ingenuity permitted indefinite expansion without danger, so that the United States could be both republic *and* empire. In the light of American innovation, the old republican prescription seemed like a futile attempt to substitute individual virtue for a lack of good laws and political institutions.[7]

Gordon Wood noted:

> The sacrifice of individual interests to the greater good of the whole formed the essence of republicanism and comprehended for Americans the idealistic goal of their Revolution. From this goal flowed all of the Americans' exhortatory literature and all that made their ideology truly revolutionary. This republican ideology both presumed and helped shape the Americans' conception of the way their society and politics should be structured and operated—a vision so divorced from the realities of American society, so contrary to the previous century of American experience, that it alone was enough to make the Revolution one of the great utopian moments of American history.[8]

The utopian moment seemed to have decidedly ended in the period before the constitutional conventions, and to have been finally buried with the new Constitution. Indeed, Wood argued that the Revolution involved a shift to liberalism that marked the last gasp of republican politics.

HAMILTON AND THE USE OF POWER

Did the establishment of a liberal republic, then, mean that Americans could and should dispense with the idea of virtue altogether? Jefferson thought that this was what Alexander Hamilton believed. He avowed, "Hamilton was honest as a man, but as a politician, [he believed] in either the necessity of force or corruption to govern men." It was true that Hamilton heartily embraced America's destiny as a commercial empire and believed that antique civic virtue among the people must give way to enterprise, interest, and ambition. His main worry was not that people would act with self-interest but that so many people failed rightly to understand their own true self-interest and to act reasonably upon it. His policies aimed, in part, at educating them. Hamilton was certainly no democrat, yet he expected to find virtue among the people's representatives, for, "the supposition of universal venality in human nature is little less an error in human reasoning, than the supposition of universal rectitude. The institution of delegated power implies, that there is a portion of virtue and honor among mankind, which may be a reasonable foundation of confidence." Like many of his famous contemporaries, he was himself a man of considerable virtue and ambition—honest, financially uncorrupt, morally and physically courageous, reverential of law and authority—and he expected to find genuine virtue and good sense only among an honorable aristocratic elite fit, like himself, to rule.[9]

Hamilton was republican only because in the United States nothing else would be accepted, but since "a republican government does not admit of a vigorous execution, it is therefore bad." "Vigorous execution" was what Hamilton desired above all. Government must be strong and stable and would be so only if the interests of men of property were tied firmly to it. The Constitution—of which Hamilton did not wholeheartedly approve though he defended it—was too much concerned with limiting power rather than with ensuring that it could be energetically used for the national interest. His view was that too little power was as dangerous as too much and could easily lead to anarchy and thus to despotism. "When you have divided and nicely balanced the departments of government," he said, "[w]hen you have strongly connected the virtue of your rulers with their interest; when, in short, you have rendered your system as perfect as human forms can be; you must place confidence; *you must give power*" (my italics).[10]

Hamilton's idea was basically to use the power of the state to further economic and national development. He had no faith in laissez-faire economics and sought to use government to actively structure markets in order to foster industriousness in the population and encourage commercial growth in both agricultural and manufacturing sectors. A mercantile nation must defend its markets and interests against powerful rivals, as well as extend them. To do so, it needed sound public credit, a secure financial system, a strong central government, and specialized military and naval forces. In responding to the objection that the ancient republics of Greece, though continually at war with each other, never acquired standing armies, Hamilton noted that the industrious habits of Americans, absorbed in the pursuit of gain and devoted to improvements in agriculture and commerce, were incompatible with a nation of soldiers such as the ancient republics in reality were. Hamilton would heartily have concurred with Locke's view that "the chief end of trade is riches and power . . . power consists in numbers of men and ability to maintain them." Military power at the service of trade made wealth creation possible just as wealth gained from trade made a strong military affordable. This was the secret of power in the modern world. Hamiltonian foreign policy therefore aimed first and always at the preservation and furtherance of a national interest conceived in mercantilist terms. His new nation needed leaders of dynamic virtue—indeed of Machiavellian *virtù*—who by an effective exertion of the national will could tame the turbulent currents of commercial fortune. Hamilton resisted the appeal of geographical expansion, fearing to stretch the national resources beyond their scope, but his ultimate ambition was to see a United States that was capable of dominating both northern and southern continents, a commercial regime powerful enough to compete with and even overbalance the empires of Europe.[11]

Hamilton's ambitions for American commerce were not motivated by avarice but rather were inspired by a vision of the power and glory to which the United States could, with all its natural advantages, attain. He hoped that America's rise to power would foster a spirit of nationalistic pride and attachment among the people, harnessing their individualistic ambition to the broader national project that their own industry made possible. He had not, therefore, altogether abandoned the idea of citizen virtue as devotion to a public interest larger than the mere aggregation of individual interests. He hoped, however, to shift it into an alternate mode by supplementing acquisitive individualism with a love of nation capable of evoking the spirit of self-sacrifice when necessary.

This combination (which may fairly be said to foreshadow American reality) could, however, equally describe the hope of Thomas Jefferson. The difference was that Hamilton's nationalism was fiercely particularistic, while Jefferson's was of the transcendent type that upheld America as the universal exemplar.

MADISON AND THE ABUSE OF POWER

Hamilton's positive view of power was considerably at odds with those of many of his most famous contemporaries, who had inherited a rather skewed perspective from radical Whig theory of the seventeenth and eighteenth centuries. The influence of the latter was evident in the general distrust of power that became a hallmark of American political attitudes and in the institutionalization of a representative form of government that Dissenters had argued would moderate official power.[12] All power was, by definition, dangerous, and any delegation of power automatically courted tyrannous abuse. Liberty and power were thus assumed to be antagonistically related. This made the principal problem of government one of how to prevent grants of power from being used self-interestedly or tyrannically, rather than that of how to ensure they were used wisely. The apparent failure of a natural aristocracy to appear—a wise and disinterested leadership that could be trusted with power—threw Americans back on an oppositional tradition obsessed with the *abuse* of power and convinced that power in any shape or form was a prime agent of corruption. Of course, it was taken as fundamental that liberty implied the rule of law—meaning the rule of general, just laws applying equally to all—rather than rule through the arbitrary will of men. The rule of law, because not arbitrary, was indeed taken to be identical with the rule of virtue. As a purely formal principle, however, the rule of law did not solve the problem of power. After all, laws themselves may be unjust and partial, and even impartial ones must be administered by partial men. An authentic rule of law could be achieved only if supported by social and political conditions that militated against the arbitrary use of power and thus preserved liberty.

The solution provided by the authors of the Constitution was a set of republican institutions designed to divide and check political power at every point where it might possibly accumulate. Informing this solution was a radically pessimistic view of human nature that sat oddly with hopes for a virtuous, public-spirited citizenry. Humanity was taken to be inevitably dominated by the passions, and the selfish passions at that. Henry Clay stated the case very clearly in 1840: "The pervading principle of our system of government—of all free government—is not merely the possibility, but the absolute certainty of infidelity and treachery, with even the highest functionary of the State."[13] But though such a system of government might *simulate* virtue by preserving liberty, it surely did not rely on the positive virtue of either governors or governed for its maintenance. Madison, to be sure, always retained hope for traditional republican virtue. As the (probable) author of *The Federalist* No. 57, he implied that even a constitutional government that balanced powers and interests must be supplemented by virtue. In the constitutional debates, Madison averred that the people must have at least enough virtue and intelligence to choose representatives of virtue and wisdom; otherwise, the forms of government would avail them nothing.

Like Hamilton, Madison often expressed the hope or belief that human nature contained as much potential for virtue as for depravity, yet in the end he placed more confidence in the mitigating effects of a suitably limited central government and on the mutual moderation of diversified interests. Together, these might preserve the American experiment even in the absence of citizen virtue. Not only would the encouragement of competing interests prevent the tyrannical domination of any, but the untethering of human acquisitiveness would inevitably ignite the hope of personal wealth in a richly resourced continent and work to the benefit of peace and stability. It seemed, to put it in the unflattering terms of Bernard Mandeville, that personal vice could be made to work to the public good, at least under American conditions of liberty and the rule of law.[14]

This morally permissive policy, according to one commentator, gave American political life a "solid but low foundation," one that lacked real nobility, the sort of founding that might seem incommensurate with any grand sense of providential mission. Yet, in practice, it proved no impediment. Despite the theoretical and practical victory of interests, popular faith in special American virtue and divine election persisted. J. G. A. Pocock insisted against Wood that the language of virtue and corruption continued to be important in shaping American thought. Republicanism, he claimed, did not expire with the Revolution but was merely transposed into a new key, with the civic independence required for republican virtue guaranteed now by the possession of freehold agrarian property. This was indeed the central theme of the political thought of Thomas Jefferson, whose ideas so deeply invested the received version of the American myth.[15]

JEFFERSON AND THE AMERICAN MYTHOLOGY

For Pocock, the tension or antithesis between virtue tied to land and corruption associated with an expanding commerce remained pivotal. He was right about this, yet there was also a competing view that saw no necessary antithesis between virtue and self-interested commerce. Most Americans thought they could be both Lockean liberals *and* good republicans (prominent Americans thought Locke *was* a republican). The predominant view became that the sterner version of republicanism was, and no doubt always had been, quite unrealistic. Virtue, properly conceived, could be seen to be perfectly compatible with, and in fact inseparable from, the free

Lockean pursuit of self-interest. As Margaret Jacob's work on the seventeenth century "Newtonians" makes clear, the English latitudinarians had already worked out a synthesis of natural religion, free will, and market forces that made virtue compatible with industry and material prosperity. Americans could also draw on the ideas of Scottish "common sense" philosophers, and of Locke himself, to envision the well-regulated pursuit of economic self-interest as conducive to the social virtues of peace and good order (it was a happy coincidence that Adam Smith's treatise *An Inquiry into the Nature and Causes of the Wealth of Nations* first appeared in 1776, the year of the Declaration of Independence). In Alan Craig Houston's summation: "Civic virtue did not grow out of the renunciation of private interests, but rather out of the recognition that the vast majority of private interests are encompassed in, indeed are part and parcel of, the public interest. To put the point somewhat baldly, self-interest was the strongest possible foundation for civic virtue." There was in fact a natural harmony between citizen duty and citizen interest. As Thomas Jefferson put it: "so invariably do the laws of nature create our duties and interests, that when they seem to be at variance, we ought to suspect some fallacy in our reasonings."[16]

The public good, in this view, was nothing more than the collective defense and protection of the right of individuals to rationally pursue their own interests, the beneficial effect of which among naturally sociable creatures capable of voluntary association was the establishment of a well-ordered and prosperous community. Collective defense would be assured, moreover, because citizens had a real stake in maintaining the conditions of their own and everyone else's liberty, most importantly as these were protected by law. Jefferson believed the American system of government to be the strongest on earth because, at the call of the laws, everyone would fly to their defense, regarding invasions of the public order as their own personal concern.[17]

But even with such a view of liberal freedom and virtue, the old fear of corruption nagged, intensified by the work of political economists of the Scottish Enlightenment who had discerned inevitable "stages of progress" in economic history. These were, typically, the hunter-gathering, agricultural, commercial, and finally manufacturing stages, each one leading to greater refinement in the mechanical and liberal arts. The problem was that, in the end, when all agricultural land was occupied, the dispossessed would drift to the cities and be absorbed into the drudgery of factory life. Here was the source of Jefferson's anxiety about manufacturing and urbanization. Laissez-faire liberalism and a market society were compatible with virtue as long as individuals owned the products of their own labor and exchanged them freely at market. But the growth of large-scale manufacturing turned labor into a commodity and the laborer into a corrupted and degraded object of industrial tyranny.[18]

For republicans of Jefferson's temper, the result would be increased luxury at one end of the social scale matched by misery and dependence at the other, in both cases implying loss of virtue. Here was the basis of a new theory of the tendency of free republics toward self-destruction, this time through natural economic development rather than through the defensive rise to military power. Madison, who thought long and hard on the matter, believed that he had found an American solution to this problem. The central government would pursue trade policies that effectively arrested development at the commercial-agricultural stage. Government would promote the household manufacture of simple necessities while securing foreign markets for U.S. agriculture, in exchange for which agrarian Americans would receive the finer manufactures of Europe. Territorial expansion would also be necessary to absorb into agriculture any excess of population that might encourage the development of large-scale urban manufacture.[19]

But land in America was first and foremost a saleable commodity, and a great deal of it was in the possession of state governments burdened by public debt, a fact that encouraged speculation on a large scale, and indeed bouts of speculative mania. Speculators (among whom were many if not most of the great names of U.S. history) had no difficulty in employing egalitarian republican rhetoric to rationalize a practice on which they grew wealthy. The Madisonian solution proved to be no solution at all in an expanding commercial republic where the small farmer was inevitably always on the retreat, squeezed by larger agrarian enterprise on the one hand and creditors and bankers on the other. The whole idea was, as Forrest McDonald says, "pie-in-the-sky political economy," yet no less influential for that. It was essentially the same agrarian-republican vision championed by Jefferson, as summarized in his famous Query XIX of the *Notes on Virginia*.[20]

The ideological success of Jeffersonianism, despite its material defeat, is a vital part of the story of American virtue. It is important to note, first, that the Jeffersonian concern with the corrupting effects of luxury and industry did not imply that civic virtue should be identified with the renunciation of individual self-interest. Certainly, Jefferson hoped that the rich western lands would support a growing republic of sturdy yeomen farmers inclined to egalitarianism and exhibiting a virtue that, at first glance, appeared firmly in the classical republican mode. The hard-working life of the independent small farmer in possession of a freehold property seemed to him peculiarly conducive to the maintenance of sober virtue, in contrast to the life in the cities ("sinks of voluntary misery") where manufacturers ("panders of vice") produced unnecessary luxuries and induced popular dissipation. "Those who labour in the earth," he declared, "are the chosen people of God, if ever he had a chosen people, whose breasts he has made his peculiar deposit for substantial and genuine virtue."[21]

Yet Jefferson was also a wholehearted believer in natural rights, a man who revered John Locke and who held to the fundamental liberal tenet that government existed solely to protect individual rights and must itself be prevented from encroaching tyrannously upon them. He did not believe that a republic, though it might call upon equal services from its citizens, could command their "perpetual service" as the ancients had claimed. His fundamental individualism was most adamantly expressed in a letter to James Monroe: "If we are made in some degree for others, yet in a greater are we made for ourselves. It were contrary to feeling and indeed ridiculous to suppose that a man had less right in himself than one of his neighbors or indeed all of them put together. This would be slavery and not that liberty which the bill of rights has made inviolable and for the preservation of which our government has been charged. Nothing could so completely divest us of that liberty as the establishment of the opinion that the state has a 'perpetual' right to the services of all its members." Nor did Jefferson hold seriously to the Spartan frugality of the republican ideal, for he was in agreement with Condorcet that the virtuous exercise of free human labor power in an abundant land would inevitably lead to prosperity. Indeed, he was sure that the Divine Being had willed it so in America for the edification of the world.[22]

Exemplary American virtue was thus connected to prosperity and happiness via an expansiveness that implied energy, industry, and an intensely practical, rather than intellectual, bent. Jeffersonian thought was resolutely naturalistic (in fact, a species of materialism) and imbued with Enlightenment faith in the power of human reason to understand and transform nature for human betterment. Jefferson's characteristically American rationalism insisted on the superiority of practical and "useful" thought over abstract or metaphysical reasoning. Pragmatic thought and invention were held necessary to master a wilderness created, as Jefferson assumed, for an agricultural paradise. Work and invention would produce an abundance that would signal God's blessing on the exemplary American experiment. Jefferson argued that Malthusian pessimism about population outstripping food supply could not apply in the United States. American freedom would produce a wealthy America and would vindicate not just Americans but the entire species. It would even vindicate God himself, for it would prove that He had created human beings in love and not in anger and had given them a capacity for self-government, virtuous industry, and earthly happiness.[23]

Jefferson's championship of this myth formed the real subtext of the famous quarrel with Hamilton that called into being America's first party system (Hamilton's Federalists opposing Jefferson's Republicans). At one level, the difference was over economic development and the proper uses and limits of central power; but at a deeper level, it was a contest over the emerging nation's very soul. As one historian noted, neither Federalists nor Republicans regarded themselves as parties but rather as embodiments of the true national will, their duty being to win and hold power from those who would illegitimately usurp and misuse it. Hamilton's hope, as we have seen, was for a conservative, hierarchical nation focused on trans-Atlantic commerce, with agriculture balanced by trade and manufacture and the propertied classes well locked in to the political system. It was a vision congenial to the merchant oligarchs of the New England seaboard who doubted the wisdom of continental expansion, but one condemned by Jeffersonian Republicans for its aristocratic, even monarchical, tendencies and English sympathies.[24]

Jefferson's opposing agrarian vision appealed to the democratic sensibilities of people in the backwoods of the South and West who resented eastern dominance and were forever pushing at the boundaries of white settlement in their hunger for land. Jefferson adamantly opposed the idea of a highly centralized power, upheld states' rights, believed in strictly limited government, and opposed standing armies and a national bank, all for the sake of maintaining the egalitarian ideal of a virtuous American yeomanry. Despite his agrarianism, his economics rested essentially on laissez-faire individualism. Indeed, the great theorist of Progressivism, Herbert Croly, would one day accuse Jefferson of laying the foundations of a perverted American individualism that turned politics into "a species of vigorous, licenced, and purified selfishness." Denying a proper role for a strong, regulative state of the kind Hamilton championed, Jefferson permitted unlimited individual economic opportunities that in the end created conditions of bondage and thus destroyed true individuality.[25]

This was a deeply ironic charge to lay against Jefferson. He could not have foreseen the rise to dominance of gigantic, exploitative corporations in the second half of the nineteenth century and surely would not have welcomed it. He might, indeed, have been doubly chagrined to observe that the Hamiltonian capitalists had taken over his own doctrine of laissez-faire, turning it into a weapon of inequality by assimilating it to Herbert Spencer's theory of civilization's advance as "survival of the fittest." He would have been surprised, at the very least, that the anomalous ideology of "laissez-faire conservatism"—the trademark doctrine of the American Right and their big business supporters ever since—would sometimes come near to displacing his own version of the defining American myth. Yet Jefferson himself had been acutely conscious of the tension between trying to preserve equality, simplicity, and virtue on the one hand and, on the other, granting the liberty to pursue economic development on the basis of private property (it being quite irrelevant whether that property was in the form of land or of some other species of capital). He understood that a strictly equal division of property was impracticable, but his travels in France had made him painfully aware that the accumulation of unlimited wealth produced levels of inequality that, as he argued on pure Lockean principles, violated natural right: "The earth is given as common stock for man to labour and live on." Though he advised American legislators to find as many devices as possible for subdividing property, and recommended a steeply progressive property tax, the American system for the most part preferred to treat private property as inviolable and therefore to place no necessary limits on its accumulation. Jefferson nevertheless hoped, with Madison, that the apparently limitless opportunities that the continent provided for new settlement would keep inequality within bounds and ensure that prosperity remained general. He believed that

American governments would "remain virtuous for many centuries; as long as they are chiefly agricultural; and this will be as long as there shall be vacant lands in any part of America."[26]

The result of this thinking was that Jefferson's vision—his dream of "an empire of liberty" in the Americas—was an expansive one. Hamilton desired economic rather than geographical expansion for the sake of increasing American strength so as to compete more effectively with the powers of Europe. Jefferson looked to inward expansion in order to *escape* from Europe (and, by implication, from the domination of the commercial eastern seaboard whose fortunes were so closely tied to trade with Europe) and its pernicious tendency to corrupt American virtue.

Jefferson always betrayed an acute sense of the vulnerability of American virtue, and of the fatal consequences to the American mission if virtue were lost. After the frights and alarums of the 1790s, he insisted on the need to protect and preserve the American experiment for the world's sake, and especially from contamination by Europe. He blessed the Almighty Being who had divided, by an expanse of water, Europe from America in order to create at least one space for peace on earth. "I hope that peace and amity with all nations will long be the character of our land," he wrote, "and that its prosperity under the Charter will react on the mind of Europe, and profit her by the example." He championed the United States as a refuge for those suffering under European misrule, expecting that their happiness would affect even the land they had left, since the very existence of an American sanctuary would tend to restrain the forces of domestic oppression. And yet, as his *Notes on Virginia* attest, he also worried that the provision of unlimited asylum for the discontented of Europe—whose character would either remain constrained by the principles of absolutist monarchies in which they had been raised or would turn licentious in throwing them off—might corrupt the principles of American society. In 1823 he advised President James Monroe that the preservation of freedom in the Americas might require that the despotic powers of Europe be excluded from the whole Western hemisphere: "Our first and fundamental maxim should be, never to entangle ourselves in the broils of Europe. Our second, never suffer Europe to intermeddle with cis-Atlantic affairs." Ironically, preserving America *for* the world meant, in practical terms, preserving America *from* the world, or at least the threatening European part of it.[27]

Yet the division of labor that Jefferson and Madison envisioned for America and Europe—agriculture in the one exchanging for manufactures in the other—implied a continued American dependence on the Old World and its allegedly corrupt concentrations of manufacture. American corruption was to be, in effect, permanently outsourced to Europe. It is difficult to see how an America so artificially preserved could be a persuasive example for economically developed Europe. The dependency on Europe that the scheme fostered was also a dangerous one, as Jefferson himself discovered during the war with Britain of 1812–1815. The experience of this conflict caused him to discard his adamant opposition to American manufacturing. Modern industry implied military power, and preserving national security seemed to require a measure of industrial self-sufficiency.

CONCLUSION

This late admission foreshadowed the eventual triumph of Hamilton's vision of a commercial empire defended by a powerful military over Jefferson's agrarian, antimilitarist ideal. Yet the latter would long remain, even in industrialized, urbanized America, the sentimental repository of republican virtue. Seventy years after Jefferson's death, its essential spirit was summarized in the slogan of an Iowan farming paper: "Good Farming, Clear Thinking, Right Living." The beliefs expressed by the chief writer were distinctively Jeffersonian: that agrarian existence engendered courage, self-reliance, honesty, industriousness, and fear of the Lord; that one could safely rely on the common sense of the common man; that the wellspring of a righteous life and American democratic principles was agricultural civilization; that privilege and trusts were detestable; that cities and big business were to be distrusted; that war was despicable and that large armies and navies benefited only special interests who profited from weapons production; that Europeans were wily, quarrelsome, and unscrupulous; and that if America properly fulfilled its role in the world, the millennium would be at hand.[28]

Ron Chernow, in his biography of Hamilton, concluded: "If Jefferson provided the essential poetry of American political discourse, Hamilton established the prose of American statecraft. No other founder articulated such a clear and prescient vision of America's future political, military, and economic strength or crafted such ingenious mechanisms to bind the nation together." I would put it thus: if Hamilton was the prophet of American reality, Jefferson remained the true keeper of the distinctive American mythology. Jefferson, steeped as he was in the European Enlightenment, had imbibed the Idea of America as a place of natural virtue in which a grand experiment in rational government could be undertaken to the ultimate benefit of all humankind. It was this mythology rather than a soundly reasoned political and economic theory (which he lacked) that conveyed a belief in American virtue into the succeeding centuries, albeit a mythology self-consciously founded on political ideas. The fact that Jeffersonianism was a rather incoherent mix of traditional republicanism and economic liberalism did not detract from the power of the mythological narrative that incorporated them.[29]

Jefferson's victory over the Federalists in the presidential election of 1800, and the long ascendancy of the Virginia dynasty that followed, ensured that his views would come to dominate America's view of itself. It determined, as Joyce Appleby wrote, "that the United States would not just be; it would stand for something. Its coherence would come from beliefs, from statements of high principles and abiding truths, from a creed which spoke of liberty and equality, natural rights and human nature." After Jefferson, American citizens came to accept without much question that superior virtue was part of their national heritage, and that their virtue was closely connected to America's providential mission. After the presidency of Andrew Jackson they would be equally certain that American virtue was closely connected to democratic government. But if the American sense of virtue proved robust, so did the belief that American virtue was vulnerable to corruption and required fortuitous or enforced isolation to ensure its preservation.[30]

Before addressing the history of American attempts to preserve virtue in foreign policy, however, I examine more closely the imagined content of the virtue that the mythology supposed Americans to possess, and which it supposed so perpetually vulnerable, and in particular that element which identified virtue with innocence.

CHAPTER FOUR

Problems of Virtue and Power

WHAT THEN, WHEN ALL IS said and done, was the supposed actual content of the virtue that Americans presumed their nation to foster and themselves to exhibit? Despite the apparent clarity of the lists cited in the previous chapter, there is in fact no simple or singular answer to this question. Our discussion of republicanism has inevitably focused mainly on civic virtue, which Montesquieu argued was quite distinct from either moral or religious virtue (though he allowed they were causally interrelated). In American conditions, however, such a separation was impossible to make. A number of different, and not wholly compatible, currents of thought and attitude flowed together to inform a popular conception in which positive and negative, active and passive, notions of virtue were commingled.[1]

Both republicanism and liberalism tied virtue to liberty and equality, though these were differently understood in each case. Republican virtue, as we have seen, emphasized frugal independence and a rough equality of condition, while liberal virtue rested on laissez-faire economic enterprise and equality of opportunity. A different and negative conception of "natural" virtue (deriving from Rousseau-the-romantic rather than Rousseau-the-republican) eulogized freedom from the contaminating and corrupting influences of highly developed, "artificial" civilization. A more positive form of intrinsic virtue was believed transmitted by history and blood from British forebears, the possession of which made the colonists ideally suited to their bold experiments in liberty. The British inheritance included Protestant Christianity, whose superiority to Catholicism or to heathen religions was taken for granted. Republicanism, liberalism, and Protestantism all stressed the capacity and readiness for hard work as a central virtue, regarding idleness as either corrupting or positively sinful. Christianity's doctrines of sin and redemption also introduced into American virtue the idea of guiltless innocence, which, though it chimed with Rousseauean natural virtue, was foreign to classical republicanism. Christian innocence was closely aligned with a doctrine of universal benevolence that Jefferson discerned in Jesus' teaching, a doctrine that conformed readily to the progressive, universalizing thought of the Enlightenment. In considerable tension with this, however, were republican virtues of martial valor and sacrifice that continued to be important to Americans whenever national pride and honor were at stake or when there was a continent to be tamed or wars to be won. Such virtue had a religious parallel, moreover, in a proselytizing Protestantism that conceived the idea of mission as a positive endeavor by active "soldiers of Christ" to spread the gospel to every corner of the world.

I now examine each of these strands more closely.

THE CONTENT OF AMERICAN VIRTUE

Liberty and Equality

Virtue's connection to liberty and equality in the republican tradition rested, as we have seen, on an ideal of citizen independence guaranteed by small, self-sufficient landholdings. Though the forces of history, society, and economy militated against this ideal, nevertheless the myth of special smallholder virtue was tenaciously maintained by farmers throughout U.S. history and occasionally emitted a powerful political impulse, as in the Anti-Masonic Party of the 1820s or the Populist movement of the 1880s and 1890s. It was romantically indulged by political sympathizers who included Teddy Roosevelt, Woodrow Wilson, and Franklin D. Roosevelt.[2] Despite the practical defeat of agrarianism, there remained in the public consciousness the idea that real virtue implied genuine independence of mind and body, the liberty and courage to think and choose for oneself. American virtue was always linked with a sturdy individualism that presumed every person was the equal of every other no matter what the difference in their conditions.

Liberalism's view of liberty likewise stressed individualistic independence from tyrannous power, particularly governmental power, though it did not tie independence exclusively to land. The productive use of liberal freedom to pursue individual advantage and well-being demanded certain personal, "bourgeois" virtues—of reason, industry, thrift, temperance, plain-dealing, and enterprise—as well as social virtues of good order and observance of law. None of these was antithetical to either Protestant or republican virtues. But the differential outcomes produced by individual effort—whether due to differences in luck, capacity, or character—meant that liberal moral equality was quite compatible with substantial material inequality as long as some faith in equality of opportunity was preserved, along with democratic forms. As we saw in the discussion of Jefferson, this meant that liberal virtue was very closely linked to just deserts in the form of material prosperity. Virtue was never simply its own reward in the American context but was always tied to economic success as cause to effect. Success, conversely, would generally be sufficient proof of virtue and failure proof of its lack. Such a doctrine was not merely compatible with, but practically definitive of, an American reality governed by the cult of success and the dream of Everyman making good by dint of individual effort (though it took on an uncomfortably harsh aspect when reinforced by social-Darwinist ideas about survival of the fittest).

Simplicity

One enduring legacy deriving variously from Calvinism, republicanism, and Rousseau's doctrine of nature was a belief in, or hankering after, the virtue of simplicity in American life. Simplicity—really a shorthand for the catalogue of virtues opposed to excessive artificiality and refinement, to deviousness and cunning, to servility and claims of inherent status—was taken to be an essential aspect of American character by Crèvecoeur, Franklin, Jefferson, Jackson, Lincoln, and many others. Nevertheless, widely broadcast European theories of American degeneration made Americans feel somewhat ambivalent about their alleged simplicity, however much they professed to value it.[3] Benjamin Franklin thought simplicity compatible with refinement and philosophical sophistication, but the tendency of American democracy and American pragmatism seemed to be toward a certain common roughness. Jeffersonian thought, by devaluing the purely intellectual and resolutely emphasizing the practical and useful, did little to discourage such a trend. Such homely Americanism seemed hardly conducive to high civilization. Americans, engrossed in occupying and exploiting their continent, covetous of material success, often determinedly isolated and insular in outlook, tended to appear to European eyes either boorish or vulgar rather than virtuously simple. Such attitudes persisted even after the United States had entered its great age of wealth and power, with Europe playing intellectual and condescending Greece to America's indomitable but naive Rome.

John Adams once noted that Montesquieu, unlike the ancients, understood virtue as a wholly negative quality, being merely the absence of ambition and avarice rather than the possession of excellent qualities. But at least republicanism, like Calvinism, presumed that virtue, to be maintained, required personal fortitude and a continuous act of positive will to resist selfish passion and the temptations of luxury, idleness, or power. Commerce and industry threatened willful simplicity only because the wealth and power they produced elevated the level of temptation. Rousseau, however, had a much more passive conception of virtue. He argued that virtue was primitive and natural, corrupted principally by the advance of human science and art, including the invention of property and class. This idea was projected by the Enlightenment onto America and (save for Rousseau's negative assessment of private property) gratefully received. Americans, in this view, were virtuous not by dint of their own continuing moral effort but merely because they had been uprooted from Europe and transplanted into a natural wilderness. Stripped of the accretions and corruptions of European culture and class, placed in closer proximity to unspoiled nature than any European could be, Americans had rediscovered natural, primitive virtue. It was significant, too, that they had safeguarded their "naturalness" by devising an ingenious political system that did not attempt to deform or reform the natural man, but rather permitted the release of his energies into safe and productive channels for his own and society's benefit. (Even Alexis de Tocqueville held to the idea that an American was more "natural" than a European, though he was ambivalent about the resultant virtue.)[4]

Industry

Jeffersonians likewise held that human nature was universal and naturally virtuous, at least under certain environmental conditions. A common nature was overlaid by regional distinctions produced by cultural and environmental influences, sometimes pernicious but in America largely pared back to a natural state in which simplicity and naiveté were indistinguishable. Natural virtue for Jefferson was hardly more than the good psychological health of a robust body, maintained by a simple life of active work and by moderation in indulging the pleasures of the flesh. The test of its existence was a practical one, namely, the ability to cope with the natural world given by God for humanity's use. As Daniel Boorstin put it, the Jeffersonian "could not imagine that the virtue of men was anything but harmonious with their effective physical functioning under American conditions." That productive work should be, to the agrarian republican, almost synonymous with health and thus with virtue reflected the American inheritance of Calvinism and liberalism (the latter itself deeply imbued with the Protestant ethic). Hamilton, for all his aristocratic pretensions, shared the positive attitude toward work and indeed thought his system better than that of the agrarians because it enlarged the range of objects of human endeavor and thus opportunities for "human exertion," which he regarded as a good in itself. Hamilton's was the commercial-entrepreneurial counterpart to the agrarian-republican valuation of work.[5]

It is important to note that the attitude of white Americans toward work allowed them to assess their own virtue as superior to that of Native Americans, a consequential distinction since, on Lockean principles, productive labor was the basis of natural property rights to land. The virtue of industriousness allowed settlers to claim superior entitlement to the territory of Native Americans, who were, it was argued, in mere "idle occupation" of it (see Chapter 7). It also served, to an important extent, to distinguish Yankee northerners and northwesterners from their brethren in the aristocratic South, where a different mythology inevitably prevailed. In the South, where the idea of freedom necessarily retained its classical sense of "nonslave," labor was unavoidably regarded as incompatible with honor, certainly among the gentry. As for the rural southern smallholder, the effect of the dominance of the plantation culture and economy, according to a famous essay on the subject, was to cause "the divorce of pride from the ideas of effort and achievement." Jefferson himself noted this difference, though he characteristically put it down to the effects of differing climate, arguing that the warmth of the South "unnerves and unmans both body and mind."[6]

Innocence

Jeffersonian virtue, being merely the absence of "disease," had no positive content; neither did vice, being merely the absence of health. Preserving virtue in this negative view was not so much a matter of exerting the individual will as of maintaining the healthy conditions under which virtue would naturally flourish. It is remarkable how often in American discourse the question of virtue's corruption is associated with the word "contamination," a medical rather than a moral category, and one demanding sanitary or preventive remedies rather than the fostering of exemplary behavior. The Jeffersonian view, in other words, has little use for the concept of sin and in this conformed to one of the general tendencies of American culture. Calvinistic belief in the inevitable sinfulness of fallen human nature, and the impossibility of attaining a state of grace by any effort of one's own, had long been giving way to more optimistic and frankly materialist views. In 1740 Jonathan Edwards had attacked the young people of Northampton, Massachusetts, for sinful self-reliance that overlooked their dependence on God. Though Edwards and other evangelists sought to reestablish rigorous Calvinism, the religious enthusiasm of the Great Awakening they ignited encouraged the view that humble sinners could gain salvation by choosing a mystic, personal communion with God. Of course, belief in innate human sinfulness did not disappear in the United States and flourishes still, along with a persistent millenarianism among conservative Christians horrified by what they regard as the modern American Gomorrah. U.S. history has been marked by periodic crusades against social or moral evils in which a puritanical and sometimes vengeful attribution of sinfulness is quite evident. Nevertheless, the dominant cultural trend has been contrary to this. The naive virtue of the American natural man was easily assimilated to the Christian conception of innocence, or sinlessness.[7]

Emotional enthusiasm and reliance on an "inner light" as evidence of religious truth reinforced the pragmatic, anti-intellectual strain of American life. It seemed characteristically American that the true test of evangelical virtue should be productivity, measured in terms of numbers of souls saved. On the whole, the progress of religion in America served to strengthen rather than constrain a culture that exalted free individual choice. American Protestantism encouraged the "epistemological freedom" to decide on the truth of religious matters for oneself. The explosion of proselytizing sects and denominations was in part a consequence of the rejection of Old World authority, and of the determinedly Protestant idea that one's own (or one's sect's own) interpretation of the word of God was as good as that of any priest or pontiff. The evangelical view of the history of the Christian church paralleled the secular story of primitive and virtuous origins corrupted by a history of gradual accretions of rank, wealth, and refinement. Americans often searched their Bibles to discern the lost, authentic teachings of Jesus in order to effect a return to true, unvarnished religion and Christian virtue. What they usually found was a means to be washed clean of sin through direct contact with the deity rather than through the intermediation of priests bearing holy authority. In the words of Richard Bushman, writing of the social effects of revivalism in Connecticut, "the men affected by the Awakening possessed a new character, cleansed of guilt and joyful in the awareness of divine favor."[8] This recovery of purity and simplicity was the religious complement of the natural virtue that Americans had regained in their Edenic wilderness.

And if heavenly salvation could be assured by an act of positive commitment and will, so also could earthly well-being. A rich continent seemed to offer ordinary human beings the chance at material prosperity and happiness if they would but industriously exert themselves. Americans were disinclined to regard life on earth as necessarily a vale of suffering and tears, or to think that true religion was incompatible with material prosperity. On the contrary, they tended to believe that getting right with God was the surest way of gaining wealth and happiness. Such optimistic linking of religious and worldly happiness was emphatically confirmed in the revivalist movement led by Charles Grandison Finney during the Jacksonian years and has been often reaffirmed to the present day.[9] In the United States, Calvinist fundamentalism was watered down until there was little left of it but a belief in divine Providence and national election, underwritten by an assurance of American innocence, that was readily harnessed to the progressive dream of America.

The idea of American innocence was of particular importance to

Americans as they contemplated the world and their role within it. It implied a benevolently Christian view of humanity that was as universalizing as Enlightenment rationalism. It is worth noting, in this regard, Jefferson's estimation of what he saw as the limitations of classical philosophy. The ancients were indisputably great, he said, in relation to precepts concerning the government of one's passions and the attainment of personal tranquility. They embraced kindred and friends, inculcated patriotism as a primary obligation, and taught justice toward neighbors and compatriots. They did not, however, inculcate peace, charity, and love to our fellows or embrace with benevolence the whole of humankind. In this respect, the teaching of Jesus (who Jefferson regarded as moral teacher rather than divine savior) was far superior, for he inculcated "universal philanthropy . . . to all mankind, gathering all into one family, under the bonds of love, charity, peace, common wants and common aids. . . . He taught, emphatically, the doctrines of a future state." The ideal Jeffersonian American would not only remain free of guilt by avoiding political entanglement and war—in which bloody hands and brutalization could scarcely be avoided—but his or her patriotism could be innocently and benevolently extended beyond the borders of the United States to enfold all of humankind. "The first object of my heart is my own country," Jefferson wrote, at a time when France threatened the United States, but the Jeffersonian could never be an *exclusively* American patriot. The Christian virtues that were part of American virtue could not be arbitrarily restricted in the range of their exercise.[10]

Missionary Spirit

The dominant, Jeffersonian version of the American myth was therefore significantly Christian while eschewing Christian doctrine. It was underwritten by the providence of a benevolent but distant Creator who differed vastly from the vengefully jealous Protestant God of many of Jefferson's contemporaries. Some of the latter gladly would have forced American minds to conform to their own narrow doctrines had they succeeded in establishing a state religion, which Jefferson, Madison, and others determinedly resisted. The Constitution of the U.S. government, whose survival and progress lay at the heart of the American mythology, was intentionally "godless" (the words "under God" in the Pledge of Allegiance were added only during the Red Scare of the 1950s). This was precisely to safeguard the liberty of Americans to believe or not to believe as they chose. Yet the struggle between devoutly religious Americans and free-thinking deists or downright atheists for ownership of the exemplary state, and thus for control over the interpretation of the American mission, has never ended.[11] In fact, a thoroughly Protestant version of mission has always mixed with the basically secular Enlightenment mythology, often reinforcing it as much as attempting to usurp it.

Indeed, the confluence of religious and secular missions in the minds of some American political leaders resulted in America's purposes in the world being readily identified with God's. Woodrow Wilson, whose name is forever associated with the missionary strain of U.S. foreign relations, proclaimed the identity explicitly upon America's entry into the Great War: America, he claimed was born a (Protestant) Christian nation in order to exemplify devotion to righteousness as derived from Holy Scripture. (Similar ideas have been attributed to George W. Bush.)[12]

Inherited Virtue-as-Excellence

America's English inheritance played an important part in forming this attitude. As we have noted, moderate Anglicans in seventeenth-century England had already argued a synthesis of views that, however it was transmitted, seems to have found a natural home on American soil. These were the notions that England was a nation elected by God to forward His providential plan on earth; true religion was compatible with and in fact confirmed by scientific discovery; Calvinistic determinism undermined the virtue of self-help; success in this world and the next depended on acts of free individual will; markets were natural and just in their apportionment of material rewards; and prosperity was therefore the proper reward of hard work.[13] In addition to such attitudes, Americans had also inherited from Britain an unusual gift for designing and operating institutions that guaranteed political liberty, an ability that their own native genius had indeed improved upon. The very wonder of their revolutionary victory over the most powerful nation on earth seemed evidence to Americans that divine Providence had been at work to ensure the baton of liberty passed decisively into more capable hands.

There was always some question and confusion as to whether the special virtues Americans allegedly exhibited were the result of cultural inheritance or of transmission by blood (of genetics, as we would now say). The universalizing assumptions of an American mission—to be forwarded by individual Americans regarded as representing the potential of all humanity—suggested the former. If the ringing words of the Declaration of Independence allowed no exception in the matter of human equality, the presumption must be that the obvious differences among peoples are cultural-historical and thus surmountable in time. Of course, progress may take a great deal of time, given the corrupting effects that rank and servility have on the human soul, but culture could be no necessary barrier. It was of the essence of "Americanism," after all, that anyone could become an American. One was not an American by virtue of birth, connection, or ethnicity but by virtue of allegiance to certain *ideas,* the idea of liberty above all. It followed that to be "un-American" was to betray, not primarily one's blood or kin, but the ideas and values to which America was committed.

Americanness was an act of willed commitment that anyone might choose to make. If the progressive dream of America were true, more and more nations, inspired by the success of the American example, would choose to adopt the ways and means of liberty and become more like Americans themselves. The virtue of Americans must therefore be merely *temporarily* exceptional, a matter for satisfaction, perhaps, but not for excessive pride. To the extent that the American mission succeeded, the exceptional nature of America and Americans must diminish, since the qualities of the guide are less remarkable once everyone knows the way. America would have achieved its historical goal, ironically, when American virtues were no longer peculiarly American. Yet the belief in special virtue was such an article of mythological faith that it was difficult for Americans to imagine it as other than a peculiar birthright and a cause for particularistic pride of the kind that the myth's universalism, reinforced by its Christian components, disavowed. The issue of pride is especially relevant when we consider virtue as a martial, republican quality, a strand that never disappeared from American life.

Martial Virtue

Martial virtue could be corrupted by softness, self-indulgence, and luxury, by a loss of virile energy and neglect of duty. Pride and honor were not just compatible with, but the very essence of, this intensely particularistic and patriotic virtue founded on devotion to a particular republic and way of life.

It was necessarily in considerable tension with the innocent virtue of the liberal Christian myth, though, as we have seen, it comported readily with that of kinship and descent, often reinterpreted in racial terms. It was the masculine virtue central to the frontier myth of "winning the West," clearly symbolized in the code of the gun and the honor of the rugged individual who, when challenged, would never back down.[14] It was the virtue that underwrote particularist American nationalism, mobilized whenever the nation's pride was slighted, its honor assailed, or its interests and assets attacked. Its martial spirit could sometimes be enlisted to support militarization and the aggrandizement of national power, though this urge was frequently tempered by the traditional republican fear that militarization would lead inevitably to empire abroad and tyranny at home. (Conservative nationalism was thus as likely to be expressed as an extreme form of isolationist withdrawal punctuated by outbursts of violent belligerence when national pride was perceived to be at stake.)

VIRTUE, POWER, AND LAW

The persistence and utility of martial virtue complicated the American attitude to power. Republican virtue presupposed the exercise of military power by a free people in the self-sacrificing defense of liberty, kin, and way of life. Liberal Enlightenment and Christian thought, however, harbored an extravagant suspicion of power as being always potentially deeply corrosive of virtue. No one denied that some level of armed power was necessary for the proper defense of the American experiment in free government, and there was a widespread belief that the growth of American power was anyway an inevitable by-product of the exercise of the liberal-Protestant virtues of industriousness, foresight, economy, and reason in an abundant land. But the facts of prosperity and power led to a perennial problem of how American power was to be best expressed and used so as to avoid corrupting the virtue that had produced it.[15] Consciousness of power tended, of course, to foster pride. Pride was natural to martial virtue but offensive to virtue as innocence, which tended toward Christian humility. The use of American power, especially military power, was a matter of honor for martial republican virtue; but even in self-defense, it endangered innocent virtue, which equated war with sinfulness and inevitable brutalization.

Thus were set the parameters of the recurring dilemma that Americans faced in understanding and deploying their power in a manner that did nothing to threaten the universal mission. For most of the nineteenth century, America's solution to this was to remain isolated from what it regarded as the primary site of corrupting power politics—Europe. But changes in the world by the end of the century, including America's own rise to wealth and power, turned isolation into a fading dream. Confronted with new temptations and opportunities to utilize their power in the wider world, Americans looked for a different solution to the dilemma, one that was based on their own domestic experience. As at home, international power would be tamed by being constitutionalized.

The extravagant fear of power derived partly, as I have noted, from radical Whig critiques, but it was reinforced by observation of war-scarred Europe. The tendency was always to equate power with force and coercion. If coercive power implied domination and therefore lack of liberty, it must be inherently corruptive. It corrupted its possessors by tempting them toward tyranny and corrupted nonpossessors by robbing them of liberty and making them servile. But if rule by force and coercion represented the demise of virtue, then its opposite—rule by deliberative agreement and rational law—must represent the exercise and preservation of virtue.

As we have seen, it was to mitigate and contain the natural tyrannical propensity of power that the U.S. political system institutionalized the principles of federalism and the separation of powers. Though the ruling idea here was that only power could check power, the whole ingenious system was further safeguarded by being authorized by, and made permanently subservient to, a written constitution. Constitutionalization created a "higher" realm of law above that of politics, controlling and limiting the latter. Abolitionists of the early nineteenth century indeed formulated an explicit "higher law doctrine," arguing that the Declaration of Independence, with its universalistic principles of natural rights, should be interpreted as a binding part of a flawed Constitution that winked at slavery.[16] Though the Supreme Court never accepted this, there was a sense in which the Constitution was always imaginatively constructed by Americans as a realm of higher law, controlling and moderating the play of political power. The rule of law, properly understood, was the rule of reason and justice as opposed to that of force and coercion.

The conservative view of the central role of federal government throughout the nineteenth century was to safeguard and maintain the

Constitution while otherwise leaving Americans free to get on with business. The Constitution was revered ostensibly because it substituted the rule of law for the rule of corruptible human beings. It preserved essential liberties by confining political power within prescribed institutional forms and by allowing for judicial review of all the "inferior" legislation that was the product of ordinary politics (the play of countervailing powers). Of course, control and interpretation of this law was the prerogative of judges who were themselves fallible, but Alexander Hamilton had explained in *The Federalist* No. 78 that the judiciary was the least dangerous branch of government, having the power of neither the sword nor the purse (which belonged to the executive and the legislature, respectively). "It may be truly said to have neither FORCE nor WILL," he wrote, "but merely judgment." Hamilton may have been too sanguine in thinking that "liberty had nothing to fear from the judiciary" as long as its powers were kept quite separate from the other branches, but nevertheless an image was established of the constitutional realm as the opposite of the realm of force and power. It was of the utmost significance that the Constitution had not been coercively imposed on the American people but was the result of agreement and vote. To be sure, the Constitution itself was in reality a flawed product of political bargaining and compromise (which is why the abolitionists wished to "constitutionalize" the Constitution by making it subject to the universal principles of the Declaration of Independence). Yet it could at least be imagined to be the consensual product of the wise deliberation, free agreement, and electoral assent of the people's own representatives.[17]

In this respect, the Constitution could be seen as solving the problem of the "general will" Rousseau set out in his *Social Contract*. Rousseau had sought to show how people might be thought to preserve their natural liberty when entering political society by being themselves the authors of the laws to which they would be subject. To be truly legitimate, however, the laws had to be more than an expression of people's particular wills, always liable to be arbitrarily swayed by passion and self-love. They must rather embody a cool general will that ensured they were the rationally best ones for preserving the common good. To be subject to laws that were simultaneously the product of one's own (highest) will and of pure deliberative reason could not be regarded as a loss of liberty.[18] Such a rule of law consequently represented the reign of virtue, not of force. It was natural enough for Americans, once they had canonized the founders, to see the Constitution in similar terms. In its transcendent role in the U.S. system of government, a deliberatively produced and electorally approved Constitution reconciled popular sovereignty with rational rule, signaling the ascendancy of reason and virtue over arbitrary will and brute force. The dangerous realm of politics and power was thus permanently constrained and tamed by the reign of virtue within the United States. No other polity had ever solved the problem of free government so efficaciously, not even Britain, which had hitherto been the model of political liberty.

CONCLUSION

The strong antithesis that the liberal myth set up between innocent virtue and power encouraged the tendency to identify the rule of virtue with an uncoerced realm of rationally agreed law. This would have important consequences as Americans considered their foreign policy options. Obviously, no super-arching agreement had ever been achieved among the nations and empires of Europe, whose interactions continued to be determined solely by the exigencies of force and cunning. International relations remained the uninhibited realm of treacherously corrupting "power politics." The prime question for early U.S. foreign policy, consequently, was how to operate and survive within this field of wickedness. As a particular nation in a world of competitively warring empires, the United States was obliged to find policies that would preserve its sovereign independence without staining its own virtue.

This would be difficult if it were assumed that any engagement in power politics was automatically corrupting. To play the same cynical, calculating game as other nations would be to descend to their level, dissolving any distinction between them and America and undermining the exemplary role. Yet how could America effectively safeguard its own proper interests *except* by playing the only game that was on offer? It would be tragically ironic if the American "city upon a hill" should be destroyed because of self-preservative actions taken in the international arena to preserve it, brought down through interaction with that same corrupt world whose last best hope it represented. Here lay the logical roots of that enduring tension between idealism and realism that has so often been noted in U.S. foreign policy, and the reason why that tension typically revealed itself in debates over international engagement versus national isolation (or "nonentanglement"). Isolation preserved exemplary virtue; engagement always threatened it.

The United States had to act in the world to protect its own interests, not just to ensure survival but to defend its pride. Yet every aggressive act of national self-assertion tended to emphasize the particularity of the nation and its interests rather than its universal nature, and sat awkwardly with a distinctly Christian-pacifist strain in the Jeffersonian myth. National pride and assertiveness in defense of justified interests was all very well, but it could too readily slide into jingoistic militarism and the desire for imperial conquest. It seemed to follow that being pulled by pride toward the pole of power meant being pulled away from the pole of innocent virtue, risking assimilation to the common brutality of ordinary nations and the failure of the universalistic mission. Transcendent American nationalism, even when expressed in isolationism, always had universalistic aims that resisted such particularism. It recognized no necessary boundaries between peoples and no necessary exclusions to Americanism: an American represented the potential of all humanity, and one became an American simply by devotion to the transcendent idea. Underlying all particularities of peoples and nations was the essential identity of human beings and the promise of liberty for individuals that the American experiment promised.

Such liberty was a form of secular salvation mirroring the salvation of souls granted by a Christian God for whom there was neither lord nor peasant, master nor slave, Jew nor gentile—only individual sinners in need of redemption. As in the Christian conception, love and benevolence were due from one soul to another rather than enmity and violence, the recognition of equality rather than superiority. Christian virtue was concerned with the cultivation of humility rather than pride, or at least not the arrogant pride associated with overweening power. When Woodrow Wilson declared there was such a thing as a nation being "too proud to fight," he signaled that Christian virtue was more concerned with preserving innocence than with defending worldly honor. This virtue cultivated peace rather than war, returned good for evil and kindness for injury. The violence of others was an occasion for displaying forbearance, while to perpetrate violence oneself was to forfeit innocence and to become brutalized and corrupt. Most remarkable, virtuous conduct was equated with selfless conduct, giving rise to an astonishing expectation among many

U.S. political leaders that U.S. foreign policy would be distinguished from that of other nations by its lack of self-interested motivation.

Yet it could hardly be denied that renouncing power to preserve innocent virtue and safeguard America's universal role left the nation exposed to humiliation and wounded pride. This must inevitably seem insupportable to a people convinced of its own special virtue. The dilemma of such corrupting entanglement might be avoided if America could remain truly isolated, but virtuous isolation was difficult to achieve as long as the United States insisted on being a great trading nation. The possibility of economic isolation based on national self-sufficiency was debated at certain points in U.S. history, but the fact was that the United States was locked at its birth into the developing global capitalist economy. How then could America preserve its virtue among quarreling nations when it was thoroughly commercially entangled with all of them? This is the subject of the following chapter.

CHAPTER FIVE

Nonentanglement

THE ECONOMIC DIMENSION

THE PRINCIPLE OF nonentanglement with foreign powers that was to characterize U.S. foreign policy for a century, and to leave significant traces even after the United States had become a world leader, was born during the first few turbulent years of the nation's history. Potentially fratricidal bitterness between Hamiltonian Federalists and Jeffersonian Republicans during the 1790s, caused by the intrusion of foreign affairs into domestic politics, gave serious pause to both parties. It caused even Jefferson to think that the American mission had to be a purely exemplary one rather than one of active engagement in foreign struggles.

Yet there were two ways of understanding the nonentanglement principle. It could denote either the prudent but temporary expedient of a weak nation striving to maintain its independence until such time as it could compete with dangerous rivals on equal terms; or a fixed intention to avoid being corrupted by European power politics, thus preserving American virtue and the sacred American mission. The first was Hamilton's (and perhaps Washington's) position, the latter broadly Jefferson's (though he was not altogether uninfluenced by the Hamiltonian reasoning). If the Hamiltonian version posed difficult but essentially pragmatic problems of survival, the Jeffersonian presented deeper puzzles. Washington had said in his famous farewell address that explicitly outlined the doctrine of nonentanglement: "The great rule of conduct for us in regard to foreign nations is, in extending our commercial relations to have as little *political* connection as possible."[1] But even the providential existence of an ocean between America and Europe could not guarantee the isolation needed to maintain innocent virtue in its purest state as long as Americans continued to trade. This seemed to present Jeffersonians with a clear choice: either strive desperately to maintain political isolation while remaining economically entangled, or pursue a strategy of economic self-sufficiency that would imply a more complete isolation.

This latter option was in fact seriously mooted at various points in U.S. history, though it was never realistically in the cards. Even Jefferson accepted that his simple agrarian republicans would need a continuous supply of the products of European civilization that Yankee traders imported in exchange for American agricultural goods. Many Americans nursed an alternate hope, however, one whose fulfillment promised to alleviate or cancel the problem. This was that the expansion of trade itself, and of free trade especially, would encourage the development of commercial republics much like the American. It was believed that such republics, bound together in webs of mutual commercial interest, would be inherently peaceful (unlike dynastic monarchies obsessed with princely honor and glory). The dangers of commercial entanglement would thus be dissolved. This was, indeed, the economic version of the American myth of mission, one that could be fulfilled simply by Americans being their true entrepreneurial selves—a compelling idea given that American liberal freedom was always tied to economic freedom. It was a hope incorporated in the very first diplomatic treaty the nation negotiated and one that would surface often in the centuries that followed, usually expressed as a wish for the spread of liberal democratic government.

In the next chapter I will begin to look at the political sense of nonentanglement. But first, I examine the economic dimensions of the struggle to preserve American virtue.

THE ECONOMIC DIMENSION I: ISOLATIONISM

William Appleman Williams claimed that U.S. diplomacy was driven principally by the commercial interests of businesses guided by the systematic imperatives of expansive capitalism. He nevertheless pointed to the consequential and contradictory ideas that generally informed U.S. foreign policy: a generous humanitarian impulse; a principle of individual and

national self-determination; and a feeling that other people must necessarily, for their own good, adopt the American way. Melvyn Leffler agreed
that the U.S. economy has always functioned as part of a world capitalist
system but argued that its participation in that system only occasionally
dictated its foreign policy decisions, which were more often affected by
considerations of national security. Yet neither national security nor the
national economy was ever separable as an issue from that of the universalistic mission. Americans have always sought, with wildly varying
degrees of success, to balance and reconcile their economic, security, and
missionary interests. At times of particular stress they have even been
tempted by the path of economic isolation.[2]

To appreciate how unlikely was the possibility that the United States
would actually ensure diplomatic isolation through economic isolation, we
might consider the fate of a comparable set of Calvinist European colonists
in another part of the world. By the early eighteenth century, Dutch settlers
in Capetown, South Africa, had given rise to a distinctive people known
as *trekboeren,* or wandering farmers, who over the subsequent hundred
years gradually dispersed eastward across southern Africa. The grim and
hardy Boers were fiercely independent pastoralists, as implacably hostile
to native tribes (whom they struggled to either enslave or exterminate) as
any American settler. Like the Americans, they saw themselves as divinely
elected, a righteous, patriarchal people chosen by God to rule over an alien
land and its backward heathen populations. Again like the Americans, the
Boers resisted the administration of the British, who took possession of
the Cape Colony during the Napoleonic wars and whose liberal policies
on slavery and the frontier threatened their way of life. The Great Trek
out of the Cape Colony between 1835 and 1843 formed the most dramatic
act of the Boers' own mythological narrative of liberty defended and a
frontier conquered. Once settled in the Transvaal and around the Orange
River, uninhibited by any founding document proclaiming the equality
of humankind, they developed a policy of apartheid that maintained the
strict inequality of black and white populations.[3]

The Boers, determinedly independent of all but the most minimal
form of state authority, provided a fair representation of the kind of frugal,
virtuous yeomanry that Jefferson idealized. Their life never rose above
subsistence level, and they seemed content to maintain it so. Was such a
fate ever conceivable for more than a handful of Americans? The relative

natural wealth of the two countries indicates the negative. Americans could and always did compare their wilderness to biblical Canaan, a land flowing with milk and honey; in the South African veldt the Boers found a promised land more akin to the desert habitat of the biblical prophets. The Cape was hardly more than a European weigh-station on the trade route to India, and until the discovery of gold and diamonds two hundred years after the beginning of white settlement, South Africa had no product to tempt traders or investors. Shut out from the international economy, it had no means of building real wealth and thus did not have to deal with the temptations of luxury.

Yet the contrast was more than one of differential abundance. In the United States, the doctrine of individual liberty made it practically a duty for settlers, ranchers, prospectors, speculators, and manufacturers to exploit to the fullest the land's natural wealth—often with ruthless disregard for environmental values—for the sake of personal prosperity and happiness. Most Americans produced, not for self-sustenance, but to sell to markets in order to achieve ever-higher material standards of living, and many of those markets were overseas. As colonists, Americans had been locked into an Atlantic trading system from the start. They were an intrinsic part of Britain's mercantilist empire, acting partly as a supplier of primary materials and partly in competition with British shipping for the Caribbean trade. Chafe as they might at their legally enforced dependence, they nevertheless enjoyed British protection from French and Indian depredations at sea and on land. This "Atlantic system" was continued even after the Revolution, mainly thanks to Jay's Treaty of 1794, which, though despised by Republicans, was ratified (under pressure from Hamilton) because it reestablished free-trading relations with Britain and heightened American financial respectability in the world's eyes. By this time a culture of determined enterprise was highly developed among Yankee traders in the North while the South had become reliant on export markets for the products of its plantations.

America was thus immersed in a globalizing economy from the very beginning, and the development of its resources, upon which any future greatness depended, made it reliant on foreign capital for more than a century. A community of interest grew between merchants of the eastern seaboard and in Britain, whose common concern was to systematically develop the resources of the United States, and whose common fear was the pell-mell, disorderly settlement of the West by feckless settlers seeking easy fortune or escape. Britain remained the principal source of the capital that developed the United States, though its metropolitan functions of control steadily migrated to the eastern seaboard as wealthy American merchants in Boston, Philadelphia, New York, and Baltimore took over the reins. Their interests found political expression in the Whig Party that succeeded the Federalists, whose program included free trade, sound money, the orderly sale of public lands to men of capital and federal and state aid for "internal improvements." New territories were to be opened up, immigrants assisted to fill the land and supply labor, riverboats constructed, canals dug, railroads laid, and Atlantic shipping built in order to provide continental Americans access to markets in the East and in Europe. This program was inherited by the Republican Party, whose defeat of the South in the Civil War freed the nation for systematic industrial development, ostensibly under the doctrine of laissez-faire but in fact crucially supported by government measures on tariffs and subsidies and other policies favorable to business. The rapid industrialization of America in the latter half of the nineteenth century—led by giant corporations like the Carnegie Steel Company, Standard Oil, the Singer Company, General Electric, the great railroad companies, and the banking interests of J. P. Morgan—locked the nation even more firmly into the international economy. The search for markets to absorb an ever-increasing volume of U.S. products, and the search for opportunities to invest an ever-growing volume of U.S. capital and savings, made the idea of an economically isolated America inconceivable.

Even so, the question of pursuing economic self-sufficiency was seriously raised from time to time in the course of U.S. history, usually under the stress of economic recession. The problem with being locked into the developing international capitalist economy, and into the complex system of cooperation and competition between capitalist states which that implied, was that the nation had to face the periodic crises that racked the whole system. Like other nations, America could respond to crisis by choosing from options that clustered around two broad poles: economic defense (economic nationalism) on the one hand and economic liberalism (internationalism) on the other. Henry Clay advocated the former after foreign trade declined in the 1820s, suggesting the creation of a self-supporting "American system," in which northeastern manufactures would be traded for western farm produce behind protective tariff walls. By contrast, President Grover Cleveland, with the support of economists and business groups, responded to the crisis of 1893 by reducing tariffs on imports in order to lower the input prices of raw materials and foodstuffs, thus making American industry more competitive. This choice between defensive closure and liberal opening of the economy seemed to parallel that between isolation and engagement in the political realm, yet what became clear during the late nineteenth century was that choices in one sphere had disturbing repercussions in, and a deep influence on, the other. Certainly, domestic political implications were inevitable either way. Clay's American system was resolutely opposed by "Cotton Whigs" of the South who depended critically on the Atlantic trade, signaling the domestic dissensions that tariff issues would arouse during the nullification crisis of 1832–1833. Cleveland's strategy in the 1890s sacrificed American farmers by removing their protections against cheap imports and portended the defeat of Populist domestic solutions like the free coinage of silver, which would have disadvantaged industrial trade.[4]

Nor could foreign policy be insulated from domestic economic issues. America had become part, an increasingly powerful part, of the Second Industrial Revolution. This meant it had given itself over to industrial capitalism's ruling principle of continuous and accelerating growth. It therefore inevitably found itself in sharp competition with foreigners for markets and investment opportunities, and frequently in conflict with indigenous populations in other lands who resented the disruption to their traditional ways of life that capitalist intrusion caused. Indeed, opting for incessant growth in production could turn even economic defense into an expansionist policy, as the example of Bismarck's Germany with its combination of high protective tariffs and aggressive colonization showed. A nation could protect its own industries behind tariff walls but still needed easy access to the raw materials of the world that fed industrialization, and these seemed best secured by colonizing the countries that possessed them. A purely domestic economy could not be self-sustaining except at low levels of production, but an empire could hope to maintain growth while remaining relatively insulated from other imperial powers. This was precisely imperialist Albert J. Beveridge's hope for America's future at the end of the nineteenth century.

The so-called Wisconsin school of historians strongly affirmed that

America's late-nineteenth-century burst of imperialism was not, as often claimed, an "aberration" but a logical and deliberate outcome of its industrial revolution.[5] Technological innovation and "forced" production led to "overproduction" and an anxious search for foreign markets in which to sell the surplus product. The problem was intensified by the long recession begun in 1873 that turned into severe depression from 1893 to 1897, causing unemployment and greater exploitative pressure on labor. This produced serious strikes and riots and an upsurge of "un-American" revolutionary ideas introduced by European immigrants. A distinct political-industrial elite, preferring forced production to "socialistic" redistributive policies, sought a solution to domestic unrest and capitalist crisis by pursuing formal or informal imperialist policies that could safely sustain continuous growth. This elite pressed for an improved American consular service that could report conditions and opportunities in foreign parts, for reciprocal treaties with Latin American countries that were the source of raw materials, for an Isthmian canal that would open the South American Pacific coast to Yankee trade and provide a route to the markets of Asia (especially China with its fabled promise of limitless wealth), and for the annexation of Hawaii and other strategic islands in the Pacific for the same purpose.

A necessary concomitant to such economic expansion was a modernized and expanded navy capable of defending U.S. gains and rights against imperial competitors, and also of forcing the door of the Open Door Policy whenever locals resisted. In a world of newly industrialized military powers, this became a pressing issue, though in truth it had always been an implication of the American commitment to external trade. Jeffersonian republicans, observing the British example, had feared from the beginning that expanding commerce would spearhead the advance of empire abroad. Protecting trade and the American citizens involved in it sooner or later required the dispatch of warships, armies, and ultimately administrations. War and entanglement seemed a direct consequence of commercial empire. Throughout the nineteenth century, American economic interests in foreign parts frequently required the protection of U.S. naval and marine forces (the U.S. Marines' Hymn, with its opening words, "From the halls of Montezuma to the shores of Tripoli," memorializes such far-flung engagements). Moreover, the precedent of using force to compel unwilling peoples to open their markets to American traders had been set by Commodore Matthew Perry in Japan in 1854 and formalized as a doctrine in the 1860s by William H. Seward, a determined expansionist who regarded the refusal to trade as a scandalous sin.[6]

The implications of expansion in an economy dominated by complex corporations also enhanced the stature of the presidency vis-à-vis Congress, the only part of government capable of pursuing and attaining the foreign policy goals and treaties that corporate leaders favored. William McKinley was the "first modern president" in this respect. In the words of Walter LaFeber: "In a centripetal-centrifugal effect, as U.S. foreign policy spread globally, authority over that policy centralized in the chief executive's office."[7] The "Imperial Presidency" was born, and ancient republican fears seemed about to be confirmed: imperial expansion led inevitably to militarization and to a dangerous centralization of power. It was hardly surprising that such developments should meet with determined resistance in the American context. Committed imperialists had necessarily to field arguments showing that these new developments were not a betrayal of American ideals but rather represented their fulfillment, a move that required a reinterpretation of the traditional mythology (see Chapter 8). Sincere anti-imperialists who opposed the thrust of U.S. foreign policy had, for their part, to show how economic development could be squared with continued diplomatic isolation and nonentanglement.

The option of isolationist self-sufficiency was not strongly expressed until the catastrophic economic collapse after 1929. The effects of the Great Depression produced general pessimism about free enterprise capitalism and the benefits of international trade. An explicit link between trade and political entanglement was drawn in a congressional investigation under Senator Gerald P. Nye in 1934, which blamed the nation's disastrous involvement in the Great European War in 1917 on the selfish pursuit of the trading interests of financiers and munitions manufacturers.[8] The Nye Committee convinced many members of Congress that America should legislate against economic entanglements, and the Progressive historian Charles Beard (who had supported entry into the war) welcomed the report and came out strongly for isolation and self-sufficiency. The policy he called "continentalism" required the imposition of even higher tariffs and large, planned cuts to domestic production.

The most considered response to self-sufficiency isolationists like Beard came from Henry A. Wallace, Franklin D. Roosevelt's secretary of

agriculture. Wallace's response is doubly interesting because he represen-
tatively embodied and defended the Progressive version of the essential
American myth. He had the traditional repugnance for European politics
and faith in America's superior virtue and was himself tempted for a
while to take the strict isolationist path to preserve it. As a quintessential
believer in America's providential mission and deeply concerned with its
economic dimensions, he wrestled long and hard with the question of
what economic policies the United States should pursue to fulfill it. In
a best-selling book, he posited a choice between economic isolation and
internationalism as alternate ways of dealing with the Depression. Though
Wallace believed Beard's was a potentially viable solution, he rejected it
because it would incur a "spiritual price" for America that was much
too high. The price would be an "army-like national discipline in peace
time" and unprecedented "regimentation of agriculture and industry."
Only severe state planning and regulation could compel overproducing
farmers and manufacturers to restrict output to serve a purely domestic
market. This ran directly contrary to the fundamental American tenet of
economic freedom.[9]

But Wallace also opposed economic isolation because it would be
harmful to the wider world. This raised an interesting and paradoxical
point for Americans, who were often insensitive to the ways in which
the measures they took in their own interests adversely affected nations
for whom they were supposed to provide a shining example. Protective
tariffs in particular frequently caused dismay and disappointment. The
highly protectionist McKinley Tariff Act of 1890 devastated the European
steel industry and placed high tariffs on sugar imports, causing American
planters in Hawaii to agitate for annexation. Such policies, indeed, played
into the hands of imperialists who sought precisely such objectives: it
may have been no accident that the sugar tariffs led to a revolution in
Cuba that impelled the United States into war and formal imperialism.
High tariffs after the Great War dismayed weaker nations wanting to
access the American market in order to earn dollars that would pay for
American food and machinery and speed recovery and development, provoking them to accuse the United States of setting a very poor example.
Tariffs of the 1920s, culminating in the Smoot-Hawley Tariff Act of 1930,
outraged feelings in countries like Japan and, according to Wallace, encouraged the defensive economic autarky that laid the groundwork for

fascism in Europe. Wallace argued that America could, by unselfishly and responsibly reducing tariffs and pursuing liberal international trade policies, use its economic power and leadership potential to guide the world to a peaceful and prosperous millennium, effectively countering the dreadful risk of war.[10]

Wallace was here advocating a course that could potentially solve the dilemma of America trying to remain politically nonentangled while being economically engaged. This was, specifically, to make economic engagement a central part of the American mission.

THE ECONOMIC DIMENSION II: ECONOMIC INTERNATIONALISM

The hope that fractious politics might be dissolved in peaceful economics could be traced to Montesquieu in the early eighteenth century. Anticipating the thought of Adam Smith by half a century, Montesquieu had said that all trading nations were, in reality, members of a single "grand Republic." In *The Spirit of the Laws* he wrote that "movable effects, as money, notes, bills of exchange, stocks in companies, vessels, and, in fine, all merchandise, belong to the whole world in general; in this respect it is composed of but one single state, of which all the societies on earth are members." Nations who bought from and sold to one another became mutually dependent and thus disinclined to quarrel. Trade therefore inclined to peace, at least in republican governments. Monarchies may love the splendors gained through trade but they distrusted merchants, and their commercial interests were always sidetracked by dynastic concerns. "Great enterprises, therefore, in commerce are not for monarchical, but for republican, governments." Montesquieu saw Britain as the great example: "Other nations have made the interests of commerce yield to those of politics; the English, on the contrary, have made their political interests give way to those of commerce."[11]

These themes were frequently rehearsed in the United States after independence. Tom Paine championed them in *Common Sense,* claiming that all wars were caused by monarchies and that republics were inherently pacific. America should therefore never make alliances that would embroil the country in the dynastic wars of Europe. Since America's market was all of Europe, no "partial connections" should be formed with any part of it.[12] The Continental Congress, however, thought these could scarcely be avoided, which was why, when it accepted Jefferson's Declaration of Independence in 1776, it also adopted Richard Henry Lee's resolution to form foreign alliances. Yet the "Model Treaty" drawn up by John Adams for a possible alliance with France was of a distinctly revolutionary kind. Adams, influenced by both Paine and Montesquieu, was determined that American relations with Europe would be founded only on "a commercial connection" and not a political one that implied "submission." The treaty suggested unprecedentedly liberal neutrality rights for third parties in situations of war between belligerent trading partners, but its overall purpose was to propose a scheme that provided French privileges to American merchants and American privileges to French. Since this was intended as a model for all future treaties, it was clear that the ultimate aim was a general trading system that recognized no nationalities at all. The plan was undoubtedly geared to American interests and American weakness, but it was argued on the novel grounds that general trade and prosperity would mitigate and perhaps ultimately eliminate the causes of war between nations.

This was a proposition, however, that the mercantilist nations of Europe refused to accept, and Adams himself was soon disillusioned by harsh political experience. Though nations might mouth the rhetoric of free trade, they were quick to prohibit imports that threatened their own industries or that upset their balance of trade. It was impossible to be economically virtuous when all around were pursuing policies of the most narrowly self-interested kind. Simple defense required reciprocal action. Hamilton, for his part, lambasted the whole idea of peaceful republics, which he said flew in the face of both historical experience and authorities as eminent as Machiavelli and Hobbes. Commerce had done nothing to alter the frequency of war but had merely changed its objects. It was time, he concluded in *The Federalist* No. 6, to dispense with the fallacies and idle theories that the United States would be exempt from ordinary imperfections and weaknesses. "Is it not time to awake from the deceitful dream of a golden age, and to adopt as a practical maxim for the direction of our global conduct that we, as well as the other inhabitants of the globe, are yet remote from the happy empire of perfect wisdom and perfect virtue?"[13] Better to strengthen one's navies and defend one's commercial interests with all the force and diplomacy one could muster.

Hamilton may have had reason, history, and experience on his side, and once again his objections prefigured American realities. Nevertheless, he had captured neither the nation's mythological consciousness nor its conscience. The idea that commerce and economic development would promote democratization and international peace would recur again and again as a theme, informing American liberal economic internationalism. President William H. Taft's Dollar Diplomacy after 1909, for example, was a move from traditional protections of American life and property abroad to the active support of overseas investment by both the diplomatic and consular corps. The idea here was that investments were good not just for the United States but for the countries invested in. They earned profits for America, improving its economic welfare, while promoting economic and social stability abroad, thus promoting world peace. Dollar Diplomacy would be, Taft said, a benign "nonimperialistic" imperialism that transcended territorial imperialism, replacing guns with gold, dollars with bullets. Taft was a wholehearted subscriber to the fundamental liberal economic faith: "The right of property and the motive of accumulation, next to the right of liberty, is the basis of all modern, successful civiliza- tion, and until you have a community of political influence and control which is affected by the conserving influences of property and property ownership, successful popular government is impossible." The policy may have seemed intensely self-serving, but it was an attempt to reconcile commercial expansion with the traditional mission. It was, however, a fail- ure. Taft too often had to back up dollars with bullets to secure American investment interests, usually by helping reactionary or dictatorial regimes to suppress domestic revolution.[14]

Taft's successor, Woodrow Wilson, also regarded the global expansion of American enterprise as a force for progress toward liberal democratic government, but he believed that the use of American power to further such expansion was an act of selfishness. He was therefore distraught to find himself caught in the same trap as Taft, dispatching ships and marines to rebellious Latin American countries to preserve American business interests that were the chief agents of upheaval.

The general blindness of Americans to the disruptive effects of mar- ketization on traditional societies and economies was hardly surprising given their belief in the universality of liberal values and the universal significance of their own example. Universalism was, anyway, a necessary assumption if their expansive commercial ambition was to be reconciled with the preservation of virtue. Herbert Hoover provided another notable example of such attempted reconciliation after the Great War had transformed the United States from a debtor to a creditor nation. Hoover, particularly as secretary of commerce in the years before 1929, consciously employed American finance in the pursuit of what has been termed "economic diplomacy." His philosophy of a new "American System," very different from Clay's, was perfectly in keeping with the traditional mythology. America was the great exemplar of democratic freedom in the world, and freedom was synonymous with economic freedom. Hoover's explicit goal was the defense and expansion of that freedom at home and abroad. This created a de facto alliance between business and free government, the latter's task being, never to coerce, but to encourage "free men" whose self-interest and civic spirit would bring national prosperity and produce surpluses that could be deployed elsewhere. The practical know-how and can-do attitudes of motivated individuals that made the United States a great industrial power could be demonstrated and implanted abroad, inspiring economic progress on a world scale and the formation of a peaceful international commonwealth of commerce. Hoover even defended America's high tariffs as being in the long-term interests of other nations on the familiar reasoning of America's mythological mission. America must not only survive but also thrive, Hoover said. If it were now to be the essential driver of global economic development and the world's banker, it needed to stimulate its own domestic production, earn more revenue, and strengthen the value of the dollar. Tariffs allegedly achieved these goals. Thus was apparent selfishness revealed to be disinterestedness, and genuine economic internationalism was essentially linked to, while being arguably compromised by, economic nationalism. The enduring tension between particularism and universalism was again displayed.[15]

Hoover tried desperately to preserve and further his noble endeavor as president after 1929, but his efforts were destroyed by the onset of the Great Depression. This worst of capitalist crises demonstrated in catastrophic fashion how dependent the global economy had indeed become on the United States. The effects of American collapse were rapidly transmitted abroad, ushering in an era of intense economic nationalism that saw the abandonment of the gold standard, the end of currency convertibility, the initiation of universal protectionism, and the formation of defensive regional trading blocs (the so-called autarkic response).[16]

Franklin Roosevelt, succeeding Hoover, showed little leadership in matters of international economy, preferring to concentrate on desperate domestic problems. Yet by 1936 American officials were again busy trying to steer economic policy back onto an internationalist path by encouraging exchange rate stability and multilateral trade. The apotheosis of their efforts was the Bretton Woods international conference of July 1944, which laid the economic foundations for a new post–World War II order, establishing the International Monetary Fund and the precursor to the World Bank. The United States thus committed itself to becoming the linchpin of arrangements aimed at guaranteeing world peace, though full internationalization was frustrated by the onset of the Cold War. American aid to Europe through the farsighted Marshall Plan, its reconstruction of the shattered Japanese economy, and its economic dominance and leadership of the West could perhaps be seen as a partial fulfillment of the grander promise. But it was difficult to argue that American Western hegemony in a nuclear world dangerously divided between two antagonistic blocs really represented a fulfillment of Montesquieu's vision of peacefully cooperative republics.

The end of the Cold War was certainly celebrated as the triumph of the liberal democratic way (the "end of history" indeed), but it also saw the emergence of tensions and conflicts between old allies that the greater conflict had long suppressed. In a rapidly globalizing world, however, the dream of peace through liberal economic progress persisted. It would be evidenced in Bill Clinton's geoeconomic foreign policy and in George W. Bush's response to the new challenge of Islamist terrorism—democratization of the Middle East on the assumption that liberal development policies would undercut anti-Western hostility (see Chapter 17).

CONCLUSION

The persistent American desire for diplomatic isolation always had to contend with the fact of original and increasing economic integration in the world economy. The central question was whether economic involvement represented primarily a threat to the American mission or an opportunity for its fulfillment. If economic entanglement dragged the United States into war or imperialism, then it threatened the virtue that was fundamental to the mission. If, on the contrary, the spread of liberal economics constituted the spread of peaceful enterprise and development, then virtue was secure and economic engagement was at one with political mission. What was clear, however, was that the United States was capitalist at its foundation and an expansive industrial and postindustrial capitalist country in its progress, despite the severe challenges of economic depression. The choice of economic isolation therefore can hardly be imagined as realistic. Hopes of liberal internationalism, on the other hand, remained still to be definitively proved even at the start of the twenty-first century. Given the nature of the American example, Americans have little choice but to cling to this hope for the long term, but the problem in the meantime has always been how to reconcile economic engagement with the preservation of virtue.

It is to this problem that I turn in the next chapter, which begins to trace the history of political nonentanglement.

CHAPTER SIX

Nonentanglement

THE POLITICAL DIMENSION

IT WAS HIGHLY SIGNIFICANT that the first major test of the new republic and of its actual or prospective character should have been sparked by events abroad that raised the vexing question of entanglement in foreign affairs. Revolutionary turmoil in Europe between 1787 and 1799 reverberated violently at home, causing ideological divisions that threatened the very survival of the young United States. A consensus was eventually reached that the only safe solution was a declaration of American neutrality as between belligerents and a policy of nonentanglement in the destructive quarrels of Europe.

The practice of neutrality was made both difficult and necessary by the fact that the United States was commercially entangled with nations at war with one another. Moreover, the demand that these nations respect U.S. neutrality was generally unsupported by U.S. military preparedness. Hamilton had warned that the rights of a feeble government would be but little respected, and "if we mean to be a commercial people, it must form part of our policy to be able to defend that commerce."[1] But republican Americans believed that building powerful standing armies and navies, even for defensive purposes, would conduce to warfare abroad and tyranny at home, ultimately destroying virtue. Yet absent such forces, avowed neutrality was not an effective solution. Powerful nations could simply ignore it, attacking at will American shipping that supplied their enemies with necessary provisions, including arms.

This dilemma raised a question of American pride and honor that tended to undermine the resolve to dispense with conventional military forces. Though power might be a danger to virtue, it was unfortunately also true that material power brought international prestige and respect. Powerlessness in a wicked world, as Hamilton had said, brought merely contempt. Unpunished foreign attacks against American interests inevitably provoked domestic outrage. Jefferson as president, finding American neutrality flouted, tried to retaliate by using economic interests as a weapon that could substitute for military power, but his strategy proved a dismal failure. It left the nation with a sense of impotence, shame, and dishonor that only a raggedly fought but ultimately satisfactory war would erase.

The successful assertion of American force evoked outpourings of pride and joy and gave a boost to a nascent sense of American parochial nationalism. The new nationalistic spirit encouraged at length the announcement of a foreign policy doctrine proclaiming the Western hemisphere to be off-limits to European colonization. The Monroe Doctrine was a precocious claim of American right that simultaneously signaled the nation's isolationist intentions with respect to Europe. The United States would be continentally strengthened through internal expansion while resisting further entanglement in corrupting European power politics. Healthy growth and material preservation would thus be assured even as American virtue was preserved. Particularistic pride and innocent virtue were in this case apparently compatible, even mutually reinforcing. Yet there loomed a troubling question: how was such a conception of virtue to be reconciled with the application of force necessary to achieve continental expansion?

These are the central themes explored in this chapter and the next.

AMERICAN NEUTRALITY

The American Revolution infused European progressive opinion with hope but naturally filled its reigning aristocrats with dread. Depending on who looked, the United States was either a magic mirror reflecting the future liberation of Europe or a horrible anticipation of the chaos to come. This divided reaction ensured that every development in U.S. politics would be closely scrutinized for the meaning it held for France and Europe for several crucial decades. Many Americans fully reciprocated this interest, eager to encourage in the Old World forces of liberty they had unleashed in the New. Whether such interest should extend beyond moral support to include material assistance was a question that arose when revolution stirred in France in 1789. It became one of urgent significance after 1793, when a coalition of European monarchies declared war on revolutionary France in an effort to crush the republican threat it presented. The very stability and survival of the new American nation seemed to depend on how the question of foreign entanglement was answered.

The events in Europe acutely sharpened the existing division between Hamiltonian Federalists and Jeffersonian Republicans. Though both parties had welcomed the start of the French Revolution as a progressive episode, the Federalists grew increasingly alarmed at the French failure to establish a stable government and at the descent into terror at home and conquest abroad. With France soon at war with Britain, both of them trading partners of the United States, the division between Federalists and Republicans turned into one of Anglophile social conservatives versus Francophile radicals. An influx of vocal English and French émigrés violently inflamed the domestic debate, and political clubs and Democratic Societies sprang up in imitation of the French Jacobin clubs. This export of violent radicalism to the United States caused shivers of horror among the ranks of the Federalists.

For most Republicans, on the other hand, the spectacle of French popular nationalism and radical egalitarianism stirred a powerful sympathy. Jefferson, for his part, championed the radicals and eulogized the French Revolution, often in immoderate terms. Republicans launched stringent attacks on the ruling elites, turning the dominant issue into one about popular participation in politics. Events in France seemed to them to confirm the significance of their own revolution, which could now be seen as the precursor of the French, the first stage in the progressive emancipation of all civilized humanity from the tyranny of rank, custom, and prejudice. In the bitter wrangling that followed, Federalists and Republicans heatedly accused one another of undermining the American republic.[2]

In these dangerously fractious circumstances, the administrations of both George Washington and John Adams strove to avoid being seen to act for or against either France or Britain. Yet it was hard to maintain a sentiment for neutrality in the country while British warships preyed on American traders bound for France. When the Federalists refused to respond to such outrages with sufficient wrath, Republicans accused them of pursuing policies friendly to Britain and of thereby revealing their aristocratic sympathies and tendencies. Jay's Treaty of 1794—negotiated with Britain by the Federalists (in truth under the manipulation of Hamilton) to settle differences and thus prevent war—particularly incensed Republicans.[3] When they tried to block its ratification by Congress, Federalists condemned them for risking war with Britain and for showing their French Jacobin sympathies.

The American accord with Britain established by Jay's Treaty inevitably incurred the hostility of France. The French viewed the eventual ratification of the treaty by Britain and the United States in 1796 as a violation of its own 1778 commercial treaty with America, not to mention a betrayal of the friendship and assistance that France had given the Americans during their own revolutionary war. They broke off diplomatic relations and launched an undeclared naval war against the United States. This caused great alarm among the public and provoked a bellicose reaction among extremist Federalists, whose feelings of kinship for Britain made the conflict at home genuinely one about the new nation's identity. Hamilton schemed to get himself put in charge of an army (ostensibly to defend the country against French invasion but perhaps equally to invade Spanish holdings in the South) while President Adams stubbornly resisted the pressure toward war and sought a negotiated solution. To Hamilton's fury, Adams eventually succeeded in ending the crisis in 1799, at the cost of his own chances of reelection and the division and effectual ruin of the Federalist Party.

The passions that this prolonged episode aroused had threatened to tear the new nation asunder, but at its end the robustness of America's experimental political system was confirmed. Jefferson triumphed over Adams in the presidential election of 1800, and power passed peacefully from one set of bitter rivals to the other. As Henry Adams wryly observed in his history of the era: "So strong was the new president's persuasion of the monarchical bent of his predecessors, that his joy at obtaining the government was mingled with a shade of surprise that his enemies should have handed to him, without question, the power they had so long held."[4]

If the events of this period had helped confirm in Americans the Enlightenment view of America's special destiny, it had also demonstrated the difficulties they would face in keeping faith with that destiny in a turbulent world. The American government represented, Jefferson said, "the world's best hope," the proof that a republic, even one of large extent, could maintain itself and prosper. If the best interests of all humanity were to be served, the particular and more immediate interests of America had to be met. Clearly, there would always be the possibility of conflict here. How was national survival to be maintained under the strain of internal dissension and external threat without at the same time jeopardizing the crucial representative, universal role?

From the very start of the Revolutionary War, the predominant American answer to this problem was a policy of neutrality. The Model Treaty of 1776 had revealed the general direction of American thinking. Commercial diplomacy rather than political treaty-making would be the rule after independence. This explained the clause in the Constitution of 1787 that discouraged treaty-making by requiring two-thirds of the Senate to approve ratification (so that it would take a mere minority of senators to defeat a treaty). None of the constitutional framers believed that the United States would need any more than six diplomatic missions abroad, since they assumed that diplomatic negotiations, as opposed to commercial relations, would be comparatively rare.[5] American leaders saw their best protection, not in forming alliances, but in adopting a policy of strict neutrality that would prevent the nation being dragged into the endless quarrels and conflicts of Europe.

Neutrality, however, is extremely difficult to maintain when the neutral country's trading partners are warring one against the other. An action that one belligerent accepts as even-handed, because it does not harm its own cause, is bound to be interpreted by the other as an instance of partiality. The problem becomes even more acute when the neutral state feels actual sympathy for one party over another, a lesson Americans learned during the French revolutionary wars and again, a century later, during the Great European War. Republicans in the 1790s, for instance, were outraged at the heavy-handed treatment of U.S. merchant vessels by British warships and demanded responsive measures that were beyond the capacity of the young country to take. Hamilton's Federalists, on this occasion, were willing to swallow their pride, believing that the overriding national interest lay with preserving peace with England. Hamilton went out of his way to defend the Neutrality Proclamation against the Democratic Societies, who saw it as evidence of American cowardice.[6] He and his Federalists, however, were in their turn outraged by the depredations of France and prepared to countenance war to correct the offense.

Indeed, such partiality was unavoidable once the universalist myth had been accepted. If the United States really represented the world as it would some day be, it must surely be automatically on the side of any nation that attempted to follow its example. This is certainly what Jefferson's Republicans believed during the 1790s. Yet siding with France automatically aroused England's enmity, and the enmity of England presented a very real danger to the republic's fortunes. If America's survival had to be assured for the world's sake, then it seemed essential to placate England. But prudently placating England ensured French enmity, thus tragically pitting one new republic against another.

These difficulties did not negate the policy of neutrality for Americans. Indeed, the domestic alarms set off by the French Revolution made strict American neutrality seem even more necessary to the administration of George Washington. In an effort to discourage U.S. citizens from passionate commitment to foreign causes, Washington first issued a Neutrality Proclamation and then steered through the Neutrality Act of 1794. The latter prohibited U.S. citizens from enlisting in foreign armies, from raising forces at home to aid a belligerent, or from arming belligerent warships in U.S. waters. In his farewell address (mostly composed by Hamilton), Washington famously counseled against "foreign entanglements" and explained that his neutralist policy had been motivated by the need to gain time for his country to settle its institutions and acquire the strength necessary to command its own fortunes. The Neutrality Act, however, proved to be much more than a temporary expedient. It was made permanent in 1800, extended to prohibit American involvement in wars of revolution in 1817, and codified in legislation in 1818. It would remain a cornerstone of U.S. foreign policy until at least World War I and a continuing forlorn hope for nonentanglement right up until World War II.

The drastic effects of foreign turmoil on domestic tranquility convinced even Jefferson of the prudence of avoiding entanglements on the basis of principled sympathies. In a remarkable statement of his principles in 1799 (principles he claimed were unquestionably those of the great body of citizens), he said: "I am for free commerce with all nations, political connection with none; & little or no diplomatic establishment. And I am not for linking ourselves by new treaties with the quarrels of Europe; entering that field of slaughter to preserve their balance, or joining in the confederacy of kings to war against principles of liberty." As president he would repeat in his own words Washington's neutralist prescription: "peace, commerce, and honest friendship with all nations, entangling alliances with none." Using force to defend liberty abroad was clearly fraught with complications and roused bitter and dangerous partisanship at home, as Jefferson expressed in a letter to Tom Paine: "Determined as we are to avoid, if possible, wasting the energies of our people in war and destruction, we shall avoid implicating ourselves with the Powers of Europe, even in support of principles that we mean to pursue. They have so many other interests different from ours that we must avoid being entangled in them. We can enforce those principles as to ourselves by peacable [sic] means, now that we are likely to have our public councils detached from foreign views."[7]

PRIDE, HONOR, AND INTERESTS

On one level, then, avoiding entanglements was a matter of simple prudence for an insecure infant nation. For Hamiltonians, such caution might be merely expedient until the United States had grown into a first-rate power (as most Americans confidently expected it would), at which time it could choose to further its interests as it might, militarily when necessary. For Jeffersonians, however, avoiding entanglements bore directly on the American libertarian mission. Entry into foreign wars, even on behalf of a worthy cause, would place intolerable pressure on civil life. The passions aroused by war and the proscriptions that always accompanied it would seriously jeopardize constitutional government and republican freedoms of speech and assembly. War and militarization would lead to centralization of power and thus to tyranny, a sequence startlingly confirmed by the transformation of the French Republic into the Napoleonic Empire during Jefferson's presidency. Foreign involvement meant the risk of forfeiting America's peculiar virtue and thus its exemplary role. It was not just the survival of the nation that was at stake, but the meaning of America for the world. While America-the-particular-nation had a good prudential reason for avoiding foreign entanglements, America-the-universal-nation had a positive obligation to avoid them.

Yet even if alliances could be avoided, the United States still had to defend its own particular interests and integrity against the encroachments and depredations of powerful rivals. A major motivation for seeking a stronger union in 1787, after all, had been a widespread concern over American weakness in the world. "There is scarcely any thing," wrote Hamilton in *The Federalist* No. 15, "that can wound the pride or degrade the character of an independent nation which we do not experience."[8] The question therefore arose of how the defense of national interests could be effectively guaranteed.

Jefferson had seen the problem clearly enough by 1785. Despite his agrarian preferences, he could hardly deny the maritime provinces their established interests in trade, nor American farmers access to the technological advances of European industry. But extensive trade inevitably left U.S. shipping open to foreign depredation and insult. In a letter to John Jay he lamented:

> And insults must be resented . . . to prevent their eternal repetition. Or in other words, our commerce on the ocean must be paid for by frequent war. The justest dispositions possible in ourselves will not secure us against it. It would be necessary that all other nations were just also. Justice indeed on our part will save us from those wars which would have been produced by a contrary disposition. But how to prevent those produced by the wrongs of other nations? By putting ourselves in a condition to punish them. Weakness provokes insult and injury, while a condition to punish it often prevents it. This reasoning leads to the necessity of some naval force, that being the only weapon with which we can reach an enemy. I think it to our interest to punish the first insult: because an insult unpunished is the parent of many others.[9]

Effective defense seemed to require the accumulation and disposal of national power in the form of military might, but elaborate military preparedness was antithetical to the republican spirit. Jefferson argued that standing armies in peacetime would "overawe the public sentiment, while strong navies would drag the nation into eternal warfare and crippling expense."[10] Moreover, war inevitably led to centralized government, a strengthened executive, higher taxes, the loss of "republican simplicity," the subversion of the Constitution, and the suppression of civil liberties. To take arms against a sea of foreign troubles was therefore to risk the destruction of American civic virtue and the end of the American mission. With Jefferson's victory over the Federalists in 1800, and the beginning of the long Republican ascendancy, this belief solidified into Republican dogma.

Yet the refusal to arm carried its own threat. The troubling question was whether a strictly limited central government lacking command of an army or extensive navy could maintain itself against internal or external threat. Jefferson put his faith for internal defense on citizen militias and for the prevention of sea-going depredations on a small navy that would present little danger to the integrity of the republic. But a small navy was also incapable of punishing offenders in the way he had prescribed. Such forces, however zealously they might respond, exerted negligible force in the day-to-day conduct of foreign relations.

Unable to pose a credible military threat to powerful nations, Jeffersonians sought to preserve U.S. interests by the use of economic incentives. Jefferson thought that governments, like people, were essentially controlled by their interests and that he could therefore prevent war by manipulating European commercial interests. As early as 1793 he was prescribing an alternative to war "which will furnish us a happy opportunity of setting another precious example to the world, by shewing that nations may be brought to justice by appeals to their interests as well as by appeals to arms."[11] Threats to withhold American commerce from one or another of the great European rivals—a commerce on which their interests were presumed critically to depend—would force each to observe and honor American neutrality. The interest of every nation would "stand surety for their justice," and trade embargos would prove an effective substitute for armies, navies, and wars.

Years of foreign policy failure during Jefferson's and his successor Monroe's presidencies would show that many things were amiss with this reasoning. Banking as it did on hard-headed calculations of interest, it overlooked the very factor to which Jefferson himself had pointed: the extent to which a lack of conventional power would leave Americans exposed to devastating slights to their national pride and honor. In the rivalrous conditions of the early nineteenth century, Jefferson's economic weapon proved a poor one. Neither Britain nor Napoleonic France, after

the resumption of war between them in 1803, was inclined to show tender respect for the neutral rights of U.S. ships carrying supplies to the
enemy. Napoleon's clearly expressed contempt for the United States was
a sting to the pride of Americans, but his maritime weakness made his
edicts against their shipping relatively bearable. Americans were much
more incensed by the attacks of British warships on their vessels, and
especially by the British habit of "impressing" American seamen (often
British deserters or emigrants) into their own service.

An attack by the Royal Navy on the American frigate *Chesapeake* in
1807, in which four seamen were removed and one hung, ignited particular outrage among Americans. ("No Nation," John Quincy Adams would
later declare, "can be Independent which suffers her Citizens to be stolen
from her at the discretion of the naval or Military Officers of another.")
Later that same year, the British government, which had already declared a
blockade on the whole of northern Europe, issued Orders in Council that
prohibited all trade with France except that which passed through British
ports and paid duties to the crown. This was seen as amounting to a re-
imposition of colonial regulation that had been removed by the Revolutionary War. By dint of it, according to Henry Adams, "American commerce
was made English." The orders were deeply resented in America and gave
the prolonged argument with Britain, whatever its real determinants, the
popular character of a second struggle for independence.[12]

Jefferson's response was first to try negotiating with Britain, at which
he proved inept, and then to attempt "peaceful coercion." The Embargo
Act of 1807 prohibiting both U.S. exports and the departure of U.S. shipping (except in coastwise trade) was widely evaded and failed to impress
either the British or the French. The Non-Intercourse Act legislated under
Madison in 1809, which aimed to close the export-import trade with belligerents, proved even weaker and aroused general contempt. The failure
of "economic warfare" caused a mounting sense of national frustration
and humiliation that came to a head after the congressional elections of
1810–1811 brought new and vigorous young leaders like John C. Calhoun
and Henry Clay to the legislature. These were men who, if they did not
exactly want war, were prepared to accept it for the sake of national honor
and independence. With the British continuing intransigent, the Foreign
Relations Committee of November 29, 1811, produced a report stating that
the time for "submission" was at an end. It recommended preparations

for war. "What are we not to lose by peace?" asked Clay; "—commerce, character, a nation's best treasure, honor!"[13] With such sentiment mounting, conservative Republicans were forced to wrestle with their faith in Jeffersonian pacifism. Acting the peaceful lamb in a wilderness of wolves had, on the face of it, proved a forlorn and misguided policy. After an agonized debate that lasted seventeen days, Congress voted for a war bill. Madison signed it on June 18, 1812, not realizing that Britain had already withdrawn the offending orders.

Thus the United States stumbled into a misbegotten war with no army, a miniscule navy, and no war plan. It was a war poorly led by Madison, often mismanaged on the ground, and only occasionally successful at sea. Moreover, it ended as ironically as it had begun, with Andrew Jackson's defeat of a British force at New Orleans occurring after a peace treaty had already been signed at Ghent a month before.[14] Yet it had several notable consequences for the United States. First, it settled the question of Canadian independence, creating the basis for perpetual peace between the two neighbors (though Americans continued to hope that Canada would grow closer to the United States in time and eventually join the Union voluntarily). Second, it marked the end of serious British interference in U.S. affairs (though Republicans could not conceive at the time that this would be so). Third, it fatally discredited the Federalists, whose actions in calling a New England convention to oppose "Mr. Madison's war" were widely regarded as seditious. Fourth, Britain's betrayal of its American Indian allies during the treaty negotiations, combined with Jackson's defeat of the Creeks at Horseshoe Bend, left the West effectively open to U.S. territorial expansion. Last and by no means least, it gave American nationalism a very decided boost; it was no coincidence that an incident in this war inspired the writing of "The Star-Spangled Banner." The experience of this war caused even Jefferson to discard his adamant opposition to U.S. manufacturing. Modern industry implied military power, and preserving national security seemed to require a measure of industrial self-sufficiency.

All these factors were important in defining the character and future extent of the United States. Principles of nationalism that had largely been the preserve of the Federalists now passed to Republicans under the leadership of James Monroe and John Quincy Adams. Moreover, these men's brand of nationalism was decidedly expansionist, unlike that of many Federalists (who had, for example, opposed Jefferson's purchase of the Louisiana Territory from Napoleon in 1803). With the British threat removed and Indian capacity severely crippled, the potential existed for the nation to spread rapidly westward.

AMERICAN NATIONALISM AND THE MONROE DOCTRINE

This more expansive attitude reflected the self-confidence gained through a war that had ended a long period of national humiliation. Jefferson's policy of economic warfare had, according to a major historian of the period, "served chiefly to convince Europe of the cowardice of the United States . . . [under a leadership that] often spoke loudly and carried no stick at all." The war washed that shame away. Though it had been fought to a draw at best, it might as well have been a famous American victory for the effect it had on national morale. The United States had taken on the greatest maritime power on earth and survived intact. A conflict that, at its start, had been rhetorically declared a second and last struggle for national freedom was declared, at its end, to have restored national honor and self-respect. A year after the war finished, Clay declaimed: "Let any man look at the degraded condition of this country before the war; the scorn of the universe, the contempt of ourselves. . . . What is our present situation? Respectability and character abroad—security and confidence at home . . . our character and Constitutions are placed on a solid basis, never to be shaken."[15]

Americans felt renewed pride and a more assured sense of place in the world. The national leadership after 1815 was determined to assert the new spirit that was abroad. Republicans were suddenly converted to schemes they had formerly opposed but that now seemed necessary to secure the nation's defense and prosperity. Madison, before he left office, took a number of initiatives that would previously have been anathema to Republicans. He chartered a new national bank (having let the first one lapse) in order to mobilize national resources; he appropriated funds for land defense and for a much enlarged navy sufficient to defend American shipping; and he imposed protective tariffs on imported manufactured goods, particularly British ones, to encourage national self-sufficiency. He also launched efforts to open the British West Indies to American ships, a long campaign motivated more by American pride than by the doubtful practical benefits that might accrue.

Madison's successor, James Monroe, the last president to have been an active revolutionary, proved in many ways an ideal embodiment of the fresh sense of American nationalism. Presiding over a brief "era of good feelings," he remained firmly above all sectional and personal squabbling to stand proudly for the whole nation. But the driving force behind his administration's nationalistic policies was his secretary of state, the son of John Adams, John Quincy Adams. Adams was a believer in the importance of the American political experiment and concerned to ensure its continuance by securing the United States as a continental entity. His continental ambitions produced far-reaching diplomatic achievements that expanded the territorial range of the nation. But Adams went further and sought to put the entire Western hemisphere under the exclusive protection of the United States, an intention embodied in a precocious declaration of diplomatic independence in 1823.

Though largely the work of Adams, this became known to history as the Monroe Doctrine. One part of it, the "noncolonization principle," was directed at European powers tempted to establish colonies in Central and South America where the Spanish Empire was crumbling. This principle asserted that "the American continents, by the free and independent condition which they have assumed and maintained, are henceforth no longer subjects for any new European colonial establishments." The noncolonization principle was later supplemented by a "nonintervention principle," a response to fears that European powers were planning to intervene forcefully to help Spain regain the colonies it had lost in a series of Latin American revolutions. Americans were obliged to feel some sympathy for these nationalist revolutions given their own history and the national myth they had constructed around it, though their attitude was in fact quite ambivalent. They doubted whether nonwhite populations had the virtue and capacity to make their revolutions succeed in the liberal manner of the American and were disinclined to offer them material support.[16]

They were even more disinclined, however, to see them crushed by reactionary European governments and therefore took the extraordinarily bold step of issuing a hands-off order to empires more powerful than themselves. Monroe, again under the advice of Adams, warned that his government would view any attempt by European powers to oppress Latin American states, or to control their destinies, as showing "an unfriendly disposition toward the United States." Significantly, though, Adams saw that this nonintervention principle had to have reciprocal effect, preventing U.S. intervention in European independence movements. The Greek struggle against the decaying Ottoman Empire, for example, was a very popular cause in the United States, and some prominent leaders favored lending it material support. But Adams had already stated his views on such matters in 1821, when he argued that the United States should be a "beacon of liberty" for other peoples but not an active participant in their struggles. In a much-cited passage he had declared: "Wherever the standard of freedom and independence has been or shall be unfurled, there will her heart, her benediction, and her prayers be. But she goes not abroad in search of monsters to destroy. She is the well-wisher to the freedom and independence of all. She is the champion and vindicator only of her own." In 1823, he reiterated the traditional warnings about the dangers of U.S. involvement in European affairs and noted that any such intervention by the United States would logically undermine its proscriptions of European intervention in Latin America.[17]

NATIONAL PRIDE VERSUS INNOCENT VIRTUE

The Monroe Doctrine was generally well received by Americans as comporting with their own views, but it was castigated in Europe. For one thing, Europeans believed that the noncolonization principle was selfishly hypocritical because it applied only to them, leaving the Americans free to extend their own internal empire as they might. Moreover, the vainglorious American "hands-off" admonition to European powers seemed like an instance of absurd overreaching by an upstart nation unaware of its own feebleness. As it turned out, the doctrine had little real influence on U.S. foreign policy until it was later revived to justify national expansion. Later in the nineteenth century it would be regarded, as Herbert Croly said, as "the equivalent of the Declaration of Independence in foreign affairs," leading an American statesman to declare that all of U.S. foreign policy could be summarized in a single phrase: "The Monroe Doctrine and the Golden Rule."[18] From the start, though, the doctrine provided an important pointer to American intentions and attitudes and also revealed the tensions and contradictions within them. The United States desired to be a great nation, recognized as such by the world, while insisting that it remain separate from that world. The Monroe Doctrine combined a claim to full American acceptance by the international community—and even to an American leadership role within that community—with the traditional insistence on diplomatic isolation. America was to be insular yet expansionist, a leader yet disengaged, nationalistically particular yet universally exemplary.

Yet maintaining innocent nonentanglement always had to be squared with preserving American commercial interests, and thus American pride, against the wiles of European rivals. This balance needed to be carefully managed if damaging conflicts were to be avoided. The cantankerous foreign policy of President Andrew Jackson (1829–1837) threatened often to upset this balance in favor of pride and honor. Jackson's policy (if it can be called such) was immensely popular precisely because he belligerently refused to countenance any real or perceived insult or injury to U.S. interests. A man sprung from the people of the West, he seemed to many Americans their ideal representative, countering the obnoxious sophistications of the Old World with his "shirtsleeve diplomacy." Pugnacious, candid, crude, vigorous, xenophobic, and disrespectful of traditional forms, he undoubtedly struck an emotional chord with his fellow citizens. The more thoughtful of them, however, rightly feared that Jackson's pursuit of idiosyncratic goals and his high-handed propensity to hurl threats at powerful empires carried the ever-present danger of embroiling the United States in unnecessary difficulties with other nations, even to the point of war (as in his dispute with the French over monetary claims dating back to Napoleonic attacks on U.S. shipping).

Jackson was always contemptuous of law and authority. He and his propagandists were adept at transforming actions prompted by his own peremptory will into expressions of the "popular will," trumping mere legality and thereby justifying his expansion of executive power. In a suddenly democratic age in which the "common man" was exalted as never before —in rhetoric if not in fact—this was a potent argument. But Jackson's representative will was an authentic product of the western Carolinas, highly attuned to defending manhood and honor against insults and injuries for which no law, it was held, could give adequate remedy. Jackson's force and violence unrestrained by law placed him, in the terms I have been discussing here, in a position antithetical to the reign of innocent virtue. It encouraged particularistic American nationalism at the expense of the transcendent. However popular at home, carrying this attitude into foreign relations with great powers—especially when combined with Jackson's oft-stated premise that the American cause was invariably just and not subject to further consideration—was a recipe for potential disaster. The instinctive defense of national pride and honor over usually minor issues did not make for a prudent foreign policy aimed at securing the safety and survival of the United States and its providential mission.

Whether through luck or the possession of more subtlety than either his friends or his enemies gave him credit, the Jacksonian style in foreign relations never did quite tip the nation into disastrous conflict.[19] Virtuous American independence from other powers was maintained and even strengthened, while the goal of continental expansion definitely had begun.

CONCLUSION

The Monroe presidency accomplished two principal things: it set a foreign policy marker for the future that enshrined Washingtonian-Jeffersonian nonentanglement as a diplomatic ideal, and it established continental expansion as America's main task for the foreseeable future. America would maintain its diplomatic isolation from Europe and, safe within its own hemisphere, would occupy and settle the continent to consolidate itself as a major power. If the assertion of diplomatic independence served to comfort American pride, its successful maintenance would secure American virtue from the corrupting influence of Old Europe.

This double goal survived even Jackson's righteous wrath and provocations, and in fact prevailing circumstances permitted Americans to keep diplomatic entanglement with Europe to a minimum until the 1890s. This allowed nineteenth-century Americans too easily to convince themselves that their nation was indeed exceptional in its isolation and moral purity. Tocqueville noted the "vanity" of Americans in this respect: "I tell an American he lives in a beautiful country; he answers: 'That is true. There is none like it in the world.' I praise the freedom enjoyed by the inhabitants, and he answers: 'Freedom is a precious gift, but very few people are worthy to enjoy it.' I note the chastity of morals prevailing in the United States, and he replies: 'I suppose that a stranger, struck by the immorality apparent in all other nations, must be astonished at this sight.' . . . One cannot imagine a more obnoxious or boastful form of patriotism. Even admirers are bored."[20]

On the question of internal empire, however, European critics surely had a point. The anti-imperialism on which Americans prided themselves, and which they had embedded in their mythological self-view, seemed seriously at odds with their determination to dispossess indigenous tribes, Mexicans, Spanish Californians, and anyone else who stood in the way of their occupation of the continent (and here Jackson played a significant role). Expansion would require an exertion of power and often a use of violent force that seemed difficult to reconcile with innocent virtue. Indeed, it would often prove irreconcilable except by means of hypocritical piety. It could be readily reconciled, however, with a conception of active republican virtue that emphasized the manly, martial qualities needed for defense and conquest, and that conduced to nationalistic pride. By the end of the nineteenth century, American expansion had given birth to an alternate version of the national mission centered exactly on this virtue, one that joyfully embraced American power and sought its aggrandizement. It was a version that momentarily displaced but could not vanquish the more universalistic version, eternally suspicious of power and dedicated to innocent virtue.

CHAPTER SEVEN

Innocent Virtue and the Conquest of a Continent

A MAJOR DISRUPTION to the general sense of international isolation that America felt during the nineteenth century occurred during the Civil War. This was because intervention by the European powers, particularly Britain, was devoutly sought by the South—because it would have the effect of confirming its independence—and stoutly opposed by the North for the same reason. On several occasions, relations between Britain and the North approached crisis point, though matters were always fortunately resolved short of war.[1] But though the United States escaped serious embroilment in Europe, it remained commercially engaged; indeed, U.S. commerce grew with the general increase in international trade after the end of the Napoleonic wars. America's rather antiquated naval fleet was deployed around the world—in the Mediterranean, in the Caribbean, near Brazil, along the Pacific Coast, and in the Far East—to afford protection, but commercial conflicts very rarely raised serious diplomatic disputes.

Most explanations as to why the United States was left largely to its own devices during the nineteenth century include an element of fortuitousness. Some point to the fact that the balance of powers in Europe, established by the settlement of Vienna in 1815, was for the most part maintained, broken only by the Crimean War of the 1850s and the brief Franco-Prussian War of 1870, neither of which had much effect on America. There was simply no major war in which the United States was in danger of becoming entangled. Nor after 1823 (the year of the Monroe Doctrine) was there much European interest or interference in America's hemisphere, save for some feeble efforts by Spain and Napoleon III's imperial pretensions in Mexico in the 1860s. The only nation that might have offered a serious threat was Britain, which had ambitions in Central America and which maintained a permanent presence in Canada, on the United States' very doorstep.[2] There were several border clashes and disputes with Canada over the years that might conceivably have led to larger conflicts, since popular hostility and suspicion could be easily aroused against the old enemy.

The fact that no serious conflict occurred was mainly due to the judicious restraint of British political leaders in the face of what many of them regarded as the arrogance and aggressiveness of their American counterparts. The British for the most part recognized that their greater advantage lay in keeping the United States as a friend rather than an enemy, and they were acutely conscious that Canada constituted a permanent and vulnerable hostage to fortune in any U.S.-British conflict. They knew too that the Atlantic Ocean made any successful projection of British power difficult and hazardous, and were anyway more often preoccupied with the serious task of maintaining the balance of power on the European continent. Not only that, but Europe, and Britain especially, had become crucially dependent on America for imports of produce, particularly cotton and foodstuffs. Britain was also by far the largest investor in U.S. securities. British prosperity therefore seemed critically tied to continuing American prosperity.[3]

What serious diplomacy there was with foreign powers, including Britain, during the nineteenth century related mainly to clashes or disputes over the possession of North American territory or over influence in nearby regions. This fact reflected the determinedly expansionist, continental aims of the developing nation.

Expansion had been an option and temptation for the American colonies from the very beginning; indeed, the colonists' belief that Britain was blocking their westward movement had been one of the causes of the Revolution. Expansion had, however, never been a universally approved policy. Many Federalists would have liked to limit westward expansion in favor of consolidating the United States as an orthodox Atlantic power. Jefferson, on the other hand, looked forward to a far distant future when rapid multiplication caused both northern and southern continents to be filled with a single people under similar government and laws (though he meant organized in free and independent states, not under a unified government). Yet even he believed that the huge Louisiana Territory he had purchased from Napoleon would take a millennium to occupy effectively. In the early nineteenth century, however, expansion toward the Pacific became a positive American passion due to a combination of nationalistic fervor, the pressure of a rapidly increasing population, anticipated opportunities for profitable capital investment, gold fever, and the southern desire to acquire more territory for plantations.[4] The question was how this expansion, which Europeans regarded as simple imperial colonization, was to be accomplished without compromising innocent virtue with its implied necessity of keeping "clean hands."

The basic mythological version has always been that American virtue naturally prospered in a virgin wilderness, the "new Eden." Even so thoughtful and progressive a man as Herbert Croly heedlessly wrote Native Americans and Hispanics out of the history of white colonization by claiming, "The land was unoccupied, and its settlement offered an unprecedented area and abundance of economic opportunity."[5] But, of course, the wilderness was neither virgin nor empty, and occupation was accomplished using varying levels of power and force. "Winning the West," as it was so often termed, required (apart from covetousness for land and wealth) energy, courage, resourcefulness, endurance, and the martial spirit to defend hard-won goals in a "savage" land. These were virtues variously displayed by pioneers who scouted the wide land and its native inhabitants; by god-fearing pilgrim settlers who followed in their wake, encouraged by government land grants; by U.S. soldiers deployed to suppress Indian tribes that menaced them; by engineers and entrepreneurs who carved the canals and forged the railroads that supplied settlers and provided access to the world for their produce; by gun-savvy lawmen capable of imposing order on an anarchic, often violent frontier. They were active republican virtues that, though often given an individualistic twist in American circumstances, were mobilized to defend the national interest and extend the national wealth and power. Such goals inevitably produced conflicts in which the preservation of clean hands was hardly conceivable.

Expansion involved Americans in four separate arenas of conflict during the nineteenth century. The first (as already noted) was with foreign powers—Britain, France, Spain, Mexico, and Russia—that occupied, or had various claims to or designs on, North American territory. The second was the civil conflict between North and South triggered by expansionism. The third was conflict with Native American tribes and confederations resisting the confiscation of their territories. And the fourth was the conflict generated in the attempt to impose orderly economic development on a violently anarchical frontier. In this chapter I will look at each in turn and the problems for innocent virtue that each presented.

INTERNATIONAL RELATIONS

The acquisition of territory from, or in competition with, other powers was achieved in various ways, but these generally included force or the threat of it. This was true even in the earliest and most important case: Jefferson's purchase of Louisiana from Napoleon Bonaparte. The sale was an unanticipated boon because Jefferson and his secretary of state, Madison, had sought merely to gain New Orleans as a free port for U.S. commerce coming down the Mississippi. Even for that, however, they were prepared to fight and had threatened to make war on France in alliance with Britain. Napoleon, preoccupied with a looming European war, unexpectedly offered them the entire territory, and a deal was finally concluded for the sum $15 million. During this whole affair, Jefferson proved extremely flexible with regard to his own republican principles: an isolationist in foreign affairs, he was nevertheless willing to form an alliance with Britain to gain his ends; a strict constructionist on constitutional interpretation, he chose to overlook the fact that the Constitution provided no authority to the federal government to acquire foreign territory, much less incorporate it into the Union. His compatriots (with the exception of some Federalists) readily forgave him, however, since he had doubled the size of the United States and set it on the path to world power.

The purchase had the added effect of opening the question of West Florida, still held by Spain but with a disputed border with Louisiana. Jefferson and Madison used threats and bribery to induce Spain to cede some territory, or even the whole of Florida, and encouraged a separatist rebellion in part of West Florida and then annexed it. Devious plotting and planning continued until Monroe finally purchased Florida in 1819, though only after an unauthorized invasion by General Andrew Jackson and threats from Secretary of State John Quincy Adams that an authorized one might follow if Spain refused to give way. In these same negotiations, Adams concluded a Transcontinental Treaty that established a boundary between Mexico and the United States from the Sabine River (now the eastern border of Texas) along 42° north latitude (now the southern border of Oregon) to the Pacific Ocean. Adams considered this an epoch-making event and the high point of his diplomatic career.

John Quincy Adams, as we have seen, was a significant figure in the history of America's western progress, embodying both the nation's largest ambitions and its deepest moral concerns. As well as gaining Florida and pushing the country's southern border to the Pacific, he was responsible for negotiating a treaty with Britain that laid down the northern boundary of the country from the Lake of the Woods to the Rocky Mountains along the line of 49° north latitude. His vision reached even to Alaska, where he sternly resisted Russian and British challenges. Adams was quite explicit about his determination to familiarize the world with the idea that the "proper dominion" of the United States was the whole North American continent. He thus simultaneously imagined America as a pure exemplary "beacon" for other nations, and as the active occupier of a whole continent.[6] The link for Adams was the need to make the United States so secure and strong that its survival as an exemplary free government would not be in question.

His belief in the importance of the American experiment, and in the consequent necessity of creating a powerful and independent United States, had been confirmed by his diplomatic experiences in Europe, particularly in Russia. He believed it was essential to sustain America's material progress by gaining recognition of her commercial rights and through the continental expansion of a vigorous and enterprising people. Yet it was also necessary to preserve moral virtue, without which the American example would be meaningless. Though Adams shared the almost universal belief in Anglo-American racial superiority, he was sympathetic to Indians and sensitive to the fact that the American empire of liberty encompassed their destruction. He was also passionately opposed to the extension of slavery to new territories, the prime motive for southern expansionism. It was for this reason that he opposed the annexation of Texas (where slavery already existed) and what he called President James Polk's "most unrighteous" war against Mexico of 1846–1848.[7] It was true that Polk had a cloth ear on the issue of slavery, but many antislavery northerners saw his achievements during his presidency—his annexation of Texas, settlement of the Oregon boundary with Britain, and conquests of territory during the Mexican War—as a fulfillment of the destiny that Adams himself had adumbrated. Polk even revived Adams's Monroe Doctrine in 1845, ostensibly in response to British and French intrigues to keep the Republic of Texas from being absorbed by the United States, but actually with the intention of warning Britain not to interfere with Polk's designs on the Spanish colony of California. (Polk's invocation of the doctrine marked the shift from a policy of U.S. protection of Latin America to U.S. domination.)

The Mexican War was started by a presidential ploy that prefigured similar manipulations of Congress in later centuries, its aim being to disguise aggressive intent as justified defense. The quarrel was over Texas, which had won its independence from Mexico in 1836 and then later applied for statehood, eventually gaining approval from Congress in 1845. Mexico opposed the incorporation of Texas into the United States on strategic grounds and disputed a Texan claim, supported by Polk, that the republic's southern boundary ran along the Rio Grande rather than the Nueces River to the north. Polk tried to purchase the disputed area, along with New Mexico and California, but when that failed he planned a war of aggression, ordering troops into the region south of the Nueces. He used a skirmish near the Rio Grande to declare that Mexico had "shed American blood on American soil" and asked Congress to declare war. Despite the voices of northern Whigs raised strongly in criticism, Congress obliged on May 11, 1846, with an overwhelming vote of approval that displayed a nationalistic sentiment, martial excitement, and the rising expansionist spirit. The same patriotic surge swept through a population in which the doctrine of "Manifest Destiny" had made deep inroads. Many thousands volunteered.

By the end of the year, however, revelations of Polk's prewar maneuvering in Congress and second thoughts about the consequences of expansion produced noisy dissent, particularly in the North. Northerners worried about strengthening "the slave power" and also about the unhappy prospect of the United States ruling over numerous nonwhite people (for Polk had not made clear his war aims with regard to the conquest of Mexico). In 1847, the Whig opposition won a vote in the House of

Representatives, declaring that the president had "unnecessarily and unconstitutionally" begun the war. The war nevertheless proceeded until U.S. forces had captured Mexico City and conquered California. A treaty concluding the war was signed in February 1848, by which time thirteen thousand U.S. troops had died, mostly of disease. For this sacrifice, Americans had gained a vast region that would contain the future states of California, New Mexico, Arizona, Utah, Nevada, Colorado, and Wyoming. Such gains through warfare were not, of course, accepted as the simple prerogative of a powerful, greedy victor. Polk claimed he "had not gone to war for conquest," yet he had no regrets over an action that had extended "the dominion of peace" over "increasing millions."[8]

This war practically concluded the expansion that gave final shape to the United States of America (apart from Secretary of State William Seward's purchase of Alaska from Russia in 1867 and the annexation of Hawaii in 1898). True, some Americans never gave up hoping that Canada might join the Union, while others, particularly slave owners, coveted Cuba and parts of Mexico and Central America.[9] But the thought of annexing Latin American countries always raised the question of what to do with their nonwhite populations. To this there seemed only two possible answers: either to admit them as citizens and give them full access to the political processes of the Union, or to rule over them as subject populations. To most Americans, these were equally unpalatable options. The first was unthinkable because inferior peoples of nonwhite or mixed blood simply lacked the virtues necessary to operate a free government; the histories of their own republics, which had mostly ended in tyranny or monarchy, had proved this to American satisfaction. To admit such people as equal citizens would threaten to dilute and debase America's own virtue and perhaps destroy the sacred Union itself, thus defeating its noble mission. The second option was just as unthinkable (at least until the 1890s) because it offended the Union's basic principle of liberty, from which grew its anti-imperialism.

It should be noted that the attitudes and arguments that seem to modern liberal sentiment so objectionable were almost universally shared by white people of all nations in the nineteenth and well into the twentieth centuries (and have not disappeared even today). Racism was widely argued and accepted as representing "scientific" truth. Such arguments no doubt supported and rationalized the existing racist arrogance of Americans, an arrogance that Latin Americans and other nonwhite peoples always resented. Nevertheless, it was possible for white Americans to combine sincere concern for liberty and republican equality with sincere belief in racial categories of superiority and inferiority—though generally with debate over how far inferiority was cultural, thus improvable, and how far inherited, thus permanent. Americans, like other westerners, would always have a hard time negotiating their ambivalence about peoples who might constitute either incorrigible savages to be beaten down or backward brethren to be helped in their growth to maturity and equality. But it was quite possible, given prevailing beliefs, to reach the seemingly paradoxical conclusion that the unequal must be excluded for the sake of preserving political equality and that political liberty could be saved only by refusing to extend it to those incapable of sustaining it. Historians of Manifest Destiny and American racism have taken a stern view of such American "hypocrisy," and certainly there was no lack of hypocrisy on display, then as now. Belief in innocent virtue could hardly be maintained *without* hypocrisy given the aggressive force required to fulfill America's continental aims. Polk was undoubtedly hypocritical in declaring conquest to be no part of his government's intention, but he was not necessarily insincere in believing that the blessings of political liberty bestowed over so large a territory made adequate amends. The American distaste for overlordship may have been informed by arrogance and prejudice, but it was also another manifestation of the wish to keep the world at a distance in order to maintain the purity of American virtue and preserve the grand experiment.[10]

But was not America's expansion westward merely a form of "internal imperialism," as it has often been denoted? No doubt, yet it must be admitted that it was imperialism of an unusual kind, for its purpose was never to extend American rule over conquered and subject nations. The peoples with whom the United States came into conflict were merely impediments to occupation and free settlement of the continent, to be swept aside or dealt with as harshly as might be, and were never intended as subjects of an imperial power. The Northwest Ordinance of 1787 and the Constitution of the United States made provision for adding new territories to the Union on the basis of equality and mutual agreement, and with a view to their potentially gaining statehood, but none for the addition of imperial possessions.

The underlying contradictions in American attitudes on this matter would only really become politically problematic when economic expansion abroad led to the necessity of foreign policy decisions regarding the annexation or control of overseas territories with majority colored populations. Certainly, the awkward consequences of indulging a more orthodox form of imperialism after 1898 would convince many Americans that they were right to resist the desire to rule directly over subject peoples. Anti-imperialists believed that the Constitution could not be extended over water and that American traditions forbade such colonization. Yet in the presidential elections of 1900, William McKinley and his imperialist supporters, defending the possession of the Philippines, reinterpreted U.S. history as one of continuous imperialist colonization beginning with Jefferson's purchase of Louisiana, claiming furthermore that its success had been due to the application of superior force. To argue thus was, however, to place the populations of overseas territories into the same category as Native Americans—impediments to expanding white civilization to be ruthlessly defeated and subjugated. Such a reinterpretation clashed dissonantly with a justification that had accompanied overseas colonization—namely, that of a "white man's burden" to civilize and elevate "inferior" peoples to self-governing capacity—and also with the fact that most administrations had no desire whatever, save in the case of Hawaii, to admit overseas territories to statehood precisely because of fears of complicating America's already existing race problems.

In the first half of the nineteenth century, however, there was a racially distinct subject population nearer and more urgently to hand, within the borders of the United States itself, whose existence constituted an enduring blot on American virtue and its ideal of liberty. Belief in Manifest Destiny to occupy the continent inevitably threw up the question of whether successful expansion would extend the empire of liberty or that of slavery.

LINCOLN AND THE CIVIL WAR

War is incompatible with innocent virtue, and the horrors of the Civil War turned some of its more sensitive participants—men like Oliver Wendell Holmes and Ambrose Bierce—into deep and lifelong cynics. If the war was ultimately transfigured as a supreme test and purification of American virtue and a confirmation of the American mission, it was thanks to the genius of northern writers and poets who believed in and celebrated the sacredness of the Union and its historic mission. It was also due to the efforts and words of Abraham Lincoln.

Lincoln was a man acutely attuned to the national mission, and one who had thought long and hard on the most glaring and enduring blot on the national virtue. The blot of slavery was one that the founders had hoped would fade with the passage of time as America developed and the institution became economically unviable. In the meantime, they resigned themselves to living with an uncomfortable contradiction between the Declaration of Independence, with its promise of universal liberty, and the new Constitution they had devised to safeguard political liberty. The foundational law intended to moderate naked power was compromised by its toleration of slavery and left the continuance or abolition of the institution for decision by individual states with an implication of no federal authority to interfere. More than unease, this contradiction provoked the fear that its full flowering would one day rend the nation apart. Jefferson, a slave owner who embodied the contradiction within his own person, remarked in his *Notes on the State of Virginia* that he trembled for his country when he reflected that God is just and that "his justice cannot sleep forever."[11]

Slavery did not die out in the South, nor was it abolished. It was maintained as the foundation of an aristocratic cotton culture forever seeking new soil to replace degraded plantations. This southern "civilization" grew steadily more distinct from the developing industrial-agricultural economy of the North even as better communications opened it to the closer moral scrutiny of northern abolitionists. Southerners, in response to moral critique, hardened their theories of slavery from necessary evil to a law of nature and prepared to defend their civilization and its "peculiar institution." Their main political defense was maintenance of voting parity in the Senate, which required keeping the number of slave states equal to the number of nonslave states, thus ensuring that no constitutional amendment to abolish slavery would ever succeed. Western expansion was thus both a tantalizing opportunity and a dire threat to the South. Controversy inevitably recurred over whether new states carved out of the territories would be slave or free, and whether Congress had the constitutional authority to forbid slavery in them. A crisis over Missouri in 1820 was defused by a compromise bill, guided through Congress by Henry Clay, admitting Missouri as a slave state balanced by the admission of

Maine as a free state and excluding slavery from the rest of the Louisiana Territory north of 36° 30″ (the southern border of Missouri).

The Missouri Compromise held for three decades, but the pressure of western migration brought it under increasing strain. Sectional conflict loomed between the southern "friends of slavery" and northern "Free-Soilers" moving into the new territories. In 1846, during Polk's Mexican War, Representative David Wilmot of Pennsylvania had introduced a proviso to prohibit slavery in any territory won from Mexico. Though it failed in the Senate, the proviso caused great southern bitterness and politicized the slavery issue once and for all. But the man who, more than any other, racked it to the point of crisis was Lincoln's political rival Stephen Douglas, the Democratic senator from Illinois dedicated to opening the western territories to settlement and a transcontinental railroad for the sake of advancing "white civilization." Douglas, hoping that preoccupation with western development would distract attention from the slavery issue, bullied an act through Congress in 1854 aimed at opening Kansas-Nebraska. To appease southern opposition to the act, Douglas divided the territory into Kansas and Nebraska and repealed the antislavery rule above 36° 30″, leaving the question of slave or free to be decided by "popular sovereignty" ("squatter sovereignty").

The Kansas-Nebraska Act galvanized northern opposition as the nation stumbled through a series of crises and alarms (including the Supreme Court's *Dred Scott* decision that implied the unconstitutionality of forbidding slavery in the territories). The political effects were profound. They included the dissolution of the Whig Party, the division of the Democratic Party between those for and those against slavery, and the birth of a new Republican Party whose presidential candidate in 1860 was Abraham Lincoln. Since Lincoln had been tarred by southerners as a "Black Republican" (that is, a fanatical abolitionist of the John Brown hue), his election was the signal for southern states to secede from the Union, triggering the Civil War. Yet Lincoln, though firmly antislavery, was not in fact an abolitionist. He had worked out a compromise policy position that drew on previous adumbrations by his political heroes, Jefferson, Madison, and Clay. This maintained a careful balance between principle (slavery was an evil that must not be permitted to expand to other territories), constitutionality (accepting the lack of federal authority to interfere with slavery where it already existed), and political realism (what southerners who were addicted to slavery and northerners who were antislavery but negro-phobic might be persuaded to accept). Lincoln had stated his general view in 1845 in his opposition to the annexation of Texas: "I hold it to be a paramount duty of us in the free states, due to the Union of the states, and perhaps to liberty itself (paradox though it may seem) to let the slavery of the other states alone; while, on the other hand, I hold it to be equally clear, that we should never knowingly lend ourselves directly or indirectly, to prevent that slavery from dying a natural death—to find new places for it to live in, when it can no longer exist in the old."[12]

The paradox of tolerating slavery in order to save "liberty itself" was the key to Lincoln's thought. The evil of slavery must not be allowed to destroy the greater good of America's example of free, democratic government, the "last best hope of earth," as he expressed it. It could destroy that good either by surviving and expanding its dominion, thus undermining the true virtue of the republic, or by causing the breakup of the Union, which would be the sure consequence of any northern attempt to interfere with it. Maintaining the Union was a paramount value for Lincoln because it would prove that "a nation conceived in Liberty, dedicated to the proposition that all men are created equal" was capable of surviving. "Must a government, of necessity," he asked, "be too *strong* for the liberties of its own people, or too *weak* to maintain its own existence?" Lincoln (and non-abolitionist northerners generally) would have accepted a constitutional amendment to entrench the hands-off policy but could never accept either slavery's expansion or the disintegration of the republic. He was willing, if agonizingly distressed, to accept war in order to preserve the Union. Here, indeed, was a test of the virtue and resolve of Americans dedicated to the national ideal and the national mission. The world must see that "those who can fairly carry an election, can also suppress a rebellion—that ballots are the rightful, and peaceful, successor of bullets."[13]

The war was longer and more destructive of human life and property than anyone could have foreseen, a cataclysm that produced a result more "fundamental and astounding" than either protagonist had imagined or intended. Lincoln addressed the issue in his second inaugural address, in which he spoke not of American innocence but of American sin. Slavery was a sin not just of the South but of the whole nation that had tolerated it, and the whole nation had paid dearly in blood and treasure. Lincoln, a pacific man, had not scrupled to mobilize northern power to save the sacred

Union, but the war had become a "fiery trial" that scarified the nation, punishing it for the national sin. Yet the war had also purified America by removing the dread stain. Sin, on the image of Christian redemption, had been washed away by blood, and the possibility of genuine innocence for the future had been founded. Lincoln could thus conclude his great speech with the words: "With malice toward none; with charity for all; with firmness in the right, as God gives us to see the right, let us strive on to the finish the work we are in."[14]

Lincoln represented in many ways the apotheosis of the American mythology. He was himself a profound exemplar of it, a self-made man who rose to highest office, who argued the right of all, even negroes, to strive similarly to achieve whatever they were capable of, free from the despotic control of others. But for Lincoln, the free pursuit of self-interest, to be virtuous, must be constrained by principles of right, as the interests of slave owners in keeping their slaves had not been. It was his hope that the war, in vanquishing the slave power and the mythology of human inequality it fostered, had refounded the nation on this proper principle. Whether the work he started has been properly completed even today is a matter for debate; nevertheless, it hardly can be doubted that the war confirmed the liberal American mythology as definitive. Lincoln has been venerated not just because he led the North to victory in the Civil War while sustaining its democracy, or because he was ultimately if inadvertently responsible for abolishing slavery, but because he found the eloquence to ennoble the war by painting it as the desperate but ultimately confirmatory test of the unique American mission. His resonant prose revitalized the mythology and transmitted it afresh to subsequent generations, leaving an example of constancy, endurance, and faith that would be the measure for every president of high ambition who followed.[15]

VIRTUE AND THE FATE OF NATIVE AMERICANS
During the war, as Lincoln was preoccupied by Robert E. Lee's invasion of Maryland, he was called upon to deal with the results of a Sioux uprising in southwestern Minnesota. More whites were killed than in any massacre in U.S. history, and Lincoln dispatched General John Pope (fresh from his defeat at the Second Battle of Bull Run) to deal with it. Pope, finding panic everywhere and fearing the outbreak of a general frontier war, declared his intention to "exterminate the Sioux" if he could, since

they should be treated "as maniacs and wild beasts." The U.S. Army put down the rebellion and took fifteen hundred Sioux men, women, and children as prisoners. Lincoln, confessing himself uninformed on Indian affairs, ordered that no executions be carried out until he had personally examined each individual case, which he did in minute detail. From a list of 303, he approved the death penalty for only the most atrocious crimes of murder and rape of innocents, and in the end 38 men were executed. Though it was the largest public execution in U.S. history, the citizens of the area were outraged at Lincoln's leniency, and the Republicans suffered a marked loss of electoral support in Minnesota as a result.[16]

The contrast between Lincoln's attitude and that of people on the frontier was an illustration of the truth that innocent virtue, encompassing a Christian concept of universal benevolence, was difficult or impossible to sustain in a struggle to dispossess a people of their ancestral lands. Perhaps unsurprisingly in the American context, an attempt to sustain innocence had nevertheless been made.

The necessary theory was provided, as so often in America, by John Locke. Locke had argued (in refutation of Spanish justifications of Spain's occupation of South America) that conquest did not provide a legitimate title to land—only industrious labor that turned land to agriculture could do that.[17] Locke (in writing a constitution for the Carolinas) claimed that, since the Indians occupied more land than they could properly make productive use of, the colonists had a right, without doing injustice to the Indians (as long as there was sufficient land left to sustain Indian life), to claim some for agricultural purposes—but only as much as they could properly till and defend given their numbers. (Land not so tilled remained "waste," an English legal term that in the colonial context founded Croly's conception of the wilderness as, at least technically, unoccupied.) Locke's theory comprehended the possibility of violence, but only in legitimate defense of property that had been justly and peaceably acquired. The basis of English colonialism would therefore, according to Locke, be peaceful agrarian settlement, not conquest.

These arguments were taken up by European writers like William Blackstone, Emmerich von Vattel, and William Paley, all of whom were influential in the United States. They were in turn enthusiastically promulgated by prominent preachers, politicians, and farmers and, most significantly, by Jefferson. After his purchase of Louisiana, Jefferson looked forward to expansion over ages to come and "contrary to the principles of Montesquieu, it will be seen that the larger the extent of country, the more firm its republican structure, if founded, *not on conquest*, but in principles of compact and equality" (my italics). Once the balance between settlers and Indians had tipped decisively in the former's favor, however, pressure on Indian lands grew more acute, and the "Indian problem" arose to full prominence. Jefferson, who always expressed concern to safeguard the rights and welfare of Native Americans, adopted a policy of persuading them to leave their supposedly "natural" and ungoverned state to adopt agriculture and civil government, in order to assure them proper title to their lands. Foreshadowing the policy of Indian removal that would become a controversial feature of Andrew Jackson's reign, Jefferson argued that Indians who preferred to cling to their old ways should be "encouraged" to swap their lands for territories farther west, beyond the Mississippi. In practice, he was prepared to harass tribes and force cessions of land or flight to ensure white expansion. Tocqueville noted the cynicism of such official American dealings with the Indians: "The states, in extending what they are pleased to call the benefits of their laws over the Indians, calculate that the latter will sooner depart than submit; and the central government, when it promises these unlucky people a permanent asylum in the West, is well aware of its inability to guarantee this. The states' tyranny forces the savages to flee, and the Union's promises make flight easy. Both are means to the same end."[18]

Legal cases involving Indian removal were defended on Lockean-Jeffersonian principles of just settlement and the alleged "state of nature" of the Indians, which implied they had no possessory title to the lands they occupied. The man who, more than any other, exploded this convenient conceit was Justice John Marshall. In three judgments of the Supreme Court, Marshall rejected the Lockean argument that Native Americans had acquired no title to the full extent of their lands because of their failure to cultivate. He argued that aboriginal Americans did not exist in a state of nature but were divided into separate independent nations with laws and governmental institutions of their own and had always been recognized as such by the United States. The entitlements of European settlers were based not on agricultural labor, therefore, but simply on *conquest*. Whether such entitlement was just or unjust in abstract terms, Marshall's Court, as a court of the conquering power, was not at liberty to speculate.[19]

The fate of the so-called Five Civilized Tribes—Cherokee, Choctaw, Chickasaw, Creek, and Seminole—provided the ironic and tragic proof of the contradictory impulses of American mythology. These nations had made every effort to Europeanize after 1800 as Jefferson suggested they should, adopting government on the American model, agriculture, writing (in the case of the Cherokee, their own form of writing), even slavery. Yet none was spared by the federal government, which forced them to march to Oklahoma in the 1830s in "removals" that were often cruelly and carelessly managed. Jackson had strongly supported the Indian Removal Act of 1830 that authorized such removal. He permitted its implementation even over Marshall's ruling in *Worcester v. Georgia* (1832) in which the tribes were defined as "domestic dependent nations" whose limits were governed by federal treaty. Jackson, with a typical westerner's attitude, thought it an absurdity to talk about treaties with Indians who, he said, should be handled by "legislative fiat." Jackson had a lifelong obsession with combating what he called the "triple-headed" menace that had always plagued frontier settlers—England, Spain, and their Indian allies—and in both his military and political careers he encountered and decisively battered each of them. The language of Jackson's presidential state papers reeks with piety over the welfare of the Indians to whom he promised a humane, just, and liberal policy, but his true purposes were transparent. The all-too-naked aim was the acquisition of twenty-five million acres of Native American domain for white settlement, and Jackson did not scruple to use bribery, trickery, sophistry, and coercion to achieve it.[20]

Though Marshall's judgment became the basis for future claims to Indian title, its real significance for our story is that it robbed American virtue of the quality of innocence that Americans claimed for it as they contrasted themselves with corrupt, power-loving Europe. Certainly, New England moralists like Edward Everett and Ralph Waldo Emerson believed Indian dispossession incompatible with moral innocence, for they were sickened by what they regarded as a reproach to the national character. But it was significant that, though Henry Clay and some of his Whigs opposed Indian removals on humanitarian grounds, Whig administrations, once in power, pursued precisely the same policy. It seemed that a continent could not be effectively won with clean hands. And yet there was a curious coda to the Indian removal cases that showed the persistence of the desire to maintain innocent virtue *somewhere* in the American system, and most fittingly in the law. Marshall concluded his *Worcester v. Georgia* judgment by asserting, Pilate-like, that the Court, having determined the justice of the matter, could now wash its hands of the iniquity of oppressing the Indians and disregarding their rights. There were apparently limits to the ability of the legalistic reign of virtue to restrain the corrupt operations of power, but American law would retain its innocence and virtue even as legally uncontrollable politicians and land-hungry farmers and speculators performed the dirty business of securing the land for white settlement.[21]

The Lockean rationale for dispossession would continue to have popular currency and was vehemently expressed by people as eminent as Horace Greeley and Theodore Roosevelt. Yet Marshall's removal of the Lockean-Jeffersonian fig leaf had exposed the facts of brute force and superior white power in all their stark nakedness. In justification, Americans could and did, of course, appeal to the brutal realities of the competition of opposing cultures over land. In the frank words of young First Lieutenant William T. Sherman, campaigning in 1842 against the Seminole in St. Augustine, Florida, one hears the authentic frontier attitude: "It is not ended by a d---d sight but about as near to it as we can come unless the population be got to fight for themselves, not only to repel the attacks of the marauding bands but to follow up & drive them out of their settlements—this the way in which the indians were always conquered in the west should have been done here but the citizens are a most dastardly cowardly set." The "cowardly" citizens of St. Augustine, the oldest town in North America, were, notably, of Spanish descent and therefore the objects of Sherman's contempt. Yet his assumption of intrinsic white superiority did not preclude sympathy for Indians or Hispanics. His attitude was not one of racial hatred but merely of grim necessity based on a desire to make the republic secure in its continental home.[22]

But what could justify American expansion in terms more transcendent than the right of conquest, or the ancient right of a strong republic to secure its own safety and ambition? Here the myth of mission was invoked: "primitive" peoples should not be permitted to block the path of human progress. America, in the vanguard of the Enlightenment, the very embodiment of its promise, would not properly fulfill its destiny unless it occupied the whole continent, and it must do what had to be done to accomplish the task. According to the American mythology, Providence had planted the United States in its western ocean fastness to be a secure laboratory for the experiment in liberty (a belief Albert Weinberg called the dogma of "geographical predestination"). The dispossession of native peoples was thus rationalized as an unfortunate historical necessity, and the perennial conflicts between land-hungry settlers and Native American tribes were elevated into the frontline skirmishes of an advancing civilization. What had formerly been known as "the backcountry" now became "the frontier," symbolically understood by Americans as the retreating border between human progress and barbarism (as embodied by Indians and Mexicans). As early as 1825 Charles Stewart Davies was arguing that the native peoples of the continent were destined to recede and give space to "American Providence."[23]

But the task of ensuring that this "receding" in fact occurred excluded faintheartedness and sentimentality of the kind indulged by New England do-gooders far from the perils and problems of the frontier. The requisite virtue here was the tough, manly, stoically martial one of ancient republicanism rather than soft, innocent virtue, now mainly consigned to the keeping of devout and loyal womenfolk. It was an image given pictorial representation in the work of Frederic Remington (himself an easterner who seldom went West), for whom the Manifest Destiny of Americans was linked by the Social Darwinism of the time to the destiny of the Anglo-Saxon race in its victory over the "scrap heap of departing races."[24]

This was the virtue that would be immortalized in America's frontier myth and the myriad popular tales that it spawned, tales in which one took for granted the intrinsic "goodness" of heroic settlers and western heroes contesting with the elements, the wilderness, the "savages," and the outlaws.

THE FRONTIER MYTH AND AMERICAN VIRTUE

The myth of the Old West began with American expansion, but in its final form it encompassed mainly that period after the Civil War when the nation turned its attention to the conquest of the Great Plains. It was on this western frontier, according to the myth, that the essential American character was formed. The movie actor John Wayne embodied its ideal type, and after his death in 1976 Jimmy Carter eulogized: "He was a symbol of many of the most basic qualities that made America great. The ruggedness, the tough independence, the sense of personal conviction and courage—

on and off the screen—reflected the best of our national character. It was because of what John Wayne said about what we are and what we can be that his great and deep love of America was returned in full measure."[25] Wayne had once himself pointed out that the character he played could be rough, cruel, tough, or tender, even immoral, but never petty or small. He or Carter might also have added "never dishonorable."

It was historian Frederick Jackson Turner who in 1893 formulated the thesis that the westward-moving frontier furnished "the forces dominating the American character," its "good as well as its evil elements." In addition to toughness, anti-intellectualism, and rough, pragmatic energy, the frontier, according to Turner, encouraged individualism and a democratic temper that was basically antisocial. Turner portrayed western settlement as the result of a tendency to confuse individual liberty with an absence of effective government, inducing a perpetual movement to escape from the oppression of the tax gatherer. The "free lands" of the frontier furnished "a field of opportunity, a gate of escape from the bondage of the past; and freshness and confidence, and scorn of older society, impatience of its restraints and its ideas, and indifference to its lesson."[26] Jackson was writing, as it were, in memoriam, for in 1893 the frontier had been officially announced closed, an era of U.S. history was ending, and the question was how the character allegedly formed by it would shape or be reshaped by the new one dawning.

Turner's frontier thesis was immensely popular for many years and remains even today the main conception of American character formation, still readily resorted to by politicians for rhetorical purposes. But it was repeatedly challenged after Turner's death in 1932. Younger historians in the midst of the Great Depression felt skeptical because, as one historiographer wrote, "An interpretation of the past that stressed agrarianism rather than industrialism, rugged individualism rather than state planning, and optimistic nationalism rather than political internationalism seemed outmoded in a one-world of machines and cities suddenly beset by a bewildering economic cataclysm." Turner's student, Frederick Merk, took up his master's theme but realistically stressed the distinction between the propaganda (Manifest Destiny) and the practical policy driving expansion for national or economic purposes. Many followed suit. Some argued that Turner got the story backwards: the frontier was not the anvil on which American individualism and democracy were forged but merely the canvas on which the frontier myth was projected by an eastern business establishment whose policies drove the western development from which they profited. America was not accidentally but purposely developed by and for eastern and English capital. Just as the original dream of America had been, in large part, a European projection, so the mythical West was a fabrication of the new metropolis in the East for its own ideological purposes. Of immense help in this process were those eastern artists whose carefully idealized works of frontier life were later taken as representations of reality.[27]

What I wish to note here is that the ambivalences contained in the American mythology were inevitably carried over into its extension and development on the far frontier. The frontier possessed from the start a highly ambivalent character, being at once a romantic escape *from* civilization and the front line *of* advancing white civilization. James Madison had argued that the main reason so many of his compatriots went west was that they were "irresistibly attracted to the complete liberty, that freedom from bonds, obligations, duties, that absence of care and anxiety which characterize the savage state."[28] Both the legendary Daniel Boone and James Fenimore Cooper's character Natty Bumppo were portrayed as either the representatives and harbingers of the new civilization or as free souls desperately taking flight from that encroaching civilization into an ever-receding wilderness. The frontier thus embodied unresolved American oppositions of nature versus civilization, rural versus urban life, liberty-from-law versus liberty-under-law, simplicity versus complexity, individualism versus corporatism, naive innocence versus sophistication.

It also embodied, and often dramatized, American ambivalence about power and virtue. As escape, the mythical West was imagined as an Edenic wilderness made fruitful by the new American Adam and Eve, with all the biblical assumptions of "original sinlessness" that this image conveyed.[29] Such a view comported readily with the Jeffersonian version of peaceful agrarian settlement that, if it sometimes strayed beyond the reach of state law, nevertheless carried the natural law within it and fostered the upright republican virtue that ensured such law would be properly observed.

The alternate image of the West, however, was that of the Wild West, a place of actual lawlessness (discounting the laws of Native Americans, which white pioneers generally did). It was a realm of ever-present danger, a thoroughly masculine milieu in which masculine virtues predominated.

If in Eden everyman had his Eve, in this West everyman was ultimately alone except for his gun and horse and the comfort of an occasional whore. Here the only law was the law of violence, and a man's virtue was measured by his willingness to stand up for himself in a way that demonstrated his courage and skill with the means of violence. The creation of heroic legends around the exploits of western gunmen, outlaws, and Indian fighters in cheap novels by easterners like Ned Buntline glorified western violence. A west that was wild must be tamed, and could be tamed only by main force. It needed powerful, larger-than-life heroes to tame it. Whatever the genuine virtues of such heroes (of which John Wayne became the filmic type), they were hardly innocent in the Christian sense, and they were almost never farmers (did Wayne ever play a farmer?). This, once again, was a story not of peaceful settlement but of conquest, and it required the warrior virtues of the conqueror.

Later western books and movies (at a time when these still dealt seriously with the mythic American soul) sometimes played on the tension between and interdependence of these two bearers of alternate American virtue: the peaceful innocent and the warrior gunman. The theme of the coming of law and order to the Wild West—the displacement of the rule of force by the rule of virtue—is as old as the western myth itself. In some versions, the lawless good man pins on a badge and becomes the symbol of the arrival of law that must be enforced against unruly or outlaw elements. The central drama is often one of conflict between two types of freedom—freedom *from* encroaching law, and freedom *under* law from the threat of force and violence. In actual history, the story had political dimensions absent from the simplistic mythical version of good guys versus bad. Richard M. Brown points to the political background in post–Civil War clashes between Republicans and Democrats, most of them recently migrated to the West, who engaged in what he calls a "Western Civil War of Incorporation"—a war between a cowboy pastoral culture and an urban capitalist one. Brown distinguishes between "incorporator" gunmen like James Butler (Wild Bill) Hickock and Wyatt Earp, mostly Republicans acting on behalf of "the conservative, consolidating authority of capital" to establish law and order, and "resister" gunmen like John Wesley Hardin and William Bonney (Billy the Kid), who were mostly southern Democrats happy to live by the anarchic values of the violent West.[30]

Yet outlaws like the James brothers, the Daltons, Butch Cassidy and the Sundance Kid, the Youngers, and many more were frequently as much admired as famous lawmen because they embodied the same masculine virtues—toughness, loyalty, courage, honor, daring, even generosity—the very virtues that the "taming" of the West required. It was unfortunate that the outlaws had pursued the antisocial path of robbing trains and banks, for this meant they must be tamed in their turn and their wild freedom destroyed by order and by law. Many Americans felt ambivalent about the closing of the frontier because the advent of law implied the establishment of effective government, and Americans had been taught to distrust the intrusive power of government from the beginning. But it was also because the loss of lawless freedom implied the loss of the individualistic, manly virtues appropriate to it, which seemed to have no place in the disciplined order of industrial production that was becoming the dominant mode of American life. The individual that Turner had pro-claimed was a product of the frontier, and which at the beginning of the twentieth century was being valorized as central to American character, was, as John Dewey observed, "in the process of complete submergence in fact at the very time in which he was being elevated high in theory." One of the most famous presidents of the United States, Teddy Roosevelt, would be deeply afflicted by this strange ambivalence and by the mythic romance of the American cowboy. Indeed, regret over the loss of pure freedom and manly virtue (synonymous with effectual power) would play consequentially in the foreign policy of the late 1890s.[31]

Yet if the martial virtues associated with honor and glory were en-dangered, innocent virtue could be regarded as having been guaranteed by the triumph of law and order. The secure bonds of law allowed the peaceful development of communities free from random violence, the establishment of the schools, churches, and productive businesses upon whose existence moral and economic progress depended. But the clear lesson of the passing of the Old West, whether one looked at the fact or the myth, was that establishing this rule of law required the exercise of force and violence, the exertion of the superior power of law-bringers over the forces of anarchy. It was a lesson that another generation of national leaders (who tended to see virtue and power as antithetical) had difficulty comprehending, and which would indeed take them half a century to apply consistently in the field of foreign policy.

INDUSTRIAL REVOLUTION

Occupation of the continent had not been managed with clean hands but rather by the often ruthless exercise of manly, martial virtue and sometimes by trickery and deceit. The American mythology, however, could not permit a nationalist expansion that was unaligned with the mission of advancing liberty or that lacked any universalistic moral content. Jefferson had imagined an extension of the empire of liberty that converted native peoples to western ways and absorbed them in the grand experiment, but that ideal had been thoroughly betrayed. The only alternative was to reinterpret egalitarian mythology in accord with a more frankly racist theory that envisaged the tide of superior white civilization sweeping inexorably westward, engulfing inferior peoples as it went. The doctrine of Manifest Destiny invoked to rationalize this expansion (which was really the doctrine of western progress under another name) could not avoid the inescapable fact that this exercise of active virtue had involved considerable force and violence, in plain contradiction to innocent virtue.

Nevertheless, America had managed to keep itself relatively aloof from Old Europe and its quarrels, always mythologically imagined as the prime source of real corruption of American virtue. It had also survived a desperate internal challenge and maintained its unity and free government, preserving its great example and keeping alive the hope of the world. With continental conquest completed, foreign powers banished, and Native Americans safely herded onto reservations; with the Union defended and firmly established, slavery abolished, industrialization growing apace, and economic power and wealth amassing; the United States could take stock of itself at the end of an amazing century of development and think, on the basis of international comparison, that it had done well to preserve its integrity, its democracy, and its mission.

Not that all looked perfectly rosy at the approach of a new century. The expansion of territory had been accompanied and fueled by a vast industrial expansion, itself fed by a massive immigration of peoples. A lengthy recession, that began in 1873 and turned into severe depression between 1893 and 1897, caused hardship, anxiety, and conflict. It encouraged a frightening concentration of financial and industrial interests as America entered the "organizational" age of the great corporation, the result of a new industrial revolution that radically transformed the old America of small agrarian communities.[32] As Americans looked inward, they saw that this revolution had come at the cost of urbanization, spreading slums, savage exploitation of labor, and a huge and growing gap between rich and poor. The rapid growth of cities produced an alliance of big business and urban political machines that made a mockery of local democracy. Yeoman farmers had been impoverished and their defensive populism roundly defeated, just as the upright representatives of honest producers who called themselves the Knights of Labor had been defeated and branded "subversive" by the forces of wealth and "progress." Such forces, though fearful of upheaval and revolt, did not themselves conduce to order and sobriety but were the very agents of social ferment. What they brought about was not a realization of the Jeffersonian dream of individual independence and healthy virtue but rather of his worst nightmare of dependence, immiseration, and corruption. The American promise of democratic control and equal opportunity for every individual appeared seriously compromised.

Whether the main political response to these severe tensions would be conservative or radical was decisively determined by William McKinley's defeat of William Jennings Bryan—champion of agrarian interests, democratic reform, and "easy money" as an answer to economic depression —in the presidential elections of 1896. Not only did the Republicans win the White House, but they swept northern Democrats from Congress and established an ascendancy that was to last for much of the following thirty-six years. Conservatism was tempered, however, by the rise of a Progressive movement that crossed party lines and would remain a significant force in U.S. politics until 1920, setting the political battle lines, practical and philosophical, for a century to come. The regulative goals of most Progressives were not meant to destroy American corporate capitalism but to tame and civilize it in order to save it from its own excesses, and from the radical, socialistic reactions it tended to provoke.[33] In many ways the "robber barons" of the late nineteenth century were the business equivalent of the heroically lawless individualists who had tamed the West, and were sometimes lauded as such. They had taken the wildly chaotic, wasteful, and often unprofitable enterprises of steel makers, railroad companies, oil wildcatters, and imprudent bankers and ruthlessly rationalized and consolidated them into great corporations that could compete with the best in the world. They had created the basis of the United States as a genuinely world-class power, but at the cost of massive social disruption and upheaval. The barons themselves thus represented a last wild frontier of lawless freedom that needed to be brought under the orderly authority of law and virtue in order to preserve the "moderation" of the American experiment. It was in this spirit that many Progressives conceived their task as the perfection of the American democracy, the preservation and purification of the American example. To the anti-imperialists among them, this was an internal task that would require most of the nation's energies for the foreseeable future.

Other Americans, including some notable Progressives, looked outward, having gained a new awareness of their nation as a world power. Between 1894 and 1896, America had thrice confronted Great Britain over South American claims and issues, and each time Britain had chosen to give way.[34] It was a de facto recognition that the United States had definitely arrived on the world stage. Political leaders and commentators, especially after prosperity returned in 1897, began to consider the directions in which the nation's own internal development and commercial interests were propelling it, and how best to secure those interests in a world undergoing great changes. Superior American virtue was simply assumed, of course, but the question was what to do with growing American power. What would ensure the future security of the United States, and what role should the nation play with respect to foreign powers competitively jostling for markets and empire? Those who thought that the only logical course was for America to enter the "great game" and join the ranks of the imperialists argued that this would be no more than a natural continuation of the expansive thrust of the nineteenth century. Such a course would have the incidental benefit of preserving the heroic martial virtue exhibited in the conquest of the West.

CONCLUSION

The imperialists would have their day but would have to contend with the objections of anti-imperialists, for whom the violence and entanglements of imperial expansion represented a serious threat to the maintenance of innocent virtue. It was a question that over of the next century would raise sharply and painfully the conflicts and contradictions lurking within American attitudes to both power and virtue.

CHAPTER EIGHT

From Imperialism to World Peace

A NATION THAT NOW spanned a continent had three main directions in which to look as it took stock of its strength and its needs and contemplated a new place for itself in the world: southward to the countries of its own hemisphere; eastward, back toward Old Europe; and westward to the Pacific, in which direction its expansionist impulses had been carrying it all along. Looking to the south it felt a resurgence of traditional distrust about European power and influence and, as the decrepit Spanish Empire finally crumbled, discerned important strategic imperatives for asserting its own dominance in the region. To the east it saw the European nations jostling competitively within the constraints of an enduring continental balance of power, each expanding its industries and armies while carving up the world among their various empires. Particularly notable was the rising autocratic, military-industrial power of recently unified Germany under an ambitious Kaiser Wilhelm II, for whom British sea power constituted the main obstacle to imperial expansion. To the west the United States contemplated the tempting market of China, a potentially unlimited outlet for the surplus product of its force-fed industrial revolution. Capturing a share of this market was a grand prize that would motivate dreams of an American-controlled isthmian canal and the acquisition of a Pacific empire. But as it looked covetously toward Asia, America also observed, along with the European empires competing for the same prize, a new Asian power arising. Japan had made a transition from feudalism to industrial-military power in a single generation, a feat at least as remarkable as America's rapid continental and industrial expansion, and it would at length become important to America as both trading partner and bitter rival.

America's foreign policy responses to this fin de siècle world would be determined partly by contingent circumstances on its own doorstep and partly by a reassessment of U.S. interests that specified the capture of foreign markets as vital to domestic peace and development. An upsurge of patriotic sentiment and nationalistic attachment was characteristic of the whole era but, in America's case, also reflected consciousness of growing power. Involvement in a putatively anti-imperialist war in Cuba would in fact see the nation set aside its traditional anti-imperialism to extend its power via an overseas empire of its own. The economic and strategic motives behind this bout of conventional imperialism were buttressed by a sentimental indulgence of that masculine virtue that Americans had exhibited on their own frontier, and which seemed in danger of being lost in a soulless industrial society. Overt imperialism, however, caused a reaction at home. Imperial occupation of the Philippines, most controversially, provoked an insurgent uprising and a U.S. military response that in many ways provided a foretaste of what would occur six decades later in Vietnam. The sullying of innocent virtue seemed hardly compensated by the thin rewards of colonization, causing disillusionment with imperial adventures even among some former enthusiasts. The presidency of Theodore Roosevelt, nevertheless, placed heavy rhetorical emphasis on active masculine virtue and power—the power of a newly dominant presidency to effect needed, progressive change at home, to police America's own region and extend its interests farther abroad (speaking softly while carrying a "big stick").

By contrast, Roosevelt's successor, William Howard Taft, was a conservative, cautious lawyer devoted to the idea of liberty under law both at home and abroad. World peace could be achieved, he believed, by negotiating treaties of unlimited arbitration with other nations. Taft also sought to reconcile assertive, often disruptive U.S. commercial expansion with a positive sense of mission by reviving a foreign policy idea that had been there at the birth of the American republic. This was a belief that economic development and trade under American tutelage would bind nations peacefully together and end the need for aggressive imperialism. Taft's Dollar Diplomacy sought to knit American business interests with the national interest and both to the cause of international development and peace. It was not a success, however, and was emphatically rejected by Roosevelt as pusillanimous and by Woodrow Wilson as inherently "selfish."

These episodes form the subject of the present chapter.

THE RISE OF AMERICAN IMPERIALISM

The Republican administration of President Benjamin Harrison was the first, in the latter part of the nineteenth century, to start flexing American muscle internationally. Harrison's secretary of state, James G. Blaine, looked into the future and saw the need of American industries for foreign markets and consequently for the naval resources to defend them. He aroused a brief flurry of national sentiment in 1889 when he stood up to Germany and Great Britain in defense of an American concession in Samoa, granted as a coaling station for U.S. shipping in 1878. President Harrison caused controversy, however, when he placed before the Senate a treaty to annex Hawaii after a coup led by U.S. sugar interests (using the modus operandi pioneered by Texas), toppled Queen Liliuokalani, and established a republic. American anti-imperialist sentiment was aroused. The Democrats blocked ratification, and Harrison's Democratic successor, Grover Cleveland, withdrew the treaty from the Senate. Cleveland had a keen enough appreciation of American commercial interests abroad but believed the nation could gain all the advantages it desired without taking on the burden of annexing distant islands occupied by people of a different race. As he later explained: "I regarded, and still regard, the proposed annexation of these islands as not only opposed to our national policy, but as a perversion of our national mission. The mission of our nation is to build up and make a great country out of what we have, instead of annexing islands."[1]

Cleveland's resolve was sorely tested, however, when a revolt by Cubans against their Spanish colonial masters broke out in 1895 (an effect, indeed, of U.S. tariff policy that caused a drastic decline in Cuban sugar exports). America's "yellow press" took up the cause with gusto, whipping up public outrage by printing exaggerated stories of the atrocities of corrupt and despotic Spaniards, but Cleveland resisted mounting public calls for American action. Again, though he understood and wished to protect and further U.S. investments in Cuba, he also saw that political involvement raised the possibility of annexation and the distasteful prospect of attempting to assimilate "inferior" peoples. Though Cleveland's successor, the Republican William McKinley, was an even more determined economic expansionist, he also initially hoped to avoid involvement. However, after an explosion on February 15, 1898, destroyed, with heavy loss of life, the USS *Maine*—sent to Havana Harbor to protect U.S. citizens—war seemed inevitable. But McKinley was determined to resist Cuba sympathizers in Congress pushing for annexation and was also worried that the Cuban Revolution was taking a more radical turn hostile to American commercial interests. A highly skilled political operator, he carefully controlled the path to war to ensure that its outcome would be de facto, informal American control of "liberated" Cuba through local, capital-friendly forces.

The war aroused rapturous public enthusiasm, and no one was more enthusiastic than McKinley's own assistant secretary of the navy, Theodore Roosevelt. Roosevelt resigned his post, formed a 1st U.S. Volunteer Cavalry regiment (the Rough Riders), and took them off to Cuba to fight. His leadership exploits, especially at the Battle of Santiago, aided by his own astute self-publicity, turned him into a national hero. The brief, victorious war against the decrepit Spanish Empire reflected and confirmed the momentous change in America's world status. Two decades previously, when Cuban revolutionaries had requested the help of the United States, the U.S. government had, for various reasons, declined. Now American arms had triumphed decisively, and the nation had its first heady taste of the potential worldly power that its possession and exploitation of a rich continent might afford. It had embarked on a veritable crusade in Cuba on a wave of moral outrage and idealistic patriotism, cheered on even by redoubtable anti-imperialists like William Jennings Bryan. Such men, however, soon regretted having ignored John Quincy Adams's axiom that the United States, whatever its sympathy for libertarian revolutions, "goes not abroad in search of monsters to destroy."

Victory left the United States with choices about the political future, not just of Spanish possessions in the Caribbean (Cuba and Puerto Rico) but also in the South Pacific (Guam and the Philippine Islands) where Admiral George Dewey had annihilated a Spanish fleet. McKinley, like

Polk before him, had declared in his inaugural address that America sought no wars of conquest and must resist temptations to territorial aggression. And in truth he was not interested in aggrandizement as such but only in reestablishing, after severe depression, domestic prosperity and stability, for which it was presumed expanding foreign trade was essential. American imperialism would therefore be strictly limited to goals that promoted this end, a view that occasioned different consequences in different places. McKinley took advantage of events to formally annex Hawaii, where American sugar interests dominated and the strategically important Pearl Harbor was located, but this was in a traditional mode, with an expectation of future statehood (finally achieved in 1959). His concern in the Caribbean and Central America was to protect rapidly growing American investments against both local dissenters and foreign interests, and to assure the prospects of a future isthmian canal by gaining strategically placed U.S. naval bases. McKinley wanted this achieved, however, without granting statehood and citizenship rights to Latin peoples situated inconveniently close to U.S. shores. Cuba was therefore indirectly controlled through a treaty that granted formal self-government by people friendly to U.S. interests, while America preserved (under the so-called Platt Amendment) a right of intervention to secure "republican" government. But the intention to annex Puerto Rico without extending full rights caused a storm among anti-imperialists in Congress, and the act, which made the island an "unincorporated territory," was only narrowly passed. The Supreme Court confirmed its underlying principle in the so-called Insular Cases, whose judgment was that the peoples of territories taken by conquest did not enjoy full citizenship rights. This marked a significant constitutional departure, the first time the United States had annexed a territory without the intention of granting full statehood.[2]

The situation in the Philippines and Guam was different again. Here the point of real interest was Manila, which could be used as a strategic location for projecting and protecting U.S. interests in Asia, particularly China. The question was whether control of Manila required control of the whole island of Luzon or even of the entire archipelago. The final decision was heavily influenced (as it had been in Hawaii) by the fear that other great powers—Germany, Russia, or even Japan—might step into the vacuum. McKinley, declaring that the territories must become U.S. dependencies, forcibly "purchased" the Philippines from Spain. America suddenly found itself in the unfamiliar role of a conventional imperial power.[3]

This caused a storm of debate between eager imperialists and horrified anti-imperialists. The realpolitik considerations may not have been negligible, but the debate was not conducted in such terms, which had little purchase on an American public educated in the corrupting effects of power politics. It was argued, rather, as a matter of competing ideals, one of which rejected the dominant American "isolationist" tradition and the other which confirmed it. The contrast was well illustrated by the following two statements from around this time, the first from arch-imperialist Senator Albert J. Beveridge, the second from arch–anti-imperialist William Jennings Bryan:

> Before the clock of the [twentieth] century strikes the half-hour the American Republic will be the sought-for arbitrator of the disputes of nations, the justice of whose decrees every people will admit, and whose power to enforce them none will dare resist. And, to me, the Republic as an active dispenser of justice is a picture more desirable than a republic as an idle, egotistical example posing before mankind as a statue of do-nothing righteousness. . . . The regeneration of the world, physical as well as moral, has begun, and revolutions never move backward.

> Behold a republic increasing in population, in wealth, in strength and in influence, solving the problems of civilization and hastening the coming of a universal brotherhood—a republic which shakes thrones and dissolves aristocracies by its silent example and gives light and inspiration to those who sit in darkness. Behold a republic gradually but surely becoming the supreme moral factor in the world's progress and the accepted arbiter of the world's disputes—a republic whose history, like the path of the just, "is the shining light that shineth more and more upon the perfect day."[4]

The common assumption here was of a redemptive American mission underpinned by superior American virtue; the dissent was over whether that virtue was an active one backed by worldly power or a purely exemplary one. The imperialists, holding to an enlarged version of Manifest

Destiny, vaunted national power and interpreted the American mission as the advancement through expansive power of white civilization on earth. The anti-imperialists (though hardly less racially conscious than their opponents) saw this as a perversion of the true exemplary and pacific American mission, whose fulfillment required a relinquishment of power and the preservation of innocence.

The imperialists appealed to the work of an American strategist, Captain Alfred Thayer Mahan, who had been converted from isolationism to expansionism in the course of his historical research. Mahan's work was profoundly "realist" in that he thought it vain to expect governments to act on anything other than the national interest, since they were agents not principals and had no right to do more. National self-interest included a relentless search for markets and the need to defend those markets and the national shipping that serviced them with far-flung outposts of empire. On the ancient grounds that aggressive action is the best defense, Mahan adopted an extraordinarily expansive interpretation of what adequate defense required. He recommended an American canal through the Central American isthmus to permit the navy to defend trade routes in both Atlantic and Pacific oceans, as well as military bases in the Caribbean to defend the canal. On similar grounds he recommended, too, the annexation of Hawaii. If this sounded more like national self-assertion than self-defense, Mahan argued that America's former isolation and immunity were bound to disappear under the impact of technological advancements in communications, transportation, and weaponry. The nation must therefore recognize that its long-term interests were bound up with regions far from its own shores, including in Old Europe.[5]

For all its realism, Mahan's work was wrapped in the familiar racist version of the American mission. Expansion was not just an American interest but a duty, for the extension of American influence would bring enlightenment to backward races as well as the blessings of Christianity and good Anglo-Saxon government. It was a view perfectly congruent with that of Rudyard Kipling's poem "The White Man's Burden," penned on the occasion of the Spanish-American War to encourage Americans in their imperial duty. This virile, expansive republican virtue was, of course, under constant threat of corruption from the evils of laxness and fleshly indulgence and would wither and waste if left unchallenged and unexercised. American mythology had always emphasized the dangers of corruption, but the imperialistic version of American destiny tied to visions of race war was positively obsessed by it. Loss of manly virtue would mean that the nation must eventually fall prey to stronger, fitter nations in the unceasing struggle for survival.

Americans were not immune to such appeals, but they had been too long conditioned to the idea that maintaining virtue implied nonentanglement to be wholly possessed by them. Though Mahan had been encouraged by the idealistic surge of support the American public showed for the Cuban war, he was deeply disillusioned by the shallowness of commitment revealed in its swift subsidence and the turning inward that followed. The Cuban war had indeed opened the way to the fulfillment of Mahan's policy of bases in Caribbean, an isthmian canal, and a Pacific frontier, but the U.S. Congress and people had not supported it for those reasons and were, at best, unenthusiastic about having the white man's burden thrust · upon them. The contrasting reception the public gave to the Open Door principles, formulated by Secretary of State John Hay in 1899 and 1900 in response to a crisis in China, pointed up the lesson.

OPEN DOORS AND IMPERIAL DISENCHANTMENTS

After a Sino-Japanese war in 1894–1895, which Japan had won, the great powers scrambled to establish their own exclusive "spheres of influence" in China, thus threatening to destroy the crumbling Qing dynasty and turn China into a series of separate colonies. The United States had sentimental attachments to China due to extensive missionary involvement, but it was also entranced by the vision of unlimited markets after the depression of the 1890s, particularly for cheap cotton goods produced (or overproduced) by U.S. textile firms. It desired, too, to have a hand in the development of Chinese railways being organized by various international combinations. The Open Door notes that Hay circulated would ensure, he said, "a fair field and no favor." They provided, among other things, that each of the great powers should maintain free access to any port open by treaty within its sphere, that only the Chinese government should tax trade, and that China's territorial and administrative integrity should be preserved. Hay saw these interlinked demands as best suited to preserving American commercial interests, since a China carved up into exclusive colonies by the great powers would be a China with many doors closed to U.S. trade. They were audacious demands from a relatively weak newcomer to the region, and they impressed none of the great powers, though for reasons of their own they eventually went along with them.[6] The Open Door became the cornerstone of U.S. foreign policy for more than forty years. Though geared primarily to U.S. commercial interests, its popularity at home was due to the fact that it combined the old American belief that unrestricted commerce was conducive to peace and prosperity with the traditional anti-imperialist principle of national self-determination. Moral, missionary, and material interests thus seemed to be harmonized in conformity with the benign mythological imperative. Liberal American politicians would long persist in representing the Open Door as the very epitome of peaceful American diplomacy, a shining example of enlightened self-interest safeguarding equal opportunity and territorial integrity (see Chapter 10).

It was hardly surprising, then, that Mahan's main influence should not be on the naive American public but on devout individual disciples like Senator Henry Cabot Lodge, Albert J. Beveridge, and Theodore Roosevelt. These men shared his contempt for isolationists and peace advocates and wished to see American greatness writ large on the material canvas of the world. To the anti-imperialists, however, the imperialist infatuation with action, honor, and glory seemed like a grotesque distortion of the American mission. Indeed, the anti-imperialists were appalled that their own moral enthusiasm for liberty had led them into error and inadvertently played into the hands of the imperialists. Crusade had degenerated into conquest. Men like Bryan, Cleveland, Mark Twain, David Starr Jordan, Carl Schurz, and E. L. Godkin could reconcile themselves to the violence of war only on the basis of the highest moral motives, yet war seemed by its very nature to subvert Christian, humanitarian, and democratic values. Meanwhile, imperial conquest bred resentment among colonized peoples and provoked a kind of violence that could only be justified, if at all, on the grounds of the grimmest necessity, as was soon amply demonstrated in the Philippines.[7]

The Tagalog people under the able leader Emilio Aguinaldo had been in armed resistance against their Spanish colonizers for years and had been inadvertently led to expect that the American triumph would mean their national independence. When they realized their mistake, they promptly began a war against their new masters. After being roundly defeated in conventional battles, they turned to guerrilla warfare of the most vicious kind, met by an equally vicious response from U.S. troops, a large number of whose officers were not just Civil War veterans but old Indian fighters. For many of these soldiers, the "liberated" people of the Philippines (who William Howard Taft called "our little brown brothers") were no more than dangerous "savages" to be tamed or exterminated just as they had been in the American West. The ruthless methods of antiguerrilla warfare devised to deal with a murderous and fanatical enemy that was indistinguishable from the general population and was operating with the widespread support of that population—methods that had become notorious in Napoleonic Spain, that the British were currently using against South African Boers, and that would become familiar to Americans again in Vietnam—were now used to quell the Tagalog. A 1903 congressional investigation into the conduct of the army in the Philippines (which Beveridge defended) would reveal details that horrified anti-imperialists and the general public. Whatever martial virtues had been displayed, innocent American virtue seemed to have been deeply compromised. A merchant financier and firm Republican informed Lodge that he and many of his fellow Republicans had begun to think "this Philippine experiment" not worth the cost in money and lives and would like to get out. Though they cared little for "the brown man," they dreaded "the demoralization to our troops of atrocities committed." In another prefiguring of Vietnam, U.S. troops in the Philippines found, to their enduring resentment, that they had ceased to be honored by their own compatriots.[8]

What saved the Philippine experiment from a Vietnam-style conclusion, however, was that the war was eventually won. It in fact had surprisingly little lasting effect on U.S. politics, and had brought neither inflation nor recession, but rather coincided with a return to prosperity at home. As Richard Welch put it: "It is more difficult to feel guilty when potentially victorious and currently prosperous. . . . To be successful in diplomacy and war was to be proven correct. At least this was so for a nation with the liberal creed and good intentions of the United States." By 1903 the main Philippine rebellion was over, and the solid if paternalistic civil administration of Governor-General Taft had considerably mollified Filipino attitudes, at least on Luzon.[9]

By this time, too, imperialism had lost its savor at home even among its former advocates, largely because the Philippines seemed to be all trouble and no reward. Business interests had enthusiastically supported the Philippine acquisition in the hope of large commercial gains that failed to materialize. Meanwhile, the strategic advantages of possession had come to appear more like liabilities. The Philippines involved the United States in a part of the world where other empires contested for dominion, the ones of most concern being Japan, which was set on a long-range course of regional expansion, and Germany, which Americans had come to regard as a hostile power because it had supported Spain during the war. Nevertheless, the administration (to the surprise and pleasure of the German government) had allowed Germany to acquire a chain of Spanish islands alongside the Philippines, right across America's Pacific line of communications. Adequate defense of the Philippines under these circumstances required greatly expanded naval assets, but the American people and their representatives in Congress were always infuriatingly reluctant to support "militarization." By 1907, even Roosevelt, who had succeeded against resistance in strengthening the navy and modernizing the army, was confiding to Taft a wish to give up the islands because they had become America's vulnerable "heel of Achilles."[10] America had had its brief, exuberant fling with power and, on the whole, had found it just as problematical, unprofitable, and dangerous to virtue as its mythology had always said it was. America kept its new empire, but the American public managed for the most part to ignore it, their indifference sustained by the fact that for a long time no truly critical danger arose to confront it.

Roosevelt had not managed a major conversion of public opinion. As president after McKinley's assassination in 1901, and after his own reelection in 1904, he had given power his best shot, for power was Roosevelt's métier. He was, like his friend Frederic Remington and his mentor Mahan, an ardent imperialist who lamented the feminization of Anglo-Saxon males behind their big-city desks and the loss of that conquering, martial spirit the race had displayed in the harsh conditions of the frontier. Roosevelt had an overriding fear of the corruption of virtue that would result, he said, from society's "decadence" and sexual laxity, its lack of the "race hardening" conditions provided by glorious warfare. He advised men to keep "mastery over their own evil passions," for "lawlessness in all its forms is the handmaiden of tyranny."[11] Himself a man of boundless energy, his presidency would exhibit the virtues he esteemed. Though often hampered by conservative fellow Republicans in Congress, he gloried in his occupation of the "bully pulpit," expanding the powers of the executive in order to pursue Progressive and conservationist causes at home and imperialist ones abroad.

Roosevelt was determined to project American power abroad through his own muscular image as cowboy, soldier, statesman, and hunter and enjoyed taking decisive actions that demonstrated the virile national will. These were sometimes symbolic—like his dispatch of the Great White Fleet on its grand Pacific tour—but others were intensely practical. He selected Panama as the site for an isthmian canal, "assisted" Panama to forcibly secede from Colombia, and ordered construction for the canal to begin at once, leaving Congress to debate, as he said, not the canal, "but me." Yet when European powers threatened to intervene in Latin America to collect debts owed by weak governments, Roosevelt was at first inclined to let them until an outraged congressional and public reaction forced him to respond differently. The result was a corollary to the Monroe Doctrine that asserted the right of the United States to police the region to guarantee that Latin American nations met their international obligations. Under this corollary, and again without congressional approval, he forced the Dominican Republic in 1905 to install an American "economic advisor" who in fact directed the country's finances. The anti-imperialists naturally abhorred Roosevelt's peremptory actions (Woodrow Wilson called him the most dangerous man of the age, and Mark Twain thought him clearly insane), but Americans generally liked his dynamic leadership; his forceful, colorful, larger-than-life personality; and his gift for dramatizing events in ways that gave a fillip to national pride. They enjoyed the "Teddy" show and cheered it on, but when it closed, they had not been significantly dissuaded from their inherently conservative view of U.S. power. Indeed, they often positively misinterpreted Roosevelt's actions and intentions to suit their more benign vision of American destiny, as for example when he intervened in affairs in the Far East in 1905.

Roosevelt fancied himself in the role of broker among great powers in the interest of achieving a balance favorable to America, though in truth he did not prove especially adept in the art. When war broke out between Russia and Japan in 1904, he immediately began calculating likely U.S. interests and advantages. Though at first favoring Japan as the more liberal power, he eventually concluded that the best result would be for the two opponents to weaken each other by slugging it out as long as possible. Japan's sudden decisive victories at Port Arthur and Mukden, however, raised the prospect of a Japanese hegemony that threatened American prospects in China and the Philippines. Roosevelt therefore intervened to try to save the balance of power. Japan, as exhausted as Russia by the conflict, unexpectedly responded by inviting Roosevelt to mediate, to which he reluctantly agreed. The outcome was not noticeably to America's long-term advantage, but Americans had been treated to the novel spectacle of a great power conflict being settled on its own soil—at Portsmouth Navy Yard, New Hampshire—with its warrior president in the role of peacemaker. Hardly had this conference ended than another crisis broke out in Europe over North Africa, involving the French, British, and Germans. This time the Kaiser asked for American intervention, and the delegation that Roosevelt sent to the Algeciras Conference of 1906 played an important part in shaping the terms of a settlement.

Roosevelt's motives in the Russo-Japanese affair were to maintain the balance of power in America's interests; at the Algeciras Conference he meant to prevent Germany from destroying a recent Anglo-French détente and possibly starting a European war that might involve the United States and ruin his plans for the Far East. He had, in other words, abandoned isolation and wholeheartedly entered the game of great power politics, even intermeddling in Old Europe on the side of the British (whose interests he saw as perfectly aligned with America's). Yet the American people comprehended none of this. At Portsmouth their sympathy was with the plucky Japanese underdog, whose intentions the Roosevelt administration now mistrusted. Moreover, they interpreted Roosevelt's mediation there and at Algeciras as acts of pure altruism in the cause of world peace. It was a supreme irony that the bellicose statesman devoted to enhancing American influence and material power—the archrealist who denounced pacifism as "moral degradation"—wound up receiving the Nobel Peace Prize in 1906 for his efforts at Portsmouth. Yet it was perhaps fittingly symbolic of the general mood of the American people.[12]

THE MOVEMENT FOR WORLD PEACE

Reaction to the Spanish-American War caused many anti-imperialist Americans to align themselves more directly with the international peace movement. This movement in its various manifestations had been, during the nineteenth century, a constant counterpoint to the rise of imperialism, a reliable barometer of continuing Enlightenment hope of progress toward human perfectibility.[13] While the imperialists glorified war, the peace movement drew inspiration from a Christian view of the supreme power of love. At the start of the twentieth century, many people began to think that permanent peace might not, after all, be a mere utopian hope but a practicable possibility, achievable through general disarmament, international law, and leagues providing arbitration mechanisms for the peaceful resolution of disputes.

Such ideas chimed naturally with the innocent version of the American mission, and indeed arose from the very same historical spring, but in the aftermath of the Spanish-American War they acquired a renewed significance that reflected the nation's altered status. The huge upsurge in popularity of the peace movements was, in many ways, a mirror image of the irruption of imperialism. Both were inspired by a new awareness of American power and the country's consequently greater responsibility for world leadership. Both sought fulfillment of an American mission that combined national destiny with universal values of democracy, order, and progress. But imperialists were nationalists who made peace with the American mythology by asserting that their pursuit of national power was, coincidentally, in the world's best interests. Anti-imperialists were cosmopolitan rather than nationalist in their outlook, taking the universal humanitarian goal of America as the key to its mythological mission.

Some of the latter, indulging the old hope of peaceful commerce, looked forward to the passing away altogether of nations and thus of narrow, destructive nationalism. David Starr Jordan, head of Leland Stanford University, wrote in 1899: "The day of nations is passing. National ambitions, national hopes, national aggrandizement—all these become public nuisances. Imperialism, like feudalism, belongs to the past. The men of the world as men, not as nations, are drawing closer and closer together. The needs of commerce are stronger than the will of nations." William Jennings Bryan believed that he spoke for the majority of his compatriots when, at a July 4 ceremony in London in 1906, he extolled the efficacy of moral example above that of violence. The world, he said, was on the threshold of a great intellectual and moral awakening in which nations would consider justice more important than physical prowess. Anti-imperialists often stressed this purely exemplary role, but their pursuit of peace was hardly less activist or militant than the imperialists' pursuit of power. Their internationalist perspective connected them to peace movements around the world, which meant they were no more isolationist than the imperialists. The essential difference between them concerned the efficacy of force, violence, and power as compared with that of rational consent, virtue, and peace. The peace movement believed the tide of history was on its side.[14]

Such views seem tragically ironic given our knowledge of the subsequent course of twentieth-century history (and imperialists, of course, ridiculed them at the time). Yet they expressed a tendency that had existed from the very beginning—in the liberal Enlightenment itself, perhaps, but certainly in American mythology—to presume a radical disjunction between power and innocent virtue, usually figured as a contrast between the rule of force and the rule of law. Power implied force, and the ultimate expression of force was war. Power and war were evil, while fraternal co-operation and peace were good. Though strict pacifists were in a minority among peace advocates, the tendency to see issues of war and peace in stark black and white was general. It became a commonplace that war was an aberration in human affairs, not the norm, an evil trick pulled by wicked people of narrow self-interest over moral, peace-loving people (always the majority). The cure was to be found in education, conversion, and the wider participation of the people of all countries in decision-making. Educated and enlightened people would one day demand that the evil reign of force be replaced by a benign reign of virtue almost always identified with international law. Just as the rule of law had constrained and ordered politics and power in the American system, so it would end the reign of power and force in the international arena if people of goodwill everywhere cooperated.

Of course, national law was ultimately sanctioned and enforced by the coercive power of the state, an overarching Leviathan not present in the international arena. But this, far from being a drawback, was taken as a mark of the superior beauty of the international law. Submission to such law would be a matter of pure rational agreement, not of forceful compulsion. No one stated this more clearly than steel magnate and peace advocate Andrew Carnegie when he told an audience: "International law is unique in one respect. It has no material force behind it. It is a proof of the supreme force of gentleness—the irresistible pressure and final triumph of what is just and merciful."[15] Such law would achieve the reign of innocent virtue indeed. This was a faith that moved large numbers of people before World War I and for some time after it. As Roosevelt, the great apostle of power, ended his presidential tenure, U.S. foreign policy moved closer to embracing this same faith. Roosevelt's own anointed Republican successor, William Howard Taft, began the shift, much to the chagrin of his former friend.

THE SEARCH FOR WORLD PEACE BEGINS

Taft was of aristocratic rather than democratic disposition and an anti-imperialist by background, principle, and temperament. When in January 1900 President McKinley asked him to head a commission to establish civil law in the Philippines, Taft replied that he had disapproved annexation because it meant "the assumption of a burden by us contrary to our traditions and at a time when we had quite enough to do at home." He agreed with his younger brother Horace who expressed both the family view and that of most antiexpansionists of the era when he stated his objections to "anything like a vigorous foreign policy. . . . It seems to me like the whole work of America is the civilization of America and the building up of the nobler democracy than has yet been seen." Taft's strong-minded mother expressed another typical view when she said, with regard to the Philippines, that she could see no advantage in gaining sovereignty over "those savages," since indeed the United States already had more aliens than it could comfortably manage. Nevertheless, now that annexation was a fait accompli, Taft believed America had acquired a "sacred duty" to govern the Philippines properly and to help develop Filipinos as a self-governing people (something he thought might take a century or more).[16]

Taft's moderate, pragmatic governorship was very much in keeping with this sense of duty. He evinced no interest in the Philippines as a strategic national asset but viewed the country wholly in terms of its political relationship with the United States, the latter's responsibility to govern for the good of the Filipino people being uppermost. He was a man uncomfortable in politics but with a high judicial consciousness, and his assumption of civil authority in the Philippines could be said to mark the advent of the rule of law in a regime where force had dominated. The military commander he displaced, General Arthur MacArthur (Douglas MacArthur's father), had acted as an imperial proconsul with both civil and military power. MacArthur, a lifelong soldier whose habit was command and whose principal means were military, looked upon the Filipinos as unrelenting enemies to be ruthlessly conquered by U.S. troops. Such an attitude merely proved to Taft that the army was at best "a necessary evil, but it is not the agent to encourage the establishment of a well-ordered civic government."[17]

It was this high respect for law that most distinguished Taft, as president from 1909 to 1913, from his colorful predecessor. Roosevelt, though he genuinely believed "lawlessness was the handmaid of tyranny," favored a Hamiltonian and even Jacksonian view of the executive. He interpreted the restraints of law as narrowly as possible so as to give full rein to the power of the presidency, which ostensibly represented the popular will. As he wrote in his autobiography, the spirit of his administration was guided by the theory that

> the executive power was limited only by specific restrictions and prohibitions appearing in the Constitution or imposed by Congress under its constitutional powers. My view was that every executive officer, and above all every executive officer in high position, was a steward of the people bound actively and affirmatively to do all he could for the people. . . . I declined to adopt the view that what was imperatively necessary for the Nation could not be done by the President unless he could find some specific authorization to do it. . . . Under this interpretation of executive power I did and caused to be done many things not previously done by the President and the heads of departments. I did not usurp power, but I did greatly broaden the use of executive power.[18]

Taft, by contrast, argued that state power should be strictly limited by law so as to safeguard personal and property rights: "The true view of the executive function is, as I conceive it, that the President can exercise no power which cannot be reasonably and fairly traced to some specific grant of power. . . . Such specific grant must be either in the Constitution or in an act of Congress passed in pursuance thereof. There is no undefined residuum of power which he can exercise because it seems to him to be in the public interest." For Taft, ordered liberty was a function of law, first and foremost. Though he did not disagree with the Progressive measures Roosevelt had so peremptorily introduced—indeed, he was a much more active "trustbuster" than his predecessor—he saw his main presidential task as putting them on a sound legal basis. He believed in the perfectibility of law, in the long run, but the restraint of law was essential to the educational process en route. Law embodied principles of right and justice that were not merely conventional but came from a "higher source," and the best instrument to preserve that law was the judicial system, not state action or any of the other popular democratic measures demanded by the people.[19]

This respect for law did not make Taft a pacifist, however. Law meant order, and order had to be enforced, sometimes sharply and with violent force, both at home and abroad. Nevertheless, given his view of the relations between power and law, it was not surprising that he should be drawn to international treaties—the basic bricks of international law—as a basis for building world peace. Indeed, this was one major plank of his foreign policy, the other being his so-called Dollar Diplomacy. Neither was successful, and it could be said that the one major foreign policy achievement of the Taft presidency was a negative one: a patient refusal to be drawn into intervention in Mexico where a revolution, begun in 1910, threatened substantial U.S. investments.

Dollar Diplomacy was, in effect, an attempt to reconcile the expansion of "selfish" American commercial interests, whose effects generally disrupted local cultures and economies, with the liberal American mission. Its failure was due in part to its being first linked to Roosevelt's expanded Monroe Doctrine and in part to the diplomatic ineptitude and arrogance with which Taft and his secretary of state, Philander Knox, pursued it. The perception was that the continuously chaotic conditions of indebted Latin American countries provided a perennial motive for European creditors to step in to protect their investments. America's need to prevent such encroachments had become all the greater with the building of the Panama Canal, an important strategic asset needing proper defense. Taft's idea was that, if the administration could encourage U.S. bankers to take up Latin American debts and turn Latin America into a monopolized preserve for U.S. capital, the cause of European intervention would be removed and the grounds for regional prosperity and peace would be properly established. This was Taft's benign "nonimperialistic" imperialism, allegedly helping countries to help themselves. Regional prosperity and peace were linked with America's strategic control of the Caribbean. The policy, Taft assured

Congress in 1912, "is one that appeals alike to idealistic humanitarian sentiments, to the dictates of sound policy and strategy, and to legitimate commercial aims."[20]

The problem was that many Latin Americans, already upset by Roosevelt's interventions and dispossessed by burgeoning American ownership of land and business, did not see it that way. They felt bullied by the administration into granting commercial advantages and establishing financial protectorates for U.S. interests. Taft eventually felt compelled to send naval detachments to Honduras and warships and troops to Nicaragua to secure "order" in favor of those interests. In the latter case a petty dictator, Adolfo Díaz, was maintained in office courtesy of American military power. Nor was the U.S. Senate impressed. Defending the more traditional policy of nonintervention, it refused to approve the treaties concluded with Honduras and Nicaragua.

Undeterred, Taft attempted to extend the policy to China but met with even less success. The policy there was fueled by hopes of making the Open Door a living reality, of pushing through grandiose railroad-building ventures in Manchuria, of building up weak American trade with China, perhaps even aiding that country to become a constitutional republic on the American model (the nationalist revolution that overthrew the Manchu dynasty occurred in 1911–1912). But Taft was trying to promote American investment in a region where other great powers had long-established security and economic interests as well as commanding military presence. While the latter either increased or maintained their trade with China, U.S. exports actually declined markedly, squeezed out by great power combinations. As Minister to China John Calhoun told Knox in early 1912, with respect to the Open Door Policy: "Diplomacy, however, astute, however beneficent and altruistic it may be, if it is not supported by the force which not only commands but demands respect and consideration, will avail but little."[21] This represented sound advice that would be very imperfectly heeded over the following decades.

Taft's other major foreign policy initiative met with no greater success. His assay at world peace was nevertheless a telling prelude to that of Woodrow Wilson's, which failed even more spectacularly.

Though Taft distinguished himself from those he called "peace cranks"—men like Bryan, Carnegie, and Senator Elihu Root[22]—he came to think, like them, that world peace could be practically achieved via the principle of arbitration of international disputes. Roosevelt, despite his bellicosity, had also favored treaties of arbitration, though he had insisted that these not cover questions relating to the vital interests, independence, or honor of the countries involved. Taft, however, insisted on unlimited arbitration that did not exclude such matters. He sounded out the attitude of the British government and received a positive response. This caused great joy among peace movements in Britain and the United States but great unhappiness among the Germans, who saw any British-American treaty as a combination aimed at them, and the Japanese, who understood it as an attempt to break up their alliance with Britain. Taft, to prove his sincerity, responded by offering a treaty with any country that desired one, spelling out proposals for neutral mechanisms to ensure fair arbitration. The grand experiment began when the American, British, and French governments signed treaties of unlimited arbitration on August 3, 1911, which Taft duly submitted to the Senate for approval. This was undoubtedly the most popular act of Taft's entire presidency, and the American press was so convinced of the importance of the treaties that it assumed approval would be a formality.

But it had underestimated the Senate's jealousy of its constitutional prerogatives in the treaty-making process (Taft and Knox had neglected to submit the treaties for the Senate's prior consent). The senators were egged on, too, by the old warrior, Roosevelt, who had sallied forth from the lists to condemn Taft's outrageous proposal that the United States bind itself to arbitrate questions respecting its honor, independence, and integrity. Roosevelt had the ear of Senator Henry Cabot Lodge, and he filled it with forebodings about giving foreigners on arbitration commissions the ability to take away legitimate powers from president and Senate. He also published his views in a series of articles that caught the eye of the delighted Germans, who embarrassed Taft by inquiring whether he intended to submit the Monroe Doctrine or U.S. immigration policy to arbitration. A majority report of the Senate Foreign Relations Committee, written by Lodge, recommended that various paragraphs be struck from the treaties and added an amendment listing issues that could not be submitted for arbitration. These were fatal alterations, and though the treaties passed by an overwhelming vote, they had been utterly emasculated.

Taft refused to give up a cause that had become dear to his heart and went on an energetic speaking tour during the campaign of 1912, arguing that the Senate had put its prerogatives above world peace. But with the Republican vote split by Roosevelt's third-party candidacy, the presidential election was lost to the Democrat Woodrow Wilson. Taft had hoped, he later said, that either the Senate would change its mind or the people would change the Senate—"instead of which they changed me."[23]

CONCLUSION

In 1898, Americans entered a war of liberation that had turned into a war of outright imperialism. If political elites, with some support from economic interests, understood this as a necessity to secure American markets and thereby American domestic stability, prominent anti-imperialists and the American people generally felt they had been led astray. If some had experienced a brief, vivid bout of enthusiasm for power, glory, and national aggrandizement, seduced by an aggressive version of their myth that emphasized active, martial virtue, they had nevertheless become rapidly disillusioned by the consequences of its exercise. The dominant American myth was too profoundly antipathetic to the idea of an acquisitive empire, and the American sense of innocence too deeply offended by the deeds the nation was forced to undertake on its behalf, to support it over the long term. The overseas empire persisted, of course, but rather through the neglect and disinterest of most Americans than with their positive backing. The whole experience had served merely to confirm a growing belief in the necessity and possibility of creating a peace on earth that was something more than the peace of the graveyard, a peace that could be reached only by pacific means.

Taft failed to fulfill this hope, but after him came a statesman with the spirit of a Christian missionary. During Wilson's tenure of office, the inherent tensions within the American mythology would come sharply into focus as a result of a cataclysmic European war. The moral-political battle would be fought in terms of allegedly sharp dichotomies: the New World versus Old Europe, New Diplomacy versus Old Diplomacy, a forgiving policy of German reintegration versus a punitive one of containment, law versus force, cooperation versus balance of power, idealism versus self-interest, disarmament versus rearmament, generous internationalism versus selfish nationalism. American virtue, in other words, would be pitted decisively against ancient power, and virtue's triumph would, Wilsonians believed, usher in the millennium.

CHAPTER NINE

Woodrow Wilson and the Reign of Virtue

IN THE COURSE OF A FEW hectic years, the presidency had passed from warrior to lawyer to priest. Wilson's presidency marked the ascendancy of innocent virtue in U.S. foreign policy, which he promised to make "selfless" and exemplary. No exercise of American power would be allowed to offend innocent virtue on his watch.

Yet Wilson was unable to keep his promises. He intervened violently in Latin American politics whose turbulence was in some degree a result of America's own policy, drawn partly by the expansionist logic established by McKinley and partly by his own obstinate moralism. He would commit the nation to participation in a cruel war in Europe, justifying it as a war to end all wars, the prelude to building world peace through general disarmament, arbitration, and a system of international law expressed in and safeguarded by a League of Nations. That this project to fulfill the national mission ended in resounding failure was in large part due to Wilson's inability to transcend the too-simple antithesis of virtue and power that his worldview assumed and the American mythology encouraged.

This important episode is the subject of the present chapter, but to begin we must look at how Wilson conceived of American nationalism and the vital American mission. These played a large part in his conception of his task in pursuing the reign of perpetual peace. The tenor of his thinking on America and its special exemplary role can be gauged from a famous speech he made in 1915 to explain why the United States should not become involved in the Great War in Europe.

> My urgent advice to you would be, not only always to think
> first of America, but always, also, to think first of humanity. . . .
> Americans must have a consciousness different from the con-
> sciousness of every other nation in the world. . . . America
> must have this consciousness, that on all sides it touches el-
> bows and touches hearts with all the nations of mankind. The
> example of America must be a special example. The example
> of America must be the example not merely of peace because
> it will not fight, but of peace because peace is the healing
> and elevating influence of the world and strife is not. There
> is such a thing as a man being too proud to fight. There is
> such a thing as a nation being so right that it does not need
> to convince others by force that it is right.[1]

WILSON ON NATIONALISM AND MISSION

Wilson, in his scholarly days, had formulated a synthesis of sorts between particularistic American nationalism and the universalist, antinationalist tendency of the American mythology. More accurately, he had developed a view of liberal nationalism that made it an essential foundation for a universally encompassing society of peaceful nations.

Wilson's own nationalism signaled his acceptance, as a southerner, of the validity of the outcome of the Civil War. States-rights "particular-ism" had been defeated and a political union established that could form the basis of developing nationhood. Influenced by German historicism, Wilson rejected the idea that nations were primordial, ethnocultural enti-ties and regarded them instead as the products of organic, evolutionary development. A nation was the historical achievement of a mixed people struggling to become a single people with a distinctive identity. Wilson's American melting pot (severely limited by a belief in racial hierarchies quite as profound as Roosevelt's[2]) described an immigrant nation of largely European origin. As he illustrated in his multivolume *History of the American People,* English, Scots-Irish, and other ethnic Europeans—in conditions of frontier freedom and under the guidance of great leaders like Washington, Jefferson, Clay, Jackson, and Lincoln—not only had assimilated but had grown increasingly democratic and egalitarian. Over centuries of struggle and interaction with one another and with their own constitutional, political forms, the American people had welded themselves into a self-determining, democratic nation.

Self-determination was thus both a historical process (in the sense that nations created themselves in history) and a goal to be achieved. Full self-determination—a stage that many peoples in the world had yet to reach—came only when national unity and moral community had been genuinely realized. When it had, other nations were obliged to respect the new nation's independence. A mixture of intrinsic racism and bitter experience convinced Wilson that most non–Anglo-Saxon nations were too immature for true independence, which was why the principle of national self-determination that he enunciated during the Great War generally excluded them (apart from Japan, and then with reservations), much to the disappointment of colonized peoples whose hopes he had raised.

It is important to note that, although Wilson was a sincere believer in constitutional government, he did not revere the U.S. Constitution as many others did (Grover Cleveland, for example, idolized it as the "ark of the covenant"). His attitude was, in fact, as Hamiltonian as that of Andrew Jackson or Theodore Roosevelt. He believed a written constitution was a mere legal document, given life and reality only by the meaning that succeeding generations read into it and by their adoption of it as the "skeleton frame" for the living organism that was the developing nation. As a Unionist, Wilson welcomed the fact that the federalist checks and balances embodied in the Constitution had been effectively destroyed by the defeat of the Confederacy, but on the other hand he expressed regret that the balance between executive and legislative branches had been upset by the usurpation of power by Congress during Reconstruction (whose progress he profoundly regretted because "the better whites" had been denied the vote while "the most ignorant blacks" had been granted it).[3]

Wilson believed that the ideal Constitution of the founders, with its nicely adjusted checks and balances, no longer reflected the reality of a government dominated by Congress. His solution to this problem (as he saw it) of American government was not to restore checks and balances but to concentrate power in the executive branch. The American people's democratic instinct, organically developed in their experience on the frontier, was best expressed in the only office that reflected the will and interests of them all: the presidency. The sovereign power of a democratic nation properly belonged to the leader who was alone accountable to the whole nation: the president.[4] (This view explained Wilson's admiration of the British parliamentary system, in which the prime minister dominated the legislature.)

Wilson thus rejected balance of power as an aim of American government, just as he would reject it in international relations. His ideal, he said, was not balance of power, but "community of power." The implications of this view for the American dilemma of power and virtue can hardly be overstated, for it logically placed the burden of free, popular government on positive virtue rather than on the limitation of power. In contrast to the founders, who devised institutions on the assumption of general rascality, Wilson presumed that institutional safeguards could accomplish nothing without citizen virtue. He believed that the virtue of democracy lay in the capacity of a free people to elect virtuous leaders and to be properly led by them. Their capacity to abide by the rule of law similarly depended on uncoerced respect for the law, not on fear. For such a people, a constitution was not the *condition* of their liberty but merely its expression. Britain had different institutional arrangements from the United States, but Britons were no less free than Americans. It was the *essence* of institutions, not their form, that mattered, and that essence was democratic liberty and citizens' capacity to use it moderately and wisely, a matter of pragmatic experience and citizen virtue rather than of theoretical conviction.[5]

The reality of American virtue was evident in the fact that the Revolution (which Wilson considered a democratic one) had been essentially "moderate," avoiding the descent into anarchy, chaos, and tyranny that was the fate of so many subsequent revolutions. It followed, then, that organic progress toward a liberal democratic nation was less a matter of right institutions or constitutions than of the moral progress of individuals toward a condition of responsibility consonant with the orderly use of liberty. A disordered, immature individual was no more capable of sustaining a democratic, constitutional nation than a disordered and immature nation was capable of sustaining an international one. The self-determination that enabled responsible individuals to create and sustain a free political community was not merely closely analogous to, but a prerequisite of the self-determining capacity of nations that made them fit to be part of an international moral community. Wilson was therefore not just a national-ist, but a *liberal* nationalist who held that national self-determination must rest on the liberty of self-determining citizens. Like most Americans, he presumed that the values of liberalism, individualism, democracy, rule of law, and laissez-faire were universal and that liberal-democratic nations tied to one another by bonds of mutual interest and commerce would, unlike autocratic ones, be inherently peaceful and antimilitarist. He was inevitably, therefore, also a liberal *internationalist.*[6]

Though Wilson presumed the equality of liberal, self-determining nations in an interdependent community of nations, he did not, needless to say, regard America as simply one nation among others. His view of a distinctive American nationhood by no means canceled the universal role. America was not just any nation, but the nation that had proved the validity of liberal and democratic government, pointing the way for the rest of the world. The myth of mission remained solidly intact and made nationalism indistinguishable from patriotism: "Patriotism is a principle, not a mere sentiment. No man can be a true patriot who does not feel himself shot through and through with a deep ardor for what his country stands for, what its existence means, what its purpose is declared to be in its history and in its policy." In an Independence Day speech in 1914, Wilson asked rhetorically, "What are we going to do with the influence and power of this great Nation? Are we going to play the old role of us-ing that power for our aggrandizement and material benefit only?" Every answer he gave to that question showed the hold the myth retained upon his mind.[7]

Though, as a liberal internationalist, Wilson was glad to see American enterprise penetrate to every corner of the globe, believing it good for both America and the world, the selfless national task was to found a just and peaceful international order to moderate the otherwise dangerous competition among capitalist nations. He therefore explicitly rejected the Dollar Diplomacy of his predecessor as a misuse of American power to back up far-flung commercial and industrial enterprises, a purely selfish impulse. He admitted that America had, despite its idealism, proved as liable as any other nation to press its selfish advantage. As president, he was determined to eliminate that selfishness. He believed that if the United States perfected its own behavior, its example would uplift the whole world. The nation had become powerful, he said, not because of expansion and industrialization but because of its enduring ideals. Other nations had been as rich and powerful, others as spirited, but Wilson hoped that Americans would never forget that theirs was created to serve, not just itself, but humankind.

This service had now to be more than purely exemplary. America's rise to world power and the increasing interdependence of nations had, Wilson believed, made a policy of pure isolation obsolete. "We are participants," he said, "whether we would or not, in the life of the world. The interests of all nations are ours also . . . What affects mankind is inevitably our affair."[8] The United States would have to maintain its virtue while assuming new obligations of neighborliness commensurate with its material greatness. Wilson thus took up the project that Teddy Roosevelt had self-confessedly failed to accomplish: to make the United States behave like a world power that was permanently, politically engaged in international security. Wilson did not think, however, that engagement necessarily implied contamination through "entangling alliances." In May 1914 he argued (against Hamilton's clear intentions) that George Washington's warning about entangling alliances did not merely apply because of passing circumstances but had a strong moral foundation. It reflected the fact that no country was yet going in the same direction as the United States:

> We cannot form alliances with those who are not going our way; and in our might and majesty and confidence and definiteness in our own purpose we need not and we should not form alliances with any nation in the world. Those who are right, those who study their consciences in determining their policies, those who hold their honor higher than their advantage, do not need alliances. You need alliances when you are not strong, and you are weak only when you are not true to yourself. You are weak only when you are in the wrong; you are weak only when you are afraid to do the right; you are weak only when you doubt your cause and the majesty of a nation's might asserted.[9]

This was why he argued that the League of Nations would have to become a genuine community of peace-loving nations associated by "covenants of justice, law and fair dealing," not a mere system of treaty alliances based on expediency and advantage. Wilson was confident that there would be no problem if America sufficiently remembered its mission to guide the world peacefully toward liberty. No nation that respected liberty and had set its foot upon that path, he said, need ever fear American power. Dismissing Roosevelt's glorification of masculinity and power as an adolescent fantasy, he insisted that America's increased obligations did not imply an extension of its physical power; it was America's character and ideals the world needed more than its military or economic might. The force of America, he said, "is the force of moral principle, . . . there is nothing else that she loves, and . . . nothing else for which she will contend."[10]

PROBLEMS WITH WILSON'S VIEWS

It may seem paradoxical, given these premises, that Wilson and his equally idealistic secretary of state, William Jennings Bryan, should apply the Roosevelt Corollary to the Monroe Doctrine more often and more thoroughly than Roosevelt himself. Though professing sincere anti-imperialism and the best of neighborly intentions, they could not help but be swayed by the same factors that had swayed McKinley, Taft, and Roosevelt: the need to protect U.S. commercial interests, to exclude European powers, and to secure the strategically important canal. Not only did they continue to sustain unpopular, despotic governors in Nicaragua and the Dominican Republic, but they eventually ordered the marines into the latter, and also into Haiti with great loss of life, to establish U.S. protectorates. Furthermore, Wilson fell into the Mexican trap that Taft had carefully avoided. This was largely a result of his disgust at Victoriana Huerta, a reactionary general who had murdered his own boss in a coup and provoked a revolutionary movement against him by constitutionalists. Moral righteousness was in the ascendant when Wilson declared he would teach his neighbors how to elect good men. Though Wilson naturally favored the constitutionalists, he was to learn that U.S. incursions into Mexico and interference in its affairs were equally unpopular among all opposing forces. The best that could be said for his Mexican policy was that he avoided, in the end, the general war that many American investors, Catholics, and ultranationalists were urging on him.[11]

Arthur Link, Wilson's most sympathetic biographer (who first labeled Wilson's foreign policy "missionary diplomacy"), argued that part of the problem was that Wilson and Bryan were largely ignorant of and indifferent to foreign affairs. They were both, he wrote,

dedicated to the American ideal, at least theoretically, and obsessed with the concept of America's mission in the world. . . .
[Their] urge to do good, to render disinterested service, was so
compelling that it motivated interference in the affairs of other
nations on such a scale as the United States had not heretofore
attempted. . . . To varying degrees, many other factors were
involved—naiveté, the desire to protect American economic
interests, imperialistic ambitions—but these operated subcon-
sciously on Wilson's and Bryan's minds. Paramount in their
motivation was the ambition to do justly, to advance the cause
of international peace, and to give to other peoples the blessings of democracy and Christianity.[12]

Later authors also argued the administration's ill-preparedness for a
global leadership role. According to Lloyd Ambrosius, Wilson's inexperience of the world caused him to fall back on his own personal experience
and to project "his conception of American nationalism onto the world,
presupposing its universal validity." He claimed that Wilson, while appreciating the growing interdependence of nations, failed to comprehend
their continuing pluralism and was consequently unable to distinguish
between the interests of the United States and those of other nations. But
of course Wilson's ignorance of the world was hardly greater than that of
most Americans, and his attitude was perfectly in keeping with the traditional myth's assumption that one day all the world would be America
and all humankind American in its individualism. He once advised newly
naturalized citizens that they must become thorough Americans and could
not do that if they thought in "groups." Cultural pluralism, within a single
nation or a community of nations, was a recipe for disunity. Though
Wilson was critical of many aspects of America's political development,
he nevertheless believed that the American experience had proved the
possibility that a nation dedicated to individual liberty could maintain
its unity and independence and that this was an authentic model for the
world. And if all nations in time moved toward American-style liberal
democracy, he expected that a society of such nations would also grow
organically into an ordered international community.[13]

Wilson assumed that progress toward the moderate ideal must itself be
moderate and orderly, which was why he found the Mexican revolution,

and also the Chinese and Russian revolutions, so deeply disappointing. Nevertheless, he continued to favor the metaphor of organic growth and hoped that the League of Nations after the Great War would lay the constitutional foundations of an organically evolving international community. Yet there was an unrealistically pacific assumption embedded in this organic image that Wilson hardly acknowledged. The myth of America obscured for him certain blunt facts of U.S. history that he himself knew perfectly well. "I have studied the history of America," he said; "I have seen her grow great in the paths of liberty and of progress by following after great ideals. Every concrete thing that she has done has seemed to rise out of some abstract principle, some vision of the mind. Her greatest victories have been the victories of peace and of humanity."[14] But this was to underplay the fact that the unity of America had been confirmed only through a terrible civil war. In his own history, Wilson had written:

> The nation, shaken by those four never to be forgotten years
> of awful war, could not return to the thoughts or to the life that
> had gone before them. An old age had passed away, a new age
> had come in, with the sweep of that stupendous storm. Every-
> thing was touched with the change it had wrought. Nothing
> could be again as it had been. The national consciousness, dis-
> guised, uncertain, latent until that day of sudden rally and call
> to arms, had been cried wide awake by the voices of battle, and
> acted like a passion now in the conduct of affairs. All things
> took their hue and subtle transformation from it: the motives
> of politics, the whole theory of political action, the character of
> the government, the sentiment of duty, the very ethics of pri-
> vate conduct were altered *as no half century of slow peace could
> have altered them* [my emphasis].[15]

War, it seemed, despite its horror, had turned out to be a positive force in U.S. history. The "organic" moral community that founded the American nation after the Civil War had been forged, not through peaceful growth, but through conflict and the coercive application of northern will. The blot of slavery had been erased and a new order produced, but the process had hardly been "orderly." The reign of virtue, if that is what the post–Civil War nation represented, had been achieved and was maintained by force as much as by the consent of all its citizens, a good portion of whom in the

South were merely bitterly acquiescent (or ultimately reconciled, according to Wilson, only by the arousal of nationalist spirit caused by another war, the Spanish one).[16]

The organic metaphor is an inappropriate one for any human organization. It obscures the inevitable social-political conflicts that must be managed and contained if the organization is to survive. A single cell of a multicellular organism has no interests or aims separate from that of the whole organism and, since there can be no conflict between the parts, growth and development may be imagined as harmonious and internally "peaceful." The "virtue" of the individual cell, if we may call it that, is precisely its utter subsumption within and subservience to the interests of the larger organism. The wish for that to be true of human societies is, when pushed to the limit, a totalitarian one, at odds with the American liberal idea of individual freedom. To be sure, Wilson thought that democratic Americans had reached or were approaching a level of maturity that enabled them voluntarily to submit to the common will and be part of the common good, distinguishing their free polity from others based on balance of power or coercion. This was the virtue that rendered the exercise of liberty safe. But the political unity that makes possible a "community of power" is always and necessarily a *political* achievement, and even when unity is the product of consent and political agreement, its maintenance always requires the existence of varying degrees and orders of coercive force. This is not to denigrate the importance of genuine consent in well-functioning polity, but only to note that such consent is invariably undergirded and guaranteed by effective power.

In 1909 the Progressive theorist Herbert Croly had declared that the foreign policy of a democratic nation must serve the cause of international peace and had foreseen that, though the American desire for peace had in the past justified its isolation and neutrality, in the future it might demand military intervention, even in Europe. "Peace will prevail in international relations," he wrote, "just as order prevails within a nation, because of the righteous use of superior force—because the power which makes for pacific organization is stronger than the power which makes for a warlike organization."[17] It was Wilson's (and America's) unwillingness fully to accept this in the international sphere that doomed the League of Nations to irrelevance.

FAILURE OF THE LEAGUE

Wilson was dragged into the Great War despite himself, and despite the reluctance of the American people. A theme of his presidential campaign of 1916 had been that he had kept America out of a war that was incomprehensible in its causes to Americans, one that seemed to be senselessly consuming the material wealth and young manhood of Europe. After his reelection he offered America's services as mediator to end the conflict, proffering an ideal of "peace without victory" that stirred liberal souls everywhere but that none of the belligerents was seriously willing to contemplate. By April 1917, Wilson had decided that U.S. entry into the war against the "undemocratic" power of Germany was his only option.[18]

Matters had gone in this unhappy direction because the traditional American policy of neutrality had proved no more viable than during the Napoleonic wars, especially after Britain placed a blockade upon Germany and the Germans retaliated with unrestricted submarine warfare (a form of warfare that Wilson considered inhuman). The loss of American lives in German attacks inflamed anger at home and threatened constantly to precipitate the nation into hostilities. Wilson's "too proud to fight" speech, made in response to such provocation, was generally well received by the public, but, as in Jefferson's day, certain influential sections of opinion viewed it as a matter of shame and disgust that the nation could not or would not defend its rights on the seas, and thus its own honor. Wilson himself, after much soul-searching, abandoned the peace camp in mid-1915 and joined those advocating war preparedness by strengthening the military and creating a Continental Army. He thus ignited a long, bitter controversy with peace Progressives who included prominent figures like William Jennings Bryan, Senator Robert LaFollette, and Jane Addams. The latter regarded America's only goal to be self-purification; believed all wars were caused by evil bankers, munitions-makers, and military men with vested interests; and saw preparedness as a glorification of force that would turn the United States into an armed camp, terminating domestic reform. The contest became one between pacifist purity (represented by organizations like the League to Limit Armament and the American Union Against Militarism) versus national honor and the need to defend it (represented by the likes of the National Security League and the American Rights Committee).[19]

Wilson achieved preparedness by the end of 1916, but the number of those positively advocating intervention remained small. For his own part, Wilson felt inexorably impelled toward war by the submarine issue, though he had no desire to move until he could be sure of determining the peace. He remained ever hopeful, too, that he might end the war through mediation and even considered using American wealth to force Britain and France to the negotiating table by threatening restrictions on loans. Britain's new prime minister, David Lloyd George, however, believed that a mediated end to the war would leave Germany as a persistent military threat to Europe and the world. Lloyd George shared Wilson's liberal aims and wished to see the democratization of Germany and all Europe, and he hoped that guaranteeing the self-determination of small nations would enable them to form a bulwark against German expansionism. But he thought these outcomes achievable only if German militarism were decisively defeated. This required America's entry into the war on the side of the French-British entente rather than its mediation of the conflict. Lloyd George, one of the canniest politicians of his age, cajoled and flattered Wilson to induce him to enter the war not so much for the sake of military victory but for the sake of winning the peace. Wilson's judgment, he averred, was the only one among world leaders not corrupted or injured by the war. Only Wilson, being unmotivated by desires for revenge or territory, could hope to impose a just and lasting peace that would properly express the moral value of free government.[20]

Wilson of course found this eminently congenial, but the mood at home was not yet decisively for war. Thanks to the opposition of a dozen die-hard senators, Wilson could not even succeed, in March 1917, in getting Congress to grant him authority to arm merchant ships and otherwise defend U.S. shipping.[21] A fortnight later, however, the sinking of three American merchantmen coincided with the first Russian revolution and the establishment there of a constitutional government. The first event gave Wilson a plausible cause for war; the second swept away the objection that the Allies could not possibly be fighting for democracy while autocratic Czarist Russia was on their side.

A last, desperate outpouring of peace sentiment failed to halt the move to war. Wilson had made the crucial decision but was as acutely, agonizingly aware of the risks to which American innocence would now be exposed as anyone in the peace camp. On April 1, 1917, the very evening before he declared war on Germany, he made quite plain what he thought the dangers were: "Once lead this people into war and they'll forget there ever was such a thing as tolerance. To fight you must be brutal and ruthless, and the spirit of ruthless brutality will enter into the very fibre of our national life, infecting Congress, the courts, the policeman on the beat, the man in the street."[22]

Wilson thus foretold the excesses that his own administration would foster in its attempt to solidify opinion behind the war and to neutralize opponents, too readily branded as "traitors." Such risks or consequences could be justified only by the elevation of the motives and ends of the conflict, and control of the peace process afterward. In his address to Congress the next day, Wilson outlined the objectives for which the nation would fight against an autocratic power, namely, to make the world safe for democracy and to found a peace on "the tested foundations of political liberty." It is worth quoting at some length from this speech:

> Our object . . . is to vindicate the principles of peace and justice in the life of the world as against selfish and autocratic power and to set up amongst the really free and self-governed peoples of the world such a concert of purpose and of action as will henceforth ensure the observance of these principles . . .
>
> A steadfast concert for peace can never be maintained except by a partnership of democratic nations. . . . It must be a league of honor, a partnership of opinion. . . . Only free peoples can hold their purpose and their honor steady to a common end and prefer the interests of mankind to any narrow interest of their own. . . .
>
> The world must be made safe for democracy. Its peace must be planted upon the tested foundations of political liberty. We have no selfish ends to serve. We desire no conquest, no dominion. We seek no indemnities for ourselves, no material compensation for the sacrifices we shall freely make. We are but one of the champions of the rights of mankind. . . .
>
> It is a fearful thing to lead this great peaceful people into war, into the most terrible and disastrous of all wars, civilization itself seeming to be in the balance. But the right is more precious than peace, and we shall fight for the things which we have always carried nearest our hearts,—for democracy,

for the right of those who submit to authority to have a voice in their own Governments, for the rights and liberties of small nations, for a universal dominion of right by such a concert of free peoples as shall bring peace and safety to all nations and make the world itself at last free. To such a task we can dedicate our lives and our fortunes, everything that we are and everything that we have, with the pride of those who know that the day has come when America is privileged to spend her blood and her might for principles that gave her birth and happiness and the peace which she has treasured. God helping her, she can do no other.[23]

American power would be purified by being deployed from pure, selfless motives and for a supremely virtuous end—the establishment of the rule of virtue worldwide. The risk of contaminating innocence was worth taking for the achievement of a great ideal: world peace, democracy, disarmament, the end of aggression—the end, as Secretary of State Robert Lansing said, of "force and selfishness" in international affairs. The phrases "league of honor," "partnership of opinion," and "universal dominion of right" all signaled the inauguration of the reign of Christian virtue on the earth, and the end of the rule of power. Just as the Civil War had been the blood price for confirming the Union that founded the exemplary liberal democratic nation, so would the European war be the blood price of laying the international foundations for world union. The outcome would be the final consummation of the American mission. "It is this we dreamed of at our birth," Wilson told Congress; "America shall in truth show the way."[24]

There is not space to relate, save in brisk outline, the oft-told story of Wilson's crusade and its ultimate failure: his seizing of the initiative on war aims with his Fourteen Points speech (on January 8, 1918) promising a nonpunitive peace with Germany, principles of equality and national self-determination, and collective security provided by a League of Nations; his decision personally to spend seven weary, acrimonious months at the Paris Peace Conference naively negotiating with the crafty Old World politicians of Britain, France, and Italy; the eventual production of the Treaty of Versailles (signed June 28, 1919), whose financial and territorial terms severely compromised the Fourteen Points but at least included the covenant of the League of Nations; Wilson's return to the United States in failing health to fight his greatest battle against "irreconcilable" Republican senators led by Henry Cabot Lodge, who wanted either to reject the treaty or to attach reservations that would strictly limit America's commitments to the league; his frustration and consequent decision to take his case directly to the people (in September 1919) in a whirlwind tour that brought on a paralyzing stroke and crippled his presidency; his rigid refusal to compromise with Lodge and the Republicans, leading to defeat of the treaty in the Senate; the election of 1920, which Wilson called "a great and solemn referendum" on the treaty and the league—lost.[25]

My purpose here is to expose how the problem of reconciling American power with American virtue played in this vivid drama. America had deployed its might for a virtuous purpose, but to complete that purpose, it must apparently be prepared to permanently deploy the power needed to support the league it had instigated. Americans had hitherto led mainly by example but must now take up a more active world leadership role. Wilson had been acutely aware, ever since the Bolshevik seizure of power in Russia in October 1917, that America was contending for that leadership with a rival universalism whose anti-imperialism and world mission were quite opposed to American principles. His own aim would always be to create an order that repudiated both imperialism on the one hand and revolutionary socialism on the other. He implicitly refuted godless communism's assumption of a vanguard role when, formally presenting the Versailles Treaty to the Senate, he claimed that America had come to this heavy responsibility through no plan of its own, but by the leading hand of God. America could not refuse the cup the Divine Will had given it, even if this meant stepping away from isolationism.[26]

The Senate battle that followed was not, however, a simple contest between internationalists, who desired the collective security system that the league represented, and isolationists concerned with preserving traditional nonentanglement. In fact, the pure isolationists—men like William Borah and Hiram Johnson—were in a decided minority. Other irreconcilable Republicans—like Lodge, Philander Knox, and Elihu Root—feared that collective security would make the United States the world's police, dragging it willy-nilly into dangerous conflicts in which it had no intrinsic stake, the very nightmare that had always informed American republicanism. Nevertheless, they were willing to support a more carefully defined commitment to continuing the wartime alliance with France, mainly as a safeguard against a resurgent Germany that remained, for them, the potential enemy of civilization. Knox thus introduced to the Senate a "new American doctrine" that contemplated a breach of isolation for the sake of some "small and natural" entente with limited and appropriate obligations, specifically an obligation once more to come to the defense of Europe should its freedom and peace again be threatened by a Germany seen as a danger to the very existence of democracy on earth. He told the Senate that "our cobelligerents need have no anxiety, for so surely as the sun rises if the Hun flood again threatened to engulf the world, we shall again be found fighting for the right, with the same complete accord and cooperation as in the past, all for the defense of civilization."[27] If it had been worth foregoing isolation in the recent war for this purpose, it was presumably worth doing so again in the future. To assume unlimited obligations, however, was going much too far.

But Wilson believed that signing an ordinary treaty of alliance with France and England to contain Germany would be merely to reinstate the Old Diplomacy, already discredited by the war. As early as January 1917, in his "Peace without Victory" speech to the Senate, he had noted that European balance of power arrangements had proved desperately unstable, collapsing into a devastating and senseless war whose submarine threat undermined America's traditional neutrality policy. If neutrality could no longer ensure America's noninvolvement in European conflicts, something else had to be found. That something had to be morally finer and more reliable than the rule of mutually opposing and balanced forces, which was really an attempt to bind evil with evil. Wilson had not accepted the terrible necessity of entering the war just to refound the order that had caused it, thereby risking more wars in the future with all the horrors and threats to virtue they entailed. Wilson's New Diplomacy envisaged a "society of nations" that would represent a genuine community of power capable of preventing war among its members.[28] This was the intent of the controversial "mutual guaranty" of Article 10 of the league covenant, a collective security pledge committing all to preventing the aggression of any member against another.

The great question to be addressed, however, was how a virtuous league could effectively discourage or prevent aggression among member nations. Wilson began by insisting that all members must be equal, and not merely in a juridical sense. It was necessary to equalize power among them by ensuring disarmament. Achieving an equalization of power—or rather powerlessness—as well as of rights would mean that none would be tempted to use superiority of force to trample the rights of others in order to achieve selfish ends. But this raised the familiar Hobbesian problem of who would, first, ensure that disarmament occurred and, second, enforce the nonaggression pact if broken? Wilson refused to commit the United States to a permanent enforcement of German disarmament (much to the chagrin of French Premier Georges Clemenceau), even though he particularly desired it. He hoped that, absent a sovereign power, moral suasion would be sufficient. But what if that failed and a rearmed nation showed aggressive intentions toward another? Clemenceau was not the only skeptic about the power of moral suasion, and even Wilson, in the end, was unwilling to put all his trust in it. He wanted Article 10 to be an "affirmative guaranty" against aggression by any member against any other, in other words, an *enforcement* clause which, by its nature, assumed that the only real deterrent against aggression was the threat or exercise of military power. For the article to be effective, therefore, there would have to be either a binding commitment of all members to use military means in cases of aggression or an international force created for that purpose. But Wilson would accept neither of these.

Secretary of State Lansing saw clearly that the "affirmative guaranty" interpretation of Article 10 implied the "establishment of a ruling group, a coalition of Great Powers" sufficiently armed to do the job required, though he disapproved of it because it would violate the requirement of equality among nations. His most trenchant objections were the same ones that energized the Republican opposition, namely, that the affirmative guaranty would compromise U.S. sovereignty by transferring Congress's right to declare war to a clique of great powers. As for Wilson's refusal to accept the logic of his own position, Lansing could only conclude that the president's plans were those of an impracticable dreamer, too dependent on altruistic cooperation and taking no account of "national selfishness and the mutual suspicions which control international relations."[29]

No doubt Lansing considered himself a sober pragmatist compared with Wilson, but his own belief that some means other than coercion could be devised to enforce international agreements hardly indicated a firm realism. Lansing noted that all the arguments over the proposed form of the league boiled down to two alternatives: a politico-diplomatic organization or an international judiciary. As a practicing lawyer, his own preference was emphatically for the latter, partly because he thought it the only one achievable and partly because he sincerely shared the American prejudice against the use of force in international relations, which is to say the American revulsion at traditional diplomacy and balance of power politics. He wrote in a note to the president: "The legal principle [of the equality of nations], whatever its basis in fact, must be preserved, otherwise force rather than law, the power to act rather than the right to act, becomes the fundamental principle of organization, just as it has in all previous Congresses and Concerts of the European powers."[30]

Lansing admitted that enforcing an international covenant based purely in law would not be easy though he imagined that outlawing an offender and applying economic pressure might prove effective. If that failed, however, he had nothing further to offer. Nevertheless, he was upset by Wilson's commitment to a politico-diplomatic version of the league guaranteed by the combined force of five great powers. The consequent primacy of these powers would, he thought, establish an aristocratic or oligarchic international order rather than a democratic one and would thus be "entirely out of harmony with American ideals, policies, and traditions." It would, in effect, be just another form of power balancing that would undermine all idealistic hopes for the postwar peace. Realizing that Wilson seldom heeded his advice, however, Lansing thought the most he might expediently achieve was to substitute a less dangerous negative guaranty for Wilson's affirmative one. He hoped to make Article 10 a "self-denying covenant" of members to keep their hands off other members. In reality this would, if accepted, have pushed the league more toward the juridical form that Lansing desired.[31]

Wilson, for his part, wanted to keep the affirmative interpretation but could not wholeheartedly accept Lansing's logic about what was required to fulfill it. He was willing to contemplate the possibility of an American commitment to force on specific occasions (the implied obligation was merely "moral," he claimed, and would be fulfilled only subject to congressional approval), but he would not submit to a legal rule that meant *automatic* American commitment. Entanglement could not go that far, for it would leave American virtue and its preservation at the mercy and hazard of the actions of other nations, dragging the United States into who-knew-what actions.

Wilson's position, ironically, was thus not so distant from that of Lodge's Republicans (indeed, had it not been for a deep personal animosity between Lodge and Wilson, some compromise surely could have been reached). Wilson had never, in fact, rejected nonentanglement altogether but had sought merely to compromise it. Indeed, his policy during the war had shown the limits of his internationalism. America had entered the war not as one of the Allies but as an "associated" power, its armies kept separate from the others and under U.S. command. This demonstrated that America could act firmly in the world, even in a leadership role, while remaining strictly its own master. Military or diplomatic freedom and independence of action (which did not of course preclude voluntary cooperation with other nations) preserved nonentanglement while allowing the nation to perform its enhanced international role.

It is important to pause here to recognize that isolationism and nonentanglement are not necessarily the same thing; though isolation implies nonentanglement, the reverse does not follow. Nonentanglement is quite compatible with unilateral American action in the world *at times of America's own judgment and choosing,* and of course always in a noble cause. It was thus that Albert J. Beveridge could be an enthusiastic imperialist (who believed that God had given it to the Teutonic peoples to be the "master organizers of the world") yet a supporter of the isolationists in the battle over the league treaty. After World War II this "engaged unilateralist" outlook would become a shibboleth of formerly isolationist conservatives newly impressed by America's preponderant power and resentful of the constraints imposed by the United Nations and other alliances. If in their hands the unilateralist tendency would often seem indistinguishable from an aggressive nationalism that threatened to transform world leadership into world dominance, it was nevertheless true that dominance was always asserted for a holy cause—anticommunism or antiterrorism. The two traditionally interconnected elements, nonentanglement and mission, were always preserved, just as they had been by Wilson.

Where Wilson differed from these later patriots was in his discomfort with power and its uses, a discomfort he could not overcome even to lay the foundations of the "community of power" that he hoped the league would become. His vague prescriptions over the affirmative guaranty seemed unlikely to ensure the believable sanction against aggressors that the league required. Wilson, not believing in the possibility of a synthesis between the terms of the virtue-power dyad, tried to straddle them—and failed. Unable to put full confidence in the sway of virtue alone but afraid of the dangers of committing fully to the use of power, he attempted a compromise that was bound to be ineffectual. Republican senators William Borah, Philander Knox, and Warren G. Harding on the Senate Foreign Relations Committee saw the flaw and rejected it. Only a full commitment of American power could realistically guarantee the preservation of each member of the league as a self-determining nation, a commitment they, of course, would not contemplate.

CONCLUSION

Friedrich Nietzsche once wrote that a future leader in a world lacking a metaphysical anchor would have to combine the mind of a Caesar with the soul of a Christ.[32] It is not too whimsical to understand America's mythological mission as expressing disbelief in the possibility of such a synthesis and a consequent failure to effect it. If there was in power-obsessed imperialists too much of the Caesar, in peace-loving anti-imperialists there was too much of the Christ.

Yet even the most Christian of U.S. political leaders had been tempted, in 1917, to assume the mantle of a Caesar and go to war. Wilson had mobilized American military power and risked American innocence in the hope of establishing the universal reign of peace and Christian virtue on earth. Nonentanglement had been compromised and domestic freedoms endangered for this transcendent cause, but as in the case of imperialist adventure, the results had been profoundly disillusioning. Instead of a new international rule of law and virtue, the postwar settlement produced only a resurgence of bad old European power politics. What was worse, Wilson, by joining in the game, had apparently forfeited his own purity. His original motives—America's motives—for entering the war were called into serious question because of the compromises he had felt obliged to make at Versailles. The American doughboys who had died in France had been "gypped . . . killed for six-percent bonds, for oil wells, for spheres of influence."[33] Shallow cynicism replaced a hope that had proved, in retrospect, hopelessly naive. The case against war and military preparedness that Progressive pacifists had made in 1915–1916 was now commonly accepted as fact: war was intrinsically evil, and its occurrence could be explained only by the machinations of powerful people with something to gain—profiteers, industrialists, armaments manufacturers, money lenders. Ordinary people could never expect any good to come of it, particularly the ordinary people of America whose exemplary mission was inevitably endangered. Only a threat to the very survival of the United States—a survival as important to the rest of the world as to Americans—could justify a purely defensive war, and few people believed the nation had been truly threatened in 1917.

It was the extreme dichotomy that the mythology posited between power and virtue, the belief that the choice came down to one of either/or, that had led to this profound popular disillusionment. It was a belief that the administration had shared. Secretary of State Lansing, who understood the logic of the dichotomization, was at least consistent in his willingness to reject coercive power outright and put faith, however attenuated, in the pure rule of law. Wilson dithered because he was torn between the belief that no good could come of the use of power and an apprehension that, in the political world, nothing moves except by the application of some force. It was this same, deep ambivalence that would characterize and paralyze American engagement with the world in the two decades that followed.

CHAPTER TEN

Disillusionment and Hope

LODGE, IN THE BRUISING Senate battle over the League of Nations, defeated Wilsonian multilateralism but also accidentally defeated his own larger goal of having the United States play a role in world affairs commensurate with its power. The senators who insisted that the country remain absolutely free to choose when its vital interests were at stake, and when to act to defend them, were staying true in effect to the nonentanglement principle. Such strict unilateralism automatically turned into isolationism when, in the prevailing postwar atmosphere of disillusionment, the bar for what constituted a vital American interest was set impossibly high. The isolationism of the interwar period thus occurred by default. Despite the rapidly deteriorating international environment of the 1930s, the conditions held to justify American intervention were never reached, at least not until the Japanese attack on Pearl Harbor shocked America out of its "emotional deadlock."[1]

It was a lesson that Franklin Roosevelt, Harry Truman, and Dwight Eisenhower would take to heart: unilateralism led to isolationism, and isolationism led to disaster. This period would also bring the final demise, under the weight of its own contradictions, of America's traditional doctrine of neutrality as a means of avoiding international conflict. The conviction would take shape that genuine domestic and international security could be guaranteed only through multilateral engagement that would require the permanent commitment of American power on a scale that neither Wilson nor Lodge had ever contemplated. Before they could arrive at that conviction, Americans had to traverse two decades during which their simple view of power and virtue as necessarily antithetical would first be hopefully indulged and then finally upturned by catastrophic events and by large failures of policy.

That there existed a policy that could fail indicates that the term "isolationist" to describe America during this period is rather misleading. Isolationism was genuine insofar as this denotes an American reluctance to commit its military power for international purposes.[2] In many other ways, particularly in the 1920s, Americans remained thoroughly engaged and even took a leadership role in trying to create a secure international environment. One of the most important avenues they explored was the economic. American industrial and financial capital was officially encouraged to deploy worldwide so as to lay the foundations of a peaceful global order secured by trade and development. In areas of more conventional diplomacy, America also took the lead by negotiating important international treaties and pacts that established the essential keynote of international relations in the 1920s. That note was peace, for this was the great and hopeful era of peace movements in the United States and Europe. But peace was to be secured not by force or through military balance but by disarmament, virtuous self-restraint, and the pressure of world opinion.

Both these strategies failed. The "diplomacy of the dollar" was shattered by the onset of the Great Depression after 1929, which caused the rapid abandonment of economic internationalism. The pious hope for peaceful diplomacy was tested and found wanting first by Japanese expansion in Asia and then by Hitler's aggressive moves in Europe. In the fascist ideology that inspired these moves, Americans encountered a wicked inversion of their own mythology, one that challenged virtually every assumption upon which the latter was based.

These are the themes explored in the present chapter.

DISILLUSION AND REACTION

Cynicism, sometimes accompanied by an affectation of aesthetic amoralism, was a common reaction in Europe to the Great War's horror and futility. Yet America, the least affected of all combatant nations, was particularly distinguished by its mood of self-flagellating critique. The widespread belief that the United States had been duped into war indicated the distance that most Americans perceived between their initial idealistic hopes and the war's actual outcomes. There were, to be sure, realists who insisted that America had, in fact, intervened to protect its own interests rather than to end all wars, but the public did not forget what had moved it most. When the ambassador to Britain, George Harvey, told the Court of St. James in 1921 that America had sent soldiers overseas solely to save the United States of America, he suffered a veritable maelstrom of abuse and vilification, especially from veterans' organizations and Gold Star mothers who felt the nobility of their sacrifice impugned. Harvey's speech, which had been cleared beforehand by President Warren Harding's administration, was intended to discount any idea that America might yet join the league and also to lay the moral basis for an insistence that Europe pay its war debts to the United States. Yet this exercise in tough realism redounded so badly at home that Secretary of State Charles Hughes felt obliged, a fortnight later, to defend the idealism of American intervention. He was wildly cheered for his effort.[3]

But if America was sure of its own idealistic motives, it was equally certain that its idealism had been betrayed and its innocence undermined. Foreign politicians, selfishly obsessed with balancing power and gaining advantage, had not been reformed by America's example or leadership. At home, meanwhile, social and economic reform had been put on hold while civil liberties were assaulted. The hatred and paranoia aroused by war had, as Wilson feared, stained the very fabric of American life. Wilson himself, in an effort to garner popular support for the war, had assisted in the contamination by setting up, under the direction of zealous reformer and idealist George Creel, a Committee on Public Information whose mission was to elevate the European war into a holy crusade for the world's very soul. Of course, Germany's autocracy and militarism made it an easy target for American demonization, and the committee's output included some crude propaganda. Creel himself tried to damp down virulent anti-Germanism my means of unbiased reporting, but many of the passions aroused among Americans were, to say the least, unedifying. When Congress passed an Espionage Act in June 1917, the full vitriolic force of super-patriotism was unleashed. Attacks occurred against "hyphenate Americans" of all kinds, but particularly German Americans. Tolerance gave way to hysterical intolerance of unconformity, encouraging witch hunts against anarchists, socialists, pacifists, trade unionists, and anyone marked as "undesirable."[4] The success of Lenin's Bolshevik revolution in Russia after 1917, and the fear that communism might spread rapidly across war-crippled Europe, heightened the mood of hysteria.

Eric Foner has commented, "Perhaps the very nobility of wartime rhetoric contributed to the massive repression of dissent, for in the eyes of Wilson and many of his supporters, America's goals were so self-evidently benevolent that disagreement could only bespeak treason to the ideas of democracy and freedom." It was an attitude that would be in evidence again and again in the course of subsequent U.S. history. Here was displayed with full force the darker potential that had always lurked in a mythology that emphasized isolation as a means of protecting special virtue and moral purity. It signaled the emergence of that narrow, fearful "Americanism" that underpinned the Red Scare of 1919–1920; fueled the rise of the Ku Klux Klan; provoked the racially oriented anti-immigration movements of the 1920s; and inspired the excesses of McCarthyism, the conspiracy theory lunacy of the John Birch Society in the 1950s, and the racist Americanist doctrines of the 1970s.[5]

"One Hundred Percent Americanism," a doctrine promoted by organizations such as the Daughters of the American Revolution and the National Security League, repudiated the liberal universalism of the American myth and displayed open contempt for foreign nations, asserting the superiority of distinctively American values that were decidedly conservative, indeed reactionary. The chauvinistic "yellow press" of William Randolph Hearst had hitherto supplied this variety of Americanism with a voice, clamorously mixing introversion with bellicosity. The Great War and the competitive ideological challenge of Soviet Russia, however, provided the ideal context for its full flowering. One Hundred Percenters were not disillusioned by the war itself—indeed, they regarded America's victory as a glorious achievement—but only by the spurious, universal ideals for which Wilson claimed to have fought. They put America and its own interests first, also last. Reactionary Americanism shared American imperialism's belief in racial theory, and thus its assumption of white moral superiority, but lacked its hubristic spirit and visionary sense of world mission to educate and elevate inferior peoples. It was altogether more inward, more defensive, more parochial.

During the interwar period, an ultraconservative brand of isolationism took hold in this movement, perverting the preservation of innocent virtue into a rejection of any foreign influence whatsoever on American life, most especially any that might affect economic liberty or racial purity.[6] The traditional distrust of devious Old Europe, which had always been companioned by a certain genuflecting respect and admiration for European culture and achievement, was here deformed into Know-Nothing contempt for anything not purely American. The movement represented a deliberate, disdainful introversion signaling that Americans no longer needed or cared about condescending Europeans and their endless quarrels. The formerly poor and ignorant American cousins were now independently rich and powerful, and not obliged to attend to genteel, down-at-heel relatives who had been inclined to look at them mockingly askance.

Reactionary Americanism represented another distortion of the foundational myth, one wrought by the encounter of parochial America with roiling international conflict. Curiously, however, this movement found itself in de facto alliance with the true defenders of the central faith on the matter of isolation. The disillusionment produced by the experience of war and its aftermath effectively stifled the active missionary impulse among liberal Americans. In sharp sequence this group had been disturbed by the degrading of American civil liberties during the war; shocked by French Premier Clemenceau's announcement at the start of the peace conference that he intended to be guided throughout by balance of power principles; dismayed by examples of Wilson's secret dealings during negotiations, an apparent betrayal of his promise of open diplomacy; and appalled when Wilson prematurely announced a new three-year naval construction program that seemed to undermine the most vital principle of his Fourteen Points—disarmament. By the start of 1919, liberal commentators were declaring the league no more than an old-fashioned alliance for the usual purposes of maintaining the economic and political status quo.

Despite this, the mood of the country at large—as even Wilson's most determined opponent, Senator Lodge, recognized—was supportive of entry into the league, though with suitable reservations.[7] Average Americans may not have fully understood the implications and obligations implied in ratifying the treaty, but they wanted something positive and hopeful to show for their idealistic investment. Voting in the Senate revealed a majority in favor there too, though in such a mixture of with and without reservations as to defeat final passage. Wilson, despite reservations of his own akin to those of Lodge, had fought an uncompromising battle for acceptance on the grounds of fulfilling, or at least keeping faith with, the triumph of virtue, which alone, he believed, could justify his having taken America to war. The defeat of the Versailles Treaty in the Senate was therefore widely taken to be a defeat for idealism. The war, its sacrifices, its dangerous entanglements, its unfortunate consequences on the home front, now seemed all in vain. The stage was thus set for a profound disillusionment, not just with the war, but with active idealism itself. Virtue had not been served by a hopeful American exercise of power, but betrayed and endangered, just as mythological prejudice had forewarned.

The influential liberal journal the *Nation,* which took a leading part in spreading the postwar mood of disillusionment, came out in opposition to the league covenant in March 1919. The journal's stance reflected that of its utopian chief editor, Oswald Garrison Villard, but it also revealed clearly the dichotomous assumptions about power and virtue that the myth perpetuated. The choice was cast as one of *either* power *or* virtue, *either* force *or* justice, *either* selfishness *or* altruism, *either* good *or* evil. It was presumed that no compromise was possible between these alternatives, far less that power might be put at the service of justice and virtue. Can war be cured by war, Villard asked, or will it be cured by the doctrines of Christianity and the brotherhood of man? Many liberal Americans thought they knew the answer to that rhetorical question. All coercion was a futile attempt to bind evil with evil, and the war had proved once more that evil could not overcome evil, at least not in any way that provided a stable, permanent peace. Many of the proponents of this view had opposed the war from the start, but after Wilson's defeat their opinions penetrated deeply the views of those who had supported it. There was much purging, purifying, and recanting among people who felt that the tenets of Wilsonian intervention had led them astray. Great American literature of the period reflected the same preoccupations: the so-called lost generation of writers—F. Scott Fitzgerald, Sinclair Lewis, E. E. Cummings, Edmund Wilson—sought to destroy all sentimental illusions, but their cynicism, realism, even nihilism expressed a painfully disappointed idealism.[8] Revisionist historians, meanwhile, questioned the reality of German guilt for the war as well as Wilson's true motives for entering, deepening the general pessimistic sense of having been thoroughly deceived.

Americans were also incensed by the apparent ingratitude of the people they had set out to save, especially regarding the controversy over repayment of U.S. wartime loans. The debt issue agitated American-European relations over several years. Europeans did not understand how rich, idealistic Americans could demand scheduled debt and interest repayments immediately after a war that had devastated their economies. Angry French people who felt they had "paid with their blood" were incensed that America should talk about mere money. The Europeans responded to American demands by pressing Germany even harder for promised war reparations, increasing distress in a nation that Wilson had promised would not be treated punitively in the postwar settlement. At length, American financiers, with official endorsement, negotiated schemes that greatly eased the reparations and debt controversies, but Henry A. Wallace would later charge that Americans were at fault in not canceling war debts. They were also at fault, he said, in following a policy of expanding exports to Europe after 1918 while placing high tariffs on imports, a lack of "world consciousness" that helped produce the dangerous international conditions of the 1930s. Yet his was a rather lonely voice. Most Americans merely felt themselves slandered by European criticism that seemed to question the reality of their unparalleled moral reputation.[9]

CONTINUING AMERICAN INTERNATIONALISM AFTER 1920

The disillusionment that characterized the United States after 1920 seemed to lead to a rejection of all altruistic involvement in international relations. Americans put the somber heaviness of war and disappointment behind them and gave themselves up to gaiety and self-absorption, withdrawing into things purely American: prohibition, movies, speakeasies, jazz, automobiles, gangsters, flappers, the roaring twenties, the Ku Klux Klan, anarchists, Wall Street. Yet to see only this is to overlook the fact that America, despite its rejection of the League of Nations, sought other means of pursuing its ideals during this period. It was notable that American business in the 1920s acquired, with official encouragement, a self-consciously internationalizing mission. Since the war had materially strengthened America and turned it, for the first time, into a creditor rather than a debtor nation, it was in a unique position to take over the central role Great Britain formerly played in sustaining an international economy. Herbert Hoover, who shared the prevailing aversion to the use of force in support of principle, and who had made his reputation conducting relief aid operations in China and Europe, was particularly influential in forwarding this internationalist economic agenda. As secretary of commerce for eight years under President Calvin Coolidge, and then as president himself, he introduced his "American system," encouraging a massive expansion of U.S. overseas investment. Hoover hoped that the organizational example of American corporate business, as well as its hard capital, would lay the foundations of a global commercial civilization able to draw into its peaceful orbit all the nations of the world, including the Soviet Union (see Chapter 5).[10]

These commercial efforts were accompanied and greatly strengthened by an enormous international dispersion of American mores, methods, and entertainments during the 1920s. The mythological hope that all the world would one day be America seemed about to become a reality, at least in a cultural sense. The war had shattered Europe and discredited and degraded its ancient mythos to the point of extinction. European leadership in world affairs had perceptibly passed across the Atlantic, despite the United States' rejection of the league. The surge of enthusiasm that Wilson's idealistic agenda had ignited in Europe had never completely evaporated, so America remained a moral leader in the popular imagination. American wealth and power commanded new prestige. American industrial organization, efficiency, and productivity were greatly admired everywhere, even by the likes of Josef Stalin. American standards of living inspired envy. American glamour incited infatuation and emulation. American music, dance, radio, movies, literature, and style—whether of language, life, or fashion—were everywhere the rage. American popular and material culture began to exert on the world that intense attractive power (recently labeled "soft power") that has distinguished it ever since. Some sophisticated Europeans reacted to this materialistic "cultural imperialism" with the kind of horror still often expressed today by French intellectuals, but to most ordinary people, American fashions proved irresistible.[11]

Such cultural attractiveness overlaid and reinforced the traditional mythological appeal of the United States as the place where anyone with native ability and determination could make good under conditions of political freedom and economic opportunity (though there was considerable irony in the fact that it was during these years that Congress introduced drastically restrictive immigration laws). Viewed from abroad, the American dream seemed to have been positively realized in America. The gigantism and regimentation that characterized American industry did not dent the individualistic myth but helped reinforce it, for efficient industry produced the material means for enriching individual life. Henry Ford's assembly line automobiles were manufactured at a price that the workers in his own factories could afford, thus granting them the freedom of the roads—at least on weekends. The American dream became universally visible, tangible, potentially achievable.

In addition to gaining influence through the dollar or through cultural dispersion, Americans also occasionally turned their attention to the more usual forms of political diplomacy, and when they did it was clear that disillusionment had not propelled them into any larger sense of realism about power. The *Nation* continued its old refrain that force was never a legitimate instrument of national policy and that war and armaments were evil in themselves. Its recipe for peace was the familiarly legalistic one of international government: the outlawing of war, the establishment of disarmament, the creation of a world court and a parliament of equal nations (such as the league manifestly was not). Many Americans nursed similarly hopeful attitudes, as their joyful reactions to treaties on arms control negotiated under U.S. leadership revealed.

The Washington Treaties of 1921 succeeded in placing agreed limitations on the naval armaments of the major powers and were enthusiastically greeted by Americans as the first real step on the road to complete disarmament. They represented, in actuality, an adjustment to the current realities of great power politics between America, Japan, and Great Britain. Japan had used its alliance with Great Britain to declare war on Germany in 1914 in order to take over German interests in Shantung Province, China, and to acquire a permanent mandate over a formerly German-held chain of Pacific islands—the Marshalls, Marianas, and Carolines. Though President Wilson did not at the time regard Japan's acquisition of German possessions as cause for particular alarm, it was clear to naval strategists that the islands dangerously flanked the United States' lines of communication with its Pacific possessions and interests in Hawaii, Guam, the Philippines, and China. Holding the islands made Japan the dominant naval force in the region, as dominant as America was in the Western hemisphere or Britain in the Atlantic and Indian oceans. The difficulty was that each of the three powers held smaller interests in the others' spheres that would, if the reigning power should threaten further expansion, be very difficult to defend short of a massive naval and military buildup. Such a buildup was just what some elements in the various governments, including the American, were urging at the close of the Great War.

In greater America, fear of military expansion and of the tax burden it would create sparked an energetic disarmament movement led by women's organizations and the churches. When Senator William Borah introduced a congressional joint resolution asking President Harding to open negotiations with Japan and Britain, he sparked off a huge wave of public enthusiasm that affected nearly every section of society. Big navy advocates in the White House and Congress, including Senator Lodge, were at length forced to bow to overwhelming public sentiment. Secretary of State Hughes became the star of the subsequent Washington Naval Conference when he dramatically proposed that the United States, Britain, and Japan halt all construction of capital ships for ten years and scrap existing battleships so that the three powers would have a ratio of 5-5-3, respectively. Buoyed by the popular fervor his proposal generated, Hughes was able to negotiate a Five Power Treaty (for the three powers plus France and Italy on a ratio of 5-5-3-1.75-1.75, respectively). Other outcomes were a Four Power Treaty in which Japan, Britain, and the United States multilaterally pledged to respect each other's rights in the Pacific, and a Nine Power Treaty in which all nations represented at the conference agreed to observe the Open Door Policy and to respect the territorial integrity of China.

The success of these negotiations reflected the fact that none of the great powers was prepared, in 1921, to contemplate the cost of an extended arms race. Moreover, the treaties contained a defect in that the limitation did not extend to light cruisers, auxiliary ships, and aircraft. It was also clear that their long-term success depended on the prudent and continuous use of diplomatic, political, and military pressure to induce the territorially ambitious Japanese to maintain the status quo, a doubtful prospect given the reception of the treaties by militarist groups in Japan. Such hard facts were, however, lost on the American public. In an outpouring of joy and relief, Americans greeted the treaties, not as a realistic exercise in great power politics, but as a signal of the approaching *end* of all power politics. They were taken as the harbinger of a larger disarmament that would end the vicious cycle of armaments, taxes, and war and usher in the reign of virtue, law, and peace. Sympathizers round the world were cheered at this apparent revival of America's missionary spirit. Hughes, elevated by his efforts to almost saintly status, proclaimed an absolute end to the naval armaments race, saying that the United States had taken perhaps the greatest forward step in history to establish the reign of peace. The Hearst press dissented, of course, as did naval strategists and a few political commentators, but they were either ignored or severely denounced as unreconstructed "militarists."

The treaties nevertheless had to surmount the opposition of determined political opponents within Congress still concerned to avoid contaminating entanglement. Indeed, the aftermath of the Washington Treaties was in some ways a mini-replay of the aftermath of the war, though with a different outcome. Some of the old "irreconcilables" in Congress—Borah, Hiram W. Johnson, and James A. Reed—attacked the Four Power Treaty as a "quadruple alliance" every bit as entangling as the league had threatened to be. Its Article II—by which the signatories agreed to consult with one another in cases of threatened aggressive action in order to reach an understanding of the most efficient way of dealing with the situation—was treated as equivalent to the league's Articles 10 and 11. The irreconcilables claimed it would drag the United States into the selfish power intrigues and conflicts of alien nations, the only difference being that the theater of struggle had now migrated from Europe to the Pacific. The treaty nevertheless passed in the Senate, ironically with the help of Senator Lodge, whom Hughes had shrewdly included in the U.S. delegation to the conference and who was therefore obliged to defend its results. Lodge well understood the balance of power basis of the treaties, but in the climate of the times he found himself defending them to Congress on wholly idealistic grounds. America thus became thoroughly entangled in the world, though its people did not quite realize it, and those who knew better did not care to tell them.

The exaggerated hopefulness with which America greeted the treaties would, in a world wholly recalcitrant on matters of power and interest, eventually suffer the same fate as the hope with which it had entered the war. Great power rivalry was not discontinued but too plainly displayed in the continued building of cruisers, submarines, and other vessels not

covered in the treaties. A new arms race led, in 1927, to another armaments limitation conference in Geneva, but this one was a dismal failure.
Freshly disillusioned, Americans began to cast about for other means to
achieve peace, and settled on the idea of outlawing war.

The notion of devising international laws against war (rather than the
traditional practice of treating war as a legal category) had been around for
some time but was only properly ignited after the French foreign minister,
Aristide Briand, proposed that France and the United States outlaw war
between them. What Briand actually sought was a bilateral pact that would
enlist American power in the defense of France's security in Europe, especially against a resurgent Germany, but influential Americans chose to interpret it as a basis for constructing a collective security system. President
Coolidge's administration, and especially Secretary of State Frank Kellogg,
resisted the concept, but like the Harding administration before them
became swept along by a great wave of public enthusiasm stoked by the
ever-active peace organizations. Briand's idea was multilateralized, much
to his discomfort, and the result was the Pact of Paris of 1928, commonly
known in America as the Kellogg-Briand Pact. Coolidge declared that this
pact promised to deliver the world from war, and the Senate approved it
in January 1929 by a vote of eighty-five to one. Some senators were, to be
sure, skeptical about the power of brotherly love to keep the peace, but
they could hardly resist a flood of petitions and letters from the public
urging the pact's passage.

Though wildly popular, the pact was no more than a motherhood
statement of breathtaking proportions. All signatories renounced war as
a means of national policy and agreed that international disputes would
be settled only by peaceful means. But the pact contained not a single
obligation for any nation to actually do anything in any circumstances.
This indeed was the beauty of it for Secretary Kellogg and Senator Borah,
who insisted that the United States was under absolutely no obligation to
come to the help of any alien power or to coerce or punish any violator.
The lack of any specific obligation no doubt accounted for the fact that the
pact was eventually signed by nearly every significant sovereign nation,
including Japan and the USSR; there were easy kudos to gain by signing
and apparently nothing to lose, especially when nations (including the
United States) began adding a reservation with regard to the defense of
vital interests that could be interpreted very widely.

The pact represented the apotheosis of the assumption that power was inherently evil and a threat to virtue, along with the corollary assumption that virtue must therefore tame power by means other than the use of coercive force. The rule of virtue would be a rule of law underpinned, not by physical power, but by every government's self-denying renunciation of force. This virtuous self-denial would be supported by the constant pressure of world opinion, meaning the opinion of the common people of the world, presumed always to be naturally pacific when not corrupted by self-serving special interests or power-hungry governments.

America in its most apparently isolationist period, then, was in fact closely and hopefully engaged with the world on several levels—commercial, cultural, and political. Indeed, at the start of 1929, Americans could be forgiven for imagining that the foundations of a new, progressive, and peaceful international order under beneficent U.S. leadership had been solidly laid.

All such expectations were rudely shattered when the U.S. stock market collapsed under speculative pressures later that year, and the capitalist world entered a deep and lasting depression. In these dire circumstances, the American dream, founded on material well-being, began to seem like a mere illusion, even to Americans. Instead of internationalism, all nations, including the United States, turned to the self-protective, beggar-thy-neighbor policies of economic nationalism and the building of exclusionary regional trading blocs. Though President Hoover struggled to preserve the international order of commercial cooperation he had helped to build, the times were against him. America was about to enter an era of disabling doubt about its ability to sustain its own national mission, at the same time as violently assertive international rivals assaulted, through word and deed, the liberal assumptions upon which that mission was founded. Americans would fail to counter effectively the ideological force of fascism abroad and would pay for that failure by eventually having to confront it with military might.

THE FASCIST CHALLENGE

Fascism represented the ultimate rejection of the Enlightenment tradition upon which the American state had been founded. It was not itself a product of the Depression (though depression greatly boosted its popularity), but rather of the general disillusionment caused by the Great War.

Fascism first achieved success in Italy where Benito Mussolini seized power in 1923 (the name, *fascism*, came from the bundle of reeds, *fasces*, that had symbolized authority in ancient Rome). Its intellectual roots lay in an anti-individualist strand of European philosophy that exalted the national state as the highest form of human development, a state to which the individual was radically subordinate and bound by ties of absolute duty. Fascism was an attempt to revive, in an extreme form, the self-denying, martial republican virtues of ancient Sparta, the same ones that the United States had rejected as inappropriate to a modern commercial republic. It valued heroism and sacrifice above peace and comfort, public action above the private, and it sought to unleash the irrational but vital instincts of human beings in order to promote collective, often violent action. Since fascism's goal was the militarization of civil society, it glorified authority rather than autonomy, obedience rather than liberty, irreconcilable conflict rather than cooperation. It rejected principles of equality, law, and reason in favor of superiority, force, and will. The will that mattered was the will of the strongest, the charismatic leader who could successfully embody national authority and formulate the national will, a leader whose commands must be obeyed instantly and without question. With the national will thus unified and effectively harnessed, a powerfully armed state given over to conquest and expansion might accomplish anything.

Fascism was, in other words, not just the antithesis but the inverted image of the pacific American mythology, an evil twin that exalted all that the former decried. Here was a "realism" that touched the outer limits of unreality, that would attempt indeed to create its own reality. Ethics, and particularly Christian morality, were dismissed as mere impediments to ruthless action and the exercise of power. Marxism, likewise, was rejected as an intellectualized version of the Christian myth, for it claimed to discern a rational pattern in history foretelling the eventual triumph of the weak over the strong. The fascists denied any intelligible pattern in history and saw nothing but a perpetual, dynamic struggle in always contingent circumstances. In such a world only the pragmatic employment of power, untrammeled by moral scruples or high-flown theory, could prevail. It followed that war was not, as the Americans imagined, an evil to be abolished but the very essence of virtuous life. A famous article attributed to Mussolini in the 1932 *Enciclopedia Italiana* stated: "Fascism . . . believes neither in the possibility nor in the utility of perpetual peace.

It thus repudiates the doctrine of Pacifism—born of a renunciation of the struggle and an act of cowardice in the face of sacrifice. War alone brings up to their highest tension all human energies and puts the stamp of nobility upon the peoples who have the courage to meet it. . . . Fascism carries over this anti-pacifist struggle even into the lives of individuals . . . it is education for combat."[12]

Fascism made its deepest appeal to societies wracked by the strains of rapid but incomplete modernization. It succeeded most in countries struggling to emerge from political fragmentation and semifeudalism in order to compete with modern, industrial, middle-class nations. In Italy, Spain, Portugal, Greece, and Romania, fascism was an attempt to use nationalism, anti-individualism, and authoritarianism to shock a backward society into rapid economic development. Its appeal was dramatically enhanced by the traumatic effects of the Great War on underdeveloped states, even on a state like Italy, which was among the victors. Italy, having gained nothing from its effort and sacrifice, found itself after 1918 mired in poverty, inefficiency, confusion, and endless industrial conflict. Such conditions presented an opportunity that Mussolini adeptly grasped.

The effects of the war created similar opportunities in the losing country, Germany. Germany was, to a far greater degree than Italy, already a significant industrial power, but it had been a unified political state only since 1871, and its archaic military-authoritarian traditions were much more powerful than its recently established democratic ones. Democracy was further weakened by the inflation crisis of 1923 and high unemployment after 1930. Like nearly all the countries that turned to fascism, Germany was also emotionally afflicted by a deep sense of national humiliation and resentment. The source of German resentment lay in its failure in the war, a failure popularly attributed, not to military defeat, but to a treasonous sellout by domestic enemies. Ineffectually squabbling parliamentarians in a multiparty democracy did nothing to allay the dissatisfactions caused by a combination of resentful nationalism, a capitalistic crash, a fear of Bolshevism, and a sense of being surrounded, after the war, by hostile neighbors. But widespread dissatisfaction among significant elements of the population could be exploited by a skillful and determined demagogue as a means to power.

To a potent brew of ultranationalist, antiliberal, anti-Christian, anticommunist, and anticapitalist rhetoric, Hitler added a poisonous leavening of anti-Semitism. The overriding stress on anti-Semitism was not a mere political ploy but a manifestation of Hitler's fanaticism. For him, both the liberalism of the capitalist nations and the Marxism of communist Russia were equally expressions of the secret power of an international organization of Jews bent on world domination. Hitler's obsession caused Mussolini to dismiss National Socialism (before he was drawn into its embrace) as 100 percent racism, potentially anti-*everything*. Yet Hitler's messianism, like America's, claimed to aim at the salvation of humankind, only in his case it was to be accomplished by the subjugation of inferior peoples and the utter destruction of the power of international Jewry. The nineteenth-century combination of imperialism and racism that America itself had briefly indulged was here pushed to fantastical limits. Hitler's Third Reich used German nationalism as a mere vehicle to express the creative superiority of the Nordic Aryan race and to preserve its pure blood from contamination by inferior races. In his political manifesto *Mein Kampf* ("My Struggle"), the first volume of which he wrote in prison in 1924, Hitler clearly stated that the maintenance of racial hygiene was one of his two central aims. His other was the conquest and Germanization of Eastern Europe accompanied by the enslavement of all the Slavic peoples. He never departed, except tactically, from these up to the time of his death.[13]

CONCLUSION

It would be difficult to conceive of a mythology more antagonistic to the American. If Nazi beliefs and aims were sincerely held and sternly inculcated—and they were—it was obvious that neither democracy on one side nor communism on the other could for long cohabit with them. Europeans would realize at length that the growing power of Nazi Germany might be briefly appeased but could not be contained or destroyed except through a commitment to total war.

But when war began in Europe, the United States was a distant spectator, emotionally involved on the side of the democratic nations against Nazism but agonizingly fearful of being dragged into another European conflict. And when it did finally enter the antifascist war, it was not as a result of German action, but of the aggression of a non-European nation. That nation was Japan.

CHAPTER ELEVEN

American Isolation

THE INTERWAR YEARS were a severely testing time for Americans and also for the mythology that sustained their faith. The evident failure of liberal democracy to deal effectively with the Great Depression caused profound distress, particularly when that failure was compared with the burgeoning success of powerful new rivals on the left and right. After 1917 the American mythology confronted a competing universalism in the shape of Soviet communism, whose mission, like America's, was to transform the world and usher in an era of liberty and peace, but on assumptions quite incompatible with American understanding. In the 1920s, European and other nations began to reveal a susceptibility to a very different, irrationalistic ideology—fascism—that pointedly rejected both Western liberalism and Soviet Marxism. America would encounter the fascist challenge most immediately in East Asia, where an aggressively expansionist Japan fostered a powerful mythology of martial virtue and citizen obedience harnessed to ambitions of imperial domination.

None of these challenges could be adequately met within the pacific construction of international relations that the United States had championed, and in the end they caused a reassessment of the validity of the power-virtue dichotomy implicit in the Christian version of the American myth. A fundamental shift occurred in American thinking toward what was described at the time as greater "realism," but which, in terms of the mythology, is better described as a turn to belief in the possibility, indeed necessity, of the virtuous use of American power. I will trace this transformation here.

JAPAN AND THE UNITED STATES

In 1930, hopes that peace might be preserved despite deepening economic depression were momentarily buoyed by the success in London of a new round of naval arms limitation talks covering auxiliary craft. Japan was party to this agreement, but the following year the Japanese army over-ran Manchuria in defiance of all existing treaties. This action sparked a crisis that fully tested, indeed exploded, the peaceful assumptions of the global order that the United States, in parallel with the League of Nations, had been trying to construct. They also starkly revealed the lineaments of America's gathering confrontation with Japan, a rising power whose national mythology presented another direct challenge to the universalistic American myth.

The growing conflict between Japan and the United States, which cul-minated in a devastating Pacific war, represented a collision of two oppos-ing and fascinatingly contrasting conceptions of national destiny. The my-thologies of both countries fostered belief in racial, cultural, and national superiority, but the Japanese tradition was internally unchallenged and thus unmoderated by any notion of peaceful liberal universalism. Both countries had adopted an isolationist foreign policy—in the Japanese case an extreme version dating from the 1630s—and in both cases isolation was instituted for the sake of preserving purity as well as internal peace. But Japan's policy was purely defensive and inward-looking, a reaction to the encroachments of Western missionaries and traders whose religion and technologies it found threatening. Japanese isolationism contained no suggestion of the need to preserve a shining example for a hopeful, watching world. It was ironic, but no doubt appropriate, that politically iso-lationist but commercially expansive America should, with Commodore Matthew Perry's famous expedition in 1853–1854, be the first to force Japan to open its markets to the world, a strategy that would in time precipitate the decisive clash between the two cultures and their respective myths.

The rapid modernization and industrialization of Japan after the Meiji restoration in 1868 was impelled by the deep desire of a proud people to catch up with the West as speedily as possible. Modernization was, to be sure, accompanied by the (sometimes forced) adoption of Western modes, manners, and dress as well as Western liberal and democratic ideas. But unprecedented change, social dislocation, and the onset of economic recession fostered a climate of discontent that reactionary movements could exploit to assert an alternate, illiberal, and distinctively Japanese destiny. Underlying the political struggles that ensued was the undeniable need for a people-rich but resource-poor country to secure the external markets in foodstuffs and raw materials that would sustain its own rise to greatness.[1] The question was whether economic security would be achieved through peaceful, liberal trade or by the more peremptory means of imperial conquest.

Numerous rightist-militarist organizations opted for the latter mode, dedicating themselves to internal purity (the rejection of "Westernization") and external expansion. These groups took a great deal of ideological and methodological inspiration from European fascists who had shown how to turn the modern state to aggressive purposes using fervent nationalism and intense public indoctrination to foster popular obedience. But their general aims, and their doctrine of absolute obedience to the emperor, had been formulated long before the rise of fascism. In fact, the militant purists made their deepest appeal to an indigenous mythology of destiny that harked back to the sixteenth century. This mythology postulated the true Japanese cause to be the completion of the failed mission of Chancellor Toyotomi Hideyoshi who, in the 1590s, had twice invaded Korea with the intention of conquering all China.

The popularity of a myth of imperial destiny in which China figured prominently was greatly stimulated by Japan's success, in 1879, in annexing Formosa (now Taiwan) over the protests of China. It was even more encouraged by conflicts with China over commercial rights in Korea. Great significance was attached to Japan's defeat of China in the war that erupted over Korea in 1894–1895, a victory that signaled Japan's decisive entry into the ranks of modern industrial powers. This war enhanced Japanese national pride and won Japan many trade and territorial concessions from China, though they were later "robbed" of these by Russian and Chinese diplomacy. The combination of victory followed by humiliating diplomatic defeat strengthened the hand of the resentful military in government. Even greater success was to follow when Korea, resisting Japanese domination, turned to Russia for support. In these circumstances, Japan and Britain found it expedient, in 1902, to enter into a treaty of alliance against a common rival, with Britain encouraging Japan to resist Russian expansion in Manchuria and Korea. In 1904 Japan attacked without warning the Russian fleet at Port Arthur, precipitating a war in which its arms were everywhere victorious. The war was, however, costly in lives and treasure, and the Japanese government was in the end glad to ask the United States to mediate to conclude the conflict. (It was thus that Theodore Roosevelt, against his own natural inclinations, found himself playing, to considerable applause, the role of arbitrator in a great power conflict.) The resulting Treaty of Portsmouth of 1905 was unpopular in Japan because it failed to gain indemnities from Russia to pay for the war, but it gave Japan primacy in Korea and forced Russia to grant to Japan its economic and political interests in southern Manchuria. Russia also had to cede to Japan the southern half of the island of Sakhalin.

For Japanese expansionists, the major lesson of this whole period was clear: the surest way to gain coveted trade concessions, territory, and the international respect that a superior people deserved was through military exertion. Such reflection encouraged acceptance of an uncompromising myth focused on the subjugation of inferior peoples by means of military conquest. It was a myth that, in its most grandiose manifestations, asserted the right of the divine Japanese emperor to rule over, not just the Asia-Pacific area, but the entire world.[2] The stage was set for a struggle within Japan between Western liberal, particularly American, influences and the forces of militant purism. With the eventual triumph of the latter in 1936, this would turn into an external struggle with the United States for control of the Pacific.

It had been highly portentous that Japan's rise to power coincided with America's own emergence onto the world stage. Despite friendly beginnings, friction developed because America's increasing interest in the Pacific in the late nineteenth century was frequently at odds with Japan's own. The U.S. annexation of Hawaii in 1898 was accomplished over the protest of Japan, which had its own designs on strategically significant islands to which Japanese immigrants had flocked in large numbers. The American takeover of the Philippines also naturally carried large implications for any Japanese government tempted by imperial ambition. America's interests in China, both missionary and commercial, were perennially frustrating to Japan. Neither the loudly trumpeted Open Door Policy, demanding equal access to trade, nor America's insistence on maintaining

Chinese unity harmonized with Japanese intentions toward its great but ailing neighbor. In 1915, with the European powers distracted by their own disabling conflict, Japan took the opportunity to force a notorious set of "twenty-one demands" on a weakened China, thereby gaining larger economic concessions and virtual control over China's internal affairs. To Japan's annoyance, Americans vehemently protested this development in the name of the Open Door. In 1917 President Wilson managed to block further Japanese economic penetration of China, while the presence of U.S. troops in Siberia between 1918 and 1920 frustrated the expansionist plans of Japan in that area. Wilson was also responsible for much obstructive wrangling over Japanese claims to German territories at the Paris Peace Conference.[3]

American opposition to Japanese initiatives was unpopular even among moderate Japanese, but it was especially galling to the militarists. Perceptive Americans saw from the start that their own interests, as well as their ideological predilections, lay with supporting and encouraging the forces of liberalism in Japan. Yet over the years many American actions seemed purposely designed to play into the hands of the nationalists. California's racially motivated legislative attempts to exclude Japanese from the western shores of the United States had repeatedly stirred indignation in Japan, and relations between the two countries had occasionally been brought to crisis point over the issue. Japanese people felt deeply insulted again when Wilson, at Versailles, deferred to British objections and refused to endorse a clause asserting racial equality in the league.[4] They were distressed in the 1920s at the damage done to Japan's exports by America's high tariff regime, and Congress's decision in 1924 to pass an immigration act that excluded Orientals caused further outrage. The ultranationalists proved adept at exploiting these issues to stir popular emotions and to weaken the position of moderate civilian governments seen as allied to America.

All the surface manifestations of a developing confrontation between the two powers overlaid a deeper conflict. The American mythology was suddenly pitted against an alternate, implacable myth of conquest, and in the course of their clash, the assumptions about power and virtue embodied in the American myth in its most Christian form would be undermined. The dominant virtues of the Japanese myth, based on the samurai code of *Bushido*, were martial spirit and absolute loyalty to the emperor.[5] It was not surprising, then, that the international regime of self-restraining virtue that Americans felt themselves to be pursuing should seem to Japanese expansionists a mere impediment to their own military goals, an attempt to constrain Japanese ambition and interest with insubstantial but nevertheless entangling threads of pure law.

HENRY STIMSON AND THE JAPANESE CHALLENGE

International experts accepted, and a league commission confirmed, that Japan had legitimate rights and interests in Manchuria, a region with a very complicated history, but no one could doubt that its means of securing them violated the Kellogg-Briand Pact. The Japanese claimed that their actions had been taken only in response to Chinese attacks on their treaty rights, but China turned desperately to the League of Nations, arguing that this was a test for the collective security regime if ever there was one. The league agreed but would not act decisively without first turning to the United States for help. America was forced to choose either to respond or not to respond, courting domestic and international censure either way. There was certainly apprehension in the Hoover administration that Japan's actions presaged larger moves against China and the region, violating the Washington Treaties, endangering America's Open Door and unified China policies, and perhaps threatening its Pacific possessions. America's response to the crisis was, however, complicated by its understanding of the delicate political situation within Japan.

The moderate Minseito cabinet had always had very imperfect control over the military and was now under challenge (frequently life-threatening) from ultranationalist and militarist politicians with direct access to the emperor. These men did not scruple to challenge the United States and even had the effrontery to label their proposed greater Japanese empire a "Monroe Doctrine for Asia."[6] Their hand had already been strengthened by the arms limitation treaty of 1930, since naval leaders in Japan did not accept the terms of the agreement that their own representatives had endorsed. They used what they called a "violation of national sovereignty" to whip up public outrage against the civilian government, with the consequence that the prime minister was assaulted and killed. The resultant weakening of the government (and a perception that the Western powers were distracted by economic crisis) encouraged the opportunistic Japanese Army to advance its own expansionist aims in Manchuria. The dilemma for the United States, once it had understood this situation, was how to protest Japan's violation of the treaties without further strengthening the militarists against the liberals. For America to fail to protest a blatant offense against international morality seemed an affront to virtue, a betrayal of principle. Yet a refusal to back protest with effective force was worse than an empty gesture; it was a course that might well prove counterproductive by further stimulating aggressive Japanese ultranationalism. This was a situation that called for the greatest tact and wisdom, that indeed required an exercise of consummate political prudence. Since President Hoover was preoccupied with financial crises, the principal responsibility fell on the shoulders of Secretary of State Henry L. Stimson.

Stimson's later account of the episode makes fascinating reading for what it reveals about his attitudes and understanding of the constraints affecting his responses. Some historians have damned those responses, but Stimson was, in many ways, highly indicative of his era and a particularly sensitive representative of elite American attitudes. A biographer noted that, for all Stimson's past experience and public service, "he came to the State Department knowing only what any man who read the daily papers knew about the nature of the disordered world. As one charged with the conduct of foreign affairs in these times, as one committed to remain in touch with the citizens of this world, he naturally sought to act on the given pretensions and common conceits." He considered himself, in comparison to Hoover (a "pacifist President" with a Quaker's soul), a tough-minded man: "I pined for a big stick more than he did perhaps but he pined for peace—at least as much as I if not more." But in his memoir he wrote: "My own tendency is to believe that . . . it is usually safer as well as wiser to steer by the steady objective of a reign of law than to trust to the varying compromises of 'power diplomacy.'" He regretted America's exclusion from the League of Nations, whose members "lived in a world purporting to be governed by law and its methods. We still lived in what was little better than the world of anarchy, governed by force or the threat of force." His opinion of the special virtue of U.S. foreign policy in general, and the Washington Treaties in particular, was the orthodoxy of the time. He claimed that John Hay's enunciation of the Open Door Policy had been a rare instance of a nation recognizing the need for justice and fair play toward a neighbor and had been responsible for breaking up the selfish attempts of European powers to carve up China in their own narrow interests. The policy stood for equality of opportunity for all nations in relation to China and the preservation of China's territorial and administrative integrity. When these principles "were successfully embodied in the formal covenants of the Nine Power Treaty at the Washington Conference, the American government had carried through in a most critical and vital portion of the world an example of the best kind of international diplomacy—a policy of enlightened self-interest, as contrasted to self-seeking aggression."[7]

Having for several years been a governor general of the Philippines, Stimson was familiar with East Asia. He shared the general American feeling of friendship for and concern over China, which, he said, was not primarily commercial but a result of the "great missionary movement— religious, educational and medical—which had been carried out in China for nearly a century by the churches and humanitarian organizations of this country." America's interest in China "was not rooted in our commercial instincts, but rather in our political and humanitarian idealism."[8] Yet he was far from unsympathetic toward Japan, whose progress toward liberal democracy he thought endangered by the strains of its remarkably rapid modernization. He had, however, been as shocked as others "that the Japanese forces and government would develop such a complete disregard of treaty obligations or world opinion as was exhibited." It had become clear that Japan wanted all disputes with China settled in its favor, "in other words that they should be settled by the power of the sword."

> This was a position quite incompatible with Japan's obligations under the post-war treaties—not only her obligations under Article X of the League Covenant and article I of the Nine Power Treaty, but also under the Kellogg-Briand Pact, viz., never to seek the solution of an international controversy save by pacific means. Thus . . . negotiations . . . served gradually to bring out and make more clear the ugly probability that, as applied to the Far East and Japan, this great post-war effort to place the world upon a higher level of international life was in jeopardy; the obligations of those treaties were being flouted and treated as though non-existent.[9]

But now that Japan *had* flouted the treaties, what could be done about it? Stimson was deeply concerned with Japanese domestic reactions to insensitive Western interference in Japan's affairs, but on the other hand he feared the consequences of allowing the military party to have its way unhindered. Yet what could he do? Here he became painfully aware of the lack of "machinery" provided in the treaties for addressing that issue. He recognized that the use of force, even had it been sanctioned by treaty, was out of the question because the United States and Britain had reduced their navies to such an extent that effective intervention in Manchuria was not possible. Not only that but, in the midst of the greatest depression the capitalist world had seen, neither Europe nor America had the least interest in going to war over such a controversy. Besides, as Stimson assured the public, it was a matter of principle that the methods used to settle the dispute would be in harmony with the treaties, and that any settlement reached would "not be the result of military pressure."[10]

His State Department discussions disclosed only three possible courses of action: collective economic sanctions; diplomatic pressure combined with world opinion to get fair play for China; or "a vigorous judgment against Japan backed by public opinion of the world, to save as much respect as possible for the great peace treaties which had been publicly flouted by Japan's actions." Stimson would have liked to apply economic sanctions but knew that, even if international agreement could be reached on them, they were unlikely to make it through Congress in the aftermath of the league battle. This was the reason, as Stimson noted, that in the Pact of Paris and the Nine Power Treaty, "the American government had confined itself to a reliance on the sanctions of public opinion alone." Without America, Japan's largest trading partner, sanctions were bound to be ineffective. Diplomacy too was problematic because it had to be carried out mostly in secret, given the sensitivities of nations, particularly those of Japan. Stimson had already been criticized for doing nothing by an irate American public unaware that quiet (but fruitless) diplomacy had been going on from the start. That seemed to leave only a strongly worded condemnation that Stimson himself realized was bound to inflame Japanese sentiment. To take such a course would contradict Theodore Roosevelt's fundamental axiom on combining quiet diplomacy with a show of punitive capacity.[11]

Stimson at any rate seems to have concluded, especially after the resignation of the Minseito cabinet, that all hope of restraining Japan had passed and that speaking out could do no further harm. It might do some good, however, as a warning of a threat to America's present and future interests and security, and as a sign that the world had not simply abandoned its adherence to the fine principles embodied in the treaties. The latter was especially important with regard to reassuring China that it had not been cynically abandoned. Stimson was quite aware that Chinese leaders already felt that China, in relying on the league and the treaties, "had depended on a broken reed."[12]

Stimson had one last card to play: a doctrine of nonrecognition of any territorial settlements made by means of aggression and forced agreement. In a famous open letter to Senator Borah, he reaffirmed America's commitment to the Washington Treaties and the Kellogg-Briand Pact and also to the new doctrine, inviting all other nations to follow. He argued, "The force of a non-recognition of the fruits of aggression when concurred in by the entire world would manifestly have a more powerful deterring influence than when used by a single nation."[13] Public and press greeted this note enthusiastically and hailed the doctrine as a fine example of enlightened statecraft. And indeed it had a certain diplomatic success, for the league unanimously adopted it in a resolution in March 1932. But events of the next decade would prove how ineffectual it was—quite as ineffectual as outlawing war without a means to enforce the ban.

STUMBLING TOWARD REALISM

It was telling that, during this period, only two things had temporarily checked Japan's further inroads into China. One was a maneuver of the U.S. fleet that brought it on course toward Hawaii as the Manchurian crisis unfolded. This exercise had been arranged before the crisis broke, but Stimson allowed it to go ahead, foreseeing its effect. The other was the unexpected resistance of lightly armed but courageous Chinese infantry to a Japanese attempt to take over Shanghai at the start of 1932. The Japanese suffered heavy losses and, even with reinforcements, could not complete their strategy. During the course of this conflict, Stimson noted that the Japanese militarists were paying a high price for their adventure. He added: "The higher that price the better the hopes for an ultimate reign of law in the world. It seemed that one of those rare moments of history had arrived when the soldier can render better service to the future of law and order than can the negotiator."[14]

With this extraordinary admission, Stimson indicated a different idea of the relationship between virtue and power than one that was essentially antinomic. In fact, Stimson's views, by the time he wrote his memoir, had shifted profoundly, and in a way that made him again representative of the slow but definite trend of American thinking. The events of 1932 had caused him to think that the "new dispensation" represented by the Kellogg-Briand Pact was nothing more than the paralysis of timid souls "too tired or too decent or too scared of the consequences to use the power at their disposal," a means of avoiding doing what they knew they had to do. As a new world war approached, he became an outspoken advocate of American interventionism and advised Franklin Roosevelt to cease trade with Japan and so correct the deep-seated error on which U.S. policy was based—"the setting of peace above righteousness." After the fall of France, Roosevelt appointed him secretary for war despite the fact that Stimson had been a lifelong Republican. In 1945, he would carry principal responsibility for recommending to President Truman that the atomic bomb be dropped on militarily important Japanese cities (though he proposed that Japan first be given a warning of impending destruction). Stimson was deeply concerned about the future of a world in which atomic energy existed, a world in which the rate of technical development surpassed the rate of moral advancement; but he would support America's use of the bomb to end a cruel war and perhaps deliver a sobering lesson to civilized human-ity about its potential destruction if it failed to mend its ways.[15]

Stimson was not the only principled American during these years to make the agonizing intellectual journey from the abhorrence of force to the belief that evil force could not be stopped except by the mobiliza-tion of equivalent, and indeed superior, force by the defenders of virtue. Joseph C. Grew, ambassador to Japan during the crucial years between 1932 and 1941, was particularly significant in his recognition of the central conundrum presented by the Kellogg-Briand Pact: *only force was likely to prevent the destruction of an international regime founded upon principles that forbade the use of force.* Grew wrestled constantly with this paradox, divided between the hope that Japan would moderate its behavior if the United States followed a noninterventionist policy and his sense that only force would be effective. After Japan resigned from the league in 1933, he noted that moral condemnation seemed only to make the Japanese more determined. In September 1940, observing the wild exhilaration caused in Japan by Germany's victories in Europe, he sent a telegram to Secretary of

State Cordell Hull that, as he later said, was his most significant message to Washington in all his years in Japan:

> Britain and America are the leaders of a large world-wide group
> of English-speaking peoples which stand for a "way of life"
> which today is being threatened appallingly by Italy, Germany
> and Japan. . . . The avowed purpose of these powers is the im-
> position of their will upon conquered peoples by force of arms.
> In general, the uses of diplomacy are bankrupt in dealing with
> such powers. . . . Only by force or the display of force can these
> powers be prevented from attaining their objectives. . . . [We
> cannot] protect our interests properly and adequately merely
> by the expression of disapproval and carefully keeping a record
> thereof. Clearly, Japan has been deterred from the taking of
> greater liberties only because she respects our potential power;
> equally is it [clear] that she has trampled upon our rights to
> an extent in exact ratio to the strength of her conviction that
> the people of the United States would not permit that power
> to be used.[16]

During the 1930s, as Japan proceeded with its piecemeal conquest of China and Hitler pursued policies of German rearmament, dissenting currents of intellectual opinion arguing greater "realism" began to flow. The influential Protestant leader Reinhold Niebuhr, for example, drew on St. Augustine to reinstate original sin as an ineradicable part of the human condition. He argued that, while moral behavior was possible for individuals, societies necessarily displayed a selfish "group egoism." Human political relations, he claimed, were therefore inevitably dominated and controlled by power rather than by morality and, contrary to the sentimental claims of Christian pacifism, only power could combat power.[17] Such views were heard more frequently in the United States as the tumultuous 1930s wore on and would ultimately have an effect on the foreign policy elite, but it was only with great difficulty that they made headway against the temper of the times. Retrospective cynicism about U.S. involvement in the Great War, the ongoing crisis of capitalism, disappointment over disarmament, the failure of American and league efforts to stem Japanese aggression—all combined to encourage a more pronounced desire for noninvolvement. Most Americans felt that their first priority should be to attend to domestic affairs and deal with the debilitating effects of the Depression.

WORLD CRISIS, AMERICAN PASSIVITY

Franklin D. Roosevelt's first term as president very much reflected this public mood as his administration concentrated on domestic renewal rather than international affairs. The administration did, to be sure, continue Stimson's nonrecognition policy of the puppet state of Manchukuo that Japan had declared in Manchuria. It also responded threateningly when in 1934 Japan announced that it would not renew the arms limitation treaties (due to expire in 1936) and that it would look unfavorably on third countries having separate dealings with China. Secretary of State Hull declared that the United States would retain its interests in the Pacific, maintain the rights of China, and pursue a policy of military preparedness. Yet his words received no significant material backing and were in fact somewhat undermined by Congress's Tydings-McDuffie Act of 1934. This promised (in response to domestic economic pressures, not strategic considerations) independence to the Philippines in twelve years, thus signaling American withdrawal from its Pacific colony. Japan felt encouraged. Though negotiations on naval armaments with Japan and Britain continued until 1935, they had no chance of success while Japan demanded parity in all kinds of vessels and the United States refused to comply. After the failure of these talks, Japan began immediate work on a strategy to control the southwest Pacific, while American naval construction languished.

Roosevelt's response to developments in Europe was no more decisive. He condemned fascist Italy's invasion of Ethiopia in 1934 but invoked a policy of neutrality designed to avoid U.S. involvement. He recognized the long-term dangers of Nazism but did little to try to stem the Nazi tide. This was partly because preliminary German demands, for rearmament and restoration of the Rhineland (demilitarized under the Versailles Treaty), seemed relatively modest compared with those of Japan and Italy, each bent on establishing an empire by force. But it also demonstrated that the dominant goal of U.S. policy remained minimization of the risk of involvement in foreign conflicts. This was the clear motive behind a Neutrality Act of 1935 that reversed traditional U.S. policy by forbidding the shipment of arms to belligerents in war. Another act of 1936 reinforced isolationist neutrality by proscribing loans and credits to belligerents. When Hitler ordered German troops to reoccupy the Rhineland in 1936, the United States responded mildly, fearing to seem to take sides. German remilitarization was Europe's business, not America's. It was an attitude that one historian justly labeled "American appeasement."[18]

Roosevelt did, however, recognize the Soviet Union for the first time in November 1933, but this was largely to benefit farmers and merchants seeking entry into Soviet markets. Nothing much followed politically, and indeed the administration dismissed as propaganda the call by the Communist International (Comintern) in 1935 for communists worldwide to form "popular fronts" with noncommunist parties against the fascists. It thereby missed a chance to influence a genuine global antifascist initiative. Roosevelt appeared more actively engaged in Latin America with his so-called Good Neighbor Policy, but apart from some regional trade agreements, the thrust here was also toward isolationist withdrawal. Hoover had already denounced the kind of U.S. intervention in Latin America that had been policy for Teddy Roosevelt and desperate resort for Woodrow Wilson, but Franklin Roosevelt and Cordell Hull announced a definite policy of nonintervention. They then proceeded to withdraw U.S. marines from Haiti and to abrogate America's right, under the Platt Amendment, to intervene in Cuba. Such moves cheered anti-imperialists but signaled an American reluctance to contemplate military engagement even in its own traditional sphere of influence.

The general passivity of U.S. foreign policy at a time when dark forces were reshaping international relations could be said to amount to an abrogation of responsibility. No countervailing cooperative order was conceivable without American involvement and leadership, which was not forthcoming. Roosevelt, after being safely reelected in 1936, began to show signs of more assertiveness, particularly by making agreements with Latin America to shore up hemispheric solidarity against outside (that is, German) interference. But there was no explicit policy of engagement, merely an apparently greater determination to react more forcefully to international events. The problem was that there were an increasing number of these to react to, and responses were hardly swift or sure.

In China the Comintern's united front strategy became a reality when nationalist leader Chiang Kai-shek was forced to cooperate with the Chinese communists (whom he had been trying to annihilate) to resist Japanese aggression. Meanwhile, the grouping that became known as the Axis powers began to form for the first time as Japan, Italy, and Germany agreed to cooperate against the Comintern initiative. It was clear that the world was shaping up to a confrontation of global proportions. In Spain, with Germany and Italy aiding the fascist General Francisco Franco's bid to oust a republican government supported by the Soviet Union, civil war threatened to turn into a full-scale international conflict. Congress's only reaction to this threat, in January 1937, was to enact yet another neutrality law that extended the arms embargo to countries engaged in civil war, again with the aim of preventing U.S. entanglement.

But the Spanish war dramatized the futility of laws that made no distinction between aggressors and defenders. American isolationists were deeply perturbed by the fact that U.S. neutrality laws actually assisted Franco. Germany, his main supplier, was not officially a combatant and therefore could continue to import American goods and pass them on. It was discouraging to think that Americans, by attempting to secure virtuous noninvolvement, were in fact strengthening the very powers that threatened the beacon of hope they sought to keep alive in the world. And those aggressive powers understood only too well the potential of an awakened, actively engaged United States to frustrate their expansive ambitions. Their diplomacy, as well as their propaganda, sought to play upon and encourage U.S. isolationism. The strategies of both Hitler and the Japanese militarists aimed at keeping America passive for as long as possible while they developed their own purposes and power. (It no doubt comforted them that even British prime minister Neville Chamberlain believed that one could expect nothing from the Americans but words.)[19]

Even when the government chose not to invoke the Neutrality Acts on specific occasions, as in the Sino-Japanese war that began in June 1937, American even-handedness proved problematic. In the course of that long war, the Japanese militarists stated bluntly their aim to push south to establish regional hegemony in East Asia (what they called a "new order" characterized by "Asian values"). By not invoking the acts, America could continue selling arms to the Chinese to help them resist this aggression. The problem was that Japan, as another major customer for arms, also benefited, a fact that former missionaries to China increasingly criticized.

Hitler, meanwhile, was moving to establish his domination over

Central Europe by uniting all the German-speaking peoples of Germany, Austria, Czechoslovakia, and Poland. Britain and France, fearing another war, were willing to appease Hitler with regard to his takeover of Austria and the German Sudetenland in Czechoslovakia, but larger moves on Czechoslovakia and Poland, countries that had been created by the Versailles treaties, were another matter. They were important symbols and cornerstones of the new international order, and their safety was guaranteed by defensive alliances with France and Britain. Hitler, however, hated that order and wished to destroy it. As France and Britain, in the spring of 1939, abandoned appeasement and prepared to stand against further Nazi aggression, leaders in the United States were forced to reassess a policy of neutrality that implied the toleration of virulently antidemocratic powers.

At home, the public mood was changing. By the end of the 1930s, Americans, having weathered the worst of the Depression, were recovering some confidence in their democratic system. But now they looked up from their domestic preoccupations only to find that democracy itself was under threat. They grew alarmed at international trends and pessimistic about the likelihood of war. Nazi racist actions against Jews, and Japanese brutality toward Chinese citizens, caused outrage. Opinion was also violently stirred against the Soviet Union after the Germans and Soviets signed a nonaggression pact in August 1939. Stalin's purpose in this cynical maneuver—one that utterly demoralized left-wing sympathizers and destroyed the antifascist popular front policy—was to stave off a conflict for which his forces were unready; Hitler's was to avoid fighting a war on two fronts.[20] Under the deal, the two powers brutally carved up Poland between them, and the Soviet Union then moved north to invade Finland, later invading the Baltic states of Latvia, Lithuania, and Estonia. It began to seem that the coming world conflict would be between democracy and the combined forces of totalitarianism, left and right.

The conviction grew that the United States must act to preserve democracy, yet the inertial force of nonentanglement remained powerful. Many people, some of them convinced pacifists, others supporters of the powerful America First Committee, remained staunchly isolationist. America First—a right-wing anti-British organization that attracted leaders like General Robert E. Wood, chairman of the board of Sears, Roebuck and Co.; aviator Charles Lindbergh; and Senator Gerald P. Nye—advocated an ultraisolationist "fortress America" policy. Opinion polls indicated, however, that more Americans were leaning toward the explicitly named Committee to Defend America by Aiding the Allies than toward either pacifism or America First (especially since the latter was accused of anti-Semitism and sympathy for Hitler).[21] The declaration of war in Europe in September 1939, immediately followed by the Japanese alliance with Germany and Italy (the Axis Pact), further strengthened this sentiment. It did not follow, however, that Americans were ready to play an active role in the looming conflict. On the contrary, most were agonizingly torn between a desire to aid the Allies and a dread of America being itself drawn into war. The heated debate that occurred over Roosevelt's attempt to repeal the neutrality legislation revealed the depth of this inner dividedness. Though the debate was conducted in the traditional terms of maintaining U.S. neutrality (a concept that had in fact become a nonsense), the real struggle was between those who would stay out of war at any cost and those who would reluctantly risk war to help the Allies resist Hitler. German military successes in Europe in 1940 only deepened the gloom and anxiety.

Roosevelt was determined to do all he could to help beleaguered Britain, though he understood the public reluctance to enter the war. In the 1940 presidential campaign he repeatedly promised to keep the United States out, but he used the increasing popular support for aid to the Allies to take a series of decisive steps. These included repeal of the arms embargo and lend-lease arrangements on arms to Britain. Along with several other measures, these spelled the effectual end of American isolationism. Arguing always on the grounds of American self-defense, Roosevelt persuaded Congress to pass the first peacetime U.S. draft in history and authorized U.S. naval ships to attack German submarines west of 25° longitude. The United States was thus involved in an undeclared war with Germany long before Pearl Harbor. Herbert Hoover attacked Roosevelt for risking drawing the nation into total war, advancing the traditional arguments about war's inevitable consequences—loss of life, loss of liberty, bankruptcy, and increased governmental control of national life. But Roosevelt, arguing that the danger in Europe threatened America itself in a way that had not been true during the Great War, was determined to turn the country into the "great arsenal of democracy." After Hitler attacked the Soviet Union in June 1941, radically altering the structure of the international conflict, Roosevelt extended lend-lease arrangements to the Russian dictator and thus made America part of the arsenal of communism as well.[22]

On the Asian front, Roosevelt took the radical step, in July 1939, of informing Japan that America was abrogating the treaty of commerce between the two countries, thus removing Japanese mercantile interests from the protection of treaty rights. The Japanese, who had been counting on continued U.S. inaction, were shocked. In April 1940 Roosevelt sought to deter Japanese advances in East Asia by ordering the U.S. fleet to remain in Pearl Harbor instead of returning to the Atlantic as planned. A series of American actions over the next twenty months were aimed at curbing Japan but in fact brought confrontation to a crisis. The point of no return came when, after Hitler's invasion of Russia, Japan made plans to invade Siberia (despite the fact it had signed a neutrality pact with the Soviets). Roosevelt sternly warned the Japanese government against such action and froze Japanese assets in the United States. Three days later, Japan recommenced its policy of "southern advance," aiming now at Indochina. Roosevelt, alarmed at the threat to British and Dutch possessions, effectively embargoed the U.S. oil shipments on which Japan depended. There was undoubtedly some bureaucratic mismanagement of this issue that exacerbated rather than ameliorated a tense situation, but the result was that the Japanese Navy felt compelled to look to Dutch petroleum sources in the East Indies.

Japan's leaders, realizing that taking these by force was bound to lead to war with the United States, decided on a huge gamble. They would try to knock out the U.S. fleet with a single preemptive strike of the kind that had succeeded against Russia back in 1904.

CONCLUSION

Not long before Pearl Harbor, isolationist Senator Robert A. Taft warned fearfully of the consequences should America again become involved in a European war. Even if the United States defeated Hitler, he said, it would have to shoulder the task of policing Europe and maintaining the balance of power for years to come.[23] This is exactly what came to pass, not just in Europe but globally. The fundamental tenets of U.S. foreign policy were transformed by the experience of the interwar years, and most emphatically by the war itself. Militarily engaged during World War II in the Pacific, Europe, and the Mediterranean as a dominant partner in the

Allied cause, America inevitably became involved in difficult geostrategic political questions as well as in plans for shaping the postwar world. The United States emerged from the war everywhere victorious and unquestionably the most powerful nation on earth. It had perforce to adopt a different view of power from that which had formerly prevailed.

Roosevelt and his successor Truman were determined that the mistakes of the interwar years would not be repeated. American power would no longer be withheld, smothered, or denied. It would be used to found and to underwrite a new international order that would realize the goals of peace and security that Woodrow Wilson had dreamed about but failed to deliver. In this grand enterprise, American power and American virtue would finally be conjoined, and justified American pride would find itself in harmony with American innocence.

CHAPTER TWELVE

American Virtue and the Soviet Challenge

PEARL HARBOR HAD SHAKEN America's confidence in its hemispheric invulnerability, while wartime technological advances in aviation, rocketry, and atomic energy finally ended any sense of geographic isolation the nation had enjoyed. Future effective defense of the homeland would have to be defense in depth and in breadth. America's new "strategic frontier" would, in other words, have to be located far from its own shores and across broad swathes of the earth. The blood and treasure expended in capturing Pacific islands from the Japanese had convinced U.S. officials and military planners, as early as 1943–1944, of the need for a comprehensive overseas base system. Plans were argued and revised over time, and not all of them came off, but the general policy remained that of creating a series of bases—in the Pacific rim, in the Atlantic, in Africa and the Mediterranean—that would protect American access to necessary raw materials while denying them to any future enemy, as well as providing platforms from which American power could be swiftly projected anywhere in the world.

This was defense thinking on a global basis that would have warmed the heart of Alfred T. Mahan. It comprehended the Far East, the Middle East (with its strategically important oil supplies), Europe, and, of course, America's own "back door," Latin America. The latter was to be kept friendly, stable, and secure by subjecting it to a more rigorous form of the Monroe Doctrine that would not only forbid foreign colonization and control but would frown on the appearance of foreign ideologies and the penetration of foreign investment or economic and military aid. Most urgent in the 1940s, however, was the European and Eurasian landmass so recently dominated by Nazi Germany and now, in a dawning missile age, seen as vital to U.S. security and to its long-term economic well-being.[1]

Yet the intention to maintain and extend rather than withdraw American power at the war's end was underpinned by the certainty that such deployment would both safeguard American security and be good for the whole world. It was this that would make the new American empire, if it was such, a benign one. Thomas J. McCormick (who, like his mentor William Appleman Williams, portrayed American hegemony as a systematic imperative of capitalistic expansion) noted that, if American leaders seemed arrogant after World War II, it was an arrogance of righteousness as much as of power: "American leaders assumed that American power was constructive simply because they believed American intentions self-evidently just and generous."[2] Yet the arrogance can be overstated. Americans could not but be aware of the differential between their power and that of other nations at the war's end, and they undoubtedly felt some pride in their superiority and achievement. But there was also uncertainty about the awesome responsibilities they were about to assume in accepting full-blown world leadership for the first time. Pride was not unmixed with a certain diffidence and wonder, and the uncharted challenges of an atomic era weighed heavily on their consciousness.

But just as the nation was preparing to use its power to create a better world, its energies were diverted by the challenge that had always been latent in the existence of the Soviet Union. Meeting that challenge would shift America's task from underwriting a cooperative world order to maintaining an international balance of power, a balance with profoundly Manichean characteristics. The compromises of innocent virtue this contest occasioned would undermine America's new confidence in the conjunction of its virtue and power as thoroughly as the interwar years had challenged the presumption of their antagonism.

In this chapter I explore the logical and practical nature of the Soviet challenge to America's mission. In the next I look at its consequences in the development of a dangerously incendiary form of domestic anticommunism. First, I must outline challenges and uncertainties that the United

States faced in an altered postwar world, and then consider the hopes and opportunities for a multilateral order that the bifurcation of the world into U.S. and Soviet blocs derailed.

THE UNCERTAIN POSTWAR WORLD

Most of the plans made to reinforce America's traditional dominance in the Western hemisphere and to extend hegemony over the Atlantic and Pacific oceans, though known and approved by Roosevelt and later Truman, originated with the Joint Chiefs of Staff. Their primary focus was therefore hard-headedly on security, with political and economic issues considered only insofar as they had a bearing on regional stability and security. Such plans seemed to lay the foundations for the sort of empire that Machiavelli had warned all republics would tend to become in their efforts to ensure security, but which the American mythology abhorred. The U.S. military elite, and a good proportion of the political, seemed to have been converted by the war to a Mahan-like realism on American power. Certainly, Roosevelt had long concluded that power was the fundamental and inescapable reality of international relations, and scholars at Ivy League universities, some of them refugees from Europe, would provide intellectual grounds for such a perspective. The United States, they said, because of its size, resources, and economic productivity, had no choice but to deploy its power abroad.[3]

Hans Morgenthau would provide the most influential presentation of the realist perspective, defining national interest itself in terms of power. Morgenthau argued that America had attempted to "escape from power" rather than recognizing that power "is an all-permeating fact" and "the value that international politics recognizes as supreme." He criticized U.S. foreign policy as being subject to the "illusion" that a "nation can escape, if it wants to, from power politics into a realm where action is guided by moral principles," and for interpreting its conflicts with Germany and the Soviet Union as crusading struggles "between light and darkness, with light bound to drive out darkness by dint of its superiority in virtue and strength."[4] There was, however, a systematic ambiguity in Morgenthau's realism, which simultaneously preached that nations did, in fact, always proceed on the basis of power and national interest, making morality irrelevant, *and* that America was remiss in *not* doing so. What was clear, however, was that Morgenthau wanted to settle the ancient dilemma of power and virtue by persuading the nation to come down decisively on the side of power. But in arguing his case, Morgenthau himself fell into the presumptive chasm that separated power from virtue and thus failed to achieve the satisfactory synthesis that had eluded American political leaders hitherto. Morgenthau's inability to transcend the limitations of his own power monism would characterize the rest of his career as he struggled toward a more morally nuanced (and therefore more "realistic") position (and see my citation of his telling stance on the Vietnam War in Chapter 15).[5]

At any rate, if America's postwar embrace of power politics, military might, and foreign engagement could be said to evidence a new "realism," it was not of Morgenthau's kind but rather a realism heavily tempered with traditional aims and assumptions. Far from eclipsing Wilsonian internationalism, a realistic appraisal of power was instead to be put to its service. American power had formerly been withheld, with disastrous consequences; henceforth it would be positively employed to secure the world's well-being. President Harry Truman, at a flag-raising ceremony in war-ruined Berlin on July 20, 1945, clearly expressed the intention in his own homely fashion, deeply moving the hardened reporters and experienced old soldiers who were present:

> We are here today to raise the flag of victory over the capital of our greatest adversary . . . we must remember that . . . we are raising it in the name of the people of the United States, who are looking forward to a better world, a world in which all the people will have an opportunity to enjoy the good things of life, and not just a few at the top.
>
> Let us not forget that we are fighting for peace, and for the welfare of mankind. We are not fighting for conquest. There is not one piece of territory or one thing of a monetary nature that we want out of this war.
>
> We want peace and prosperity for the world as a whole. We want to see the time come when we can do the things in peace that we have been able to do in war.
>
> If we can put this tremendous machine of ours, which has made victory possible, to work for peace, we can look forward to the greatest age in the history of mankind. That is what we propose to do.[6]

American leaders seemed to have achieved a synthesis that might be described as a recognition and acceptance of the need for *virtuous power.* The great lesson they had learned since 1919 was that power should not be regarded as antithetical to the reign of virtue but must be clearly understood as essential for its support. Woodrow Wilson had never conceived of power, particularly military power, as anything but a necessary evil, to be employed only when absolutely unavoidable and only for purposes that could justify the resort to evil means. The outcomes of the Great War had seemed to confirm that evil means were self-defeating. World War II, on the other hand, seemed to have demonstrated conclusively that power was not bad in itself but could be used for either good or evil purposes, depending on the virtue of the wielder. When Americans surveyed the ruthlessness and cruelty of the Japanese, or the indescribable depths of inhumanity in which the Nazis had sunk the German people, they could not doubt that their own power had been virtuously employed to preserve some portion of goodness in the world.

Americans in 1941 had not gone to war in a fever of jingoistic exultation over imperial acquisition, or buoyed by enthusiasm for a shining ideal. They had gone, not in the hope of gaining a perfect world—they were too chastened for that—but only to prevent the world falling into utter darkness, to preserve some sense of ordinary decency. They had gone in a mood of inevitability after suffering an outrageous sneak attack, a people shouldering a heavy burden that could no longer be shucked off. They had stowed their cynicism and departed with a sense of duty and grim purpose to do a long and difficult job that might, individually, cost them their lives but that nevertheless had to be done. And they had done it. The forces of evil had been defeated, destroyed, and Americans had returned home not in a mood of triumph, but with a sense of relief and satisfaction at a hard task completed.

They returned to a country whose strength and vigor had been enhanced by war, whose might could no longer be denied. The United States towered over devastated nations whose power had been broken or impaired. The war had not destroyed American democracy (elections occurred as normal during the war) or undermined individual rights (though the internment of Japanese Americans was a blot). In fact, war had awoken a sleeping giant to realization of its true stature and ushered in the atomic age. Even the war's effects on innocent virtue were debatable. The war had been cruel indeed and individuals had been forced, as in all wars, to do terrible and traumatizing, even if heroic things. Certain strategies or tactics were morally questionable and would be questioned for many years afterward—the terror bombing of civilians in Germany and Japan, the atomic bombing of Hiroshima and Nagasaki. Yet there was always on the other side of the ledger the conscious cruelty and aggression of the enemy, the fact that the United States had not started the war but tried desperately to stay out of it, and the necessity of shortening the conflict to save both Allied and enemy lives in the long run. And in the end the prime American image to emerge from the war was of the friendly gum-chewing G.I. with a ready smile and candy for the grateful populations he was helping to liberate.

If any war could be justified, this one had been. And it had taught America that power, even preponderant military power, was not a thing to be deprecated or necessarily distrusted, but something to be respected and positively used to secure virtuous ends. Only virtuous power could defeat wicked power, and it was dereliction on the part of the virtuous to decline to use power in desperate circumstances for the sake of defending its own purity. American power wielded to its fullest extent was indeed a terrible thing, an awesome thing, as the fall of atomic bombs had demonstrated, but a necessary thing. And if its violent employment was to be avoided henceforth, American power must establish and secure patterns of peace and development that would prevent the future rise of brutally aggressive nations. The development of atomic weaponry had made the matter more imperative than ever. As Henry Stimson put it, "Unless we now develop methods of international life backed by the spirit of tolerance and kindliness, viz: the spirit of Christianity, sufficient to make international life permanent and kindly and war impossible, we will with another war end our civilization."[7] America's now unparalleled power would be used to achieve the ends at which Wilson had aimed and which the withholding of American power had doomed.

The intention was one thing; practically fulfilling it was another. Americans were aware that the world after the war was a very different one from that which had existed before. Certainly, they regarded the atomic bomb—the most striking symbol of the change—with deep foreboding, but there was more to it than that. All the political and socioeconomic parameters of the old world were dissolving. The former great powers of Europe, France, and England had been weakened to the point of collapse; communists in France and Italy, who had been the backbone of the Resistance, were making notable political advances; Germany was abject and divided; India, the former jewel in the British crown, was demanding independence; the incipient nationalism of Asian colonies had been stirred dramatically into life by Japan's humbling of their European masters; Japan itself lay in ruins, its future uncertain; China was under armed contention between communist and nationalist forces; Zionists were laying claim to part of Palestine and arousing Arab resentment, inducing concern over Western access to oil; the Soviet Union now dominated Eastern Europe and was an important influence in East Asia, where it gave support to Chinese communists and established a communistic North Korea. Even while U.S. leaders made extensive plans for defense in depth, and even as they showed a new preparedness for a world leadership role commensurate with American power, they could not be sure which actions would be most appropriate and effective in this shifting world. Here are the words of one prominent, strong-minded American, Dean Acheson, who was directly involved at the highest level of decision-making between 1941 and 1952:

> The period . . . was one of great obscurity to those who lived
> through it. Not only was the future clouded, a common enough
> situation, but the present was equally clouded. . . . The signifi-
> cance of events was shrouded in ambiguity. We groped after
> interpretations of them, sometimes reversed lines of actions
> based on earlier views, and hesitated long before grasping
> what now seems obvious. The period was marked by the dis-
> appearance of world powers and empires, or their reduction
> to medium-sized states, and from this wreckage emerged
> a multiplicity of states, most of them new, all of them largely
> undeveloped politically and economically. Overshadowing
> all loomed two dangers to all—the Soviet Union's new-found
> power and expansive imperialism, and the development of
> nuclear weapons.[8]

Acheson's belief in the "expansive imperialism" of the Soviet Union was itself both cause and effect of the radically divided world that came into existence after World War II. As Americans planned for their own future security and contemplated an international system that might provide for the security and development of the whole world, they had perforce to ponder the likely role of their wartime ally, the Soviet Union. The puzzle was whether that role would be cooperative (or at least acquiescent) or hostile and, if the latter, how to measure the actual danger that a powerful but hardly dominant Soviet Union constituted to U.S. plans. In 1945–1946, all options, including cooperation, were considered possible. After 1946, the common assumption was that which Acheson expressed—an aggressively expansive Soviet Union that Americans would have to resist, but in a world made infinitely more dangerous by the possession of atomic weapons.

VIRTUOUS POWER AND A NEW WORLD ORDER

If the United States after World War II displayed a radically altered attitude to the possession of great power, it remained theoretically possible to debate whether constructive use of that power should take a primarily unilateralist or multilateralist form. Conservative Americans would argue for unilateralism, but as far as the Truman administration was concerned, the answer was clear. American unilateralism had led to destructive isolationism, the failure of the League of Nations, and the rise of aggressive dictatorships. It must therefore be rejected. The choice was for multilateralism, though a multilateralism of course heavily dominated by the benign power of the United States.

The return to multilateral order had been foreshadowed as early as August 1941, when Winston Churchill and Franklin Roosevelt, meeting aboard warships off Newfoundland, produced a document that asserted the fundamental principles for which the war would be fought. The so-called Atlantic Charter plainly reiterated Wilson's Fourteen Points by expressing allegiance to self-determination, noninterference in sovereign nations, the Open Door, disarmament, global economic cooperation, freedom of the seas, and the peaceful resolution of international disputes—principles that the Axis powers were, by their actions, violently repudiating. The charter, however, went even further than Wilson had done by enunciating such values as freedom from fear and want, improved labor conditions, and social security for all peoples. Fifteen other nations, including the Soviet Union, endorsed this document. The more essential difference from 1919, however, was signaled in May 1942 when Roosevelt suggested to the Russians that four powers—the United States, the Soviet Union, Britain, and China—might act cooperatively as "policemen" after the war to ensure the charter's principles were upheld. Power, and more specifically American power, would serve the order of virtue.

At the famous wartime meetings of the Big Three—Stalin, Churchill, and Roosevelt (and later Truman)—at Tehran, Yalta, and Potsdam to discuss the shape of the postwar world, most of the bargaining concerned territorial adjustments and balance of power politics.[9] At Yalta, Roosevelt quietly acquiesced in Stalin's and Churchill's pragmatic bargains over spheres of influence, so typical of sordid great power politics, but could not explicitly endorse them because of his justifiable sensitivity to public opinion at home. In fact, these deals, especially those concluded at Yalta (which were seen as abandoning Poland to tyrannous enslavement) were a stick with which conservative anticommunists would beat liberal internationalists throughout the postwar period. Roosevelt knew the danger and had, as a sop to American conscience, extracted a promise from Stalin that the Poles would be allowed to be self-determining. But he was conscious that Russia had borne the brunt of the fighting against Hitler's armies and understood Stalin's anxiety to prevent a future resurgence of German power. More importantly, though, he was keen to maintain an alliance he hoped would form the political foundation of the postwar international order.

Of course, such an order would have to be established on a right footing if it were not to repeat the failures of the interwar period. The latter had already been analyzed by such prominent figures as Cordell Hull at the State Department and Henry Morgenthau at the Treasury and two main factors identified: the absence of the United States from the league, and the destructive effects of defensive economic nationalism and discriminatory trade practices. Economic defense was seen to have led to penury and class conflict at home and war abroad, while open doors and expanding international commerce conduced to peace and plenty. Hull and Morgenthau had, since 1936, been trying to steer economic policy back onto an internationalist path by encouraging exchange rate stability and multilateral trade. During talks on the Atlantic Charter and in negotiations with Britain over lend-lease, they had worked hard to push the British into relinquishing their discriminatory imperial preference system in trade.[10]

The defining moment for this American vision was the Bretton Woods international conference of July 1944 that laid the economic foundations for the new order. The central institutional innovation here was the establishment of an International Monetary Fund that would extend relief loans to countries with trade and exchange difficulties to save them from having to resort to devaluation, protectionism, or domestic austerity measures that caused unemployment. An international bank was also proposed that would invest the funds of richer countries in developing and transitional economies. These ideas foretold a new era of international cooperation that went far beyond mutual security and disarmament, but it was clear, especially after the devastation of the war, that only the United States would have the resources to realize them. The nation was committing itself to becoming the linchpin of a revived and improved international economic system. If this were to succeed, however, it would also have to lend its considerable and indispensable weight to a new international political order.

By 1943 the American public, and even some formerly intransigent isolationists, favored U.S. participation in a postwar international organization that would accomplish what the league had failed to do. True, many "Old Republican" politicians from the West and Midwest kept the traditional faith, while in the South, deeply conservative Democrats (Dixiecrats) remained fearful of international influence on their segregated society. Such conservatives would have an important influence on U.S. foreign policy in the postwar period. It would be a long time, however, before they had the organizational strength to wrest power from New Deal Democrats and their de facto New Republican allies, sometimes derisively labeled "Me-too Republicans" (mostly from the Eastern seaboard). An elite "liberal consensus" had formed that would dominate U.S. foreign policy until after the Vietnam War.

Roosevelt bowed to the wishes of Wilsonian colleagues for a new, improved league—to be called the United Nations Organization—but his prime concern was that any new order be underwritten by the great powers acting in combination. It was significant that the delegates to the Dumbarton Oaks Conference, which met in October 1944 to draft the outlines of the United Nations, came from the United States, the Soviet Union, China, and Britain. These were the four powers that Roosevelt had hoped would act in concert to police the organization's members and protect the principles of the Atlantic Charter, and that would sit on the controlling Security Council of the new organization. Yet by the war's end, Britain was bankrupt and enfeebled, dependent on the grace of America for any influence or stature it might maintain. China, of course, was not a great power at all, but Roosevelt had declared it to be so because he wished it to be America's leading partner in Asia after the defeat of Japan, and also because it might provide an effective counterweight to Britain's imperial plans for East Asia. But the Chinese nationalist leadership had quarreled with the Americans and, as the Japanese threat receded, were preparing for a bitter power contest with the communists.[11] Neither nation was in a position to be an effective world police force. The Soviet Union remained a great power, if not as great as the United States, and any real hope for a concerted guarantee of postwar peace and stability lay in the maintenance of the wartime alliance between the two.

But here, of course, lay the greatest challenge and the greatest problem of the postwar settlement. It was clear that the postwar order Roosevelt envisaged was a liberal capitalist one that would have been anomalous for the Soviet communists to support and therefore strengthen (though they were in fact half-heartedly invited). Whether they could withhold themselves from the economic order while playing a constructive part in the new political order represented by the United Nations was another question, and many Americans hoped they would. But with the surrender of Germany in May 1945, the two allies lost the common enemy that had bound them together. As the USSR ruthlessly and unilaterally pursued its own interests in the territories it occupied, the alliance came under increasing strain. It began to crumble rapidly after February 1946, when Stalin made a bellicose speech blaming World War II on "monopoly capitalism" and forecasting many future conflicts with the capitalists for which the Soviet Union must be powerfully prepared.[12] The result was that the United Nations Organization was virtually crippled as an effective global institution before it really got under way. The world became dangerously divided once again as the Cold War began.

The effects of the Cold War will be examined in Chapters 13 and 14. To set the scene, the rest of this chapter will explore the underlying logic of the Soviet challenge.

THE NATURE OF THE SOVIET CHALLENGE

The success of the Bolshevik revolution in Russia after 1917 presented a profound challenge to America's world mission. Woodrow Wilson immediately realized this, and his Fourteen Points were formulated with that challenge specifically in mind. There now existed another nation with its own universal doctrine and its own sense of world mission, antithetical to America's own. Lenin dismissed Wilsonian internationalism as mere bourgeois sentimentalism or false consciousness, the ideological façade of a capitalist mode of production whose death knell had been sounded by the sudden irruption of Bolshevik communism. For Wilson, free enterprise, suitably moderated, was the system most conformable to human liberty, equality, and prosperity, and he anticipated that its successful spread would ultimately bring global peace. For Lenin, capitalism in its late imperialist form was no more than a passing stage in world history, an episode in the global class war that would end in the triumph of an international proletariat, the first truly universal class. Lenin was, like Wilson, an anti-imperialist, but he mocked Wilsonian anti-imperialism as nothing more than a cloak covering the capitalist exploitation of foreign peoples. Communistic ideals would instruct the exploited as to their true interests and instill in their national struggles a larger sense of international revolution.

There were many interesting parallels between the United States and Soviet Russia with regard to their respective missions. Each had been created in revolution, and each had discovered its world significance in the task of inspiring similar revolutions elsewhere. Russia, representing the eventual triumph of a universal proletariat, was necessarily antinationalist; American universalism had also fostered a strain of antinationalism, albeit a more ambivalent one (and Wilson, as we saw, had tried to synthesize liberal nationalism and liberal universalism). For each country, the ultimate end was the global triumph of a system of human liberty—individual liberty and economic liberty in America's case, liberty from class oppression in Russia's. Each regarded itself as an exemplary country whose survival would demonstrate to the world the truth, justice, and success of their different doctrines.

Soviet communism even harbored its own version of purity and its own intense fear of corruption, namely, ideological corruption, and this from within its own body. It was inevitable that a hard-headed, highly

intellectualist movement that believed it had penetrated the effectual work-
ings of history, one that prided itself on its "objectivism" and dismissed
morality as mere bourgeois obfuscation of class antagonism, should conduct its internal political battles not as unavoidable disagreements over
means and ends but as struggles over theoretical truth. Since truth was
taken to be singular, it was also natural that dissent should be interpreted
as the heresy of obstinate schismatics, or even traitors, who were attempting to impede the path of true progress.[13] Eventually, when even different
socialist countries began in the 1960s to dissent from one another to the
point of armed conflict, the inherent difficulties of communist universalism were clearly demonstrated.

The situation after 1917, therefore, was that each universal doctrine
found itself confronting a rival backed by a significant power whose intention was, in theory, to extinguish the other's flame as thoroughly as
possible wherever it happened to catch light. This is important for understanding the nature and progress of anticommunism in the United States,
and for appreciating how American virtue came to be rigidly and damag-
ingly identified with anticommunism during the Cold War.

A long scholarly controversy over the origins of, and blame for, the
Cold War was refreshed by the opening of Soviet archives in the early
1990s. Most of the controversy related to the interpretation of Soviet intentions after World War II, though this was in fact a matter that had puzzled
U.S. leaders ever since 1917. The central conundrum was whether Soviet
actions in the international arena revealed intentions that were militantly
expansionist or primarily defensive.[14] If the former, the Soviet Union could
be regarded as a powerful nation that existed to serve a dangerous ideology, and no final accommodation could be expected; if the latter, it was
merely a typical great power, albeit with a distinctive ideology, desperately
seeking its own security via a sphere of influence, in which case deals
were possible.

The historical record aside, it seems plain from a logical point of view
that the either/or nature of this question is unhelpful. Melvyn Leffler has
analyzed the start of the Cold War as an example of the "security dilemma,"
in which actions reasonably taken by one state to increase its security automatically but inadvertently decrease the security of the other, causing
escalating tension and liability to conflict. Such a dynamic was undoubtedly in play, but the mutual mistrust that set it in motion was not merely

the result of potentially corrigible misunderstanding. Bolshevik Russia's ideological reason for existence was not just incompatible with America's but necessarily hostile to it. Marxist theory performed a fundamental critique on the economic conditions on which the United States was based and foresaw their inevitable defeat and supercession by something higher and better. A national power dedicated to Marxist theory must necessarily contemplate the eventual annihilation of the American way and the defeat of the American mission. The failure of the international revolution to eventuate might force tactical Soviet accommodation to Western powers but could not alter ultimate aims as long as the Soviet Union maintained its ideological allegiance, and the Soviet Union could not abandon that allegiance without abandoning the raison d'être that legitimated its entire system of party governance and structure of authority. Even when that structure became one of totalitarian terror, ideological faith (which was taken to be identical to faith in the Communist Party of the Soviet Union) remained central to its maintenance. Thousands of individuals, even entire classes of people, might be sacrificed on the whim or the cold calculation of a tyrant, but all such sacrifices were ideologically sanctified as necessary for historical progress.[15]

The practical intentions of particular leaders from Stalin onward were always crucially important and always difficult to read, but their ideological sincerity or otherwise was of limited relevance. For the Soviet Union to relinquish its ideological core while maintaining its political structure would be to attempt to transform itself into an "ordinary" authoritarian regime (the modern Chinese route), but also to risk precipitating a new revolution with unforeseeable consequences (the Soviet Union's ultimate historical fate). The contest was, in other words, mortal. Americans were not wrong to apprehend this from the beginning. The Soviet Union arose as a challenger by the very fact of its ideology, and America (along with other capitalist nations) was from the start inevitably in a reactive posture. The question was, from a practical point of view, how to react.

This depended, in part, on how the Soviet Union behaved with respect to its ideological aims. If it assumed that its mission, like the American, was merely to survive and thrive to show the viability of its principles, leaving revolutions in capitalist nations to ripen in their natural historical course, then accommodation even over a long term might be feasible. If it decided to use its power and resources to undermine or conquer its ideological foes, then real accommodation would be either difficult or impossible. For the Soviets, this choice could not but be affected by the political realities they faced in the turbulent course of establishing their revolution. Their faith in an imminent world revolution sparked by their own example and arguably essential to its success, strong in 1918, proved illusory, forcing doubt about any short-term historical inevitability. In the 1920s Russia felt forced by a plural, intransigent, and largely hostile world to compromise its universalistic goals and concentrate on national survival.

Lenin and Stalin both argued that the survival of the Soviet Union was of primary importance because a successful communist state was the essential foundation for future world revolution. In the meantime, it was necessary to endure a period of coexistence and trade with the capitalist countries in order to strengthen Russian socialism. Stalin's proclamation of "socialism in one country" therefore signaled the end of the Soviet Union's expectation of imminent global revolution and its intention to consolidate internal Russian gains and pursue industrial modernization. Leon Trotsky famously disagreed, believing that genuine socialism was impossible in one country and insisting that the main thrust of Soviet policy should be toward encouraging international revolution. His loss of this argument was one of the main causes of his defeat in the leadership struggle of 1924. When the crunch came, the dominant view was that the first imperative was to preserve the pure exemplary flame by preserving and strengthening the nation that purportedly kept it burning brightest.[16]

COMPETITIVE COEXISTENCE

Accepting a limited coexistence, however, did not mean that ideological contest must be suspended throughout the world. Unlike America, Soviet Russia from the start tried actively to export revolution via propaganda, secret diplomacy, and material aid to radical movements worldwide. To say "unlike America," however, is to underestimate the real significance of America's reciprocal challenge to the Soviets. America's political non-entanglement, as we have seen, went hand in hand with continuous commercial entanglement and, by the end of the nineteenth century, state-sponsored commercial expansion. John Foster Dulles argued in 1948: "The only permanent defense against communist revolutionary tactics is a moral counter-offensive of the kind that Woodrow Wilson prescribed. Our major job is to make our own society such that no people will want to pull it down, such that people everywhere will want to copy it." In the 1950s, conservative American Leonard Read would agree, saying that the way to defeat socialism was not to beat down examples of its moral, social, political, and economic errors but to faithfully uphold its opposite, the example of liberty: "The technique for libertarians is to uphold the free market, voluntary society, private property, limited government concept. Uphold it expertly, proudly, attractively, persuasively." Since part of the essence of American faith in the nation's historical example was that trade, commerce, and investment, if allowed to develop naturally, would effect virtuous liberal change internationally, it followed that Americans, in addition to the use of propaganda, could spread their faith merely by pursuing their ordinary business around the globe. The Soviets, even had they been temperamentally inclined to adopt a purely passive exemplary policy, could hardly afford to let this happen uncontested. With the victory of world revolution indefinitely postponed, it could not be wise to allow capitalism to triumph by default in other countries.[17]

The Soviets presumed, just as the Americans had done, that their own interests were identical with the real interests of all humankind, but they were much more single-minded in trying to make sure that others behaved as though this were true (at least until Cold War America took up the communist challenge on a global scale). Their aim was to compel communist parties and governments around the world to follow the Russian party line, thus ensuring that parochial interests were subservient to those of the Soviet Union. Control was to be managed through an organization set up by Lenin, the Third Communist International.[18] This organization enabled Soviet leaders to manipulate, and on occasion ruthlessly to sacrifice, local radical interests for their own geostrategic ends. Disappointed comrades sometimes experienced such sacrifices as a cynical betrayal, but they were always justified by the omnipresent need to preserve the great experiment in the world's first communist state.

Great power accommodation therefore did not, and by the nature of things *could* not, preclude continuing ideological contest, which is why it is rather fruitless to try to separate ideological from realpolitik factors in Soviet behavior. The Soviet Union, like the United States, was simultaneously a particular nation among others, obliged to act according to strategic balance of power considerations, *and* an ideological exemplar obliged to pursue more distant and more idealistic objectives. Of course, this was as difficult a balancing act for the Soviets as for the Americans. The doctrine of socialism in one country supported a particularistic national identity that inevitably sat in tension with the universalizing mission. There were moments, indeed—as for instance during the Nazi invasion of Russia—when the appeal of nationalist sentiment was much more effective in mobilizing the population than a universalist ideology. Moreover, the establishment of socialist governments in other countries—Yugoslavia, China—did not produce a solidaristic international alliance tempered by deference to the first great exemplar, but rather nationalistic dissent and hostility. Nevertheless, the centrality of ideology could not be abandoned without risking political destruction.

Yet because Russia's post-1924 program of national consolidation required some measure of "normalization" of relations with capitalist nations, inherently antagonistic ideologies did not automatically lead to overt hostility. Indeed, the Soviet Union was a signatory to the Pact of Paris (the Kellogg-Briand Pact) in 1928, thus committing it to foreign policy restraint and legal support of the new international order. World revolution was still on the agenda, pursued by planting spies and agents abroad and through Comintern influence on communist and leftist groups in countries as far-flung as Europe, Latin America, and Asia. Such activities were always irritating and sometimes alarming to Americans, especially when they occurred in neighboring states like Nicaragua or, worse, Mexico (where Soviet agents were suspected, in the 1920s, of encouraging the government to deny long-standing U.S. property rights to mining and petroleum interests). Yet the Soviet Union, for the sake of its industrialization, was as keen to trade with the United States as with other nations and, business being business, Americans were no less willing to trade with and invest in the Soviet Union. Despite the fact that the U.S. government did not recognize the legitimacy of the Soviet administration until 1933, Americans had leased oilfields and invested in manganese mines, while Henry Ford had famously built tractor factories in Russia. These were the years when American finance and trade seemed to be laying the essential economic foundations of a newly integrated world order, one within which it was hoped even the Soviet Union might be able peacefully to coexist.[19]

The Great Depression undermined the foundations of this internationalism and set the world on a more destructive path of economic nationalism, just as the diplomatic failures of the Hoover years in Asia and Europe destroyed its political foundations. So severe and unexpected was the prolonged economic slump, and so incompetent were the political and business establishments in countering it, that traditional American liberal values, and American democracy itself, seemed threatened. It was a moment of great crisis for the fate of the American mission. Americans were sobered to observe that totalitarian Russia and fascist Italy seemed to cope far better with the consequences of Depression than free America, and Hitler's brutal but effective control of the German economy after 1933 served to underscore the point. Fear that the United States was losing ground against alien ideologies fed the suspicions of reactionary Americanists, causing them to search more fervently for signs of domestic corruption that they could root out and destroy. Less paranoid Americans, however, were liable to feel an increase of sympathy for the Soviet Union, especially since communists in the 1930s provided the only solid, principled opposition to the rise of fascism.

It was a disheartening blow to the latter group, therefore, when Stalin, on the eve of World War II, revealed himself the supremely cynical realist by signing the Nazi-Soviet Non-aggression Pact, which effectively carved up Eastern Europe between Germany and Russia. In using the security of the pact to attack Finland and the Baltic states, the Russian state seemed to be behaving more like its old nineteenth-century self—an expansive autocratic power—than an ideological standard-bearer. Roosevelt, who did not believe the pact could hold for long, tried to pursue diplomatic moves to detach the Soviets from Germany, but he could do little against the tide of public anger aroused by Russian aggression in Poland and the Baltic. Hitler's assault on Russia in June 1941, terrible as it was, therefore came as a relief to the Roosevelt administration. The communists were now de facto allies in the cause against Nazism, and Russia became a recipient of the kind of American aid that had been supporting Britain in its lonely stand against all-conquering Germany. When Germany declared war on the United States in December, following the attack on Pearl Harbor, Russia became an official U.S. ally and Stalin became Uncle Joe for the duration. Americans were now encouraged by Hollywood-produced propaganda to put aside their mistrust of the Soviet Union and view it sympathetically.

It is questionable how well such propaganda succeeded among the general population, but the war certainly muted the voices of isolationists and anticommunists. To be sure, some conservatives never accepted the necessity of American participation in the European war and urged leaving the two totalitarian regimes to fight it out between them, hopefully to their mutual destruction. Even those who did accept the war remained unsentimental about Stalin, viewing the American alliance with the Soviets as just as much a matter of political expediency as had been the Nazi-Soviet pact. Indeed, many were inclined to see the communists as, in the long run, a far greater threat to American virtue than was either Nazism or Japanese imperialism, and the ruthless actions of Stalin in Eastern Europe after the war seemed to confirm their view. For such people, the beginning of the Cold War marked a return to a condition of open enmity that was much more comfortable than the forced alliance had been. The natural hostility of Americanism to communism could now be vented and the great contest between good and evil undertaken both at home and abroad.

Military planning at the time devised scenarios for all possibilities, but even on the assumption of enmity, all analyses of the Soviet Union considered it highly unlikely that it would seriously challenge the United States for a long time to come. Nevertheless, with the development of hostile attitudes during the later 1940s, the question naturally arose as to what practical policies the United States should adopt in response. Roosevelt, and to some extent Truman, had hoped for cooperation with the Soviet Union for the sake of world peace after the war, but with the hardening of U.S.-Soviet relations, the choice was posited as one of either "containment"—preventing the spread of communism beyond its existing boundaries—or "rollback"—pushing communism back wherever possible. Advocates of rollback (sometimes denoted "liberation") included John Foster Dulles who, as President Eisenhower's secretary of state, introduced the art of "brinkmanship" to U.S. foreign policy. Dulles always carried with him Stalin's *Problems of Leninism,* claiming it was as much a blueprint for conquest as Hitler's *Mein Kampf* and that appeasement was as much folly in one case as in the other.[20]

Dulles was sincere, but he was also concerned to appease the opinion of a bellicose Republican Right for whom anticommunism was a holy crusade that precluded faint-heartedness. Many fearful Americans, on the other hand, felt that containment, though perhaps morally compromised, was the more prudent option in a world where adversaries possessed nuclear weapons capable of demolishing the planet. When relations between Communist China and the Soviet Union cooled to the point of enmity in the late 1960s, American leaders rediscovered the possibility of peaceful coexistence, mutual trade, and arms reduction and pursued a policy known as "détente," much to the anger of opponents on the right who never accepted the idea of a "realistic" accommodation with communists. In this they were probably correct. Champions of détente saw it as a means of effecting liberal change within the Soviet Union over the long run, whereas the Soviets—whose own version of détente after 1956 was labeled "peaceful coexistence"—viewed it as American acceptance that nuclear parity meant the equality of the Soviet Union, giving it a right to exist and to pursue "progressive" policies that would usher in a new, non-American age. In 1968, after the Soviets had brutally suppressed Czechoslovakia's experiment in "socialism with a human face," Premier Leonid Brezhnev claimed the right of the USSR to intervene in any communist state to put down "counterrevolutionary" elements. His Brezhnev Doctrine stated that Russia's Communist Party, "is responsible not only to its working class and its people, but also to the international working class, the world Communist movement"—a rationalization that alarmed communist Chinese, who condemned it as "social imperialism."[21]

Given this Soviet perspective, it was hardly surprising that containment remained the safe fallback position for Americans whenever rollback seemed to risk direct confrontation with Moscow, and thus the holocaust, or when détente collapsed under pressure of events. The latter occurred on President Jimmy Carter's watch when Soviet moves in Africa and Afghanistan in 1979 were argued to provide proof of an expansionist agenda and enabled the conservative opposition to regain the field. President Ronald Reagan reinstated the holy war against the "evil empire," causing genuine fright among the Soviet leadership. For all his aggressive posturing and military spending, however, containment remained the reality until the advent of Mikhail Gorbachev as Soviet leader. The latter's program of reform led eventually to internal collapse that finally brought the long contest to an end in 1990–1991.

CONCLUSION

The effective demise of international communism seemed to represent a triumph of the American mission and mythology over the Soviet, of American virtue over communism.[22] Yet the actual moral tale was much more complex. American triumphalism was severely constrained by the fact that waging the Cold War had caused a moral crisis from which Americans, by the end of it, had still not fully recovered. Though the problem of reconciling American virtue and power had seemed simplified by the Cold War—they were necessarily conjoined in the great crusade —that conflict merely exposed its lineaments more painfully. Even at the start of a new "war on terror" in the twenty-first century, few final or satisfactory answers had been provided to the problem, with the result that Americans stumbled headlong into a new era of conflict entangled less by damaging alliances than by their own continuing moral confusion, now masquerading as moral certainty.

An important part of the problem was that Americans remained severely bound by their own archaic mythology. World War II had confirmed a growing conviction that the power of the virtuous must be mobilized to counter the power of the wicked, encouraging a greater sense of responsibility for using American power to create and sustain a peaceful world order. Yet no one had explained how to justify, in American terms, the sordid compromises and often cruel actions or omissions that engagement in great power politics inevitably demanded. Americans, taking for granted their own selfless virtue and good intentions, presumed that the rest of the world would accept them at face value and all would be well. If America was self-evidently good, its power could not be used for anything but good purposes. But this idea of virtuous power was both simplistic and optimistic. Other peoples would not invariably see America's power as benign, and Americans themselves would be bewildered and confused when their own actions seemed less than innocent. Even theorists like Morgenthau presumed that acting for justified national interests was generally compatible with clean hands. It would not be until the 1970s that someone would attempt a "realist" justification of grubby American bargains to support petty tyrants, and even then the necessity was couched not in terms of pure national interest but of fighting a great crusade.

It was this crusade, more than anything else, that unhinged the American rapprochement with power. Had the great ideological bifurcation not occurred, had the United Nations been able to work as intended, had a concert of great powers assured a stable world system, it is conceivable that America's confidence in its virtuous power would have been confirmed rather than shaken. But domestic and international factors interacted in the Cold War in such a way that American virtue came to be identified almost exclusively with anticommunism. The result was that the nation was driven into alliances, compromises, and conflicts in which belief in innocent virtue could not be sustained and in which even preponderant power could not prevail. Great damage was done to both pride and innocence, and a crisis in U.S. politics was precipitated.

To understand how this damaging identification was forged, we must trace the interplay of domestic politics and foreign policy over time. We must look particularly at how anticommunism became indelibly associated in the 1930s with the conservative response to Roosevelt's New Deal. The reaction of conservatives to the New Deal planted the seeds of an extremely bitter partisanship in the United States that marred and complicated political life for the rest of the twentieth century and into the twenty-first (climaxing perhaps in the 2004 reelection of George W. Bush and his unsuccessful efforts to finally dismantle the coalition and policies of the New Deal). It also rebounded in foreign affairs with devastating effect.

CHAPTER THIRTEEN

Anticommunism and American Virtue

IT FOLLOWS FROM what has just been said that the United States, to remain the nation it was born to be, must necessarily be anticommunist and that the defense of American virtue must necessarily imply resistance to communism. And, despite reckless accusations hurled by conspiracy-minded people on the ultraright, most of America's leaders and a vast majority of the American people have always been solidly anticommunist. Yet the threat of communism has been registered with varying degrees of intensity ever since it became clear that Soviet Russia was not (as Woodrow Wilson and many after him hoped) about to collapse and give way to a more moderate and frankly American-style liberal revolution.

In situations of profound enmity, there is of course a perennial temptation for each side to paint the other in demonic terms. Communist leaders regularly whipped up public hatred of capitalist enemies as a means of maintaining ideological commitment and social control. In the more open, pluralist system of the United States, the demonization of communists was seldom quite so straightforwardly engineered. The work of private individuals, groups, and party factions with an anticommunist bee in their bonnets could sometimes have a significant impact on American society and even on policy.[1] Certainly, the populace was amenable, as always, to elite manipulation in the interests of property protection, and certainly, unscrupulous politicians sometimes used virulent anticommunism as a means of making a career or building a constituency. But "Red Scares" occurred even against the wishes and best judgment of many U.S. leaders, with the press usually playing a large part. The first major scare of 1919–1920 resulted from numerous factors that combined to inflame public fear and anger and subsided only after it became clear that the Bolshevik revolution had failed to take hold in Europe.

This scare left a lingering sense of public antipathy toward foreigners, radicals of all kinds, and labor organizations. It demonstrated that communism had the power to stir into dramatic life an American propensity for paranoia always latent in the enduring fear of corruption by external forces (and no doubt encouraged by an eschatological tradition that divided the world starkly into absolute good and evil). It was not that the Soviet Union constituted any serious physical threat to the United States, and no American believed that it did until the Soviets developed serious nuclear weapons in the 1950s. The reactionary Americanism that grew to virulence during and after World War I showed that virtue remained, in the American imagination, perennially fragile, vulnerable to the secret work of alien contagions. Many Americans could explain the success and spread of communism only by imagining it as an insidious germ capable of contaminating otherwise healthy human beings and infecting their minds with alien doctrines. It was a germ that attacked liberty, enslaving first the individual intellect and eventually subjecting whole societies to its tyrannous control. It had enslaved the basically decent people of Russia, and it was feared that even individual Americans—"un-American" Americans—could prove as disastrously susceptible as anyone else.[2] Communism was, in other words, a fundamental threat to American liberty and therefore to the maintenance of American virtue.[3] The social and psychological conditions thus existed for the creation of an anticommunism that amounted to more than just an occasional symptomatic outburst, one that was indeed a genuine political movement capable of shaping and distorting U.S. political life over many years.

This dogmatic anticommunism, when it arose, enfolded American virtue in a rigid embrace, dangerously compromising the requirement of innocence and putting American power at a moral disadvantage. That it was able to do so was in large part a consequence of the association made between Roosevelt's New Deal and communism. The attack by conservatives on communists in government (or in any sphere) was always an attack on the New Deal. Though the political supremacy of Roosevelt and the advent of world war substantially contained the conservative reaction, liberal Democrats remained vulnerable to charges of either encouraging communism or failing to combat it with sufficient energy. Though many liberal New Dealers after the war were as fervently anticommunist as any conservative, the Right was nevertheless able to make considerable political capital out of the alleged affinity of the New Deal with communism.

Yet anticommunism was by no means the political weapon of the Right only. The liberal establishment could invoke it for its own purposes when necessary, and more effectively, given the Right's peculiar stress on the matter. The anticommunism of conservatives was sometimes as much a point of vulnerability as of strength, for it could be manipulated to win support for domestic expenditures and foreign policy initiatives that they were congenitally indisposed to consider. But anticommunism was a double-edged sword for liberals, too, that cut back in unanticipated ways. Indeed, the anticommunist consensus established in the 1940s and 1950s concealed a dynamic of domestic struggle that had important long-term effects. The often inflated rhetoric of both liberals and conservatives (not to mention of more extreme anticommunist organizations) produced something of a self-reinforcing pattern that, in Cold War circumstances, helped paint American virtue into a constricting anticommunist corner.

ANTICOMMUNISM AND THE NEW DEAL

However frightening the communist infection might be, it had been easily contained throughout the 1920s. The Communist Party of the USA remained a small, obscure, faction-ridden organization. Things began to change, however, with the onset of the Great Depression and the apparent failure of liberal-democratic America to cope as well as totalitarian rivals with massive unemployment, stagnating production, and falling prices. In these circumstances, some Americans began to wonder whether a strongman, whether of the Left or Right, in charge of the state might be the only answer. Stephen Vincent Benét, in an imaginary conversation with Walt Whitman on the fate of the American democracy, concluded with the words: "Now they say we must have one tyranny or another, and a dark bell rings in our hearts." Whether the advent of Franklin D. Roosevelt in 1933 signaled the arrival of the feared but anticipated strongman, and whether his Democratic New Deal policies introduced a form of socialism or "Hitlerism," or whether alternately they had "saved capitalism" were questions that divided Americans then and ever afterward. Thus the Communist Party opposed the New Deal as an attempt to prop up capitalism (though they would turn to support it after 1935 in accordance with the Popular Front policy). Herbert Hoover, on the other hand, had no doubts that the New Deal was "creeping socialism."[4]

Roosevelt, who described himself as simply a Christian and a Democrat, was in reality a pragmatist with little interest in ideology as such. Nevertheless, his administration's vast expansion of federal governmental programs to tackle unemployment, regulate industry, provide farm relief, and introduce social security marked a repudiation of the strict laissez-faire, small-government policies dear to traditional Americanism. The New Deal was in fact a version of the welfare liberalism (also called "social liberalism" or "Left liberalism") that had been developed theoretically and practically in Europe after 1880.[5] Its repudiation of laissez-faire, its concern for the weak and underprivileged, and its emphasis on the enlargement of governmental power for the sake of exerting a measure of popular control over industry and finance also revealed lines of descent from indigenous American populism and clearly drew on the intellectual capital generated by Progressivism. New Dealers argued that the Great Depression proved that nineteenth-century laissez-faire liberalism was inappropriate for complex industrial capitalist societies. They expanded central government powers in order to achieve what they conceived to be a fairer balance between the forces of labor and capital and in order to create programs aimed at assisting the marginalized and underprivileged. The New Deal could not be antibusiness, for it depended on the health and growth of business for its success. Its basic aim was not to redistribute existing wealth but to allay class conflict through stimulating growth, providing unequal shares of an ever-bigger cake rather than equal shares of a fixed one. It did not seek to abolish markets but only to control market excesses and supplement market failures for the sake of public policy goals. If to people on the left, therefore, New Deal ideas were insufficiently radical, to conservative Americans aligned with corporate interests (whose status had plummeted because of the Depression) they were "cryptocommunist." The latter were aghast that Roosevelt was, as they saw it, leading the United States down the slippery slope to the "collectivization" of society.

Roosevelt had argued with Hoover that it was perfectly proper to apply the term "liberalism" to this new welfarism, indicating continuity with, and authentic development of, an American tradition rather than a rupture. He emphasized the sense of liberalism as liberality, or generosity, in order to defend a governmental duty to find and apply remedies beyond the means of individual initiative and philanthropy. His liberalism, he said, protected private property by correcting the injustices that arose from it. Roosevelt effectively won this argument, with the curious result that "liberal" thereafter took on permanently left-wing connotations in U.S. political discourse. People like Hoover now became "conservatives," even though what they sought to conserve were the pure principles of classical liberalism. Robert A. Taft, son of President Taft and Republican leader in the Senate between 1935 and 1953, could still, in the early 1950s, style himself a "liberal conservative," but by then "conservative" had been equated with "reactionary" and become a general term of opprobrium. Eventually, of course, the word *liberal* would become anathema to all conservatives. Liberalism, resting on the support of the "disinherited, dislocated, and disgruntled," was now centrally defined as belief in a positive view of the state as a means to pursue social change; conservatism, resting on the support of people "with a sizeable stake in the established order," became defined as opposition to the use of such means and a yearning for the minimalist night-watchman state and social order of the nineteenth century. According to Theodore Lowi, this ideological opposition, fixed before 1937, ended any real dialogue between liberalism and conservatism so that public debate thereafter became purely ritualistic.[6]

What is significant for the present argument, however, is that liberalism became for conservatives synonymous with big-spending big government, and with social and economic regulation that was a mere step away from socialism and therefore, by a further imaginative leap, from communism. But if New Deal liberalism was taken as akin to communism —a foreign, distinctly un-American creed—it was inevitable that opponents would associate it with the ideological threat represented by the Soviet Union. Such an association could be made more easily because of the huge upsurge in the mid-1930s of leftist social and political activity aligned to New Deal values. The darkening threat of Nazism in Germany and militaristic fascism in Japan turned many Americans into actual or virtual fellow travelers with communists, whose fundamental hopes for humanity seemed relatively benign by comparison and whose forces on the ground were the only ones positively and militantly arrayed against fascism. The Communist Party grew in numbers, reaching one hundred thousand members at its peak, with many other people passing through en route to either disillusionment or alternate commitments. (Such idealistic flirtations would haunt the careers of many later on when they faced the question "Are you now, or have you ever been . . . ?" in congressional inquiries.) Though Roosevelt rejected Stalin's Popular Front policy as a trick, there arose in the United States an informal but vigorous cultural front involving the Communist Party, the Congress of Industrial Organizations (CIO), various organizations for the unemployed, black civil rights movements, and numerous individual writers, dancers, musicians, and filmmakers.[7]

It is fair to say that most of those involved (apart perhaps from the upper echelons of the party) were less interested in defending the Soviet "workers' state" than in addressing the ingrained evils of U.S. society—notably the sharp and enduring discriminations against organized labor, women, foreigners, Catholics, Jews, and blacks. The celebrated black singer Paul Robeson was a communist in large part because the Communist Party was the only white organization of the period that made fighting racism a priority. It was characteristic of America that the ideological contest between Left and Right should be fought as one over the meaning and ownership of the essential American myth. The proclaimed aim of the cultural front was the genuine fulfillment of the American dream, a guarantee that the promise of America be extended to all Americans. The front had a general invigorating effect on intellectuals, artists, and social activists, who spearheaded an attempt to rescue the American mythology from the clutches of reactionary Americanism, stereotypically portrayed as a combination of mean-spirited fundamentalism and crass commercialism. The aim was to reemphasize American equality by making the idea of Americanism genuinely multiethnic and multiracial, the property of union members as much as of acquisitive entrepreneurs, of immigrants as much as of "natives," of Catholics and Jews as much as of Protestants. The American past was revisited to recover the promise of its great founders, but also to expose and criticize the causes it had provided for national shame.[8]

The circumstances of Depression America thus produced an efflorescence of activity that could be described as broadly of the left. It inevitably also produced a reaction from the right, and indeed from the very far right. If some on the left went so far as to become, temporarily or permanently, communists, there were those on the right who flirted with or openly embraced fascism or Nazism with its combination of economic national-ism, racism, and anti-Semitism. America housed more than one hundred fascist organizations in the 1930s and 1940s, the most prominent being the pro-Nazi German American Bund, though the adherents extended well beyond Italian Americans or German Americans. The radio broadcasts of Father Charles E. Coughlin, for example, preached the usual fascist conspiracy theories involving Wall Street bankers, communists, and Jews and gained millions of regular listeners. The same message was conveyed by a series of popular demagogues with substantial followings across the country. These were mass-based phenomena, but there was also signifi-cant involvement by elite businesspeople (including some who devised a bizarre plot to oust Roosevelt in a coup d'état).[9]

During the war, the Justice Department successfully prosecuted several leading fascists for sedition, but it was a fact of American life that, though there was never a serious prospect of fascism succeeding in America, fascist sympathizers could be accommodated in a way that communists could not. It was easier to regard fascism's crudely racist ideas as extreme or deviant variants of genuine Americanism, or at least of white American social realities, than to accommodate an ideology that was *defined* as un-American. To be sure, Attorney General Tom Clark placed the Ku Klux Klan on his list of "un-American" political groups in 1947, but the Klan was only ever mildly repressed by federal and state authorities and was an undeniably American phenomenon. Communists, on the other hand, inevitably owed their first loyalty to the true keeper of the communist flame, the Soviet Union, and were therefore not merely un-American but downright traitors. Fascist sympathizers, after the war, could find a home on the right of U.S. politics precisely by emphasizing anticommunism.[10] Communists or leftists, by contrast, had nowhere to run where they would not be hounded and harried. For this reason, the taint of communism would prove to be the Achilles' heel of the New Deal and of liberals generally, whether they were Democrat or Republican.

The general intention of the leftist cultural front was to make the United States more genuinely and more thoroughly democratic: America was to be neither the fief of ruthless plutocrats nor the preserve of traditionalists dedicated to maintaining existing social, racial, and sexual hierarchies; it was to be the egalitarian domain of the "common man." The movement's affinity with the New Deal was therefore unsurprising because Roosevelt had proclaimed that his deal was precisely one for the common man (also called "the forgotten man"). The cultural front attracted the sympathy and support of numerous New Dealers and also had a very significant effect on policy, most notably on the expansion of civil liberties beyond the idea of individual rights to be protected from state interference: the Wagner Act of 1935 aimed at protecting freedom of speech, assembly, and organization from concentrated *private* power.[11] Naturally, none of this was pleasing to conservatives and their traditional corporate sponsors, who watched their own influence and prestige ebb among a public that held them collectively to blame for the Depression. Their chagrin and humiliation were ideologically expressed as despair at seeing American liberty—negatively defined as liberty from government interference—threatened and diminished. They grew increasingly suspicious of the forces influencing the New Deal's programs and priorities and began to claim that communists or communist sympathizers were at work within government. They argued that, if the alien infection had gained a foothold in the body politic itself, the danger must be regarded as extreme. Whether or not the New Deal was itself communist, it at least provided the climate and conditions suitable for breeding communists and gave them access to the inner secrets of government.

A large proportion of corporate America and a conservative bloc in Congress were determined to exploit liberal vulnerability on this matter. Nor was the congressional bloc by any means purely Republican; in fact, some of the most influential anticommunists were Democrats. Representative Martin Dies, for example, initially supported the New Deal but turned bitterly against it and in 1938 established the committee that became popularly known as the Dies Committee. Dies's attitude to communism was well expressed in the title of his 1940 book *The Trojan Horse in America*, and his committee conducted highly publicized hearings into the activities of alleged subversives in New Deal agencies, labor unions, and other organizations. It was supposed to investigate fascist subversion, too, but in fact concentrated exclusively on communist infiltration of the United States, signifying less an obsession with espionage than a burning resentment of the New Deal. The Dies Committee, which would eventually become the House Un-American Activities Committee (HUAC), pioneered the investigative techniques that conservatives applauded as the rigorous pursuit of dangerous communists and that liberals denounced as smear tactics or witch hunts. Senator Pat McCarran, another Democrat who opposed Roosevelt's expansions of federal power on the grounds that they were Bolshevistic, was more influential than Dies in legislative terms (the McCarran Act of 1950 virtually outlawed the Communist Party in America). During the era that goes under Joseph McCarthy's name, McCarran, as chairman of the Internal Security Subcommittee and as head of the powerful Judiciary Committee, was as industrious in interrogating witnesses as the notorious senator from Wisconsin.[12]

Democratic administrations could not ignore their vulnerability to the accusations of the anti–New Deal, anticommunist bloc in Congress and felt impelled to take their own actions against known or suspected communists. Indeed, "McCarthyism" was already firmly in the field before the senator himself stepped up to the plate to raise the game to a more dangerous level. Truman in 1947 felt compelled to initiate checks on all government employees and to urge the Justice Department to prosecute Communist Party leaders under the Smith Act. Nor was this a witch hunt entirely without witches. The leftist surge of the thirties and the wartime alliance with Stalin guaranteed that some people in government and many more in the labor unions had had, and may retain, some association with communists or left-wingers. Moreover, Stalin's agents were very busy recruiting among such people, as the opening of the Soviet archives has clearly shown. The prosecution of former State Department employee Alger Hiss for spying and the condemnation of Julius and Ethel Rosenberg for passing atomic secrets to the Russians, the most sensational of cases, convinced America that the threat was real and gave domestic anticommunism a vital impetus, putting liberals permanently on the defensive.[13]

THE CONSEQUENCES OF CONSERVATIVE ANTICOMMUNISM

Truman's Democratic administration oversaw a huge expansion of the U.S. military, initiated support for anticommunist movements in distant nations, provided massive grants and lending to European nations on the verge of economic collapse, and negotiated the North Atlantic Treaty Organization (NATO) pact to defend Western Europe from Soviet aggression. Yet to hear conservatives tell the story, the liberal establishment that

Truman represented remained imbued with communist sympathies and was possibly even corrupted by communist influence from within. During an era in which practically all U.S. foreign policy was oriented round anticommunism, the Right would be determined to be more anticommunist than thou. Its reason for being so went beyond natural antipathy. Anticommunism was not just a club with which conservatives could beat liberals: it was an essential instrument for creating a coherent conservative movement capable of capturing the Republican Party and seriously challenging Democrats, who had been in the ascendancy since 1932.

The problem for conservatism during the New Deal era was that it was broadly divided between two groups with conflicting views: libertarians and moral-traditionalists. The former opposed any government regulation of business and economic redistribution; the latter wanted government to enforce narrow moral norms and maintain existing class, race, and gender hierarchies while resisting the distribution of civil rights to subordinate groups. The contradictions between the aims and assumptions of these two strands might have prevented the formation of a common cause had it not been for the anticommunism they shared. If individualistic libertarians naturally opposed any form of collectivism, traditionalists were instinctively opposed to godless communism.[14]

The "fusion" between libertarians and traditionalists that activists explicitly pursued during this era, and which laid the essential foundation of the so-called New Right of the 1970s, inevitably gave a powerfully reactionary cast to modern conservatism. Libertarians found themselves compromising their ideals of individual freedom by deferring to states' rights when it came to the 1954 Supreme Court decision mandating the desegregation of public schools. Arch-individualist William F. Buckley Jr. defended existing political arrangements in the South using nineteenth-century white supremacist arguments that placed the claims of "civilization" above those of universal suffrage. Senator Barry Goldwater, in his challenge to Lyndon Johnson for the White House in 1964, argued the "unconstitutionality" of requiring states to desegregate. Though he lost the election, Goldwater carried five Deep South states that had been Democratic since the Civil War, thus inaugurating the Republican "southern strategy" that George Wallace's powerful third-party challenge in 1968 would further encourage.[15]

But though resistance to civil rights provided a political opportunity, it was anticommunism that was the crucial cement binding "fusion con-servatives" together. Anticommunism served the libertarians by opposing state interference in the free market and served traditionalists by allowing a role for the state to enforce existing class and power relations, the latter being taken as defining their Americanism. Since both market regulation and the extension of civil rights were associated with Left-liberalism, an anticommunist crusade was the ideal vehicle with which conservatives could mount an assault on New Deal America (an assault that had been effectively delayed by World War II and the Soviet alliance).[16]

But a consequence of this fusion was the association of reactionary, often racist, Americanism with conservative anticommunism. A broad American consensus formed about the idea that communism was an evil and abomination that must be discovered, confronted, and defeated in the world by the forces of American virtue. It followed that anything that could be defined as anticommunist must be on the side of true virtue, and anything that could be described as vaguely communist must be on the side of evil. Using this crudely distorting moral lens, Christian evan-gelical anticommunists could attack liberal Protestant churches as fellow travelers, communist spies, or at best unwitting dupes. Worse, southern segregationists could condemn central government "intrusion" into local community affairs as a communistic form of state control. As during the time of southern secession, the preservation of social and political con-ditions of human inequality was described as the defense of American liberty from tyrannous central control. Resistance to civil rights was now characterized as virtuous anticommunism. In foreign affairs, this would turn into strident conservative support for white regimes under threat from left-wing black organizations in Rhodesia, Angola, Mozambique, and South Africa. Anticommunism in this arena became, in effect, an argument in support of the traditional white colonialism that had so often troubled the American conscience.[17]

The American civil rights movement could plausibly be seen as, among other things, a struggle to cleanse American virtue of a stain that the Civil War and a century of ensuing history had not managed to erase, but it could not avoid contamination by the prevailing anticommunism. The latter provided a cloak under which social conservatives could purvey an alternate, reactionary brand of Americanism in order to defend en-trenched hierarchies. The movement was therefore also a struggle over the "real" meaning of America, and over how America should properly pursue its role as the standard-bearer of freedom in the world. The association of anticommunism and racism in fact caused significant embarrassment for U.S. leaders as they conducted their leadership of the Free World, an embarrassment the Soviets happily exploited by lambasting American hypocrisy and proclaiming the superiority of their own nonracist egalitarian virtue. Conservatives of course interpreted such attacks as proof that antiracist civil rights measures were nothing more than a stalking horse for communism.

Nevertheless, conservatives forgot race when there was no white overclass to defend and were fierce in advocating support for Chinese, Vietnamese, African, or Latin American anticommunists confronting indigenous procommunists. Pursuing anticommunism at home seemed logically to imply the pursuit of anticommunism abroad, whatever the complexion of the protagonists. To be sure, some groups on the extreme right—the xenophobic "Americanists" of the John Birch Society and the Liberty Lobby—managed to circumvent this logic by interpreting all U.S. entanglement in foreign affairs as evidence of conspiratorial communist plots at home.[18] Mainstream conservatives, however, found themselves drawn inevitably into anticommunist commitments overseas. Anticommunism, in other words, had a natural tendency to pull conservatives out of their traditional isolationism on foreign policy and toward an insistence on the maximal use of American state power to defeat what they had identified as pure evil. If the postwar liberal establishment had concluded on its own reasoning that American power must now be determinedly and permanently engaged to secure world peace and order, right-wing conservatives were, sometimes despite themselves, drawn in the same direction by the presumed need to combat the communist menace wherever it appeared. This was a tendency that liberal administrations, as we shall see, sometimes found it expedient to encourage.

Robert Taft, who embodied postwar conservative Republicanism (his sobriquet was "Mr. Republican"), was very much a transitional figure in regard to the conservative movement from isolationism to red-blooded scourge of international communism. He had been a "fortress America" isolationist and remained generally opposed to American interventionism abroad even after the war, opposing military conscription and warning that NATO would drag the United States into an unwanted war with the Soviet

Union. Yet he reluctantly supported the Truman Doctrine of military aid to Greece and Turkey, the Marshall Plan of aid to Western Europe (though he wanted it severely trimmed), and even voted for NATO in the end. As Taft himself made clear, his concessions to interventionism were made solely to aid "the battle against communism." The distance that such a concession could carry someone was shown by Taft's responses to the Korean War. At first he seriously questioned intervention while offering reluctant support, and at a later stage he even called for U.S. withdrawal. Finally, however, he came around to the view that, since America had become thoroughly embroiled, it made little sense to turn off the war at the 38th parallel. Better to go the whole hog and settle the entire Far East question "in one bite," bombing Communist China, encouraging a nationalist Chinese invasion from Formosa, and forcing the communists to lay down arms in Malaya and Indochina as well.[19]

Taft's example demonstrated how natural was the move from righteous anticommunism to an embrace of the full use of America's power abroad. Taft, however, remained a reluctant interventionist compared with some of his fellow and successor conservatives. Pat Buchanan would be among the very few to resist the trend, but when he attempted in the 1990s to revive the isolationist nationalism of America First, he found little support and much criticism from New Righters and neoconservatives committed to pursuing a heavily interventionist "new world order." New conservatives were forthright in acknowledging the fact of supreme American power and the altered role it both enabled and arguably required. They supported massive military buildup while approving activities of U.S. agencies like the Central Intelligence Agency (CIA) aimed at subverting or eliminating leftist regimes abroad.

All that would remain of right-wing isolationist sentiment among such new conservatives was the principle that had underlain isolationism all along—namely, that America must preserve its independence at all costs, both for its own sake and, since the nation was self-evidently on the side of good against evil, for the world's sake also. A significant transformation occurred here, encouraged by the reconciliation of American power with American virtue. Innocent virtue in conservative hands turned into wrathful righteousness. American power was to be purified and concentrated into a terrible swift sword that could smite the godless communists wherever they appeared. For conservative Cold Warriors, the primary moral imperative had been reduced to saving liberty from the unmitigated evil of expansive communism, and nothing—including the meddling of suspect liberals at home and the entangling alliances of friendly powers—should be allowed to stand in the way of the use of American power for that end. During the postwar era, new conservatism's main difference with the liberal establishment was not, therefore, over the assumption of American leadership of the Free World, but over rollback as opposed to cowardly containment, and over unilateral as opposed to multilateral deployment of American power. The great battle was an all-or-nothing affair, and true conservatives would stomach no mealy-mouthed compromises or prudent moves toward coexistence, rapprochement, or détente. Thus William Buckley, who was among the press corps that accompanied Richard Nixon on his historic first trip to China, reported in tragic tones, "We have lost—irretrievably—any remaining sense of moral mission in the world."[20]

Yet neither the utility of anticommunism for conservative political unity nor the consequent conservative conversion to a muscular foreign policy would by itself have established the holistic identification of American virtue with anticommunism. Conservative obsessions and aims would have had little impact had they not affected the actions and aims of the long-dominant liberal establishment. The fact that they could do so revealed the force of the association previously made between the New Deal and socialism-communism. In the interaction of domestic politics and foreign affairs during the immediate postwar era, Cold War confrontation fueled domestic anticommunism and vice versa. Aided and abetted by the paranoia of McCarthyism, anticommunism poisoned the political atmosphere by placing liberal Democrats and "moderate" Republicans under suspicion of being, at the very least, "soft on communism." Any apparent failure by U.S. leaders to take the most stringent line with foreign communists—any effort to placate, bargain, or appease (appeasement of Hitler being the great negative example here)—was liable to provoke accusations of softness or even of treachery at the very heights of government. Despite the fact that liberals had led the United States successfully in a war that most conservatives had opposed, the former became perennially open to the charge of un-Americanism and unpatriotic negligence on matters of defense. It was a charge to which all the presidents before Reagan—Truman, Eisenhower, Kennedy, Johnson, Nixon, Ford, and Carter—were vulnerable and highly sensitive.[21] When external events made the issue of communism more salient, the clamorous voices of domestic anticommunists became politically more potent, putting supporters of the liberal consensus on the defensive concerning their patriotic credentials—with unfortunate results.

CONCLUSION

A humorously wise rabbi once defined anti-Semitism as "hating Jews more than is absolutely necessary." The anticommunism of those who so often made the running in U.S. politics could be similarly defined. The United States as a nation was always going to be anticommunist, but the crude reduction of American virtue to the singular mode of absolute opposition to communism was not just morally constricting but morally dangerous.

Anticommunism in foreign affairs was a significant electoral theme as early as the congressional elections of 1946, in which the Republicans gained majorities in both houses. During the campaign, the "betrayal" perpetrated at Yalta was repeatedly condemned, with Taft declaring that the Democrats' policy of "appeasing Russia" had sold millions of people in Europe and Asia into slavery. In tones that would be sounded again and again in years to come, he claimed that the Democratic Party "is so divided between Communism and Americanism that its foreign policy can only be futile and contradictory and make the United States the laughing stock of the world." Truman, however, turned the tables in the presidential election of 1948 (which he was widely expected to lose to liberal Republican Thomas Dewey). He declared that the communists were hoping for a Republican victory because it would mean a weak United States (a reference to Republican isolationism): "and that is exactly what I think. . . . But I'm going to beat them and there won't be a weak United States."[22]

Truman's sally may seem ironic from today's perspective; after the 1970s, the machismo style of foreign policy became increasingly associated with Republicans while Democrats acquired a scarcely deserved reputation for wimpishness.[23] Yet it is important to understand that the liberal elite's anticommunism was both sincerely held and an important political tool at the start of the Cold War. After World War II, that elite was intent on deploying American power in the service of future American security and the peaceful world order promised by Bretton Woods and the United Nations. Such initiatives, not to mention the military occupations of Japan and Germany, could not be achieved without substantial long-term funding.

There was, however, a curious irony here with respect to the disposition of virtuous American power. The main problem facing a foreign policy elite convinced that power must be consolidated to prevent future aggression was the postwar mood of the American people themselves. Though generally favorably disposed toward the United Nations and supportive of international cooperation to prevent a recurrence of what happened in the thirties, they were more immediately interested in swift demobilization and readjustment to a peacetime economy that would deliver the rewards that wartime sacrifice deserved. They remembered the Depression and looked forward to higher wages and a brighter future for themselves and their families that the GI Bill of 1944 promised.[24] Conceding to this (as in a democratic system any administration was bound to do) meant placing expensive defense and foreign policy measures in abeyance. After 1946 the Democratic administration was also faced with a hostile Republican Congress tempted to slip back into introverted Americanism, its primary attention focused on "rolling back" the New Deal and on lowering taxes rather than increasing spending on foreign aid. The onset of the Cold War provided the perfect means to shock both public and politicians out of their domestic absorption and induce them to support international expenditure and greater militarization.

CHAPTER FOURTEEN

Cold War Ironies

SUCH AMITY AS HAD EXISTED in the expedient friendship between the United States and the Soviet Union during World War II was already somewhat fractured before the war had ended. In such a complicated and wary relationship, it was perhaps inevitable that the only dimly transparent actions of one side would cause offense to the other, leading to reactions that were as poorly understood and equally offensive. A deepening rift thus laid the seeds of the Cold War that followed. Whoever was ultimately most to blame for this (about which argument still proceeds), it was clear that the Americans by the end of 1945 were eyeing the Soviets with growing suspicion. Roosevelt had died with his optimism severely dented by what he saw as Stalin's breach of the understanding to allow Poland to be politically self-determining.

Truman, succeeding Roosevelt, was told by his ambassador to the Soviet Union, Averell Harriman, that the Russians were overrunning Europe like a "barbarian horde." He vowed to uphold traditional American principles and "stand up to the Soviets." Despite this bluster, Truman felt sure that he could make relations with Russia work and, on meeting Stalin at Potsdam in July 1945, became convinced that on balance he could "deal with him."[1] The new and inexperienced president was undoubtedly naive in his estimate and understanding of the wily Soviet leader, and his early trust would be dashed in the mounting misunderstanding and disagreement of the following years—over the occupation of Germany, the communization of Eastern Europe, the management of atomic energy, control of Iran and its oilfields, territorial adjustment in Turkey, and failure to negotiate the reunification of Korea. Such issues gave the lie to this confidence and led to the profound mutual mistrust between Americans and Soviets that turned steadily into Cold War. It was an international confrontation that recoiled with bitter effect on U.S. domestic politics.

The cumulative shocks of the late 1940s and a long unsatisfactory war in Korea created conditions in which McCarthyism flared and flourished until the habitually reckless senator overreached and precipitated his own political downfall in December 1954.[2] Over that period, Truman and his cabinet suffered, personally and politically, the most intense and disabling attacks from the senator and his cronies, and even the universally loved Ike Eisenhower felt the sting of their anticommunist lash. The hysteria cooled eventually, but anticommunism as a force by no means died and was in fact strengthened by the role it played in uniting conservative forces in their challenge to liberalism. The prolonged Red Scare left a legacy of fear and distrust in U.S. political life and ensured that no U.S. leader could afford to appear other than resolutely anticommunist. Though many liberals were themselves sincerely and fiercely anticommunist, domestic conditions had the effect of confining liberal administrations in a more narrowly constricted foreign policy box than they would have wished.

The ways in which the complex interplay of domestic and foreign factors produced the Cold War and determined its course have been the subject of many revisionist and postrevisionist histories.[3] My intention in this chapter is to clarify how the Cold War abroad and anticommunism at home eventually brought about a crisis for the expected happy conjunction of American power and virtue.

Ironies abound here. Having worried for so long about the corrupting effects of power, particularly military power, on virtue, American leaders had at last come to accept that the virtuous deployment of their power was essential to preserve the world from madmen and tyrants. Their determination to create a new international order was, however, weakened by the domestic preoccupations of a war-weary population and residual isolationists. Faced with this general reluctance, the administration found it expedient to interpret Soviet actions and intentions as constituting an urgent communist threat that demanded immediate action and expenditure. The tactic worked, but the threat that justified increases in military power was soon greatly magnified by events at home and abroad, deflecting that power from its original purposes. Instead of underwriting a universally cooperative order, symbolized and realized in the United Nations, American power became dedicated to the defense of the Free World against expansive communism. In a nuclear age, this led to the militarization of American society on a scale hitherto unimaginable. Yet the nuclear weapons at the heart of U.S. military power also made direct confrontation with the enemy impossible, encouraging ideological wars by proxy in small peripheral countries of otherwise small interest to Americans.

What's more, the combination of U.N. internationalism and anticommunist crusade abroad interacted with U.S. politics to induce what was in effect a civil war at home, fought out first over black civil rights and then over Vietnam. What began as a noble effort to found the peace and stability of the entire world ended by producing internal dissension and furious turmoil. This domestic conflict (even now not concluded) could be variously figured as one between internationalists and nationalists, or between liberals and conservatives, or between North and South, or between younger and older generations, or between eastern intellectuals and heartland anti-intellectuals, or between tertiary-educated Americans and high school dropouts, or between establishment conformists and radical libertarians, or between cynics and idealists, or generally between the forces of progress and reaction. All of these categories had salience, yet the cross-flowing currents generated in the 1950s and 1960s did not allow for any neat compartmentalization. Divisions were often deep not just within categories but within single individuals of any category struggling to understand their own conflicting attitudes and allegiances. The noisy and often violent confrontation was, at bottom, a confrontation of America with itself or, more accurately, of actual America with mythological America. The anticommunism with which American virtue had become too rigidly identified had become the catalyst for an extended struggle over the true meaning of America, reflecting and deepening a crisis of faith in the reality of American virtue and the limits and purposes of American power.

THE COMING OF THE COLD WAR

Henry Kissinger once complained that liberals seemed to believe that the Cold War was no more than a product of a feverish Republican imagination.[4] He was right to protest, for liberals themselves were deeply implicated in the generation and conduct of the extended contest. Though hopes for rapprochement and cooperation with the Soviet Union lingered in the Democratic administration for some months after the war, they dwindled steadily as suspicions of Soviet intentions mounted. A signal event was the famous and influential "long telegram" that foreign-service officer George Kennan sent from Moscow in February 1946. This warned in sweeping and hyperbolic terms that Soviet political culture and Soviet insecurity (born of a long-standing Russian sense of inferiority to the West) inevitably motivated an expansion of power and influence. Since the Soviet leadership understood nothing but the logic of force, it could be countered only by a firm, unyielding stance on the part of the United States. Such a stance must be held long enough to allow the whole system to decay and collapse from within, as any system must that denies freedom. This was the first iteration of the doctrine that would be known as containment. Though Kennan believed a direct military challenge was unlikely, he argued that the Soviets would wage a quiet and indirect war at many points.

Here Kennan had resort to the usual American image of communism as a contaminant infection: the extensive international communist underground network, he wrote, would locate "diseased tissue" wherever it could and feed on it like a "malignant parasite." Expanding on his theme in a later article in *Foreign Affairs,* Kennan also deployed the language of the American mission: the Soviet challenge to the West's free institutions posed a test to the worth of the United States as a "nation among nations," a test for which it should thank Providence, for in meeting the implacable challenge Americans would rise to "the responsibilities of moral and political leadership that history plainly intended them to bear."[5]

The looming Cold War was thus outlined in the traditional terms of the American mythological narrative, terms that Harry Truman fully accepted. Truman had been raised in the Jeffersonian faith and was, moreover, an old Wilsonian, a proud veteran of World War I who had been deeply stirred by Wilson's moral call to action. He had regretted America's postwar withdrawal, was contemptuous of America First isolationism, and anxious lest the same spirit be reawakened to prevent the nation assuming its proper responsibilities. He also supported a new international organization that would overcome the old, futile system of power politics. Instinctively distrusting Stalin as a brutal dictator, he had nevertheless come to hope that the Soviet Union could be incorporated into the new order, but that hope rapidly faded under the pressure of events. Truman thus found himself national leader at a seminal period between 1945 and 1950. His main task would turn out to be not the construction of a fully cooperative international regime—made impossible by Soviet "intransigence"—but rather resistance to a new, powerful, and dangerous rival.

Truman conceived this task in the grandest of historical terms. He believed that the United States, a nation that had arisen to greatness even while renouncing national self-aggrandizement, must save the world from totalitarianism. The inevitable forces of internal corruption had to be overcome, of course, and the temptations of selfishness, greed, and power resisted. Also, the pacifism of the twenties and thirties was still abroad and must be repudiated. American power must be deployed on behalf of liberty and morality against the amoral, materialist forces of communism. Truman had taken to heart the lesson from the 1930s that not responding firmly to acts of aggression merely encourages aggressors to further conquests, rendering the task of fighting them later all the harder.[6]

The question was how, practically speaking, such a historical challenge should be met. Here Truman proved himself a realist. Despite his pugnacity and "buck stops here" grit, despite his initial impulse to "get tough" with the Soviets and to address them with undiplomatic bluntness, his general attitude was more cautious than bellicose, and his actions more geared to containing the Soviets, or even to coexisting with them, than to fighting them. He understood that American power, though great, was far from unlimited, and that heroic responsibility would have to be tailored to capacity. It would also have to be balanced against justified domestic demands that cut further into that capacity. Sufficient military power must be maintained to counter any Soviet threat, but Truman resisted the tendency of the military to infinitely absorb available public funds on the grounds of beefing up security. His crusading spirit was also heavily tempered by a wish not to be the one responsible for starting World War III, a war whose destructiveness in the dawning atomic age would be beyond imagining. Within those limits, however, the Soviet challenge would be positively met. Truman's pragmatic views were not, in principle, different from those of Kennan, who, not believing the Soviet Union would ever be militarily expansionist, had meant his idea of containment to be more a political and economic strategy than a purely military one. But events would drag Truman much further than he had intended to go, or that Kennan thought was wise.[7]

The first real occasion for serious decision came early in 1947 when an impoverished Britain declared its incapacity to sustain anticommunist governments in Greece and Turkey. The American administration found itself confronted with the choice of either picking up the reins or leaving these countries to their presumably communist fate. At issue here was a momentous shift in U.S. foreign policy toward assuming responsibility for maintaining the *balance of power* across the world. It was a decision that presupposed that the cooperative order promised by the United Nations was already compromised, if not utterly defeated, by the Western-Soviet split. The "Truman Doctrine" proposed precisely this historical move but was poorly received by the Republican-dominated Congress.

Anticommunism, however, gave Truman and Undersecretary of State Dean Acheson the lever they needed to pry reluctant conservatives out of their domestic preoccupations. Acheson addressed members of Congress in apocalyptic terms, warning of an aggressive Soviet Union on the march, potentially into three continents. He advanced a prototype of the falling domino theory—first Greece, then Turkey, then Iran. Asia Minor would provide the communists with a route into Africa through Egypt and into Europe through Italy and France. Truman requested $400 million of aid and outlined the doctrine of U.S. support for "free peoples to maintain free institutions and their national integrity against aggressive movements that seek to impose on them totalitarian regimes." The rhetoric was overblown, as military intelligence officials argued and Acheson later admitted, and risked being seen by Stalin as a provocation and threat that might induce him to respond aggressively. It served, however, to persuade a grudging Congress to approve the funds.[8]

It worked again after Secretary of State George Marshall proposed a European Recovery Program for a Western Europe on the brink of economic collapse. The aim of this program, the most massive foreign aid program ever contemplated, was to forestall communist challenges from within or without the European countries. It would also create the conditions of growth essential to the Bretton Woods plan, whose implementation had been delayed by economic chaos. But members of Congress were extremely reluctant to spend billions abroad that most thought could be better spent at home, while conservatives disliked its commitment to tariff reduction and tended to see it as an extension of the New Deal internationally. Truman was inadvertently aided here by Stalin, who resolutely opposed the Marshall Plan because it would incorporate a reconstructed and probably rearmed Germany in an anti-Soviet bloc. Stalin created the Communist Information Bureau (Cominform), in part to control and coordinate communist resistance to the plan in Western Europe, and at the same time engineered a clampdown in Eastern Europe. In February 1948 the Czech communists performed a coup in which the pro-Western foreign minister Jan Masaryk died. It seemed conceivable that the communists were on the march. A war scare ensued, heightened by a U.S. military seeking additional congressional appropriations. The scare was exploited by Truman, who exaggerated the threat in order to gain congressional approval for the Marshall Plan, the restoration of the draft, an increase in defense spending, and the inauguration of universal military training. A later communist coup in Czechoslovakia, and fears for Norway and Italy, would similarly assist the acceptance of the NATO mutual security pact that insecure Western Europeans had pressed on the Americans.[9]

But if pushing the conservative anticommunist button was highly effective, it was also liable to produce uncomfortable blowback. The universalistic tone of the Truman Doctrine was particularly troublesome as it seemed to promise worldwide defense against communist aggression, whereas the administration had wanted to confine its reach to the Middle East. Pro-Chinese members of Congress, however, wanted to know why, if Greece could be defended, China could not, especially since nationalist leader Chiang Kai-shek was engaged in a civil war with Moscow-backed communists. But the administration's anticommunist foreign policy was very Europe-oriented, and Acheson demurred, arguing weakly that each case would be treated on its merits. Conservatives thereupon voiced the suspicion that the apparent anticommunism displayed by the administration in the Mediterranean and Europe was a mere sham, belied not just by the failure to support China but by the failure to prevent the advance of communism (that is, New Deal welfarism) at home.

Truman managed to ride the "soft on communism" charge largely because of his resolute stand against the Soviets in 1948 when they blockaded the only road into West Berlin (jointly occupied by the United States, Britain, and France but wholly within the Russian occupation zone). The massive airlift that he ordered to supply Berliners caused Stalin to back down after several tense months, a success that undoubtedly helped Truman gain his unexpected win in the 1948 election.[10] By the start of his second term as president, Truman could indeed be forgiven for thinking that the sting had been thoroughly extracted from the communist tail. If Stalin's stand over Berlin had revealed his deep fear of a revitalized, rearmed Germany, his refusal to press it to the point of war revealed his caution when faced with American power. The successfully independent stand of Yugoslavia's Marshal Josip Tito against Stalin (for which he was expelled from the Cominform in 1948) also argued that the Soviet leader was primarily guided by realistic calculation and showed that communism was not necessarily as monolithic as routinely pictured. All this suggested the possibility of a mutual if adversarial tolerance. As in 1929, or again in 1945, U.S.-Soviet relations seemed at a point where prolonged coexistence combined with ongoing ideological competition among countries at the periphery was a conceivable option.

Several occurrences in 1949 caused domestic anticommunism to flare, making this possibility more remote. One was the victory of Mao Zedong's communists over the nationalist army of Chiang Kai-shek, which fled for safety to the island of Formosa (later Taiwan). Another was the sensational trial of alleged communist Alger Hiss. A third was the Soviet Union's detonation of an atomic bomb in August, which made the communist threat seem far more formidable than previously imagined.

The domestic impact of communist victory in China was at first radically underestimated by Acheson. He calculated that China was so weak as to be more a burden than a boon for Moscow and was anyway liable to go the Yugoslavian route of nationalistic independence. But he reckoned without the ever-vociferous China lobby which howled that the Democrats had betrayed Chiang and "lost China." Republicans who cared little about China jumped on the bandwagon and berated the administration, even suggesting that government officials who had criticized Chiang for corruption were communist agents. The full vitriolic fury of the anticommunists was directed against an obscure Far East scholar who had had the misfortune in 1941 to be listed on FBI files as "procommunist" because of his membership in a civil liberties group and to be sent, in the same year, by Roosevelt to Chungking as an emissary to Chiang Kai-shek. Owen Lattimore, on slender or concocted evidence, was labeled by Senator McCarthy a "top Soviet spy" who had been primarily responsible for the loss of China, which fact had then been covered up by a "liberal conspiracy." The "loss of China," said Joe McCarthy, was the consequence of "twenty years of treason" by the Roosevelt and Truman administrations. It was added to "betrayal at Yalta" as an anti-Democratic battle cry, emphasizing the domestic political danger of apparent softness on communism and ensuring that presidents would thereafter be obliged to espouse a tough anticommunist line in foreign affairs.[11]

Alger Hiss was a graduate of Harvard Law School who had been clerk to Oliver Wendell Holmes, served in Roosevelt's Agricultural Adjustment Administration and the solicitor general's office, moved into the State Department, and eventually become president of the Carnegie Endowment for International Peace. He was, in other words, the very type of an eastern establishment liberal. His New Deal credentials gave a boost to anticommunist hysteria by convincing many of the truth of conservative charges of communist influence on liberals in government. Dean Acheson, by now secretary of state, came under particular attack because Hiss was a friend whom he had resolutely refused to fire from the State Department. Even after Hiss's conviction for perjury in 1950, Acheson (for whom loyalty was a prime virtue) stated publicly he would not abandon him, provoking McCarthy and fellow anticommunists into a fury of denunciation. It was in many ways a defining moment for the Truman administration, leaving it permanently vulnerable to charges of disloyalty and cover-up conspiracies. Shortly afterward, Klaus Fuchs, an atomic scientist who had worked at Los Alamos, confessed in London that he was a Soviet spy, further stoking the powder barrel to which McCarthy would apply the spark.[12]

The detonation of a Russian bomb surprised and alarmed Americans and helped touch off an arms race. Life magazine wrote a feature claiming that Russia now vastly exceeded the United States in conventional military capacity, and intense fear of war gripped the country. Truman, under pressure to act, ordered development of the hydrogen bomb (an issue that had been subject to much controversy) and a reappraisal of

U.S. security policy. In early 1950 this reappraisal resulted in an epoch-making document from the National Security Council, NSC-68 (produced mainly by Acheson and chief of the Policy Planning Staff Paul Nitze). The document adopted an apocalyptic tone, sketching the challenge facing America in terms of great power history—the decline of Britain, the twice-failed challenge of Germany, the disintegration of the old European empires, and the present competition between the USSR and the USA for hegemony. The latter competition was not, of course, painted as an ordinary imperialist contest fueled by ambition and greed, but as a mortal conflict between a fanatical ideological power bent on world domination and an opposing power dedicated to the defense of freedom. Kennan and others objected that this drastically overstated actual Soviet intentions, but Nitze and Acheson reasoned once again that exaggerating the threat was the only way of convincing Congress and the budgetary offices of the bureaucracy to dispense the funds that they claimed an adequate response to the Russian bomb required. They called for a tripling of defense spending, to be financed by tax increases and cuts to social welfare and other nonmilitary programs.

Truman was unconvinced and frankly appalled. He had been stoutly resisting pressure from the military for increased spending for two years, having put his faith in the Marshall Plan and existing U.S. superiority in weaponry to deter Soviet expansion. He confessed still to believe that real peace was achievable and at hand. In the event, it took another major communist scare—the invasion of South Korea—to persuade him that a bloated defense budget was justified. The Korean War would positively foreclose on the option of coexistence and fix the main outlines of the Cold War for the next two decades.

THE KOREAN WAR

The defeat of the Japanese at the close of World War II had left the Korean peninsula divided, supposedly temporarily, at the 38th parallel, with Russian occupiers to the north and Americans to the south. The Soviets had set up a communistic state under Kim Il-sung, while the Americans had reluctantly acquiesced in a right-wing regime under strongman Syngman Rhee. Both great powers had subsequently withdrawn their forces, but with the onset of the Cold War the border between North and South Korea had turned into a potential flashpoint. It was clear that any reunification, which both North and South desired, must be a matter of either/or: either communist dictatorship or right-wing autocracy (despite the American hope that the Rhee regime would develop in democratic directions). Nevertheless, the Americans had shown small interest in or concern over the fate of Korea, being more concerned with the Soviet challenge in Europe. Their main strategy in the Far East turned on reindustrializing Japan as the region's "toolshop," supplied with raw materials from peripheral East Asian countries. It was hoped that Japan, especially after the "loss" of China, would become the heart of an integrated trading sphere to form an economic bulwark against communism in the region. Preoccupied after 1948 with policies to make this a reality, American administrators paid little attention to Korea and were taken wholly by surprise by the North's invasion.[13]

Kim Il-sung undoubtedly had the go-ahead from Stalin and Mao Zedong for his invasion, and it is probable that both communist leaders underestimated the likely U.S. reaction. The Truman administration had, after all, declined to intervene in the Chinese "civil war" and had acquiesced in the fall of Chiang, even if it had afterward refused to recognize the legitimacy of Communist China. Acheson, in a speech that did not even mention Korea, had declared Formosa outside the perimeter of U.S. interests in the Pacific. Yet the North Korean invasion, coming after a series of shocks that had inflamed American anticommunism, was immediately apprehended as a direct challenge by Moscow to America's containment policy. Truman interpreted it in terms of Japan's attack on Manchuria and Italy's on Ethiopia in the 1930s, when the democracies had so signally failed to act. Just as those failures had encouraged further aggressions, Truman was convinced that abandoning the Republic of Korea without opposition from the Free World would discourage resistance to communist attack elsewhere and bring on World War III. The loss of Korea would produce a hundred Koreas. Though worried that the Russians might intervene, he believed that the risk must be taken. He had not wanted to go to war; everything he had done had been aimed at evading war, and he certainly did not want to start another world war, but in consideration of the historical precedents, he could not avoid the decision. Aggressive power must be met by the resolute power of the virtuous, or disaster would follow.[14]

Truman also saw this as the first great test for the United Nations, which, as he said, was "our idea" and must not be let down as the League of Nations had been let down. The U.N. Security Council, benefiting from a boycott by the Soviet representative (he had walked out earlier in the year when the council had refused to unseat Nationalist China), avoided a veto. It first condemned the invasion and called for the North's withdrawal and then voted to confront armed force with armed force. It would not be a war, said Truman, but a "police action" (which did not therefore require a declaration of war by Congress). The initial response of the American public was overwhelmingly approving. Support from both the Left and Right of politics was almost unanimous. Truman had shown what Free World leadership was all about. General Douglas MacArthur was made commander of the U.S. and U.N. forces and ordered to halt the North Korean advance.

The causes and course of the Korean War have, like all other parts of the Cold War, been widely debated.[15] It is enough to note here that the outcome did not satisfy any of the protagonists, save perhaps the Chinese. After the United Nations and Republic of Korea forces had been pushed into the heel of Korea, MacArthur executed a brilliant and daring landing at Inchon that cut off the North Koreans and forced a retreat northward above the 38th parallel. At this point, the U.N. allies of the United States thought the police action concluded, but the emboldened MacArthur wanted to enlarge the objectives to encompass the destruction of the North Korean Army and occupation of Pyongyang. Truman and his entire cabinet, exhilarated by the miraculous reversal of fortune, supported MacArthur without hesitation (Truman was also thinking, perhaps, of strengthening his anticommunist credentials before midterm elections).

Containment thus turned into rollback, albeit a strictly limited rollback, for Truman did not want to enlarge the war dangerously by involving China or Russia. MacArthur was certain this would not happen, but a suspicious Chinese administration did not trust American assurances and sent a clear warning that the Americans ignored. A massed attack of Chinese troops across the Yalu River caught the U.N. forces by surprise and turned triumph into disaster, the greatest disaster of the Truman administration, according to Acheson. The conflict finally stalemated around the 38th parallel to the frustration of the United Nations' commanding general. America's allies now became doubly alarmed as MacArthur, declaring there was "no substitute for victory," appealed over Truman's head to the American public for an escalation of the war into China, even to nuclear proportions. Truman thereupon relieved MacArthur of his command—undoubtedly the most unpopular act of his presidency—and began protracted truce negotiations with North Korea.[16]

The negotiations were still dragging on when Eisenhower came to office in 1953 with Richard Nixon as his vice president. During the presidential campaign of 1952, Republicans including Nixon had attacked the Democrats' defensive containment policy as "cowardly," arguing instead for the offensive policy of rollback, causing even more intense alarm among America's U.N. allies. Eisenhower's own secretary of state, the sincerely anticommunist John Foster Dulles, adopted the rhetoric of rollback, and Eisenhower supported him. This, however, was primarily a defense against their own anticommunist Right, which distrusted the two East Coast liberals, however impressive their credentials. Eisenhower was himself a cautious internationalist who probably had no intention of ever really implementing the policy (though its false promise would have tragic consequences in 1956 when Hungarians fatally relied on it in their rebellion against the Soviets).

As far as Korea was concerned, Eisenhower had made a campaign promise to end the war and favored the stalemated truce, though he was prepared to blackmail the Chinese into conciliation by threatening MacArthur's nuclear option. Many Republicans, however, were appalled that the United States seemed to be allowing itself to be pushed by its allies toward a "soft peace." Dulles argued that no settlement should be concluded until America had shown all of Asia its clear superiority by giving China "one hell of a licking." Republican Ralph Flanders told the Senate, "it was with sickness of heart that we heard anew the proud boast that we had successfully 'resisted aggression' as if the loss of hundreds of thousands of lives and billions of dollars had been well spent in bringing us back to the starting ground of June 25, 1950."[17] Eisenhower ignored such sentiment until the truce was concluded, after the death of Stalin, in July 1953.

Such was the ambivalent outcome of the Korean War, but what were the consequences? Historian William Stueck has written that, despite the fact that Korea remained divided after three years of terrible destruction to life and property, "from a broader perspective the conflict may be seen as a turning point in which, unlike the 1930s, the political system of the United States and Western Europe rose to the challenge of authoritarianism in a manner that averted the global bloodbath of the previous decade and positioned the West advantageously in the ongoing Cold War."[18] This view rather begs the question, since it merely affirms the validity of Truman's reasons for engaging in Korea in the first place—the deployment of American power to stand up to aggressors. It would seem impossible to prove, and perhaps intuitively unlikely to suppose, that the war prevented a global bloodbath. Stalin had proceeded with his usual caution throughout the war, showing no intention of being drawn in and taking no opportunity to make advances in Europe. As for "advantageous positioning," Stueck himself notes that the war was largely responsible for freezing the parameters of the Cold War into the policy of perpetual but indirect confrontation known as containment, putting hopes of peaceful coexistence out of contention. It was no doubt true that Stalin had miscalculated in encouraging Kim, and that the outcomes of the war were, on balance, unfavorable to the Soviets. The war had promoted the massive U.S. military buildup that NSC-68 had recommended, and an arms race had begun that would be almost impossible for the Soviets to match without severely damaging and distorting their economy.

AMERICAN VIRTUE AND THE UNITED NATIONS

Nor had the Korean War, by and large, proved the efficacy of the United Nations in preventing war or, for that matter, in conducting one. It was inevitable that the United States as main guarantor of the multilateral organization should use it as a vehicle for what it deemed necessary purposes. Though the Americans criticized the United Nations for the meagerness of its military support (only a few small contingents from Australia, Britain, and Turkey), their own dominant role nevertheless suited their desire to control the conduct of the war. But their use of the organization for legitimizing purposes was possible only because of the sheer accident of the Soviet boycott. Under normal circumstances, and with a Cold War in progress, the United Nations was incapable of acting as originally intended.

Under the U.N. compact, the member states had accepted constraints on their use of force with a binding system of collective security, much as had the League of Nations. But unlike the league, the U.N. Charter had acknowledged and respected the realities of power politics by establishing the Security Council and granting the right of veto to its permanent members. It was argued that this was necessary to ensure the practical commitment of the great powers and to avoid the impotence of the egalitarian league. The charter's positive vision was one in which the Big Five—the United States, Britain, France, the Soviet Union, and China—would seek common ground and concur in their votes, utilizing the veto power only as a last resort to protect vital security concerns. The existence of the veto would mean that every issue would have to be carefully deliberated and negotiated so as to satisfy or placate all major powers, thus giving any agreements reached a decent chance of success. The aim was to make the council both effective and responsible by enabling a genuine concert of power rather than a clash of powers. Even if, as today, there were only a single superpower, such an arrangement might provide value by encouraging the dominant power to seek diplomatic support for its desired actions, thus providing legitimation and improving efficacy while softening the experience of practical hegemony.

But in the context of the Cold War, negotiated agreements were generally impossible. As long as the East-West ideological split prevailed, the veto power of the permanent members of the Security Council, always exercised along partisan lines, would be decisive. The United Nations would be, in other words, not a cooperative organization for the maintenance of peace and the settlement of differences, but merely a grandstanding forum in which the main conflict of the age would be conducted by other means.

The Korean War also brought to the surface the ambivalence or outright hostility of conservative Americans toward the United Nations. Truman was right to say that the organization was "our idea," but it did not follow that all Americans were enthusiastic about it. The traditional fear of "entangling alliances" and loss of sovereign control of America's foreign policy agenda had not disappeared. In the days of the League of Nations, the main concern had been that collective security conditions would automatically draw the United States into conflicts where no national interest was at stake. This fear persisted after World War II, but in the Cold War context it was supplemented by the obverse fear that treaty obligations might prevent America pursuing whatever actions abroad it deemed necessary or desirable. The often strained relations with U.N. allies during the Korean War illustrated the point. Moreover, Truman had gone straight to the United Nations to prosecute what he called a "police action," thus bypassing Congress and arguably subverting its authority to declare war. Eisenhower's insistence on a negotiated truce was also taken as proof that U.N. influence was pernicious. The president could not extinguish the conviction of many in his own party that the United Nations had impeded ambitious, necessary, and righteous U.S. action abroad. Some, especially on the Far Right, felt that the world's only true superpower should not have to endure the humiliation of international constraints upon its foreign policy. Herbert Parmet argued that this opinion revealed a new kind of isolationism, based less on avoiding "entangling alliances" than on "an arrogant indifference to how foreigners viewed the American superpower."[19] This, as I argued in the last chapter, is quite true, except that arrogant indifference to external opinion was morally bolstered by the persistent (no doubt equally arrogant) conviction that American power necessarily served the good of the world. It therefore followed that inhibiting American power inevitably disallowed the virtuous ends at which that power aimed.

The very structure of the United Nations seemed to anti-internationalists anomalous and contaminating. The Security Council, for all its faults, might possibly safeguard peace by mutually engaging the great powers in continuous dialogue, but from a conservative viewpoint, this was to force the United States into a form of partnership with regimes that, on Cold War assumptions, were inherently evil. Certainly, conservatives found it hard to stomach the veto powers it gave the Soviets over any multilateral actions that the United States might wish to promote. In the General Assembly, meanwhile, smaller nations, many of them newly independent as a result of postwar decolonization, frequently displayed antipathy to the United States, allegedly through envy or because they were dupes of Moscow or Peking. Their Lilliputian attempts to bind the American giant seemed thoroughly misguided to Americans, who knew where the balance of moral virtue in the world lay.

The U.N. Charter was also held to endanger American virtue in more insidious ways, notably through its potential effect on American law. In 1948 the president of the American Bar Association, Frank Holman, began a crusade to save American domestic law from subversion by "internationalism." Holman's particular concern was with the powers reserved to the states by the Tenth Amendment of the Constitution. He wanted to amend the treaty-making provisions of the Constitution so that the treaty power could not be used as an instrument of domestic legislation overriding the will of the states. He also targeted executive agreements (a foreign policy device to which presidents since George Washington had often resorted because, unlike treaties, they did not require congressional approval). Holman wanted to bring these agreements under the same limitations as treaties. Between 1952 and 1954, Senator Paul Bricker fought in Congress for a constitutional amendment that would achieve Holman's aims. In its original form, the Bricker amendment would have left decisions on the enforceability of international obligations to the political discretion of Congress or the state legislatures, a reversion to conditions under the eighteenth-century Articles of Confederation. Faced with this acute challenge to its authority over foreign affairs, the executive branch naturally resisted. Despite the opposition of the Eisenhower administration, the amendment gained significant support in Congress and among sections of the public, and in the end it was only narrowly defeated in the Senate.[20]

The majority of the American public was too confused by the legal intricacies of the Bricker amendment to care much about its failure. The controversy was nevertheless important for the breadth and depth of hostility it had uncovered toward the United Nations. Holman declared that his motivation had been the fear that the rights of Americans would be violated by U.N. covenants. Bricker himself had introduced the amendment by pointing to the dangers inherent in the Universal Declaration of Human Rights. This consideration gained him significant support among southerners, who trembled to think of the effect that such rights would have, if enforced, upon their own peculiar social and legal arrangements. Southerners accused "internationalists" of wanting to use U.N. membership to interfere with their internal affairs. After all, Congress had, in ratifying the U.N. Charter, pledged America to promote respect for rights "without distinction as to race."

What was at stake here was not, of course, the preservation of American virtue but the preservation of conditions that constituted an enduring stain on American virtue. In attempting to maintain racial segregation, Americans could not but feel the sharp inner edge of the human rights sword. Most Americans preferred to believe that those who criticized the United States for imperialistic policies in the Third World were either un-American or, at best, communist dupes. Racial segregation, however, was too inconveniently near at home and too undeniable to allow so easy a gloss. It provided an inviting target for America's foes, doubly so since the charge of immorality was combined with one of egregious hypocrisy given the nation's vaunted egalitarian promise.

As early as 1948, the National Association for the Advancement of Colored People (NAACP) had tried to charge the United States before the United Nations for violation of its charter. The Soviet Union argued that the matter should be considered but was voted down. Nevertheless, the issue would prove to be a fruitful one for the communists, particularly in the ideological competition with America for the allegiance of Third World countries. It was difficult to spread the gospel of democracy among "peoples of color" while the U.S. democracy accommodated so large and enduring an injustice against its own colored people. In the ideological battle of the 1950s and 1960s, segregation was America's Achilles' heel. Any American criticism of communist regimes for violation of human rights was immediately countered with, "Physician, heal thyself." Nor was it just the legalized racism of the South that was at issue, for segregation was widespread throughout the nation. In 1960, Nikita Khrushchev cited the racism of New York City as one reason why the United Nations should be moved to another location. Many U.S. leaders chafed under the realization that their nation's record on race relations put them at an ideological disadvantage, but domestic politics prevented effective action until a combination of legal activism, the civil rights movement, and federal legislation had decisively altered the political landscape.[21]

Conservatives had other reasons, too, for resisting U.N. covenants, particularly the Universal Declaration of Human Rights adopted by all nations at the U.N. General Assembly in 1948. Though this was, in fact, heavily indebted to the U.S. Constitution's Bill of Rights as elaborated and developed by the Supreme Court during 150 years of interpretation and application, its list of rights went far beyond what conservatives could accept. It asserted (Articles 22–26) substantial economic and social welfare rights to healthy development of the child, environmental hygiene, jobs for all, fair wages, and continuous improvement in living conditions. *Time* magazine of July 1953 argued that fulfilling these would require an enlargement of government that would make it "even more totalitarian than . . . the Soviet Union."[22] Moreover, the rights to which conservative Americans had been most devoted—especially individual rights to private property—received only a brief mention in the declaration (Article 17). The Universal Declaration seemed to them an extension of the New Deal abroad, which, since it was drafted under the leadership of Eleanor Roosevelt, it no doubt was. Though conservatives often found human rights rhetoric useful to embarrass their communist enemies, it was undoubtedly a double-edged sword. In general, conservatives preferred to speak about "American values" rather than human rights, but this rhetoric would become seriously devalued during the Vietnam era.[23]

The basic conflict over America's role and America's true values, then, was in part one between liberal-internationalist anticommunists and conservative-nationalist anticommunists. Yet not all the offense to Americans' sense of their own innocence would come from reactionary resistance to internationalism's potentially corrosive effects on property rights and segregation. The liberal commitment of American power abroad inevitably raised questions that the American mythology was ill-equipped to answer. The Truman Doctrine (which the Eisenhower Doctrine of 1958 extended to all anticommunist governments in the Middle East) already contained the seeds of the contradiction that emerged clearly in Korea and would be most painfully exposed in Vietnam.

VIRTUE TAINTED

The United States had benefited from a European balance of power in the past but had never had a major responsibility for maintaining it. After 1947, however, it was committed to operating in terms that its foreign policy had traditionally repudiated as corrupting of virtue. America had already conceded Eastern Europe to the Soviets at Yalta, but the Mediterranean and the Middle East (with its important oil reserves) had never been in the Soviet sphere of interest. The United States was determined to warn the Soviets off. Even if the principal motive was the quarantining of malevolent communism, the practical result seemed indistinguishable from the policies Britain and the other great powers had pursued in the past.

Moreover, in the realpolitik logic of great power strategy, the moral and political complexion of one's clients and allies was of negligible importance compared with their value as a bulwark against the larger threat. The anticommunist government of Greece was very far from savory, as the leading figures in the Truman administration well knew, but the decision to exclude the Soviets dictated that it be supported. However sound this might have been in strategic terms, it was at odds with an American conception of virtue that disdained all sordid bargains. It was notable that in the same year that the Truman Doctrine was announced, Congress created the National Security Council and the CIA under its direction. The establishment of a foreign spying service in peacetime (or at least in the absence of a hot war) was also contrary to American traditions, and the CIA would one day become a byword for the type of secret deals, dirty tricks, and covert support of tyrannous regimes that U.S. foreign policy traditionally opposed.[24]

Of course, America in the past had found itself, against its better intentions, supporting corrupt dictators and U.S. business interests in countries like Honduras, Nicaragua, and Cuba. But the anticommunist crusade gave a new lever to any ambitious would-be dictator who knew how to manipulate America's ideological sensitivities and its open political system. South Korea's Syngman Rhee was especially talented in using his knowledge of U.S. political anticommunism to gain and hold power. As anticommunist fervor grew at home, liberal elements within the Occupation Authority and the State Department who opposed Rhee found themselves in a very weak position. Any attempt to accommodate left-leaning forces in Korea risked accusations of supporting communism. Rhee understood this and waited patiently until his chances were ripe. When the Soviets in occupation of the North sent Korean patriots from the war against Japan into the South as communist organizers, the Americans countered with people like Rhee. About the latter, General John R. Hodge, commander of the southern occupation forces, said: "these people have embarrassed our efforts more than anyone else. It is a case of those who might benefit by American success, refusing to help us in our fight to bring democracy." And yet, he concluded, the United States could not break with them because "they are the bulwark against communism." However logical in great power terms, U.S. military-backed support for Rhee and other authoritarian leaders through to the 1980s left a legacy of bitter anti-Americanism in South Korea that persists to this day.[25]

Bruce Cumings argued that the American leaders he researched in his study of the occupation of Korea were not ill-intentioned, nor conspirators, nor exploiters. Understanding what happened, he said, would have been simpler had they been evil hypocrites, but they were not. They were merely sincere men shaped by American assumptions so universal and ingrained as to need no acknowledgement: "that American views on society and the good life are those of all peoples; that Americans had the right to remake Korea in their own image; that American motives are beyond question."[26] This may be well be true, but it overlooks what Cumings himself makes clear, namely, that Americans were unable to establish the American-style democracy they themselves wanted. This was largely because they were outmaneuvered by clever anti-Democrats capable of exploiting American ideological propensities in a Cold War context. Syngman Rhee's U.S.-supported authoritarian regime proved to be a precursor to similar ones in countries as various as Iran, Guatemala, and Vietnam. Tin-pot dictators around the world, however corrupt, however repressive of their own populations, could be assured of U.S. backing as long as they declared themselves firmly anticommunist and opened their economies to U.S. capital. Any principled opposition to political and economic domination or exploitation within such nations, particularly by movements self-labeled or accused of being "socialist" or "Marxist," automatically fell on the wrong side of the good-evil axis and became liable to American-assisted suppression.

This created the potential for criticism of U.S. foreign policy as, at best, inconsistent with the nation's proclaimed values or, at worst, informed by values that served U.S. interests at the cost of the violent repression of subject populations. Americans have traditionally assumed, of course, that American values are universally valid and therefore exportable to other lands and peoples, perhaps with the assistance of American economic and political power. But moral self-confidence would be tested if such exportation were reinterpreted, at home and abroad, as the *imposition* of peculiarly American values, closely linked to capitalist ones, on unwilling foreign peoples. Such a reinterpretation occurred during the Vietnam era, with severe consequences for both the American myth and the national psyche.

CONCLUSION

A necessary corollary of America's acceptance of a geostrategic role was an increase in defense spending, but the militarization that finally occurred was on a scale that would have horrified old-time Jeffersonians to the depths of their souls. The tripling of the defense budget during the

Korean War, as well as requiring increased taxes and cuts to welfare programs, greatly expanded the weight of the military in political affairs and the clout of arms manufacturers, often accused in the past of causing wars for their own gain. It stimulated the development of powerfully interlocking interests that became known as the "military-industrial complex," the dangers of which a departing President Eisenhower warned the nation in 1961. Enlarging the defense apparatus also greatly enhanced the potential power of the chief executive, who was, after all, commander in chief—the so-called Imperial Presidency, begun in the time of McKinley, that was approaching its zenith.[27] Militarizing the Cold War meant militarizing U.S. foreign policy, producing a long-term trend in the State Department toward greater reliance on military than on diplomatic responses to international problems.

But if the Cold War had allowed the United States to build such huge military resources and to deploy them globally, it also constrained their use. The interweaving logic of Cold War and domestic politics caused American virtue to be too restrictively redefined as anticommunism, implying an oppositional and defensive stance rather than a constructive one oriented toward building and sustaining a fully cooperative international regime. Of course, American power was hugely constructive in funding and promoting the recovery and growth of what became known as the First World. Liberal American political leaders, indeed, had succeeded in locking a perennially reluctant nation firmly into the international system through commitment to international institutions—Bretton Woods, the United Nations, the General Agreement on Tariffs and Trade (GATT), NATO, and so on. And if America was the hegemonic power of that system, other nations had acquiesced willingly because they shared America's democratic and capitalist-development values and benefited in innumerable ways from the new international order. Nor had these nations much reason to fear American coercive power, since the hegemon had voluntarily bound itself in an array of rules, entanglements, and multilateral institutions that limited its ability to deploy its power unilaterally or to always get its own way (a process G. John Ikenberry labeled "security co-binding" that was in stark contrast to power-balancing). America's reward for its self-restraint and multilateralism was a stable, self-balancing Western system that did not demand the continuous effort, nor incur the considerable costs (in terms of both material means and reactionary resentment), involved in managing a traditional empire. Ikenberry named this system "structural liberalism" and pronounced it well suited to America's historical predilections, however much conservative Americans might resent it.[28]

On the other hand, American power was often a highly destructive force in the Third World. The larger context that linked these two disparate effects was opposition to and defense against the communistic Second World. For all its virtuous effects in the West, American power after the onset of the Cold War was reconceived as primarily a *defensive* force dedicated to resisting communist evil. Since this larger evil could not with safety be confronted directly, Americans were led into dangerous entanglements with lesser evils that the American mythology was ill-equipped to underwrite and justify. The eventual result was a humbling of American power and loss of faith in American virtue that, combined, had a shattering effect on the nation's mythological soul.

CHAPTER FIFTEEN

Vietnam

VIRTUE STAINED, POWER HUMBLED

HENRY KISSINGER USED THE LABEL "Wilsonianism" to designate what he regarded as a regrettable but persistent strain of moralism in U.S. foreign policy: "As an approach to foreign policy, Wilsonianism presumes that America is possessed of an exceptional nature expressed in unrivaled virtue and unrivaled power. The United States is so confident of its strength and the virtue of its aims that it could envision fighting for its values on a worldwide basis."[1]

I have argued that this supposed unity of power and virtue was in fact a post–World War II phenomenon rather than characteristic of Wilson and his era. But I affirm Kissinger's later observation that moralism was rooted in the American exceptionalist tradition, and that this tradition was one of the most important casualties of the Vietnam War. Characterizing Vietnam twenty-five years after the fall of Saigon as a national "tragedy," he claimed that the war had opened a rift, still unhealed, in American society and destroyed faith in the uniqueness and universal relevance of American values. One unfortunate consequence was a continuing failure to develop a new, rational foreign policy consensus. Americans after Vietnam could no longer confidently assert their own values or feel comfortable about imposing them on others, and they were consequently at a loss as to what to do with their own predominant power.[2]

The Vietnam War was a fruit of containment policy complemented by the falling domino theory—the belief that communist success in one Third World nation would inevitably cascade into neighboring countries. But the war sharply revealed the pitfalls of containment logic. The problem of American power in a world where direct confrontation with the main foe was unthinkable lay not in its extent but in its *credibility*.[3] How was America to demonstrate to friends and enemies alike its determination and capacity to resist communism internationally? The answer was to support resistance in peripheral countries of little interest in themselves but susceptible to communist or leftist takeover. Material and technical aid on its own was relatively unproblematic, but to go a further step and commit conventional U.S. forces to an unconventional guerrilla war in an unfamiliar country, the loyalty of most of whose population could not be taken for granted, was courting danger. Failure would mean that credibility was destroyed rather than confirmed. The Korean War had hardly been a glorious victory, after all, and the defeat of French colonial armies at the hands of the Viet Minh had already shown the potential for disaster in Vietnam. By the 1960s, however, U.S. military might far exceeded that of the French and was vastly superior to anything the Vietnamese communists could deploy. U.S. military commanders were confident of a swift victory. Very few in politics foresaw the difficulties of defeating an enemy inspired by nationalistic feeling or of making a real nation out of South Vietnam, and no one dreamed of the civil dissension the war would spark at home.

I will argue in this chapter that the reason Vietnam was so traumatizing for Americans was because it crippled faith in America's virtuous power. Innocent virtue was fatally injured because power was used to conduct a cruel war whose justifications failed; fewer and fewer people believed, as time went on, that the cause for which Americans and Vietnamese were dying was either right in itself or necessary for the national interest. The war was doubly damaging because American might was not only perceived to be employed in a wrong cause but was effectively vanquished. America's martial virtue was humbled by an inferior but determined foe, with the result that pride received as deep a wound as innocence. In these grim circumstances, traditional belief in America's special mission was severely shaken, deep national divisions were opened, and an era of foreign policy uncertainty began.

I begin by looking at the prelude to war, and at the significance of John F. Kennedy in the deepening crisis that followed his assassination.

VIETNAM, KENNEDY, AND INJURED INNOCENCE

The Vietnam conflict began in 1941 as an uprising of Ho Chi Minh's nationalist Viet Minh organization against the Japanese occupation. It continued against France after the latter's refusal to accept its former colony's declaration of independence directly upon the defeat of the Japanese in 1945. Though the Viet Minh did not openly proclaim themselves communist until the mid-1950s, Americans assumed that it was a client state of China whose "loss" it did not want to see repeated in Vietnam. America therefore began providing aid to the French in 1950. After the French were decisively defeated at Dien Bien Phu in 1954, an international conference at Geneva negotiated a ceasefire and withdrawal of the Viet Minh northward above the 17th parallel, with free elections to be held in 1956 to unify the country. The communists confidently expected to win these elections, but when the time came, the American-backed interim prime minister of the noncommunist South, Ngo Dinh Diem, refused to hold them. Frustrated, the North Vietnamese turned once more to military force, using southern guerrilla forces trained in the North (the Viet Cong) to infiltrate the South in order to terrorize and proselytize.

Secretary of State John Foster Dulles persuaded the Eisenhower administration to provide Diem with economic and military assistance, but as a client, Diem proved a liability. He alienated southern villagers by displacing their elected village councils with Saigon administrators, alienated Buddhists by placing fellow Catholics in all top positions, and caused widespread resentment with a policy of relocating the rural population to isolate the communists. Though constantly seeking and acquiring more American aid, he failed to turn the Army of the Republic of Vietnam (ARVN) into a force capable of dealing with the insurgents despite its greatly superior numbers. When Buddhist monks began public protests of self-immolation in 1963, the support of the U.S. administration under John F. Kennedy was withdrawn. Kennedy, a previously determined supporter of South Vietnam who had grown increasingly dismayed by Diem, secretly approved an army coup in which Diem was killed.[4] Thus, by the time of Kennedy's assassination on November 22, 1963 (three weeks after Diem's), the American effort in Vietnam had already taken on the aspect of a hopeless cause.

The tantalizing and much discussed question that later arose was whether Kennedy, had he lived, would have committed the military forces that his successor Lyndon Johnson did. It is, of course, impossible to answer with complete certainty one way or the other. Even firmly stated political intentions can be poor predictors of future decisions that are liable to be critically influenced by unforeseeable events and circumstances. Nevertheless, the issue has an important bearing on our topic because of Kennedy's rekindling of American idealism and because of the consequent effect of his assassination on the national sense of innocence. Certainly, Kennedy was under intense and almost uniform pressure from his national security advisers to undertake a major military engagement in Vietnam, and indeed the number of American "advisers" to South Vietnam and neighboring Laos was increased on Kennedy's watch from about 800 to 16,500. This would seem to support the conventional wisdom that grew among historians and commentators that an essential policy continuity existed between the Kennedy and Johnson administrations.[5]

Such wisdom, however, discounts the evidence of National Security Action Memo (NSAM) 263 signed by Kennedy on October 11, 1963 (and confirmed three weeks later in a news conference) that outlined a program of "Vietnamization" of the war (essentially identical to that which Nixon was later to rely on). The memo recommended that

> [a] program be established to train Vietnamese so that essential functions now performed by U.S. military personnel can be carried out by Vietnamese by the end of 1965. It should be possible to withdraw the bulk of U.S. personnel by that time . . .
>
> In accordance with the program to train progressively Vietnamese to take over military functions, the Defense Department should announce in the very near future presently prepared plans to withdraw 1000 U.S. military personnel by the end of 1963. This action should be explained in low key as an initial step in a long-term program to replace U.S. personnel with trained Vietnamese without impairment of the war effort.[6]

It also discounted the recollections of Kennedy's political operative, Ken O'Donnell, who reported private conversations in which the president told how the arguments of Senator Mike Mansfield (who advised the earliest withdrawal) had altered his previous judgments. According to O'Donnell, Kennedy had come to believe that expanding military involvement in

Vietnam was throwing good money after bad. Kennedy was adamant that he would never give in to pressure from the military and members of his own cabinet to send in combat units of draftees. He was, however, acutely sensitive to charges of being "soft on communism," which was why he felt he could safely carry through withdrawal only after he was reelected. He told O'Donnell: "In 1965 I'll become one of the most unpopular Presidents in history. I'll be damned everywhere as a Communist appeaser. But I don't care. If I tried to pull out completely now from Vietnam, we would have another Joe McCarthy red scare on our hands, but I can do it after I'm reelected. So we had better make damned sure that I am reelected." Asked how to do this without damaging American prestige, he replied: "Easy. Put a government in there that will ask us to leave."[7]

This version is strongly supported by the recollections of Arthur Schlesinger and Theodore Sorensen and by the record of John Kenneth Galbraith, the famous economist and, under Kennedy, ambassador to India. Galbraith had early and accurately foreseen the danger in Vietnam and embarked on a long and fruitless quest for a negotiated settlement and a U.S. exit. Trusted and admired by Kennedy, he provided a singular and blunt voice supporting the president's resolve to resist the hawkish proposals of his own advisers. After Kennedy's death, the same advice delivered to Johnson was greeted with stony silence.[8]

If such evidence is allowed to provide an at least plausible account of Kennedy's policy intentions, it would follow that Johnson, sometime in the first few months after assuming the presidency, altered course. As vice president, certainly, Johnson had expressed the opinion that it would be "disastrous to pull out," that it was essential to win the war. In this he had the support of Secretary of Defense Robert McNamara, National Security Adviser McGeorge Bundy, and Secretary of State Dean Rusk, all hawks on the issue, as were most of the military and the CIA.[9]

According to Noam Chomsky and other skeptics, however, affirming Kennedy's intention to withdraw is an act of hagiography, evidence of a wistful desire to save the shining image of the hero-president from posthumous tarnishment by the Vietnam fiasco. Some of the affirmers, on the other hand, claim that the deniers have an ulterior motive of their own. If one assumes an essential continuity on Vietnam, then one need not consider the possibility that Kennedy's murder was connected to Johnson's reversal of policy, since no such reversal occurred. This is the malignant connection posited by a famous book by Jim Garrison and the later film by Oliver Stone. Of course, the conspiracy theorists conclude that such a connection must be causal (that is, that Kennedy was killed in order to effect the reversal) and hardly entertain the view that it might be purely contingent and opportunistic (Kennedy's death providing the chance for the hawks to follow inclinations formerly overridden by the president).[10]

These are, of course, oft-plumbed but perennially murky waters in which it is neither wise nor necessary to plunge too deeply here. It is important to observe, however, what was really at stake in this argument over historical interpretation with respect to the ongoing drama of power and virtue. The underlying issue was whether the damage done to American virtue by the use of American power in Vietnam was in principle avoidable, in which case virtue was potentially redeemable; or whether Vietnam revealed that American virtue had been bogus all along. The retention of hope or the confirmation of cynicism depended on establishing or refuting the wisdom of Kennedy on Vietnam, which meant determining how far the general promise that he represented had been true or false.

Kennedy's advent was one of the great moments of American renewal, of rediscovery of the higher purpose and meaning of America, a revival of the essential mythology of mission. According to Arthur Schlesinger, who was responsible for applying the Camelot tag to the Kennedy "court," Kennedy reestablished the republic as the first generation of its leaders had seen it. He symbolized the feeling of youthful hope and idealistic promise abroad at the beginning of the 1960s. Kennedy's admonition— "Ask not what your country can do for you, but what you can do for your country"—reinstated a republican conception of citizenship, demanding service rather than promising services. Under Kennedy, there would be moral renewal at home and a rededication to service abroad.[11]

Domestic renewal focused on civil rights and organized crime. Though Kennedy was initially a "moderate" on civil rights, the dramatic developments within the movement in the 1960s produced in him a determination to tackle what he called the nation's "moral crisis." He mobilized the Alabama National Guard to secure the admittance of two black students to the University of Alabama and called for extensive civil rights legislation against the inevitable opposition of right-wing Republicans and southern Democrats in Congress. In this effort he was supported by his brother Robert, as attorney general, who also set about tackling the problem of organized crime. Abroad, Kennedy promised to "pay any price, bear any burden, meet any hardship, support any friend, oppose any foe, to ensure the survival and success of liberty." His inaugural address was given over entirely to foreign affairs. He established a Peace Corps to encourage young Americans to contribute their time and skills to bringing a decent way of life to peoples around the globe. He resisted communism, becoming indeed a Cold War hero. He took a stand over Berlin, where the communists had thrown up a wall to divide East physically from West. He emerged victorious from a dramatic standoff with Nikita Khrushchev after the discovery of Soviet missiles in Cuba and an attempt by a Russian fleet to deliver nuclear warheads to arm them. He had stood, resolute, on the brink of Armageddon, and the Soviet premier had blinked first.[12]

Despite such confrontation, and despite his sincere anticommunism, Kennedy was no reckless Cold Warrior. Indeed, he hoped as president to defuse nuclear tensions by establishing better relations and negotiating arms limitation treaties with the allegedly mortal foe. His inaugural vow to combat the scourge of war virtually required such an aim. His dual aims of perfecting American democracy and securing international peace and prosperity were thus entirely traditional, a restatement of the aims established by the national mythology. What's more, Kennedy's telegenic appeal, enhanced by that of his glamorous First Lady, convincingly projected these aims across the globe. Not since Woodrow Wilson had the world greeted a U.S. president with such eager hope, supplemented, in Kennedy's case, with genuine love. More than either Truman or Eisenhower, the entire noncommunist world wholeheartedly acknowledged Kennedy as its true leader. This made his assassination deeply shocking not just to Americans but to people everywhere.

It was hardly surprising, in retrospect, that the drastic curtailment of this brief, shining moment should signal a decisive fracture of America's dream of peculiar innocence. It caused a cruel dashing of hopes raised too high, too fast, a savage bewilderment of aroused idealism. The assassination itself left a bitter legacy, partly through the precedent it set for the killings of Robert Kennedy, Martin Luther King, Malcolm X, and the attempted killing of Ronald Reagan; it seemed that no notable U.S. leader of whatever stripe could walk safely in his own land even when surrounded by a Praetorian Guard. Worse was the miasma of suspicion that arose around the Kennedy and King killings. No conspiracy theory was too improbable, too inconceivable, or too bizarre to be entertained. An unassuaged, perhaps unassuageable, suspicion grew that government was manipulated by secret and sinister forces beyond democratic control, that it was the seat not of virtue but of sin. Trust diminished as a gap opened between schoolbook accounts of American democracy and popular perceptions of its actual operations.

But the great catalytic event that widened this gap into a yawning chasm was the war in Vietnam. In the domestic maelstrom whipped up in the prosecution and protestation of that conflict, it was hardly surprising that some would wonder whether things might have been different had Kennedy lived. What if he had survived to win a landslide in 1964 against Barry Goldwater, gaining a liberal Congress (as Johnson did) that enabled him to push through his civil rights agenda? What if he had done as he supposedly intended and used the security of a second term to withdraw from the hopeless trap of Vietnam?[13]

Such counterfactual thoughts tempted those who wished to believe the promise had been real and not illusory, yet they were somewhat undermined by the posthumous tarnishing of the Kennedy legend. The endemic suspicion of "the Establishment" induced by the war and the consequent desire to unmask the sordid truth of all U.S. politics were directed at the end of the 1960s toward the martyr himself, indeed to his entire family. Laudatory accounts gave way to an obsessive unraveling of the golden image as revelations were made of Kennedy's illness and frailty; his obsessive womanizing; his alleged Mafia connections; and his covert attempts on the lives of leaders in Cuba, South Vietnam, the Congo, and the Dominican Republic. Richard Nixon's envy of Kennedy, it turned out, reflected his belief that the latter could get away with supposedly greater crimes than Nixon's own while maintaining a pristine reputation.[14]

The so-called Kennedy myth, therefore, assumed two contradictory but connected forms, neither of which has ever wholly banished the other. One embodied a nostalgic might-have-been, a world in which American virtue was possible but tragically betrayed; the other held that Kennedy proved the bitter "truth" that American political virtue would always turn out to be a cynical sham concealing deep and abiding corruption. Balanced accounts of his presidency became difficult to make under these circumstances. Yet it was precisely this bifurcation that made Kennedy such an apt symbol of the American conundrum of virtue and power. It was the allegedly illicit use of American power in Vietnam—a use that Kennedy, had he lived, either may or may not have authorized—that brought on the moral crisis that would afflict the American psyche and thus U.S. foreign policy until the end of the twentieth century and beyond. As in the years after World War I, but even more bitterly, Americans were left nursing a disappointment that turned to cynicism, but this time the wound went far deeper. Vietnam caused Americans to question, not just the motives of the leaders who had led them amiss, or of a military-industrial complex for whom war was good business, but the truth of the allegedly special nature of their nation and its noble mission.

INTO THE QUAGMIRE

In South Vietnam, a succession of coups followed Diem's assassination, making a mockery of America's expressed aims of building democracy there. U.S. advisers struggled desperately to create a viable state and to build the ARVN into a fighting force capable of defending it. By the end of March 1964, President Johnson had determined that the deteriorating situation required a military buildup, and even lip service to phased withdrawal was abandoned.[15]

Johnson professed himself keen to get his "fellas" out into the jungles of Vietnam to "whip hell out of some communists" in order to prevent the Chinese and "the fellas in the Kremlin" from thinking Americans were "yellow and don't mean what we say." American credibility and the policy of containment were apparently both at stake. But Johnson's lumping of the Chinese in with the Soviets ignored the fact that relations between the two had deteriorated into bitter rivalry since early 1960, a fact on which Americans failed to capitalize until the Nixon years. All that had happened after the Sino-Soviet split was that a new containment policy was settled on China and its clients in Southeast Asia. It is doubtful how much credence Johnson really put in containment, but he was deeply concerned with American credibility. His undersecretary of state, George Ball, warned him in July 1965 that a protracted war would expose U.S. weakness, but Johnson worried about the loss of national credibility if he failed to honor commitments to South Vietnam. Ball had responded presciently, "The worse blow would be that the mightiest power in the world is unable to defeat guerillas." Yet Johnson felt unable to extricate himself, despite growing unhappiness with the Vietnamese entanglement. As the White House tapes later revealed, even as he drove relentlessly on with the military buildup in Vietnam, Johnson thought that country "the biggest damn mess" he ever saw and not worth fighting for.[16]

Johnson's main concern was to win the war as rapidly and decisively as possible so he could concentrate on the domestic Great Society project that was to be his real legacy—the grand culmination of the reform process inaugurated at the start of the century. He was in Vietnam partly on the advice of the same old hawks of the Kennedy administration, but he was also, like Kennedy, haunted by the memory of Truman, China, and McCarthyism. He feared what Congress and the country would do to a president who showed himself "soft on communism," who would "lose" Vietnam as Truman had "lost" China. Commitment in Vietnam was the price Johnson paid for his domestic program (though he could not in truth afford both, and his inflationary spending would have dire economic consequences in the 1970s). The rigid identification of American virtue with anticommunism thus dragged the nation into a decade of futile warfare that devastated a Third World country and provoked unprecedented (save for the Civil War) strife at home.[17]

Trust declined because, in the end, Congress and the people felt that Johnson had deceived them. He had obtained a "blank check" from Congress for the contingent use of force in an area where U.S. interests had been threatened by a local disturbance and then, in 1964, used an "incident" of North Vietnamese aggression in the Tonkin Gulf as a pretext for what was in effect an undeclared war (shades of James Polk). Having committed U.S. forces, he then sought to conceal the real extent and cost of their deepening involvement. Certainly, he was badly let down by generals too arrogantly confident of American power and a swift triumph. Victory was forever at hand and forever postponed, but the military brass's tone of optimism remained; "pacified" villages and regions were exhibited and the infamous body count adduced to demonstrate the enemy's superior and unsustainable losses hence its ultimate, inevitable defeat. To protect his domestic program, Johnson felt compelled to back his generals' estimates and to obscure the truth of the war's progress. He also concealed the failure of bitterly feuding South Vietnamese governments to establish a nation that could fight its own fights. Whatever short-term political maneuverability Johnson's strategy of deception bought him, the long-run result was erosion of public and congressional confidence. Strong congressional suspicion would lead, in Nixon's time, to attempts to monitor more closely the activities of the executive and its intelligence agencies.

All Johnson's cunning, blustering, and bullying could not conceal forever the fact that the United States was hopelessly stuck in Vietnam, and in the end his own presidency sank in the quagmire. By 1968, with victory apparently no nearer and the cost in American lives mounting, American public opinion, though bitterly divided, was turning increasingly against the war. Richard Nixon came to the presidency promising to end it and to restore American "unity."[18]

"PEACE WITH HONOR"

Despite his own anticommunist credentials, Nixon blamed the fiasco he inherited on Wilsonian crusading against communism. During his presidency, he moved steadily and stealthily toward reestablishing U.S. foreign policy on the realistic basis of America's strict interests. He and Kissinger, his secretary of state, formulated a new strategic policy known as détente, a realpolitik approach in accord with nineteenth-century balance of power notions. The idea was to de-moralize international relations by promoting coexistence with the old enemy.

Détente appalled anticommunist crusaders on the right but was generally welcomed as a positive development in a dangerous nuclear world. Yet it put Nixon in the absurd position of continuing to prosecute an anticommunist war against an impoverished Third World country while extending the hand of friendship to the centers of world communism in the Soviet Union and China. Worse, Nixon's long drawn-out withdrawal "with honor" from Vietnam necessitated further lies and prevarication that heightened anger among demonstrators at home, in turn provoking a beleaguered mentality in the increasingly paranoid president and his administration. The moral climate in the White House declined to the extent that dirty tricks by the president's "plumbers" were routinely deemed acceptable, until exposure of their criminal break-in at Watergate brought about Nixon's fall. His resignation in 1974 marked the close of an episode in U.S. history that bore many of the hallmarks of a revolution.[19]

It is important to understand the precise logic underlying the crisis of these years. The reason Vietnam proved so intensely traumatic for the

United States was that it was catalytically responsible for shattering the post–World War II reconciliation of American power and American virtue. This reconciliation had been based upon an assumption that, because Americans were beneficently virtuous, American power would be used only for virtuous ends. Further, American power should not be withheld lest evil triumph as it had in the 1930s. The coming of the Cold War denied America the chance to be part of a genuine concert of power guaranteeing world order. Instead, the interaction of foreign affairs and domestic politics caused American virtue to be redefined as anticommunism, ensuring that virtuous power would be resolutely pitted against the greatest evil of the day—expansive, totalitarian communism. The thirties were replayed but this time with American power fully engaged against the aggressor, with Korea providing the first challenge and opportunity. Of course, the Korean War had hardly been a triumph, but at the end of the day the devil had at least been contained above the 38th parallel. In Vietnam, however, the too-close identification of American virtue with anticommunism caused the nation to overstep the bounds of political prudence. There, American virtue and American power were severed and undermined.[20]

American virtue (in the guise of innocence) demanded that in any conflict, America be on the *right* side; American power (and therefore pride) demanded that it be on the *winning* side. In Vietnam, pride received a heavy blow because of the American inability—despite carpet bombing, napalming, and defoliating—to achieve a decisive victory over a poor, relatively weak but ruthlessly determined foe. Even more seriously, innocence was affronted by the unprecedented characterization of Americans as bad guys. Let down by the corruption and ineptitude of their South Vietnamese ally, unable to distinguish friend from foe on the ground, frustrated at being denied an easy victory and with the body bags mounting, American draftees found their anticommunism shading into racism. They were being killed and maimed by slopes and gooks in miserable paddy fields far from home, and whether the people around them were communist or not, friend or foe, who could tell? As uncertainty and questioning about the purposes of the war increased, atrocities large and small occurred that could not be redeemed by a noble or even necessary cause.

The question of American atrocities in Vietnam remains a sensitive subject to this day, as became clear during the presidential election of 2004 when a controversy erupted over statements made years before by

Senator John Kerry. To suggest widespread atrocities, as Kerry had done, was apparently to do a disservice to honorable serving men and to smack of anti-Americanism. The infamous massacre at My Lai, some claimed, was the exception not the rule. Yet the evidence to the contrary is overwhelming. The conditions of guerrilla war, combined with the awesome firepower of even a single, young, frightened, and potentially irresponsible soldier and official reliance on the body count, created what has been called "an environment of atrocity." An army psychiatrist wrote at the time, "Terrified and furious teenagers by the tens of thousands have only to twitch their index fingers and what was a quiet village is suddenly a slaughterhouse." The scale of potential mayhem was much greater for a helicopter gunship armed with grenade launchers, miniguns capable of firing six thousand rounds a minute, two 7.62 mm machine guns, and rockets, especially if the rules of engagement said "anyone taking evasive action could be fired upon." A memorandum to aviation commanders early in the war regretted the number of "friendlies" killed by such weapons and asserted that helicopter crews had "no unilateral hunting license." American soldiers, it said, "cannot afford to be criticized as indiscriminate killers" if they were to have local populations join them in a common struggle. Yet indiscriminate killing and popular alienation characterized much of the U.S. effort in Vietnam. American tactics such as the clearing of "strategic hamlets" and creation of "free fire zones" were themselves problematic, as was the use of napalm, phosphorus, gas, artillery, and bombs on occupied villages. Nor were all the atrocities the result of undertrained and poorly motivated conscripts from the less-well-educated classes. The much-decorated Col. David H. Hackworth created an elite Tiger Force unit from the 101st Airborne Division in 1965 to fight the Viet Cong using their own tactics of terror and intimidation. This force raged across the Central Highlands for seven months in 1967, killing civilians, torching villages, raping, mutilating, and collecting trophy ears. "Vietnam was an atrocity from the get-go," Hackworth said. "It was that kind of war, a frontless war of great frustration. There were hundreds of My Lais. You got your card punched by the numbers of bodies you counted."[21]

Theodore Draper argued that this was the inevitable outcome of a mistaken American belief that Vietnam could be a "limited war": "As soon as the United States took over the main function of the war in 1965, it condemned itself to fighting either an unlimited war from the outset—and horrifying the world and its own people—or fighting a 'limited war' which it could not win without exceeding the limits that would make the other side fight an unlimited war." It was impossible to win hearts and minds in such a context, among either Vietnamese peasants or opponents of the war at home. Paul Kattenburg noted that the simplest way to explain America's failure in Vietnam was also the best: "the United States lost the war when Americans overwhelmingly ceased to accept it as right and came to regard it as wrong." More and more people became convinced that, whatever justifications had initially existed for the war, the means by which it was being pursued were indefensible. American servicemen were not honorable warriors in an honorable conflict but indiscriminate "baby-killers" slaughtering untold numbers of innocents to support an illegitimate and corrupt regime.[22]

What became known as "the Vietnam syndrome" after the war was generally taken to indicate the reluctance of the American people to accept casualties in distant wars that were not clearly related to definite American interests—what might be differently stated as the "body-bag syndrome." This interpretation was always, at best, only partially correct. It is undoubtedly true that a people are most firmly and easily committed when a cause aligning with their own defense is also judged to be, in wider terms, morally righteous. Americans were not, in the end, convinced that the sacrifices they were making in Vietnam served any important national interest, but they recoiled as much from the moral injury inflicted by the war as from its physical costs. It was not just that Americans were being killed and maimed, but that Americans themselves were induced to do terrible things for an unjust cause. As Kerry said in his 1971 congressional hearing, "the crimes that *we* commit threaten our country."[23] The issue had been clearly stated by that supposed arch-disciple of realism, Hans Morgenthau, in 1965 when he argued that the political and military risks the United States faced in Vietnam were not the most important ones. There existed, he said, a greater risk than the loss of the prestige gained from the appearance of power. Because his words encapsulate so succinctly the theme of this book, it is worth quoting them at length:

> It is the risk to ourselves, to our identity, to our mission in the world, to our very existence as a great nation. . . . [T]here is another kind of prestige: the image *we* have of ourselves. That

image will suffer grievous blemishes as we become ever more deeply involved in the war in Vietnam. This is a guerrilla war, and such a war, supported or at least not opposed by the indigenous population, can only be won by the indiscriminate killing of everybody in sight—by genocide. . . .

The brutalization of our armed forces would be a serious matter for any nation. . . . It is intolerable for the United States. For this nation, alone among the nations of the world, was created for a notable purpose: to achieve equality in freedom at home and thereby set an example for the world to emulate. This was the intention of the Founding Fathers, and to this very day the world has taken them at their word. It is exactly for this reason that our prestige has suffered so disastrously among friend and foe alike; the world did not expect of us what it had come to expect of others . . .

War, the wanton killing of human beings, can only be justified by a transcendent end; that makes a war just. There is no such end and there is no justice here.[24]

On this evidence, Morgenthau's realism—his insistence that American power should aim cleanly at identifying and defending the national interest —was really meant to serve a mythology whose idea of the national interest far transcended material selfishness. The ruthless and unjust use of power in the absence of genuine interests swiftly corrupted American soldiers and citizens and jeopardized the national mission. Yet many years would pass before Americans would act in accordance with Morgenthau's warning. In the meantime, they struggled among themselves and with their own consciences over what should be done.

In humbling American power and staining innocent American virtue, Vietnam confronted the nation with an agonizing choice: which partner to the broken marriage was to be served and restored, pride or innocence? If innocence, then America should act virtuously and withdraw from Vietnam immediately. If pride, then whatever the moral status of American involvement, American power (including even nuclear power according to the hawks) should be used to the utmost to win the war. This choice established the main lines of division at home between the Peaceniks, who would restore American innocence through immediate withdrawal at whatever cost to pride, and the Patriots, who would secure a victory at whatever cost to virtue. "My country right or wrong," the Patriots cried, but to deploy this ancient slogan was already to admit defeat in American terms. It gave the final victory to power over innocent virtue, and thus destroyed the exemplary myth.

Nixon, for all his alleged realism, instinctively understood this dilemma. He saw that his promise to restore the unity of the American people could be fulfilled only if he could give them *both* victory *and* virtue. But, as he noted in his first speech on Vietnam in May 1969, he was caught between two unacceptable alternatives: the imposition of a purely military solution on the battlefield or a "one-sided withdrawal" (or, what amounted to the same thing, acceptance of terms at peace talks in Paris that would be a disguised American defeat). The first was impossible because he knew that public opinion would not tolerate the actions and extra commitments that would be necessary to achieve outright victory. The second was unacceptable because it would mean abandoning the South Vietnamese, who had depended on the Americans, to their fate, and also for the familiar reasons of avoiding loss of American prestige and encouraging aggressive communism.[25] Nixon had no doubt that he must withdraw; only the *pace* of withdrawal was in question. He decided on a protracted lie that he hoped would give Americans both victory and virtue, if only in appearance.

The lie was "Vietnamization"—teaching South Vietnamese forces to win while withdrawing U.S. troops. This may well have worked politically when Kennedy first proposed it, for then the American commitment was relatively small and American casualties slight. But by 1968 the nation was too far steeped in blood, its prestige and power too fully invested, and South Vietnam was still too weak and unstable to make a convincing hero. Nixon rhetorically mobilized a "silent majority" of Americans to support this "peace with honor" plan against what he regarded as a liberal conspiracy bent on destroying him. His plan, he said, would "end this war in a way that will bring us closer to that great goal to which Woodrow Wilson and every American president in our history has been dedicated—the goal of a just and lasting peace." The problem was that Nixon and Kissinger, to give the lie a semblance of reality, felt it necessary to carry on the war for four more bitter years—even extending it into Cambodia with ultimately tragic results—in order to force the North into a more pliable negotiating mood (though Nixon resisted Kissinger's desire to deliver a "knockout blow" using tactical nuclear weapons or bombing the Red River irrigation dikes). Americans were steadily withdrawn, but by the time Nixon had concluded a settlement that differed little from the one on offer in 1968, casualties had nearly doubled and domestic upheaval had been further inflamed by the shedding of student blood on America soil. The inevitable finale came in 1975 after "a decent interval" that Kissinger had negotiated with the communists. The fall of Saigon was deeply humiliating for the United States and devastating for its Vietnamese allies. Amidst the wreckage, it was hard to discern where American "honor" lay.[26]

CONCLUSION

Throughout this period, the institutional moral capital inherent in the U.S. government, and particularly in the presidency and executive agencies like the CIA and FBI, was severely depleted.[27] Public trust remained a problem when Jimmy Carter was elected in 1976. Worse, national self-confidence had by then been further negatively affected by the end of the postwar economic boom and by relative American decline. The growth of vocal anti-Americanism abroad and in the chambers of the United Nations added to the confusion and frustration. Most worryingly, anti-Americanism seemed to have permanently infected a significant minority of Americans themselves. Though interim President Gerald Ford assured the people that the national nightmare was over, America seemed still to be suffering a deep moral malaise.

Carter provided an interpretation of that malaise in his own religious terms: it was the result of the sin into which the United States had fallen by virtue of its Cold War foreign policy. He would offer a solution that he hoped would redeem the sin and set the nation on the path of true virtue.

CHAPTER SIXTEEN

Putting Humpty Together Again

THE PROBLEM WITH U.S. military power after Vietnam was not that it had been significantly diminished—it had not. The fearful arsenal of nuclear weapons was intact, and the great military bases around the world were maintained. American power was still preponderant, yet somehow useless. American might had not been crushed as had that of Germany and Japan in World War II; it had simply been emasculated. The full extent of American power had not even been employed in Vietnam, and if it had, that nation might have been annihilated. This truth gave rise to a legend similar to that which had been current in Weimar Germany: "we were not defeated but betrayed by our own cowardly politicians." America had fought with "one hand tied behind its back." Victories had been misrepresented as defeats by a hostile media. The 1968 Tet offensive in Vietnam that had decisively turned American opinion against the war had in fact resulted in the almost complete destruction of the Viet Cong.

The feelings of nationalists with a preference for the untrammeled use of American power—untrammeled not only by squeamish politicians but by pesky alliances or importunate multilateral organizations—were thus intensified by a long, smoldering resentment. Robert McNamara might claim that in Vietnam the United States had learned the "humbling" lesson that it had no God-given right to shape other nations in its own image as it might choose.[1] But resentful nationalists were less concerned with humility than with wiping out the humiliation of the war through convincing and wholehearted assertions of American power. Their desire would have to contend with the persistence among populace and politicians of the Vietnam syndrome, but their influence would be increasingly felt as various types of conservatives gained ascendancy over the liberal wing of the Republican Party. Meanwhile, the Democrats, after the candidacy of George McGovern in 1972, moved further left to become the party of injured American innocence, as suspicious and fearful of military power as had been the isolationists and peace activists of former times. The severance of power and virtue, pride and innocence, that occurred in Vietnam had thus painfully exposed the enduring tension within the American mythology between parochial and transcendent nationalisms. The result seemed to be a final and permanent division between those who would insist on power and pride at all costs—to hell with the morality of the thing—and those who would insist on innocent virtue to the utter neglect of power and its uses.

This was certainly the caricatured view that each camp took of the other, and there was no doubt that attitudes between "hawks" and "doves" had hardened considerably. It was said that Vietnam had forced Americans to choose, once and for all, between realism and idealism, with the Right holding out strongly for the former and the Left for the latter. Yet the matter was hardly so simple. Even as the Republican Right tried to articulate a more realistic view of imperialistic American power, they could not escape the gravitational pull of a traditional mythology so deeply implanted in the American consciousness. Americans after Vietnam experienced confused feelings of hurt pride and injured innocence, and most might have liked to see pride reinstated by a convincing use of righteous U.S. force. But Vietnam had shown that there were moral limits they were disinclined to overstep. The "liberal Establishment" or elite "liberal conspiracy" that conservative hawks so despised, and who they blamed for corrupting the martial republican spirit of the masses, represented merely the crystallization of a powerful tendency of the mythology that all Americans had imbibed with their mothers' milk. Power could not be used simply because it was possessed, nor for pointless aggrandizement. If it was to be used for anything other than for strict defense, it must be for a right purpose, preferably a larger, universal one. The conservative view of American power could not dispense with the idea of crusade as a justification. Fortunately for conservatives, communism was not yet dead.

Democratic doves, meanwhile, could not ignore the sheer, blatant fact of American power. The massive militarization that had occurred after World War II had caused military-industrial interests to become deeply entrenched within society and in the various bureaucracies that served or channeled them. Globally dispersed military assets in support of alliances for the containment of communism meant that American power was inextricably engaged in a multitude of countries either sheltering under the American "nuclear umbrella" or acting as anticommunist bastions in specific regions. The continuing dependence of world trade on the dollar (even after Nixon devalued and effectively floated it in 1973), the increase of trade as a percentage of the U.S. gross national product, and the growing reliance of the United States on foreign energy sources all served to deepen the nation's global interconnectedness. The great American heartland might find the world as troublesome, incomprehensible, and dangerous as their forebears had, and they might desire to turn inward and away insofar as they were able. But America's vast human and material engagement could not simply be wished away. Moreover, events in the world would inevitably present economic and political challenges to which a permanently engaged United States had no choice but to respond. Liberals, certainly, could not avoid the question of how to use without abuse the great power that existed and upon which other peoples relied. Despite allegations of conservative critics to the contrary, none even tried. Post-Vietnam liberals saw their task not as diminishing global involvement but as moralizing and purifying it.

Most commentators have pictured the chief problem of U.S. foreign policy after Vietnam as one of building a new consensus to replace the fractured liberal one. Regret is often expressed that no such consensus has emerged.[2] Yet the liberal consensus is generally seen as constructed primarily around multilateralism, which was true, but it had also congealed around a militant anticommunism that impelled the nation into the very situation that caused the consensus to crack. It had, too, been premised on an acceptance of presidential leadership in foreign policy with congressional acquiescence. But congressional trust, along with public trust, had been forfeited in the deceits perpetrated over Vietnam. If presidents after Johnson and Nixon were to reassert their dominance in foreign policy, they had to address the problem of distrust in the office itself. In their efforts to do this, they articulated policies that tried either to cater to wounded pride or to turn it into redemptive remorse, and to reassure Americans that their virtue was either not lost or recoverable. The emergent dissensus did not result from one side choosing realism and the other idealism, but from different answers being given to the same problem: how convincingly to reunite the sundered partnership of power and virtue and thus make America—mythological America—whole once more.

CARTER'S HUMAN RIGHTS SOLUTION: PROMISE AND FAILURE

Even Nixon, in his way, had tried to square the power-virtue circle with his so-called Nixon Doctrine. This had attempted, in effect, to "Vietnamize" all of foreign policy. Nixon promised to maintain all treaty commitments, to provide a shield for any ally or strategic interest threatened by nuclear aggression, but in all cases of nonnuclear aggression to give material and economic assistance while encouraging the ally to defend itself. Critics were divided about what this would practically mean in specific circumstances, though the general intent was clear enough. Preponderant American power would be virtuously disposed to defend the Free World but would avoid being dragged willy-nilly into conflicts that, though mere sideshows, could cause severe damage to prestige, moral reputation, and domestic tranquility. There would be "no more Vietnams." Nixon hoped that good management of his détente policy, with its balance of power, coexistence, and arms-reduction precepts, would anyway sharply lessen the tensions and reduce the possible conflicts, great and small, in which the United States might become involved. It might even provide, he said, a century of peace.[3]

Détente was intended to contain communism by other means—the use of "carrots" in the form of trade deals, technology transfers, and arms controls as well as "sticks"—and did not aim at altogether abolishing competition at the periphery. That such competition still carried dangers of great power conflict was demonstrated by the 1973 Yom Kippur War between U.S.-supported Israel on one side and Soviet-supported Syria and Egypt on the other. Such danger arose from the very inability of either great power to control the often-warring states stretching from Egypt to Pakistan on the USSR's southern border. By 1978, Zbigniew Brzezinski was referring to the region as the "arc of crisis." In addition to its inherent instability, détente was also vulnerable to persistent attack from both Right and Left at home. The conservative critique focused predictably on the policy's alleged effect of weakening American power, claiming specifically that strategic arms limitation talks (the SALT negotiations) were being exploited by the devious Soviets to improve their strategic advantage in missiles. Conservative Cold Warriors argued that such an outcome was only to be expected and that the administration was naive to believe that genuine coexistence and mutual trust were possible between right-thinking Americans and atheistic communists bent on global domination. Détente, in the conservative view, amounted to the appeasement of evil, a return to the pusillanimity of the 1930s.

Liberals, on the other hand, welcomed the general thrust of détente: the arms control talks, Nixon's opening to China, his liberalization of trade with the Soviet Union, his formulation of a code of conduct for the superpowers to prevent drift into crisis and conflict. They were less happy about the insistent focus on East-West relations at a time when the world seemed to be changing rapidly, and when transnational economic, resource, and environmental issues, as well as questions of the justice of unequal North-South relations, were coming increasingly to the fore. They were also predictably chagrined to find that the Nixon Doctrine did not preclude support for the overthrow of a democratically elected government in Chile or large-scale arms sales to unsavory regimes in Iran, Nicaragua, and the Philippines, or that Kissinger could invoke it to justify CIA involvement (on the anticommunist, anti-Cuban side, of course) in Angola (though a Vietnam-shy Congress denied Kissinger extra funding for his Angolan clients). They were unhappy with the underlying emphasis on hegemonic control upon which the Machiavellian Nixon-Kissinger style of international politics was predicated and suggested that what was required was a genuine multilateralism that recognized the inescapable interdependence of nations in the late twentieth century.[4]

Nixon's self-serving manner of "selling" détente—his paranoid secrecy and deception, his long continuation of the war, his insistence on presidential supremacy in foreign policy and failure to appease a hostile Congress, above all his entanglement in the Watergate scandal—all militated against the long-term success of the policy forming the basis of an enduring consensus. President Gerald Ford, assuming office after Nixon's resignation, tended to downplay détente to placate right-wing Republicans critical to his chances of reelection. The man who surprisingly defeated Ford, Jimmy Carter from Georgia, was not hostile to détente—indeed, he tried to extend it to former enemies like Vietnam and Cuba—but he was generally hostile to the Nixon-Kissinger *style* of foreign policy.

The nationally unknown Carter came to power on an "antipolitical" platform, promising to restore trust, honesty, and openness to government and to make it more instrumentally efficient. He was, in many ways, ideally typical of the liberal American response to the moral and spiritual crisis (as he himself identified it) the country faced after Vietnam and Watergate. Carter promised to resist the influence of special interests that he saw as corrupting his own Democratic Party, and he set out to solve the complex problems of government through dedicated work, deliberation, and the power of rational analysis. Like religiously minded presidents of yore, Carter sought a real public good that could triumph over selfish interests. He was sure of his own born-again goodness and as convinced as Woodrow Wilson had been that good intentions and hard work would succeed politically. Yet his most persistent theme was that good legislation alone would never solve America's greatest problem, which was its moral and spiritual crisis. This was evidenced in "the growing doubt about the meaning of our lives and in the loss of a unity and purpose for our nation." Carter pointed to the recent history of political assassinations, to Vietnam, to Watergate, to economic inflation, and to increasing U.S. dependence on foreign energy. Renewal at home was desperately required, but the loss of American faith had its chief source in the sins of U.S. foreign policy.[5]

American political leaders from Jefferson to Hoover would have nodded sagely at Carter's diagnosis: foreign entanglement and militarization had led inexorably to domestic corruption, undermining the meaning of the United States and sullying the purity of its mission. Yet Carter no longer had the choice of relative isolation. He had to find a way to put America back on the path of virtue while maintaining deep entanglement in foreign affairs. He explicitly rejected the view that America must choose at last between idealism and realism, between morality and power. He repudiated the realpolitik views of Nixon-Kissinger as lacking the moral foundations that any U.S. foreign policy must have and that it needed now more than ever to heal the national wound. No foreign policy was viable that failed to balance idealism and realism. It was Carter's contention that America could no longer dominate a world that had become more complicated

—and more dangerous, thanks to the spread of both nuclear and conventional weapons—than Cold War Manicheism allowed. It should no longer want to try. North-South relations were becoming as important as East-West. America had even neglected its relations with allies in Europe and Japan and had not yet understood that transnational issues of resource depletion, the environment, and inflation could not be tackled alone. American experience in Southeast Asia and Soviet experience in Egypt and Syria seemed to prove that superpower manipulation of Third World nationalist movements was counterproductive. And if the example of the United States had been somewhat degraded during the years of turbulence, it could hardly be said that the example of a Soviet-style economy and society provided an attractive alternative. The Cold War might not be quite over, but it was as good as.[6]

If America could not hope to dominate this new environment, it could nevertheless share world leadership with other nations. Carter's new order would be emphatically multilateralist and made safer through the pursuit of nuclear nonproliferation treaties. What he really sought was a realization of the hope of a community of international power that had been destroyed at the start of the Cold War. To avoid the trap that the nation had fallen into through too-zealous anticommunism, however, it must have principles that could order and justify the commitment of its power. Carter therefore took up an idea that had already been advanced by the House of Representatives Committee on Foreign Affairs in its search for a new, post-Vietnam basis for U.S. foreign policy. This was to raise high the banner of human rights (the "wave of the future").[7]

Resorting to a language of human rights that had broad international currency and acceptance was a way of avoiding imperialistic connotations. Human rights could not, by definition, be tied to a particular state but were rather "universally legitimate and recognized claims by every individual upon his or her national society, which that society is duty-bound to recognize and to realize, to respect and to ensure." True, international human rights principles have sometimes themselves been accused of simultaneously furthering and masking the particular selfish interests of Western countries, but such claims have had to contend with a powerful international consensus created under U.N. auspices (no nation, for example, reserved against Articles 55 and 56 of the U.N. Charter, which mandate cooperation on human rights). Rights may often be more honored in the breach, and controversies may flourish about the application of specific rights, or about their extension to new areas such as the environment and economic development. Yet such questions are aired within an arena where their broad legitimacy is accepted. Members of Congress and Carter saw that this gave human rights discourse considerable traction on the world stage. "American values," though they are but the same human rights interpreted and modified by two hundred years of American judicial and political history, could not be guaranteed a similar level of international acceptance, especially after Vietnam.[8]

The beauty of human rights was that they seemed simply moral, unideological, almost apolitical. They could not, by definition, be purely American though their presumed general validity meant that any decent American government or citizen must wish to preserve and uphold them. The defense of American values could be, and painfully had been, interpreted as mere cultural imperialism, a bad-faith assertion of U.S. interests over those of weaker nations. The defense of human rights, on the other hand, could be argued to be the common responsibility of humankind with particular responsibilities determined by capacity to intervene, American capacity being commensurate with the global reach of its power. In place of a standard too firmly attached to nationalist sentiment, therefore, human rights seemed to provide a genuinely external and independent measure against which American virtue itself could and should be effectively judged. Most significantly, it was a standard that could be applied to Latin American dictators as easily as to communist tyrants. America, by adopting the human rights doctrine as central to its foreign policy, would no longer hypocritically and systematically betray its own ideals by supporting unfree regimes for the sake of their anticommunism. The foreign policy contradictions that were the cause of dissensus at home would thus be avoided. If the use of America's power were guided by, and exerted on behalf of, human rights, its foreign policy would possess that virtue the American myth had always claimed for it.

Carter's intention was not to replace the rhetorical tradition of American exceptionalism. Far from undermining the national myth, he hoped that his human rights doctrine would heal the nation by fully realizing it. Under it, American power and American virtue would at last be properly united. In his populist discourse, Carter retained the theme of the special virtue of the American people, arguing, "The people of this country are inherently unselfish, open, honest, decent, competent and compassionate."[9] But a virtuous people's government, he said, had proved itself unworthy of them, betrayed them, and therefore must be reformed. This was flattering to the people but ignored one of the bitterest moral lessons of Vietnam, that American citizens were as capable of being bad (or good) as any other people on earth. Yet what people took as most typical of the Carter attitude was his emphasis not on the virtue of Americans but on their sins. He accepted the humbling experience of Vietnam as salutary, teaching that the United States should be aware of the limits of its own power in an increasingly multipolar world. The characteristic belief in America's difference was reaffirmed, though Carter claimed that its unique virtue had been sadly compromised by its association with false Cold War doctrines.

In place of ideological division, therefore, he envisaged a "global community" governed by the moral responsibilities encoded in international law. Potential conflicts in the world, he claimed, could be dealt with through cooperative and proactive "preventive diplomacy" that addressed them before they became critical. In response to doubters who inquired about the continuing challenge of communism, the Carter administration appealed to the traditional exemplary role by arguing that the success of liberal democracy was a sufficient retort to that. Yet the administration also saw an element of tactical expediency in focusing on human rights. As Carter's national security adviser, Zbigniew Brzezinski, later admitted, it provided "a powerful ideological weapon in the struggle against the Soviet Union and its communist doctrine." Indeed, it was this aspect of the doctrine that would give it continuing appeal and utility after Carter's political demise, even to Republicans who had castigated him for his emphasis on human rights.[10]

Yet the very "neutrality" of human rights discourse meant it could be wielded equally effectively by anybody against anybody, including against the United States. A necessary implication of Carter's doctrine, therefore, was that it would have to be applied at home as well as abroad, and indeed, Carter was very sensitive to possible charges of hypocrisy. Domestically, human rights were to be safeguarded by the actions of an unimperial, responsive, and open presidency that promoted the "common good" (reducible to the good of individuals as bearers of rights guaranteeing dignity, welfare, and equality) and defended that good against the encroachments

and secret machinations of divisive special interests. If domestic application inevitably caused problems (as when Carter's own U.N. ambassador,
Andrew Young, embarrassed him by labeling continuing poverty in the
United States a contradiction of human rights), this was a price that had
to be paid. Before Vietnam, Americans had been too arrogantly certain of
the validity and universal reach of their own values and of their own virtue
in sustaining them. Applying the test of human rights would expose the
realities and make possible a humble acceptance of shortfall followed by
a determination to do better.

Carter's presidency was, of course, beset by many difficulties—economic stagflation, oil and energy shortages, internecine administrative
feuding, resurgent Soviet colonialism, an accelerating arms race, the hostage crisis in Iran—and above all, perhaps, his own inexperience. There
were definite foreign policy successes—the Camp David Accords between
Israel and Egypt that led to peace between those countries, the formali-
zation of relations with the People's Republic of China, the satisfactory
conclusion of a Panama Canal treaty—but such was the aura of gloom
over the nation that Carter's record acquired a sense of abject failure. The
question here is how much of the failure was due to the application of the
human rights doctrine to international affairs. Certainly, polls at the end
of Carter's single term showed that Americans felt less a sense of failed
virtue than of baffled pride. They had been bullied by the Organization
of the Petroleum Exporting Countries (OPEC), humiliated by Ayatollah
Khomeini, out-traded by Japan, and out-gunned by the Soviets. The shocks
of 1979, particularly, had decided the fate of Carter's policy: the left-wing
Sandinistas had won in Nicaragua; a Soviet brigade had been discovered
in Cuba; U.S. diplomats had been seized in Tehran; and, most alarming of
all, the Soviet Union had invaded Afghanistan. Conservatives were quick
to charge the Democratic administration with having "lost" Nicaragua
and Iran, but it was the Soviet action in Afghanistan that pushed Carter
over the edge. The Soviets had acted hubristically and, as it turned out,
very unwisely in entering a backward but fiercely warlike country to prop
up a friendly leftist regime. It was an overreach that proved immensely
costly and ultimately humiliating. From Carter's point of view, however,
the action had decisively answered the lingering question about whether
the Soviet Union was a "status quo" power or one bent on expansion. It
was undoubtedly the latter.[11]

The differences within the administration on how the United States should respond to these developments or provocations were sharpened. Secretary of State Cyrus Vance urged holding fast, arguing that U.S. military intervention abroad should be a last resort to be used only when definite U.S. interests were clearly threatened. Brzezinski advocated a return to Cold War imperatives, including the swift and judicious use of American power in Third World countries to deny them to the communists. His then aide, Madeleine Albright, argued against Vance: "I think that's one of the lessons of Vietnam—we are afraid to use power. The tragedy of Vietnam is that there are a series of people that were in government who felt that the use of power was something alien to America, because it had been misused. I think that what we needed to do was to get at the selective use of that power instead of saying, 'we can't do that.'"[12]

Carter moved closer to the Brzezinski line and away from Vance, leading to the abandonment of the human rights doctrine and the substitution instead of a new "Carter Doctrine" that effectively ended détente. Carter promised to defend America's vital interests wherever and whenever threatened, militarily if necessary, and to punish the Soviets with sanctions for their transgressions. The retreat to Cold War containment was confirmed when Carter began to supply arms and aid to *mujahadin* defying the Soviets in Afghanistan (thus initiating an historical trajectory that would have terrible unforeseen consequences for America in the twenty-first century). The new containment was made more dangerous by daring to think the unthinkable, that the United States might be able to win a "limited" nuclear exchange. Vance resigned and condemned Carter's betrayal of the ideal. Carter himself regarded his policy reversal, even in the midst of it, as a merely temporary, if necessary, postponement of his global community agenda. Nevertheless, the sudden and dramatic volte-face (judged by many even at the time to be a panicky overreaction to Afghanistan) followed by electoral defeat proved the effective death knell for the human rights doctrine as the cornerstone of U.S. foreign policy.[13]

The doctrine had achieved a measure of consensus during Carter's first two years in office and a good deal of public approval, but support ultimately proved shallow. Too many conceptual and practical obstacles lay in the way of instituting it as a moral basis for the conduct of foreign relations. The doctrine was so imprecisely formulated that it proved difficult to operationalize effectively without falling into either naiveté or cynicism. Numerous technical questions—concerning how to obtain human rights data, how to rank countries, how to justify differential responses to states of different power, and so on—also were never to receive satisfactory answers. Furthermore, there was the problem of the resistance of bureaucratic agencies wedded to older imperatives, long-standing clients, and other agendas. The result was that the Human Rights Bureau had been largely marginalized as an agency well before the political maelstrom of 1979–1980 threw everything into frantic disarray.[14] Part of Carter's failure was also certainly due to the fact that his vision of a global community was premature in a world still divided along ideological lines. The USSR's increasingly imperialistic assertion in Africa and the Middle East and the continuing competitive nuclear arms race inevitably heightened American anxiety. This caused domestic political vulnerability that drew U.S. policy inexorably back toward the implacable great power logic of the Cold War: "My enemy's enemy must be my friend whatever the condition of human rights within his borders."

The problem was most dramatically demonstrated in 1979 after Islamic fundamentalists took control of a successful revolution in Iran. Iran was an oil-rich nation of strategic importance both in Middle Eastern politics and as a bulwark against communism in the region (several U.S. military bases were sited there). This was why the United States had installed the Pahlavi dynasty in 1953 and consistently supported it thereafter despite its dismal human rights record. This still-existing strategic imperative gave Carter little option but to pursue the same policy, though he comforted himself with assurances that the shah was moving rapidly toward liberalization. He strained credibility on a 1978 visit, however, when he imprudently toasted the shah as an "enlightened monarch." Iranian opposition members, who had greeted Carter's human rights doctrine with optimism and hope, were deeply disappointed. The exiled Ayatollah Khomeini condemned the president as a hypocrite, foreshadowing the subsequent Iranian hostage crisis that, probably more than anything else, ensured Carter's defeat in 1980.

POWER AND PRIDE: THE REAGAN PRESIDENCY

In the 1980 presidential campaign, Ronald Reagan lambasted Carter for undermining national security and failing to defend America's interests.

Republicans in general disparaged his human rights policy as stressing virtue and morality at the expense of power. George Schultz called it a "cop out," a way of "making us feel better." Kissinger dismissed the policy as "romantic" while Jeane Kirkpatrick called it a conception of the national interest in which U.S. power was, at best, irrelevant.[15]

Kirkpatrick, a former Democrat whose ardent anticommunism pushed her steadily toward the Republican camp, came to Reagan's notice through a 1979 *Commentary* article titled "Dictatorships and Double Standards." This was a harsh critique of Carter for his short-sighted condemnation of President Anastasio Somoza of Nicaragua for human rights violations. Carter had also attempted to establish "normal" diplomatic relations with the Sandinista-dominated revolutionary government that toppled Somoza. Kirkpatrick's attack was ostensibly on "utopianism" and "moralism" in U.S. foreign policy, an attempt to inject greater "realism" with regard to American allies. In fact, it merely sought to substitute the "soft" moralism of Carter for a tough moralism that rationalized conservative anticommunism. She distinguished between "rightist authoritarian" and "totalitarian Marxist" regimes, arguing that the former could be peacefully democratized in time while the latter never could; they could be changed only by supporting anticommunist opponents: "In the final analysis these enemies of freedom can only be deterred from greater aggression . . . by the military capacities of the United States."[16] Kirkpatrick was reiterating the lessons learned from the 1930s except that, unlike postwar leaders, she placed little confidence in institutionalized multilateralism of the kind represented by the United Nations. Though Reagan would appoint her as ambassador to the United Nations, she could see no reasonable ground for expecting the governments of that organization to transcend permanently their own national interests in favor of another country. If salvation, justice, and virtue were to be had, it would be because unhampered American power was selflessly deployed on their behalf. This was an authentic early sounding of themes that would one day gain dominance in the Republican administration of George W. Bush.

They were also themes congenial to Reagan's worldview (and Kirkpatrick would always be an influential adviser to him). As he took office, therefore, it appeared that the human rights strategy had comprehensively failed. Yet human rights rhetoric was not abandoned after Carter. Indeed, the Reagan administration publicly committed itself to the defense of human rights internationally because they remained a convenient weapon for embarrassing the Soviets. Congressional activity on human rights issues of the kind that had predated Carter also continued. Significantly, the logic supporting such congressional initiatives was the same as that which had motivated the Carter administration: "The fact that the [Universal] Declaration [of Human Rights] is formally universally accepted by U.N. members, except Saudi Arabia, has enabled members of the House and Senate not to be seen as cultural imperialists, imposing U.S. standards on other states, but as promoting a common standard of achievement for all peoples."[17]

But human rights were a subsidiary theme for Reagan. His foreign policy emphasized, rather, American machismo. Reagan seemed more intent on reasserting American power and pride—"standing tall" in the world—than in reinventing its virtue. Indeed, the theme of the comprehensive national strategy that his national security team belatedly produced in 1982 was dubbed "prevailing with pride." The first essential foundation for this was revival of the U.S. economy. Yet in the effort to restore economic strength and thus American power, virtue was certainly not ignored. Carter's Christian response to the consciousness of collective sin had been to admit guilt and seek reformation by finding decent grounds for the reestablishment of virtue and self-esteem. This redemptive strategy having failed, Reagan took the simpler course of denial. What "the great communicator" communicated, even more than his simple conservative philosophy, was a huge sense of emotional reassurance conveyed through an attitude of buoyant optimism that the country seemed to crave. He bluffly reassured people that there was nothing fundamentally wrong with America or Americans, nor ever had been. He was alert for any example of individual heroism to which he could point to prove that "America never was a sick society," but rather its heart was strong, good, and true. Any problems they had could easily be fixed if all acted together.[18]

Reagan's second inaugural address was indicative. He summoned the American myth via the spirits of Valley Forge, of Lincoln, of the Alamo, of the settler pushing west with an echoing song: "It is the American sound. It is hopeful, big-hearted, idealistic, daring, decent, and fair. That's our heritage; that is our song. We sing it still. . . . [We are] one people under God, dedicated to the dream of freedom that He has placed in the human heart, called upon to pass that dream on to a waiting and hopeful world."[19] Americans need not encumber themselves with the sense of guilt on which Carter had needlessly dwelt, for they had nothing serious with which to reproach themselves. There was indeed corruption in the land, but that was to be found in a bloated, overweening, over-interventionist, over-taxing national government held hostage by special interests and elitist secular humanists. It was Reagan's mission to deliver a nation of free, virtuous, and godly individuals from these oppressive forces. Reagan's conservatism thus had a distinctly populist hue.

No doubt there was a contradiction in his insistence on enhancing U.S. military power while rhetorically decrying the corruptive power of big government, one that any traditional Jeffersonian would have instantly pointed out. Yet military might was justified by the necessity of continuing and completing the great moral crusade against communism. Reagan constantly compared the 1970s to the 1930s, an era of economic decline at home and appeasement of evil abroad. In his speeches he enlisted presidents from Franklin Roosevelt right through to Johnson to his cause, leaders, he said, who had demonstrated strength, wisdom, fortitude, generosity, and firmness in the great fight (though he conveniently overlooked the fact that, as an advocate of rollback, he had been a consistent critic of their policies). Reagan refused to be chastened by Vietnam, at least in his rhetoric. That period, he claimed, was an aberration in U.S. history. The war had been "a noble cause" justified on anticommunist grounds, and only the confusion wrought by unrepresentative (un-American) radicals had made it seem otherwise. If U.S. troops had come home without a victory, it was not because they were defeated but because they "had been denied permission to win."[20] But Americans must now cast aside weakening doubt and self-recrimination. In June 1982 Reagan proclaimed an era of democratic revolutions in the world that the United States had a sacred duty to defend and further.

Reagan's rhetorical strategy was an unabashed return to the Cold War version of exceptionalism in which virtue equated to anticommunism, with the latter now supplemented by antiterrorism shading into anti-Muslimism. His solution to the problem of the loss of virtue was effectively to deny that it had ever happened. It was not a matter of proof but of assertion and attitude. All that was needed was an optimistic will and the nation would be reborn to its true self. With virtue and innocence complacently assured, Reagan began to address the issue of power and pride by beefing up military spending (gaining "peace through strength"). The logic of his foreign policy position, however—which was rollback cautiously tempered by the Nixon Doctrine—was that the United States should support right-wing regimes facing challenge from radical groups in Latin America and elsewhere. What became known as the Reagan Doctrine proclaimed the right to proceed against Marxist governments because they had gained power illegitimately, that is, undemocratically. Reagan asserted that "we must not break faith with those who are risking their lives on every continent, from Afghanistan to Nicaragua to defy Soviet-supported aggression and secure rights which have been ours from birth."[21] He drew consciously and repeatedly on the traditional mythology to assert that, not only was the exemplary American mission intact, but it must be supplemented by positive support for the rights of others. Commentators usually refer to this as Reagan's reinstatement of Wilsonian internationalism, and certainly, it made the defense of democracy central. Yet Reagan exhibited none of Wilson's fear of the corrupting effects of military power; in the simplified Reaganite view, American power could not be other than virtuous. Nor was Reagan particularly insistent on Wilsonian multilateralism; indeed, his administration was divided on this issue. Secretary of Defense Caspar Weinberger was especially impatient with multilateral approaches that made American decisions subject to constraints from European allies enamored of détente.

Weinberger was impatient, too, with the loss of national will after Vietnam that disabled the use of U.S. military intervention. This indeed acted as the main constraint upon the Reagan Doctrine, for the public's ruling motto was "no more Vietnams." The doctrine had only one major success, in 1983, when Reagan initiated an invasion of the tiny island of Grenada. This was ostensibly on the invitation of the Organization of Eastern Caribbean States and allegedly to accomplish a "rescue mission" of American medical students caught up in the chaos of a leftist revolution gone haywire. Reagan had, before that point, strained to elevate the overthrow of parliamentary democracy in Grenada to a geopolitical level, using the usual imagery of a Marxist "virus" that the revolutionaries would inevitably attempt to spread throughout the region. Many Democrats strenuously opposed the invasion, at least until Soviet and Cuban weapons were uncovered on the island, but the general public greeted it with a surge of enthusiasm.

The public also vigorously applauded the bombing raid that Reagan ordered on Libya in April 1986 to punish its ruler, Colonel Muammar al-Gaddafi, for his support of terrorists in the Palestinian Liberation Organization. Such actions were swift, decisive, and relatively cheap in human and material terms. Robert Tucker noted that their real significance was "demonstrative and symbolic," by which he meant "designed to demonstrate American resolve to the main adversary, the Soviet Union." But an important part of their purpose was to allay the ghost of Vietnam at home, and the response certainly revealed how keenly the public desired that end. Yet rather than rebuilding genuine self-esteem, such actions merely pandered to injured pride, partly because they were so small compared with Vietnam (though smallness was precisely part of their attraction, given the fear of extended and uncontrollable entanglements and sacrifice that Vietnam had bequeathed). Worse, the invasion of Grenada had been immediately preceded by the murder by suicide bomb of 241 U.S. military personnel in Lebanon, an attack that prompted a speedy U.S. withdrawal. (This was one of the incidents that encouraged Osama bin Laden to think the United States weak and ready to crumble if firmly enough pushed.)[22]

More widespread application of the Reagan Doctrine was hampered by opinion polls showing huge majorities opposed to sending troops to places like Nicaragua and El Salvador. Reagan, however, persisted. Indeed, the obsession of his administration with leftist takeovers of Latin American countries, and particularly with Nicaragua, where material American interests were slight, has puzzled many commentators. Much of the answer surely lies in his desire (and that of the Right generally) to replay Vietnam with an outcome more satisfactory to American pride and purpose in the world. The administration deployed all the arguments of the 1950s and 1960s that Vietnam appeared to have discredited: the domino theory (threatening even Mexico), the credibility of the United States as a beacon of freedom, the need to draw the line somewhere to encourage allies and discourage enemies. Secretary of State George Schultz went so far as to state that the administration's goals in Central America were precisely those of Vietnam: democracy, economic progress, and security against aggression. Whether Reagan really wished to send U.S. troops to achieve these aims is, however, very doubtful; indeed, he always promised that his goals were achievable without substantial American sacrifice.[23] But even his attempts to provide material support for right-wing resistance movements (which he lauded in absurdly excessive terms) encountered a major impediment in congressional refusals to extend funding. The desire to circumnavigate Congress undoubtedly led to the National Security Council's imprudent shipment of weapons to Iran in violation of congressional prohibitions and stated policy. This was done in the hope of gaining the release of American hostages in Lebanon, but also to secretly fund Contra forces opposing the Sandinistas in Nicaragua. The Iran-Contra scandal that ensued seriously tainted an otherwise popular president's last years in office.

Reagan remained fruitlessly preoccupied with the periphery even as relations with what he had dubbed the "evil empire" of the USSR—after 1985 under the leadership of Mikhail Gorbachev—shifted rapidly toward a new and sturdier détente. His direct opposition to the Soviets up to that point had been largely confined to tough rhetoric. His practical hope was that American support for anticommunist forces around the world would give the Soviets a lesson in costly imperial overreach; and indeed, in Afghanistan the USSR had found its own Vietnam. Believing the Soviet regime rotten at its core, the Reagan administration considered it only a matter of time before decay turned into collapse. Gorbachev by and large confirmed this script, partly by identifying the desperate need for domestic reform and partly because change moved beyond his control. In seeking more internal openness (*glasnost*) and restructuring (*perestroika*), he inadvertently precipitated the fall of communism and the breakup of the Soviet Union.

TOWARD A NEW WORLD ORDER

Perhaps the most remarkable aspect of Reagan's part in ending the Cold War was how easily his anticommunist intransigence melted before Gorbachev's personal charm and reforming promise. Reagan, it turned out to everyone's surprise, hated nuclear weapons as evil-in-themselves and wished to abolish them, replacing dangerous nuclear deterrence with something else (the main purpose of his Strategic Defense Initiative, so-called Star Wars).[24] In December 1987 he signed an agreement with Gorbachev to destroy all existing stocks of intermediate-range nuclear-tipped missiles. Reagan moved so swiftly on these matters that he alarmed his own staff. Indeed, the suspicions of some harder-headed leader might well have forestalled the changes under way in the Soviet Union, as was demonstrated when the more cautious George H. W. Bush took over the reins of power in 1989.

Bush as vice president had been privately dismayed by Reagan's "sentimentalism." He immediately initiated a "pause" in the progress of the increasingly cozy relations between the Kremlin and the White House, causing Gorbachev extreme anxiety over the effect on his domestic plans for reform.[25] The Bush administration was determined to "go slow" because of its abiding suspicions about the Soviets' real intentions, worry about Gorbachev's longevity, and a concern to strategically advance a policy that would redefine American-Soviet relations for the next century. Its reaction to the democracy movement in China in the spring of 1989, and to the massacre in Tiananmen Square, showed how firmly locked it remained in Cold War thinking. Bush, National Security Adviser Brent Scowcroft, and Secretary of State James Baker worried about the stability of the Chinese government and the potential loss of a counterweight to the Soviets. He aroused public criticism and congressional anger when he merely "deplored" the massacre but preserved close relations with Chinese leaders, refused residency permits for Chinese students in the United States, and granted China most favored nation trading status. The Bush team failed to appreciate, up to the very last moment, how swiftly the old foe would collapse, and in fact tried to prevent the Soviet Union's disintegration. But once the collapse occurred, the world in which traditional Cold War thinking made sense disappeared.

If Cold War rivalry had had one advantage, it was simplification. By apparently fusing America's interest in opposing communism with its responsibility for doing so, it settled foreign policy on a more or less global scale.[26] In the changed geopolitical landscape, this relative simplicity was irrecoverably lost. In many ways, Bush was well suited to such a changed world, being a man of broad diplomatic and administrative rather than political experience. He was in fact always distrusted by the right wing of the Republican Party as a man of too moderate instincts, one with no clear conservative convictions, and certainly not given to overblown rhetoric —"vision," as he said, was "not his thing." He was in fact determined to lower the ideological temperature after the bluster of the Reagan years. His style was labeled "practical intelligence" by its practitioners and "patrician pragmatism" by scholars. In the unpredictable world he had inherited, there was much to recommend such a prudential approach. Bush was, nevertheless, as committed as Reagan to American leadership and the credibility of American power. He showed his willingness to use that power by ordering an invasion of Panama in December 1989. The purpose was to topple that country's leader, General Manuel Antonio Noriega, a former servant of the U.S. government who had become notorious for his brutality and drug trading, but the invasion was condemned by the Organization of American States and the U.N. General Assembly. Bush was unabashed. In August 1990 he made a speech in which he said the world was still a dangerous and unstable place—with terrorists, renegade regimes, and unpredictable rulers—that required a "strong and engaged America" with "military forces able to respond to threats in whatever corner of the globe they may occur."[27]

This speech was made on the very day that Saddam Hussein invaded Kuwait, potentially threatening Saudi Arabia and providing the first great test of Bush's intent. It was somewhat ironic that the uncharismatic Bush should initiate the event that demonstrated decisively that Reagan's avuncular denial had merely soothed the dilemma of American power and virtue without solving it. The Gulf War was truly Bush's war, and the national catharsis produced by victory caused Bush himself to exclaim, "By God, we've kicked the Vietnam syndrome once and for all." The lengthy title of a *Time* magazine piece put it plainly: "Exorcising an Old Demon: A stunning military triumph gives Americans something to cheer about—and shatters Vietnam's legacy of doubt and divisiveness." What had made it work, the article claimed, was a combination of "the rightness of the cause and the swiftness of the victory." Virtue and power had, in other words, been restored and reunited.[28]

Yet the aftermath was less than completely happy. Part of the problem was that Bush had felt the need to go into uncharacteristic rhetorical overdrive to "sell" the war to the American public. He had initially presented the danger of an expansive Iraq to traditional U.S. strategic and economic interests in the region, but immediate public and congressional reaction indicated an unwillingness to go war, as it was seen, for the sake of oil. Obviously, given the character of Kuwait and Saudi Arabia, he could not argue the defense of democracy or, with the end of the Cold War, defense of the Free World. Bush therefore overleaped the Cold War and returned to World War II for his imagery, promptly substituting the story of a dictator as cruel and dangerous as Hitler, one who must not be appeased. His strategy worked (though he only just managed to get Congress to pass resolutions of support), mainly because Saddam was suitably villainous and had undoubtedly broken the peremptory international law against aggression. Yet the story omitted the fact that Saddam had recently been an ally armed by the United States in his war against a common enemy, Islamist Iran. Worse, Bush had painted the butcher of Baghdad in such fiendish terms that his legalistic halting of allied forces at the Iraqi border—a de facto refusal to topple the villain—smacked of absurdity. It was as though the Allies in World War II had turned around and gone home once Hitler had been pushed back inside Germany.[29]

Bush's failure to support a rebellion, which he himself had encouraged, by Shi'ites in the south and Kurds in the north of Iraq, and his tardy provision of an American air shield for the latter in their desperate exodus, made a far messier ending than his simple scenario required. There were good realpolitik reasons for his decision—the divisions between Sunnis, Shi'ites, and Kurds that might cause the breakup of Iraq; the possibility of neighboring Iran exploiting a power vacuum; the unwelcome prospect of a prolonged U.S. occupation and the uncertainties of nation-building; the likelihood that he could not anyway have held together his winning alliance for the sake of such far-reaching goals—but none of them squared well with the simple moral narrative he had constructed. The unsatisfactory conclusion left his son, as a president in very different circumstances, with dangerous feelings of "unfinished business" in Iraq.

Even so, the success of the remarkable international alliance that Bush had masterfully constructed through the United Nations to prosecute the war caused him suddenly to talk in visionary terms about a New World Order. Bush did not precisely elaborate the terms of this order, and as the economy began to slide and the 1992 election approached, he found it expedient to downplay a theme that had aroused public controversy. In many ways, however, it resembled Carter's "global community" and could be seen as a continuation of the structural-liberal, multilateral order the United States had established among Western allies during the Cold War now extended to include former enemies. Bush told National Security Adviser Scowcroft that the Gulf War had crystallized his thinking on foreign policy. The sight of the Americans and the Russians acting as partners for global security had raised the possibility, he said, that the United Nations might finally be able to promote international cooperation to prevent aggression, the role for which it had been created in 1945.[30] If Carter in a time of national retreat had stressed interdependence and shared leadership, however, Bush as president of the only superpower left standing was more inclined to stress America's "global leadership." The Pentagon began studies of strategic alternatives adapted to possible futures that emphasized the readiness of U.S. forces of substantial size and global capacity.

More controversial was a leaked document known as Defense Planning Guidance (DPG) 1994–1999, prepared by, or with input from, Department of Defense intellectuals, many of whom would play important roles during the administration of the second President Bush (Paul Wolfowitz, I. Lewis Libby, and Zalmay Khalilzad, who were all aides to then–Secretary of Defense Dick Cheney). The DPG recommended strategies to maintain U.S. hegemonic power by positively preventing the reemergence of a multipolar or bipolar world and envisaged no significant role for the United Nations. It rhetorically raised the options of isolation, collective security, and balance of power, only to dismiss them for quite traditional reasons: isolation disregarded vital U.S. interests overseas; collective security dangerously entangled U.S. interests with those of other nations; and balance of power historically tended to collapse into major wars. The collective obverse of these was, obviously, an engaged but diplomatically unentangled United States whose preponderant power would secure permanent peace. This was "global leadership" indistinguishable from imperial dominance. If American power remained unchallengeable, and was used to protect the interests of others, it could prevent the resurgent ambition of countries like Germany, Japan, Russia, and China, thus creating a *Pax Americana* and permanently securing the conditions of global economic development. This was manifestly the post–World War II conservative wish for the unhampered deployment of virtuous American power translated into a policy proposal. The DPG also outlined a strategy for dealing with the threat of the spread of weapons of mass destruction that went beyond deterrence and containment to approve preemptive, possibly offensive military action. It thus proved to be highly prophetic (and was highly praised by Cheney as defining America's new role in the world), but at the time its hawkishness raised such a storm that it was quickly shelved. A revision some months later softened the more offensive language about keeping allies down, but its ideas were essentially the same.[31]

Bush himself, in the freedom provided by a lost election, outlined his own position, which was much more circumspect than the DPG and made multilateral institutions central. He recommended "collective engagement" to prevent regional aggression. His stated goals were distinctly Wilsonian—the security of the international community of democratic nations against unpredictable threats and the encouragement of emergent democracies everywhere—as was the insistence on American moral and material leadership. "Leadership" did not mean unilateralism, however, for the United States would soon exhaust itself if it attempted to be the world's sole police officer. Whenever possible, it should lead international coalitions, each nation contributing in a manner appropriate to its strength and stake in the outcome. Yet the sole superpower must be prepared to act alone if necessary. Military force should not be a first option and should not be instantly employed against every outrage; a prudent judgment of particular sets of circumstances would always be required. Despite Bush's commitment to the United Nations and its role, collective engagement did not necessarily imply a system of *collective security*. The decision to act militarily would be solely a matter for Americans, not one automatically triggered by multilateral commitments. But in that case, some set of criteria would be needed for determining when military commitment was appropriate. Here, Bush drew on principles previously enunciated by Caspar Weinberger (they would eventually become known as the Powell Doctrine because of Colin Powell's adoption of them in his rise to chairman of the Joint Chiefs of Staff). In a 1984 speech titled "The Uses of Military Power," Weinberger had argued that the United States should send combat troops overseas *only* if doing so was vital to U.S. national interests; when the nation had a clear intent to win in the shortest possible time (which meant assembling sufficient, indeed overwhelming, force to do the job); if there were clearly defined and regularly monitored political and military objectives and a clear plan of withdrawal upon victory; with reasonable assurance of the support of the American people; and as a last resort after all other options had failed.[32]

These were stringent conditions that counseled extreme caution, clearly reflecting the continuing desire to avoid another Vietnam-style trauma. They were hardly the principles of a rampant superpower intent on imposing its will upon the world. Before his ignominious electoral defeat in 1992, Bush had demonstrated the appropriate caution by refusing to intervene in post-coup Haiti or to contribute U.S. troops to a

U.N. peacekeeping force in Yugoslavia, which was breaking apart in an ethnically murderous civil war. Colin Powell, under both the Bush and subsequent Clinton administrations, was especially adamant that pressure to intervene in Bosnia to protect Muslims from Serbian atrocities should be resisted because the action would not meet the necessary criteria and risked escalation and entrapment. There would be no Bays of Pigs, Beiruts, or Vietnams on his watch. For political reasons, however, he did reluctantly agree in the closing days of the Bush administration to the sending of twenty-eight thousand troops on a "humanitarian" mission to Somalia, where anarchy and warlordism had created conditions of acute famine.[33] The mission violated nearly all the principles of the Weinberger-Powell Doctrine and in the end was deeply disillusioning, but by that time it was Bill Clinton who had to bear the consequences.

CONCLUSION

During the 1990s, traditional themes persisted. It remained a commonplace that the United States, as the world's first great democracy, must remain a leader of some sort in the international quest for peace, democracy, and economic development. Its latter-day economic recovery, coinciding with the weakening of formerly strong competitors, sustained its role as the main anchor of the international economy. This, along with its military might and its global extension, meant that American leadership must be of the engaged sort rather than the purely exemplary. What's more, it was clear during Clinton's tenure that most nations still wanted and sought U.S. economic and political leadership, even if they were less patient with signs of U.S. domination. America remained, as Madeleine Albright was fond of saying, the "indispensable nation."

Meanwhile, the end of the Cold War had relieved the nation (and indeed the world) of much of the anxiety of a nuclear conflict triggered either intentionally or accidentally. The issue of American power therefore seemed during the Clinton years less fraught with catastrophic consequences. With the nation apparently secure in itself, the main foreign policy questions that arose were ones of when to intervene for humanitarian reasons in regional conflicts where U.S. interests were not obviously at stake. Conflicting attitudes toward this issue showed that the United States had not yet become comfortable with its own great power nor confident of the conditions in which it could be safely disposed.

One interesting development was that many liberals who had regarded American military power since Vietnam as dangerous and illegitimate became converted to the possibility, or even necessity, of its use
for preventing genocidal crimes or supporting democratic governments
abroad. Who else, after all, had the means?[34] Thus 1994 witnessed the
surprising sight of liberals who had opposed the Gulf War pressuring
Clinton to order an invasion of Haiti to replace the democratically elected
leader Jean-Bertrand Aristide, overthrown in a military coup, while Senator Bob Dole, ex-President Bush, James Baker, and Dick Cheney warned
against it on the ground that no important U.S. interest was at stake.
Clinton reluctantly succumbed to liberal pressure on this occasion, and
would do so again later over the Bosnian issue. But such interventions in
highly complex problems with no easy or swift solutions remained deeply
problematic for policy makers still operating under the long shadow of
Vietnam. No reliably settled position had been reached on this when the
attacks of September 11, 2001, thrust the United States into a new era
of conflict that raised sharply once more the old dilemma of power and
virtue.

CHAPTER SEVENTEEN

Offended Innocence, Righteous Wrath

AMERICAN MYTHOLOGY fostered suspicion of power in all its forms but harbored a special fear for the corrupting and brutalizing effects of militarization. Yet Americans always understood that military strength was a source of both national pride and worldly respect, and after World War II they came to accept that it was also necessary for combating evil. But Vietnam destroyed the reconciliation that world war had effected. The misjudged commitment in Southeast Asia corroded innocent virtue and humbled republican pride. The result was not just confusion but an obsession with the dangers of military power that, in the long run, elevated the military dimension of international relations above the diplomatic. Discussions of foreign policy after Vietnam tended to revolve endlessly around the question of when and how the use of military force was justified. It did not matter which of the two hurts, to pride or to innocence, was most deeply felt—the effect was much the same. The mortification of wounded pride instilled a desire to restore self-respect through a buildup of military strength and demonstrations of its effective use. Concern with the loss of virtue, on the other hand, produced a preoccupation with the legitimacy of U.S. military power and ways to keep it safe and pure in the future. (It is sobering to think that the Powell Doctrine, with its insistence on a swift victory and a clean exit, might have precluded American participation in World War II.)

The preoccupation with pride and power found a natural home on the conservative wing of the Republican Party, converted from America First isolationism after World War II by a combination of American supremacy and anticommunist crusade. The paralysis of American power after Vietnam caused red-blooded Republican patriots to gnash their teeth in frustration. The restoration of American pride and honor depended, for them, on strength, and strength was measured first and foremost in terms of available weaponry—more and better missiles, planes, submarines, tanks, and so on. They depended, too, on a frank willingness to use that strength whenever necessary for the defense of clear U.S. interests. For this to be possible, it was necessary to remove the trammels that had been placed on the executive branch of government after Vietnam, and to restore the authority of the so-called Imperial Presidency. As conservatism gained political ground among Republicans, this muscular attitude enabled the party to present itself as the party of strength. It has often been said that Americans came to distrust Democrats in foreign policy because they had led the nation into Vietnam, but it was rather that post-Vietnam Democrats, with their anxious liberal consciences, were tarred as weaklings. Though Democrats had successfully led the nation in two world wars, had taken it into conflicts in Korea and, yes, Vietnam (both rather ignominiously terminated by Republican administrations), though they had stared down the Soviets over Cuba, people nevertheless came to trust the Republican Party more in foreign policy. It was a field, it seemed, in which an image of John Wayne toughness carried more persuasive power than a historical record. True, a Republican president had led the United States to triumph in the Persian Gulf and nevertheless had been defeated by a Democrat whose foreign policy pronouncements sounded positively Carterish. But Clinton's victory could be explained (aside from a vote-splitting third-party candidate, Ross Perot) by the very fact that foreign policy was not an important issue in an election focused determinedly on the economy and on Bush's broken tax promises.

It was not surprising, then, that when an ultraconservative administration came to power in 2000, its foreign policy team should be made up of figures whose predilection was for military rather than diplomatic affairs. Most were people who had spent their government careers either in the armed forces or as Defense Department bureaucrats striving to build America's military strength (in Donald Rumsfeld's case, to reshape it for a new era). It was strange but telling that those with actual army or navy experience—the State Department's Powell and Richard Armitage, respectively, who had both served in Vietnam—were the cautious ones with respect to military force, while the men they contemptuously referred to as the "chicken hawks"—Vice President Dick Cheney and Rumsfeld, Wolfowitz, and his aide "Scooter" Libby, all at the Defense Department— were conservative ideologues ready and willing to wield it. None had the background of a Dean Acheson or an Averell Harriman or the propensities of even a George Marshall, who, though an indomitable old soldier, left his most considerable mark in the field of diplomacy.[1]

Yet the George W. Bush administration, though determined to keep America strong, and perpetually stronger than anyone else, initially con-ducted a self-willed foreign policy rather than a bellicose one. The attack of September 11 changed everything. It forced the United States to defend itself against an unconventional enemy but also provided an opportunity for conservative hawks to implement strategies they had devised under the first President Bush. If this development appeared to end the shuffling uncertainty about American power that had marked the presidency of Bill Clinton, it also plunged the nation back into the dilemma that had been somewhat muffled for most of his tenure, that of how to exercise military power effectively while preserving innocent virtue.

THE CLINTON INTERLUDE

Though Bill Clinton, in campaigning mode, repeatedly hammered the theme of Bush's economic mismanagement, he also criticized the presi-dent's foreign policy for being unprincipled, realpolitik pragmatism, much as Carter had earlier attacked the Nixon-Kissinger regime. He spoke elo-quently of the moral themes traditionally embodied in U.S. foreign policy and seemed to promise, via U.N. action, the advancement of democracy around the world. He even supported the idea of a standing U.N. force to fight terrorism and prevent ethnic violence. He also rhetorically raised high the banner of human rights, vowing to link China's trading privileges to its human rights record and to apply economic sanctions in response to Chinese violations. He promised relief for the Muslim inhabitants of Sarajevo in the Balkans, under siege in the Bosnian civil war, and accused Bush of betraying democracy by siding with tyrants in order to maintain the status quo.[2]

Once in power, however, Clinton, the ambitious New Democrat, was less interested in foreign policy than in domestic measures aimed at carving a centrist "third way" between conservatism and Left-liberalism. Events abroad soon forced him to pay attention, but even then, he made no serious effort to revive Carter's human rights doctrine.[3] An initial attempt to link China's human rights record with its trading status produced a harsh Chinese backlash and anyway contradicted the administration's designation of the developing Chinese market as central to its geoeconomic strategy. The disastrous experience of intervention in Somalia further discouraged emphasis on human rights as a basis for foreign policy. Clinton had contributed eagerly at first to this mission, altered at the request of the United Nations from a purely humanitarian to a military one. But Somalia provided a bitter lesson in the difficulties of effective peace-making in a poor but armed, anarchic country. Pictures of the bodies of U.S. soldiers being dragged through the streets of Mogadishu in October 1993 caused revulsion at home, and the Vietnam syndrome returned with a vengeance. Though polls showed a plurality of people believing that warlord Mohammed Aidid, responsible for the violence, should be hunted down, many in Congress demanded immediate withdrawal. Clinton, fielding familiar objections about American credibility and the need to provide global leadership, refused to be stampeded and conducted an orderly withdrawal over six months.

Nevertheless, he had been once-burnt and would never again show enthusiasm for committing U.S. forces where no overwhelming U.S. interests, other than moral ones, were at stake or no prior obligation existed. He withdrew the promise of support for a U.N. army and laid down strict conditions for any future U.S. involvement in peacekeeping missions. If he was nevertheless sometimes pressured by domestic and international forces into commitment—as he was in Haiti, Bosnia, and Kosovo—it was only very reluctantly and after much foot-dragging, then typically opting for a limited engagement in time or tactics that risked the fewest American lives. Ironically, Clinton downplayed human rights issues at the very time they were emerging as a major theme in world politics. The rest of the developed world, and sometimes the United Nations itself, became positively Carterish in making human rights a cause for intervention, including armed intervention, in the internal affairs of sovereign states.[4]

The Clinton administration's reactive stumbling from crisis to crisis made it appear to lack any consistent foreign policy, but in fact Secretary of State Warren Christopher had laid out three priorities for U.S. foreign policy in the post–Cold War world. These were to strengthen the domestic economy, to modernize the military within budgetary constraints, and to encourage the spread of democracy in the world. Most important with respect to the last priority was the future of post-Soviet Russia (whose reform process might still fail) and the newly independent states of the former Soviet Union (whose relation to their former imperial master might turn hostile). Russia and the Ukraine still possessed nuclear weapons systems whose integrity would be endangered by political upheaval, and their newly impoverished scientists might be tempted to sell their services to "rogue states." A prosperous and democratic Eastern world, on the other hand, would be a partner for the United States in the quest for international stability and would moreover act as a bulwark against radical Islam. The Clinton administration was not unaware, either, that a resurgence of Russian enmity would play into the hands of the Republicans, whose triumph in winning the Cold War was considerably tempered by the fact that it had robbed them of the prime external threat that united their various constituencies and justified large military budgets. For all these reasons, the administration was determined to use its diplomatic strength and economic assistance to encourage Russia to become a modern pluralistic, democratic, market society.[5]

Unfortunately, Russian political instability, economic chaos, defaults on loans, and involvement in a bloody war in Chechnya over the following years undermined administration hopes for a stable partnership. Relations were not helped when the Clinton administration, responding to pressure from former communist states, decided in 1996 to expand the NATO alliance by admitting Poland, Hungary, and the Czech Republic over strenuous Russian protests. In 1994 Russia had joined the Partnership for Peace, a cooperative security agreement between NATO and East European countries, and even participated after its own fashion in peacekeeping in Bosnia, despite its sympathies with Slobodan Milosevic and his aggressive Serbs (fellow Slavs). But expanding NATO to their very doorstep was too much for Russians, who interpreted it as evidence of a new containment policy—which, in part, it undoubtedly was. Their feeling of insecurity deepened in 1999 when Clinton, fearing Russia's inability to control its own ballistic missile facilities, approved a scaled-down version of Reagan's "Star Wars" missile shield project (though danger from rogue states was advanced as another reason).

The policy toward Russia, though disappointing in its results, was merely a logical application of the administration's broader foreign policy program. Even NATO expansion was justified as creating the security architecture within which Euro-Atlantic countries could be encouraged toward greater democratization and liberal economic development. The general aim was to keep the United States fully engaged in the world and to support that engagement by promoting a healthy, growing economy at home and an enlarged "zone of democratic peace" abroad by facilitating the processes of economic globalization. It was perfectly in line with the extension of the structural-liberal Western order that President Bush had envisaged and encouraged. Geopolitics would be supported, as always, by geoeconomics, retooling America to meet the challenges of the global economy while strategically positioning the nation so as to be able to direct it through free-trading agreements with emergent regional blocs. American leadership would aim at encouraging emerging nations to liberalize their economies, open their capital markets to the world, and reform their banking, financial, and trading institutions.[6]

Clinton was here drawing most immediately on an economic strategy produced during the Bush administration by Robert Zoellick to underpin the proposed New World Order. This strategy identified big emerging markets (China, Indonesia, India, South Korea, Mexico, Brazil, Argentina, Poland, Turkey, and South Africa) into which U.S. trade could expand to the mutual benefit of all. It was an idea that went back, of course, to the very foundations of the republic. Liberty, in the guise of economic liberty, advanced prosperity and peace, as the American example had shown—a principle that could be extended globally. What was good for America was, coincidentally, good for the world, and vice versa. What made this old dream seem now possible and plausible was the end of the ideological cleavage of the Cold War. Clinton's undersecretary of commerce for international trade, Jeffrey Garten, said, "We are entering an era when foreign policy and national security will increasingly revolve around our commercial interests, and when economic diplomacy will be essential to resolving the great issues of our time."[7] On these assumptions it made sense to elevate the status of zealous Secretary of State for Commerce Ron

Brown and to create new agencies devoted, on the example of Herbert Hoover, to the active promotion of U.S. enterprise abroad.

The geoeconomic project encountered several international financial emergencies that seemed to show that global interdependence, however promising in theory, was extremely dangerous in practice unless international institutions and mechanisms existed to prevent the instant transmission of crisis from one region to another.[8] It remained, nevertheless, distinctive of the Clinton approach to foreign policy. There still existed after the Cold War, to be sure, recalcitrantly undemocratic rogue regimes that were hostile to the United States and threatened to disrupt peaceful progress if not properly managed. Cuba was identified as one of these for purely traditional and domestic political reasons, but the countries of real concern were Iraq, Iran, Libya, and North Korea. All, save Libya, which made conciliatory moves during the Clinton years, would remain thorns in the side of the subsequent administration of George W. Bush. The fear that each or all of them might be developing weapons of mass destruction (WMDs) to threaten neighbors or deliver to terrorists deeply concerned the Clinton team. Clinton saw it as an American duty to neutralize, contain, and eventually transform or "normalize" these states. The rise of moderate forces in Iran in 1997 raised hopes that it might indeed prove reformable in the long run. North Korea was more problematic, and Clinton felt it necessary to threaten air strikes against suspected atomic installations there. In the end, however, he chose to engage the country by offering trade openings and the eventual lifting of economic sanctions if Kim Jong-il, the "Dear Leader," renounced nuclear weapons and ballistic missiles.

In Iraq, Clinton accepted the legacy (in fact a low-level war) that George H. W. Bush had bequeathed him. He affirmed the Bush position that normal relations were impossible while Saddam Hussein was in power, which was in effect a demand for "regime change." Yet there was a good deal of incoherence, if not outright absurdity, in trying to encourage a result that Bush had declined to effect in his early curtailment of the Gulf War. The hope of both Bush and Clinton was that an internal uprising (of the kind Saddam had often brutally crushed) or a leadership coup (that Saddam was adept at countering) would accomplish the task against a leader weakened by a combination of economic sanctions, U.S.-imposed "no-fly zones" in the Kurdish north and Shi'ite south, and the work of

U.N. weapons inspectors trying to locate and dismantle WMD programs. After Saddam's refusal to cooperate further with the inspectors in 1998, U.S. and British planes bombed Iraqi missile defenses for four days, and regime change became official policy (though military action was explicitly excluded as a means). This was containment policy of a very active kind, but it was not noticeably effective in attaining its ultimate goal. A decade after the end of the Gulf War, Saddam's grip on power seemed as strong as ever, even if the country was more impoverished. It was perhaps little wonder, then, that members of the new George W. Bush administration should come to power harboring desires, bordering on obsession, to bring the tyrant down.

Iraq remained a persistent irritant during Clinton's tenure, an annoying itch that could not be satisfactorily scratched. It was never in the cards that Clinton would launch a full-scale war and invasion of Iraq unless Saddam renewed his attacks on Kuwait or other neighbors. As commander in chief, Clinton proved a rather reluctant warrior (his relations with the military were always strained because of his alleged draft-dodging in the Vietnam years and his efforts to have gays openly accepted in the armed forces). What small stomach he might have had for military intervention had been definitely lost in Somalia. The most disconcerting thing about Somalia was precisely that it had been a humanitarian intervention supported by the United Nations and popular with the public, one in which no suspicion of an imperialistic motive could be raised. Yet it had ended in disappointment and disillusionment, further increasing American diffidence with regard to the use of its military power. There thus remained during the Clinton presidency great uncertainty about how to match, in any general and theoretical way that the American public would support, American power to American interests and responsibilities in a changed world. Clinton, though a glib rhetorician, capable of drawing on any and every traditional source of persuasion as it suited his immediate purposes, never convincingly enunciated any central guiding doctrine that would solve this problem.[9]

Nevertheless, it was remarkable the extent to which Clinton managed, in an undoctrinaire way and despite his own domestic scandals, to reinstate the United States as the honest power broker of first resort in the world's trouble spots. This was a tribute, not just to American power, but to a restoration of international trust in the good offices of the president. The relative freedom of U.S. foreign policy under Clinton from the symbolic issues of pride and virtue that had so highly colored it for thirty years proved a blessing. Polls in 1998 showed that the public rated his competence in foreign affairs very highly. Clinton, for all his personal embarrassment at home, could be trusted to put on a bold face as leader of the most powerful nation on earth while nevertheless avoiding empty triumphalism. A majority of the public credited him as standing appropriately for both U.S. interests and the general right. It was hardly his fault that his relentless brokering of negotiations between Israel and the Palestinians, upon which he placed such store for his own posterity, came to naught in the end. True, there were still people out there who hated America, particularly among freelance Islamists resentful of the presence of U.S. troops still stationed after the Gulf War in the land of the Prophet. Some of these people, emboldened by their success against the Russians in Afghanistan, went so far as to declare war on the United States in 1998. They perpetrated lethal terrorist attacks on U.S. targets at home and abroad to which the Clinton administration (and, it must be said, a Republican Congress) responded only very ineffectually.

But few Americans fully appreciated the depth of the hatred involved, and no one seems to have anticipated the terrorists' capacity to deliver a massive physical and psychological blow to America on its own soil. The attack of September 11, 2001, provoked an instant reactive sense of offended American innocence and produced a foreign policy reversal by George W. Bush that plunged the nation into new, uncertain adventures abroad. These would dramatically raise, once again, the perennial dilemma of U.S. foreign policy that is the subject of this book.

SEPTEMBER 11 AND AFTER

I began this book by pointing to Bush's initial promise to demonstrate both "strength" and "humility" in his foreign policy. "Strength" turned out to mean using the freedom of action afforded by superpower status to pursue a narrowly conservative view of U.S. interests. The suspicion that "humility" might likewise turn out to be of the Uriah Heep variety appeared to be confirmed by Bush's demonstrated preference for unilateral American action. His out-of-step stances on a variety of issues—the Kyoto greenhouse gas accord, trade and tariff agreements, long-standing arms treaties, an international criminal court—upset and offended even traditional allies. But if this was arrogance, it seemed motivated more by a determined selfishness and a pandering to domestic corporate interests —Bush's "base," as he called them—than by a desire to impose on others.[10] Humility seemed best interpreted as a rejection of well-meaning Clintonesque "meddling" in other nations' business; even after the Afghan phase of the "war on terror," Bush stressed his opposition to "nation-building" in defiance of what seemed like necessary policy. Yet the event that had produced the war against the Taliban and their Al Qaeda allies, the attacks of September 11, inevitably changed the thrust of the Bush foreign policy agenda.

Bush quickly labeled the terrorist assault an attack, not just on America, but on "freedom and democracy" generally. More plausibly, it was a reactionary religious attack on the foremost power of a materialistic, infidel, and increasingly global civilization, and thus a potential threat to any established state whether democratic or not. And Bush, in his initial period of international coalition-building for intervention in Afghanistan, had to persuade undemocratic nations like China, Pakistan, and Kazakhstan that the enemy was indeed common. He also had to gain the acquiescence of nondemocratic Arab states to make persuasive his claim that the war on terror was not a religious crusade against Islam. A war fought with such a disparate coalition against a difficult, nontraditional enemy was better argued on straightforward collective security grounds than as a general defense of freedom or democracy. In fact, Bush's rhetoric to justify U.S. actions and build support oscillated insecurely in this early phase of his diplomacy, but the general tendency was to stress the common threat within a simple good-versus-evil scenario. The terrorists, and terrorism generally, were repeatedly branded "evil" and "inhuman," a danger to "civilization." Such unmitigated evil arguably justified any and all attempts by the United States and its allies to eradicate it from the earth.

Of course, the good-against-evil stance fell squarely within the Manichean anticommunist mode, but the altered situation at home also induced a collateral impulse to revive, in a more forthright manner, the appeal to specifically American values that Vietnam had discredited. The surge of popular patriotism that followed the shock of September 11 bemused Americans themselves; it was suddenly okay again to be American and proud of it. The questioning of liberal intellectuals became suspect if, in trying to understand why America should be the object of such hatred, "understanding" carried the implication that America was some-how to blame. The national expression of unembarrassed patriotism was premised on a general experience of the United States as clearly the inno-cent victim. Not since Pearl Harbor had the case been quite so clear, had righteous horror and defensive retaliatory action been so plainly justi-fied. In 1991, the unprovoked aggression of Saddam Hussein had made America seem right in fighting the Gulf War, but psychologically, nothing could put a nation so firmly and categorically in the right as suffering such aggression itself. The appalling acts of fanatical terrorists restored to Americans, more viscerally than anything had done since the end of World War II, a feeling of innocence, albeit in the form of innocence offended. American power, judiciously employed to correct the offense and to counter further danger, had the opportunity to be once again the servant of American virtue rather than its betrayer. More thoroughly than any foreign war, however just, more than any facile rhetoric about strength and humility, an attack on innocent civilians in the homeland had appar-ently rejoined the partnership of power and virtue sundered by the Cold War and Vietnam.

Bush responded in the immediate term with restraint and then with decisive action that momentarily routed (though, ominously, it failed to eliminate) the Taliban and Al Qaeda in Afghanistan. He therefore quite properly reaped the political benefits of the tragedy. As the bulk of the nation aligned itself behind his administration's antiterror policies, the Democrats found themselves effectively stymied. The perceived necessity for bipartisan unity was something on which no president could or would fail to capitalize politically, especially one who, after a hung election de-cided in his favor by a conservative Supreme Court, had had the shadow of illegitimacy hovering about him. The surge of popular patriotism and confused pride encouraged Bush to rekindle faith in American values at home and to reaffirm abroad American uniqueness and the importance of the American example. When he promoted American values on a visit to China, the press pointedly challenged his officials on whether this con-flicted with his vow to conduct a humble foreign policy. National Security Adviser Condoleezza Rice replied that it did not. Bush had rallied his coalition against terrorism, she said, "not by speaking in shades of gray about what it was we're facing, but in speaking in sharp, morally clear terms."[11] Yet there was reason to doubt that the moral clarity lost in the mid-twentieth century could be so easily restored by a national tragedy, or that the danger that American values might again become identified with imperial arrogance was thereby dissolved. It was significant that Bush's new rhetorical strategy coincided with a decidedly aggressive turn toward Iraq as the main target of choice after Afghanistan.

Insider reports reveal that the question of Iraq arose immediately after the September 11 attacks, with the president and top officials exhibiting a strong desire that a link between them be sought and found. Bob Woodward notes that Bush asked Defense Secretary Rumsfeld to start a war plan for Iraq on November 21, 2001, but to do it in secret to avoid "enormous international angst and domestic speculation." In his State of the Union address in January 2002, Bush identified Iraq, along with Iran and North Korea, as part of an "axis of evil," states capable of supplying WMDs to terrorists (despite Iran's having been politically supportive of the U.S. action in Afghanistan). This immediately shifted the war on terror to a potential war on states allegedly supplying terrorists. Divisions between Powell, who was against a preemptive (or preventive) war, and Cheney, who was determinedly and even obsessively for it, reportedly became bitter in the months that followed. Bush took the final decision in January 2003, but by then the preparatory buildup of troops and materiel in the Iraq theater had reached such levels, and the pressure from key figures within the administration had become so intense, that a decision *not* to go would have been the surprising one. Yet clear justification of the invasion had yet to be provided. Absent convincing proof of Saddam's relationship to September 11 or Al Qaeda, the plan to preemptively strike a fully sovereign state in contravention of international law predictably encountered more international resistance than had the Afghan operation, whose motives were generally understood.[12]

Bush, arguing that containment was not working and was anyway not appropriate in a post–September 11 world, responded with a take-it-or-leave-it attitude. His threat of unilateral American action alarmed even staunch allies in the governments of Britain and Australia who could not be certain of carrying their populations outside a multilateral approach through the United Nations that had exhausted all diplomatic avenues. Meanwhile, polls at home showed that the American people had an inclination to trust the president but little real conviction or enthusiasm for attacking Iraq, however evil its government, without U.N. legitimation.

Encouraged by Powell, Bush was reluctantly forced to approach his goal by seeking a new, stronger U.N. resolution on weapons inspections in Iraq that would allow armed intervention if, as expected, Saddam failed fully to comply. To demonstrate U.S. solidarity and put pressure on the U.N. Security Council to confirm such a resolution, he contrived to win a congressional resolution approving executive military action against Iraq if deemed necessary. The politics were very adroitly managed. Despite an increasing array of dissenting or warning voices—from Democratic senators like John Kerry and Robert Byrd, from voices within the CIA, from General Anthony Zinni (who had been Bush's own envoy to the Middle East), and from members of Bush-père's administration, Brent Scowcroft and James Baker—Bush triumphed over a cowed Democratic leadership.

Bush's arguments dwelled mainly on the security risk of a mad, bad, and dangerous dictator who was flouting U.N. authority by building WMDs that might be handed on to terrorists, though the bringing of freedom and democracy to the Iraqi people was often noted as a subsidiary benefit. The United Nations (and most crushingly the French) failed to be convinced even after Colin Powell, in his most inglorious hour, displayed to the General Assembly the alleged evidence of Saddam's continuing weapons program. The administration thought the international organization had showed it deserved the contempt with which American conservatives habitually regarded it and, disdaining its strictures, pressed on with its plans. It managed successfully to create the impression in the minds of many Americans that Saddam and Al Qaeda were linked, and even that the dictator was behind September 11, which no unbiased commentator ever believed. Yet devious if effective politics did not substitute for a clear explanation of the pressing need to invade Iraq. Very little, or only belated, attention was paid to questions about the real imminence of the threat Saddam posed; the likely consequences of war for the stability of Iraq and the whole Middle East; whether attacking Iraq was the best way to prevent the sorts of terrorist incidents then occurring in places like Kuwait, Pakistan, the Philippines, and Bali; the nature of the government that was to replace Saddam; the nature of long-term U.S. commitment to post-Saddam Iraq, its real costs, and how these were to be met; or why Iraq was a different case from North Korea (which, in the midst of the debate, had embarrassingly confessed to having broken its nonproliferation promises and produced nuclear weapons) or Iran (which also seemed to be heading down the nuclear road). What *was* certain was that the originally hands-off president had been replaced by one willy-nilly committed to intervention on a large scale. The question therefore arose as to the real strategic goals of an administration dominated by neoconservative idealists and conservative hawks of a strongly ideological bent.

The definitive story of the genesis and progress of the second Gulf War is a subject for future historians, who will have to assess the genuine weight of fear that the thought of implacable terrorists armed with WMDs aroused, and to consider the reasons behind what appears, on the face of it, to be a piece of bold but imprudent political opportunism. (A flood of revelatory and mostly highly critical books and articles by insiders and others began to flow, however, long before the final exit of a severely lame-ducked president.[13]) The failure to find any WMDs after the invasion did not mean that the fear was not real, but the constant shifting in the administration's justifications for the war strongly indicated that the real reasons were ones that could not be easily sold to the American people. The influence of Paul Wolfowitz, who had been prescient during the Soviet era about the strategic importance of the Middle East and about the dangers of Saddam afterward, has often been pointed to with respect to what amounted to a semicovert but elaborate and ambitious geopolitical enterprise. This involved remaking the Middle East via a democratic Iraq that would replace Saudi Arabia as America's chief Arab ally in the region, thus providing a powerful boost to moderates in Iran, thus leading to the withdrawal of support for Hezbollah and other radical groups, thus isolating Syria and reducing pressure on Israel, thus also undermining Yasir Arafat and allowing a permanent solution to the Israeli-Palestinian question. It was a goal and a justification that Bush himself would increasingly stress after the failure of the WMD justification and the onset of an intransigent Iraqi insurgency. Yet by concentrating publicly on the alleged immediate threat and not addressing the long-term costs of the more grandiose plan, the administration had failed to build the political support such extensive national commitment would require, and which, of course, they must have had little confidence in attaining.

Before the invasion, some commentators had no doubt that September 11 had provided both the impetus and the opportunity for the Bush administration to reshape Middle Eastern politics in a way that better aligned them with American interests and American values. Neoconservative writer William Kristol, formerly of Bush-père's administration and now editor of *The Weekly Standard*, lambasted erstwhile colleagues Scowcroft and Powell as "appeasers" who "hate the idea of a morally grounded foreign policy that seeks aggressively and unapologetically to advance American principles around the world." Conservative columnist William Safire similarly railed against "appeasers," arguing that one of the administration's purposes was to make the Middle East safe for democracy—to free all Persians and Arabs repressed by monarchs, dictators, and militant mullahs. It was a goal, he said, driven not by lust for global domination but by Wilsonian idealism. Democratic senator Evan Bayh concurred, arguing that invading Iraq would allow the United States "to begin to rebuild that country in a way that will provide a positive example to the people of that region about the principles and ideals upon which America stands." The eventual victory in the war against terror, he claimed, "will be won as much by the values and principles we embrace and advocate as by the force of arms. This gives us an opportunity to put those principles and values into action." It was perhaps less strange that a Democrat should support such active and dangerous missionary activity than that professed conservatives should do so. As John Lewis Gaddis noted, a conservative Republican administration had responded to September 11 "by embracing a liberal Democratic ideal—making the world safe for democracy—as a national security imperative."[14]

The blame could perhaps be sheeted to neoconservatives with ideological and moral outlooks quite distinct from those of more traditional conservatives (including George W. Bush). These new-style conservatives brought with them a crusading missionary spirit with regard to the uses of American power that was foreign to traditional conservatism. Two of their leading lights, Kristol and Robert Kagan, had produced a book in 2000 that argued for benevolent American hegemony on the grounds that the world had little to fear from a nation whose foreign policy was so infused with morality. The impact of September 11 allowed their influence to spread. Republican representative Mark Souder of Indiana, for example, described his district as part of Robert Taft/Paul Harvey America, with a high army enlistment rate and a long tradition of isolationism: "The idea is," he said, "you build a fortress and go after them if you have to." Souder had opposed U.S. intervention in Bosnia, but "Sept. 11 was an eye-opener

for areas like mine and for me. You can't escape your international interests. At some level we have to be the policeman of the world. We have an
ethical responsibility."[15]

But in Iraq, Bush was courting danger for uncertain gains, as more
sober commentators pointed out. All the political conditions that had
made his father choose the path of caution still existed in the Middle East.
Moreover, the proposed adventure displayed some disturbing parallels
with a former era. First, Bush's congressional resolution was eerily reminiscent of the "blank check" that Johnson extorted from Congress after the
Tonkin incident in 1964; the executive had once again trumped a supine
Congress and assumed war powers with no clear built-in limitation.[16] Second, Vietnam provided a worrying precedent for a commitment that was
open-ended, lacked clearly defined goals or an exit strategy, and depended
on a future Iraqi government of unknown democratic credentials. Third,
failing to provide the American people with a convincing rationale that
prepared them for a long, expensive, and possibly bloody commitment
risked eventual public disillusionment and protest. And, last, the fact
that a presidential proclivity for the unilateral use of American power
had been combined with a rhetorical revival of American values invited
a reidentification of the latter with overbearing American imperialism
motivated by oil and profits and aimed at hegemonic control of the Middle
East. This last danger was exacerbated by the explicit use of the doctrine
of preemption and a failure to obtain final U.N. authorization because of
the opposition of France, Russia, and Germany, who had supported action
in Afghanistan but drew the line at Iraq.

Of course, success always silences doubters and provides its own ex
post facto justification for particular political decisions, but the administration stacked the deck against its own chances of success in its war preparations. Kenneth Pollack, in a book that appeared in 2002, had examined
the choices facing the United States in Iraq and concluded that of three
options—containment, deterrence, and regime change—the last probably
carried the least risk. Yet if invasion were not to create greater or equal
dangers, he said, certain conditions would have to be met: an overwhelming force of between two hundred thousand and three hundred thousand
troops; the support of key governments in the area—Kuwait, Saudi Arabia,
Turkey, and so on; support from European allies and, ideally, the authority of the U.N. Security Council; a generally quiescent situation between

Palestinians and Israelis; a commitment to postwar reconstruction of Iraq and the establishment of a stable democracy, which would require a large occupation force over an extended period and a great deal of money. One has only to cite this list to see how imprudent the Bush administration's action plans were. Jack Matlock, reviewing these conditions six months before the invasion began, doubted that any U.S. administration could clear a bar set so high. He wrote: "The idea that Congress would be willing to finance a long occupation of Iraq and appropriate billions of dollars for Iraq's reconstruction at a time of recession and rising budget deficits seems irresponsibly optimistic. So is the idea that the United States and its allies would be capable of creating a prosperous, free, democratic nation out of Iraq's fractured and critically injured society."[17]

The extraordinary hubris and mispreparation of the administration has been attributed to a variety of factors: the poor quality or bias of U.S. intelligence on both WMDs and existing socioeconomic conditions in Iraq; overreliance on suspect information from self-serving Iraqi exiles like Ahmad Chalabi who hoped to ride to power on America's back; jealousies and suspicions between the State and Defense Departments that led to failures of communication and coordination; overconfidence in U.S. military superiority and in the effect of "shock and awe" tactics; the expectation that, with the return to full flow of Iraqi oil, the war and occupation would be relatively costless. What was clear was that none of the main drivers of the enterprise—Rumsfeld, Cheney, and Wolfowitz—expected either the conflict or the occupation to be lengthy. The general expectation was famously summed up in Cheney's remark: "I really do believe that we will be greeted as liberators." Rumsfeld, in an interview on the eve of the invasion, said it might be as little as six weeks but not more than six months before the troops had completed their task and come home. He was keen to test his "new army" theory, which, contra the Powell Doctrine, held that the future of warfare belonged to swift, efficient attacks by small, highly mobile units. With regard to the conventional stage of the war, he was right. Rumsfeld would claim, after years of the stubborn guerrilla war that ensued, that the problem was precisely a result of America's initial "catastrophic success." This was another way of saying that he had failed to prepare adequately for an aftermath he had not foreseen.

Yet the puzzling question remained: how could such an extraordinary miscalculation have occurred at such a high level? Undoubtedly, a contingent but potent mixture of forces and events lay at the heart of the decision on Iraq: tough-minded conservative officials nursing an enduring refusal to accept the humbling of American power in Vietnam and the consequent diminishment of the executive branch of government; neoconservative ideologues who dreamed great dreams that American power, if made permanently dominant and positively employed, could be used to set the world on a new and better foundation; a president with genuine leadership ability and character but limited knowledge and no sustained interest (one often euphemistically described as "incurious"); an unusually forceful and determined vice president able to shape arguments effectively to capture the presidential agenda; a common memory and continuing grudge among many of these participants concerning the unsatisfactory outcome of the first Gulf War conducted by Bush Sr.; and, of course, the seminal events of September 11 that became the catalyst for fusing all these forces to a common purpose.[18]

As the Iraq adventure degenerated into what one author labeled a "fiasco," many of the neocons who had been strong supporters expressed deep regret, not over the original plan, which they argued was sound, but over its abysmal execution by an administration they had thought would prove eminently competent. One of the leading members, Kenneth Adelman, commented sorrowfully: "The whole philosophy of using American strength for good in the world, for a foreign policy that is really value-based instead of balanced-power-based, I don't think is disproven by Iraq. But it's certainly discredited." Whether or not the project was wise to begin with is, of course, a debatable point, but it seems indisputable that whatever chance it may have had was nullified in the execution. Nor was the neglect of postwar planning a mere accident, oversight, or consequence of interagency rivalry between the Defense and State Departments. It was (as George Packer's book, *The Assassins' Gate,* makes clear) consciously willed by the administration. Rumsfeld stubbornly insisted (no doubt with Cheney's and perhaps Wolfowitz's approval) that the United States could engineer regime change but was not into "nation-building" in the Clinton mode, or in the manner undertaken by the State Department in Bosnia and Kosovo. This was a war of liberation, and the liberated would respond like good Americans by grasping economic opportunities to further their interests and by establishing the stable democratic government that such freedoms required. Rumsfeld expected to hand over government to the

Iraqis within three months. American power could be, in other words, supremely efficacious in removing evil-doers but should not get indefinitely
bogged down trying to establish and nurture new nations.[19]

The attitude displayed here was none other than the old fear of contaminating entanglement that had survived the demise of conservative isolationism. It was an attitude evident also in the conduct of the war, which
spurned the authority of the United Nations and scorned the disapproval
of old allies. Multilateral entanglements were merely a dragging anchor
on the beneficent exercise of American power, and the chain could be
severed without regret. The American superpower, it appeared, need not
feel bound by alliances, diplomatic niceties, or the opinions of others; it
could lay down its own path, rewarding those who followed and punishing
those who did not. The administration forged ahead with a unilateralist
single-mindedness that was hardly disguised by a decidedly subservient
"coalition of the willing" assembled for the purpose (denoting the "rush of
the vassals," as one commentator put it). American power would be used,
without significant cost, to liberate a nation, thereby beneficially affecting
a whole region and ultimately the world, without the United States having to become entangled in the prolonged occupation and government
of a foreign state.

The trouble was that the failure to assert immediate authority in the
liberated region left a vacuum in which an incipient insurgency began
and in which ancient hatreds found expression in deadly intercommunal
struggles for power. As violence escalated, more U.S. troops were committed, units were rotated again and again, and reservists were "stop
lossed" from returning to civilian life; the word "quagmire" was increasingly voiced only to be repeatedly rejected by the administration and its
supporters. Iraq, they indignantly insisted, was *not* Vietnam. And indeed
it was not. There was no equivalent entity to North Vietnam (certainly
not Syria); there was no ideologically opposed great power supporting the
insurgents (save for Iran once the Shi'ites took up arms); there was no
ideological coherence among the insurgents themselves (a mix of resent-
fully dispossessed Sunni Ba'athists, foreign Islamists intent on wounding
the United States, opportunistic criminals, and Shi'ite militia, some with
Iranian backing, seeking power for their long-oppressed sect). Yet such
differences were beside the point. Instead of the grateful population, brisk
house-cleaning, and swift exit they had anticipated, Americans and their

hapless allies found themselves indefinitely mired as they had been in Vietnam, struggling to cope with the usual dilemma of a counterinsurgency campaign—how to win the hearts and minds of an increasingly alienated population while cracking down violently on the enemy in its midst. As ever, the power of American weaponry made "collateral damage" often counterproductively extensive—the city of Fallujah, for example, was destroyed in the process of its liberation—especially since troops had not been prepared or trained for the job they found themselves confronting. The policy of not counting civilian casualties in Iraq, and that of forbidding the photographing of returning coffins of fallen Americans, revealed the administration's and the military's continuing sensitivity on the bad news aspects of such warfare and, by implication, its consciousness of its inability to justify the war in terms the American people would understand and support.

There was bitter irony in the fact that a prolonged entanglement that had never been in the least desired or anticipated was interpreted by foes, and even by suspicious friends, as evidence that occupation for the sake of empire and oil had been the American goal all along. Such impressions were not helped by the favorable treatment accorded, in the reconstruction effort, to U.S. corporations with links to the administration—especially when lucrative contracts were not matched by effective performance—or by the administration's intense pressuring, even in the midst of ongoing mayhem, of Nuri al-Maliki's Iraqi government to pass legislation opening Iraq's nationalized oil industry to the big four private oil companies. But if the goal had truly been empire, even economic empire, the entire affair seemed to confirm Niall Ferguson's argument that what was wrong with America was not that it was an imperial power, but that it was so bad at being one. The military adventure, far from demonstrating the fullness and righteousness of American power as the administration and its neocon allies had anticipated, had once more revealed its limitations and the perennial problems to which its use in uncertain causes was always subject.[20]

It was notable, too, that overconfidence in the swift and beneficent use of power was not accompanied by any very tender concern with the potential effects of power's misuse on innocent virtue. It was, of course, in the nature of conservatism to take American goodness as unproblematically given while smiting evil enemies mercilessly, and generally to be more interested in upholding pride than preserving innocence; the latter could always be safely left to the wimpish care of bleeding-heart liberals. Even so, a self-consciously tough administration seemed almost preternaturally blind to the dangers presented, in the context of U.S. history, by offenses to innocent virtue. They could scarcely ignore the blow to moral credibility dealt by the revelations of American abuse of prisoners at Abu Ghraib, the very facility in which Saddam had conducted his worst tortures, though they tried to minimize it by blaming underlings. President Bush said: "I share a deep disgust that those prisoners were treated the way they were treated. Their treatment does not reflect the nature of the American people. That's not the way we do things in America."[21] Yet it seemed to be increasingly the way Americans did things abroad. The administration and the military hastened to blame the scandal on a few bad eggs poorly trained for their task, and to prevent its connection to a general policy, begun by Rumsfeld, of limiting the application of the Geneva Conventions to "unlawful combatants" while starkly narrowing the definition of "torture." Yet the approval of "expanded interrogation techniques" for prisoners taken in Afghanistan or held indefinitely without legal representation in the legal limbo of Guantánamo Bay, or the practice of "extraordinary rendition" (the trans-shipment of suspects for periods of detention in countries, even Syria, well known for the use of torture), all seemed to indicate that individual rights and freedoms and legal protections applied only to Americans in America and even there were being circumscribed by provisions in the antiterrorist Patriot Act.[22] The administration's respect for law, whether national or international, appeared most manifest in its efforts to find ways of getting around it. The "gloves-off" approach was justified, naturally, by the exigencies of the fight against a ruthless enemy who would not hesitate to detonate a nuclear device in a U.S. city, yet such practices inevitably clashed dissonantly with Bush's ceaseless harping on America's love of freedom and his own intention to spread that commodity around the world. Innocent virtue was sacrificed and a propaganda coup handed to the very enemies that such brutal tactics were meant to help destroy.

For much of the world, abuses and collateral casualties were merely additional proofs that the United States had forfeited the moral high ground by choosing war in Iraq, a war disapproved by majorities even within the countries making up Bush's curiously disparate "coalition of the willing." It was an issue that could win an election for one party in Germany, lose it for another in Spain, and ruin the reputation of Bush's staunchest ally, Prime Minister Tony Blair in Britain. The broad sympathy for America that September 11 had evoked, and that had been sustained during the pursuit of Al Qaeda in Afghanistan, evaporated as the administration gave needless offense to erstwhile friends. A willingness to believe the worst about American intentions and motives, to perceive hypocrisy rather than moral clarity in the promulgation of American values, now became widespread. A wave of anti-Americanism of an intensity not seen since Vietnam washed around the world, taking sometimes virulent forms in Muslim countries. Bush's moral leadership was derided by traditional allies whose opposition had provoked the defense secretary into gratuitous insults of "Old Europe." The United Nations and its secretary general, Kofi Annan, felt snubbed and scorned. It was hardly surprising that, as America's initial "mission accomplished" triumphalism faded with the onset of intractable guerrilla war, Europe and the United Nations should indulge a certain Schadenfreude. Yet satisfaction at U.S. discomfort constituted an impediment to finding solutions to a problem of stabilization that it was in everyone's interest to find, save those of the insurgents.

At home, the country was initially divided on the war more or less along the lines of division that marked the so-called culture wars. Yet even those who supported the war did so not out of any enthusiasm, but rather from an inclination to trust the president (whose pronouncements had routinely cast it as the front line of the ongoing war on terror) and a patriotic desire to support U.S. troops once engaged. Despite the mounting costs in blood and treasure, and despite dangerously low approval ratings, Bush survived his misadventure in Iraq to gain a second term —for a number of probable reasons. First, the fear and insecurity caused by September 11 remained potent, and Bush's initial responses to it had won him credit that continued to play in his favor. There was also the usual reluctance to change a commander in chief in the midst of a war. American casualties, though mounting, remained low by the standards of the Vietnam War, and the absence of a draft (aside from the so-called backdoor draft of stop-lossing reservists) meant that the most direct pain of casualties was experienced by a limited section of the population. Most importantly, perhaps, the Democrats failed to turn disgruntlement with the war and its conduct into effective opposition, a failure that was a consequence of their own initial authorization of the invasion. Howard Dean, who had opposed the war, might have succeeded in making it a viable election issue had he not crashed and burned in the Democratic primaries. John Kerry, who had approved it, could never surmount the moral disadvantage under which that decision placed him.

Bush's electoral triumph, which saw both houses returned in Republican hands, seemed complete; his policies appeared mandated. He assumed his usual resolute, square-jawed, never-deviate-from-the-right-path stance and promised to be in Iraq "for as long as it takes." Yet the desire to extract the United States from an intolerable situation was palpable. Conciliatory moves were made toward old allies to repair fractured friendships; an attempt was made to mollify the United Nations, whose assistance in Iraq was now deeply desired. Some of the most conservative hawks—Douglas Feith, John Bolton, Wolfowitz—were moved out and on. Condoleezza Rice took over at the State Department, overbalancing a now chastened and weakened Rumsfeld, who remained at the Defense Department until his demise immediately after the Democratic victory in the midterm congressional elections of 2006. In Iraq, a handover of "sovereignty" to the interim government of Ayad Allawi was followed at length by an election—boycotted by Sunnis but generally embraced by the rest of the population—that was declared a triumph for the cause of freedom. Recruitment and training of Iraqi police and military units, which were especially targeted by insurgents, was intensified to hasten the day when "Iraqification" of the conflict could become a reality. Meanwhile, events in the larger Middle East provided some hope that U.S. intervention had indeed provoked the democratization that the Bush agenda had contemplated. Arafat died, and the peace process in Israel-Palestine moved uncertainly back on track; Saudi Arabia promised some very limited democratization, and Egypt promised somewhat more. The murder of a former prime minister in Lebanon brought the Lebanese people onto the streets to demand the withdrawal of Syrian troops and influence from the nation after twenty-nine years of occupation.

The administration tried to make the most of these developments, but in truth they were fragile and uncertain straws that, in the case of Israel and Lebanon, soon collapsed into violence and renewed fragility. The Bush presidency declined drastically under the accumulated weight of policy failure abroad and administrative failure at home (most notably, the poor response to Hurricane Katrina and the scandal of the treatment of injured troops at Walter Reed Hospital). In Iraq, murder continued unabated, with mounting communal strife between Shi'ites and Sunnis adding a grisly, and apparently unmanageable, new dimension to the mayhem. The difficult issue of shaping a future state that could satisfactorily accommodate Sunnis, Shi'ites, and Kurds as well as various other minorities seemed no nearer practical resolution four years after Saddam had fallen. With Democrats now in control of Congress, a beleaguered president put his small remaining capital on a last throw in Iraq, a "surge" of troops in Baghdad under new and allegedly more enlightened generalship; but the effort seemed forlorn from the start and perhaps merely the prelude to an eventual Nixon-like "withdrawal with honor."

Meanwhile, the problem of nuclear proliferation in Iran and North Korea (which tested a nuclear device in 2006) also pressed, partly because the lesson of Iraq for these countries was that Saddam had been attacked precisely because he did *not* possess a nuclear deterrent. The squandering of lives, dollars, prestige, and moral authority in Iraq had put the United States into a weaker negotiating position than it otherwise would have held. Iran, emboldened and strengthened by the Iraq disaster and by the relative success of its clients, Hezbollah, in a short, sharp war with Israel, took a defiant stance against international demands to cease its uranium enrichment program. The Bush administration rattled what sabers it had left (mostly naval and air power) and indicated a potential strike against the country, but eventually its hitherto implacable refusal to deal with what it regarded as foes beyond the pale of diplomacy would crack under the force of necessity. As the president's stock dwindled and the vice president's influence waned, the effective conduct of foreign relations fell more and more into the grasp of a team of professional diplomatists assembled by Condoleezza Rice. Their traditional caution and pragmatism infuriated the almost neutered ideologues, but at length they would reach an agreement with North Korea on essentially the same terms that the administration had castigated the Clinton administration for conceding in 1998, and begin talks with Syria and even Iran.

There was little doubt that even the most die-hard members of the administration, continue as they might to put a brave face on all this, understood what a colossal misadventure Iraq had been. Humility had given way to arrogance, strength had been exposed as weakness, innocent virtue had been stained once more, and American leadership had been undermined. Iraq had shattered a smug conservative assurance of the virtuous efficacy of American power, and the nation seemed as far as ever from solving the perpetual dilemma of its own foreign policy.

CONCLUSION

Condoleezza Rice, who in her academic career as a Soviet specialist had styled herself a hard-headed realist, claimed to have been converted to the moral dimension of foreign policy by the "clarity" of George W. Bush. Immediately after her Senate confirmation as secretary of state, she embarked on an extensive world tour to display to other nations the diplomatic makeover the second Bush administration had undertaken. The trip was about reassurance and fence-mending, but to make it seem less like eating crow, Rice reaffirmed, in the strongest possible terms, the Bush commitment to freedom and democracy abroad. She had already set the tone at the hearing before the Senate Foreign Relations Committee, where she promised to strengthen alliances and support friends but also justified the path already taken using a rhetoric drawn directly from the traditional mythology:

> The work that America and our allies have undertaken, and
> the sacrifices we have made, have been difficult and necessary
> and right. Now is the time to build on these achievements . . .
> to make the world safer, and to make the world more free.
> We must use American diplomacy to help create a balance of
> power in the world that favors freedom. . . . in these extraor-
> dinary times, it is the duty of all of us—legislators, diplomats,
> civil servants, and citizens—to uphold and advance the values
> that are the core of the American identity, and that have lifted
> the lives of millions around the world. . . . One of history's
> clearest lessons is that America is safer, and the world is more
> secure, whenever and wherever freedom prevails.

Rice drew a parallel between the Bush administration and those post–World War II leaders whose "vision, courage and boldness of thought" had enabled them to confront a tyrannous ideology with free trade prosperity and a message of hope and truth, a message that had ultimately triumphed. Despite the contempt shown for international organizations by the Bush administration during its first term, Rice offered a high Wilsonian vision of the "three great tasks" of American diplomacy in these "momentous times":

> First, we will unite the community of democracies in building
> an international system that is based on our shared values and
> the rule of law. Second, we will strengthen the community of
> democracies to fight the threats to our common security and
> alleviate the hopelessness that feeds terror. And third, we will
> spread freedom and democracy throughout the globe. That
> is the mission that President Bush has set for America in the
> world . . . and the great mission of American diplomacy today.

Rice pointed out that, in the Middle East, President Bush had already explicitly broken with "six decades of excusing and accommodating the lack of freedom in the hope of purchasing stability at the price of liberty." On Rice's watch, this principle was going to be universally extended to powerful friends and allies—including Russia and China—whose politics were less than democratic. President Vladimir Putin took offense at being chided for veering in an undemocratic direction, and China's leadership had to suffer encouragement to extend civic freedoms to its people.[23]

The general idea was, apparently, to try to do with freedom and democracy what Jimmy Carter had attempted with human rights, that is, to make U.S. foreign policy consistent and consistently moral, thus ending hypocrisy and bad faith. The question was, how far beyond exhortation the administration was prepared to go to fulfill its declared mission after the limits of its power had been painfully exposed once more. September 11 had demonstrated the proposition upon which Thomas Hobbes had founded his dictum of human equality, namely, that the most powerful person is always vulnerable to the murderous wiles of the weak; the deployment of U.S. armies in Iraq had further illustrated how impotent great military power can sometimes be to achieve desired goals. The military option had aroused contempt and hostility rather than awe and respect among America's foes. It had proved costly and intensely dangerous even in Iraq, and it was hardly conceivable that its preemptive use would ever be contemplated against a more considerable power. So desperately did Iraq overstretch the U.S. military and the U.S. budget that it was almost equally inconceivable that this option would be used again even against

North Korea or Iran (though nerves were jangled by the ominous building of a case for action, reminiscent of the lead-up to Iraq, during 2007, a case drastically undermined by the release of a CIA analysis asserting that Iran had ceased its nuclear weapons program in 2003). Economic sanctions were hardly less problematical in respect of nations with whom the United States had extensive trading links, for instance China, and their effectiveness was anyway always subject to severe doubt.

That left only the usual diplomatic repertoire of persuasive techniques using whatever range of carrots and sticks might be wielded without undue blowback, and with military power a distant, quiet backstop rather than a threat of first resort. The Bush administration had not shown much adeptness at or even interest in the subtle and complex art of diplomacy, but Rice and her experienced team set out to make comprehensive amends as the Bush tenure shortened. It remained a question whether this art could aptly be applied to "spreading democracy" rather than, for example, securing international cooperation among police agencies to counter terrorists, or halting the spread of dangerous weaponry, or defusing tensions between North Korea and other countries, or between China and Taiwan, or China and Japan, or aiming to restart the peace process between Israel and Palestine. There were plenty of signs, certainly, that overt moralizing generally did more harm than good, and it became harder for the administration to moralize without having its own sins thrown back in its face by the likes of Vladimir Putin. The general tendency, despite the predilections of Bush and Cheney, was to reinstate the essential role of determined diplomacy.[24] This produced results in the case of North Korea, which agreed to suspend its nuclear program, and raised some fragile hopes for progress on the Israeli-Palestinian front as Rice revived talks in a last desperate effort to establish some positive legacy for the Bush administration.

Yet it was noticeable, and hardly surprising, that Rice deployed the brave rhetoric of American mission less and less as time went by. Such rhetoric evoked, while failing to resolve, the perennial question of how to ensure that the means chosen to achieve desired ends in foreign policy did not, paradoxically, undermine the virtue upon which the missionary role was premised.

Epilogue

SAMUEL HYNES, reporting on a gathering of veterans at the new World War II memorial on the Mall in Washington, D.C., on the sixtieth anniversary of D-Day, wrote:

> American wars since the Second World War have been different: lost, or not won or even finished, or trivial, and morally ambiguous at best, though brave men fought in them. The Second World War was our last just and victorious war, the last war a man could come home from with any expectation of glory. The old men must be thinking about that as they gather together, must be glad that their time of testing came when it did, in a war where the Americans were the good guys beyond question, and the bad guys were absolutely evil. Perhaps that new memorial down on the Mall is our national monument to that last time of national goodness, before we lost our way.[1]

This book has tried to explain in terms of virtue and power why it has been so important for Americans to be among the "good guys," and yet how they could manage so frequently to "lose their way."

The American mythology established an ambivalent, even antagonistic relationship between power and virtue that made their reconciliation—necessary for preserving the essential national mission—perennially prob-

330

lematic. This was so even if one took an ancient republican view of virtue as martial readiness and self-sacrifice, but more so if one accepted the Christian-Enlightenment view of virtue as benevolent innocence. Power was necessary to defend the virtuous republic and its interests, but power always tended eventually or immediately to the corruption of virtue and thus to defeat of the mission. This presented Americans with three apparent choices, none of which seemed acceptable or feasible. The first was to choose innocent virtue and to eschew altogether the temptations of power and its uses—an impossible option if isolation was impracticable and soiling foreign entanglements were unavoidable. The second was to choose power and pride and forget about virtue and innocence—an appealing option for hairy-chested realists but scarcely likely to play for long among a democratic populace deeply imbued with certain moral and religious attitudes and a belief in the American example. The last, which could be argued to be necessary given the failure of the other two, was somehow to unite power and virtue in U.S. foreign policy, thus genuinely realizing the exceptionalist mission.

At the end of World War II, this goal appeared to be on the point of realization (though the temptation then was too readily to assume that American power must be virtuous because Americans were inherently so). Yet maintaining the unity of power and virtue in fact proved difficult in a complex world in which the United States had to play a great power role, especially after that role had been transformed by events from essential anchor of a cooperative world community to anticommunist crusader. This new role demanded endless political compromises, inconsistencies, and downright betrayals, inevitably bringing into doubt the virtue of American policy and eventually degrading the credibility of American power. In Vietnam the contradictions exploded spectacularly, severing power and virtue and undermining both.

After Vietnam, one of the main tasks of U.S. leaders (though it was never quite expressed as such) was to find a way of reestablishing the union of power and virtue, thus reinstating the American libertarian mission. But rather than being reunited, the sundered elements of the myth became twin poles between which administrations tended to oscillate. The human rights strategy seemed to concentrate too much on maintaining virtue and innocence and too little on deploying power and preserving pride. An emphasis on American values, on the other hand, became associated with an aggressive assertion of American power and pride that lent itself too readily to accusations of imperial domination of the kind that innocent virtue deplored, a danger grievously realized in the presidency of George W. Bush. In practice, the choice always tended to devolve into the unsatisfactory, indeed impossible, one of *either* virtue *or* power.

Melvyn Leffler wrote, regarding George W. Bush's alleged moral clarity: "Moral clarity doubtless helps a democratic, pluralistic society like the United States reconcile its differences and conduct policy. Military power, properly configured and effectively deployed, chastens and deters adversaries. But this mindset can lead to arrogance and abuse of power. To be effective, moral clarity and military power must be harnessed to a careful calculation of interest and a shrewd understanding of the adversary. Only when ends are reconciled with means can moral clarity and military power add up to a winning strategy."[2]

This implies that the way out of the traditional impasse is to reconceptualize the nature of both political realism and virtue in order to transcend the (basically Protestant) either/or mentality in favor of one that better comprehends the complexity of the world and the practical wisdom required to cope with it. This was part of the message of a leading neoconservative intellectual, Francis Fukuyama, who roundly repudiated the theory of benevolent American hegemony that he and his fellows had advocated before Iraq. They had been misled, he said, by attributing the fall of the Soviet Union principally to a virile show of American strength, thus taking the lesson that the virtuous progress of history toward democracy could be accelerated by American agency. But the disastrous actions of an administration that took this literally had caused the world to doubt American goodness. Future administrations would have to persuade the world, not just that America was good, but that it was *wise* in its application of power and thus able to achieve the goals it set for itself. Fearing that this failure would encourage the revival of "realism" in foreign policy, Fukuyama called instead for a "realistic Wilsonianism" that emphasized military power less and "soft power" more. The United States, he declared, was "at the crossroads."[3]

Yet the argument of this book has been that the nation has been perpetually at this same crossroads with regard to its foreign policy precisely because of its inability to achieve a lasting synthesis of the elements of power and virtue that Fukuyama desires. The either/or mentality goes too deep: either virtue or power, either good or evil, either law or force. It can be seen in the automatic assumption even of one of the muscular neo-conservatives that Fukuyama criticizes, Robert Kagan. Kagan, in a curious historical reversal, defended the virile American attitude toward power against the allegedly effeminate pacifism of modern Europe, which was devoted to international law: law and force are again taken as antonyms rather than necessary partners. Kagan's outlook reminds us, however, that the negative version of the virtue/power dichotomy is weakness versus strength, a theme that plays volubly and effectually in the culturally divisive U.S. politics of red and blue nations, making the emergence of a wise synthesis more problematic even as it is more necessary.[4]

The American task is more pressing and perhaps more difficult because of the weight of world expectation that the country must bear. Americans are, in a real sense, victims of the exceptional historical success of their own myth, whose currency has always run well beyond their own shores. Even in the midst of widespread, reflexive anti-Americanism, a hopeful attitude to America is contradictorily nourished. Indeed, an underlying strain of disappointed hope almost always lives within anti-Americanism. Even as nations bitterly criticize the United States, measuring it by its own high standards, they continue to hope for its wise and effective leadership. Listen to the words of Tim Kreutzfeldt, a bar owner in Germany, on the subject of George W. Bush: "Bush took away our America. I mean we love America. We are very sad about America. We believe in America and American values, but not in Bush. And it makes us angry that he distorted our image of the country which is so important to us. It is not what America stands for—and this makes us angry and it should make every American angry, because America lost so much in its reputation worldwide."[5]

Or consider the chapter headings of a book titled *What Does the World Want from America?* written by contributors from China, Japan, Africa, India, Britain, and America: "To Be an Enlightened Superpower," "First among Equals," "The Keystone of World Order," "Participate in the African Renaissance," "Justice for All," "What Is Right Is in U.S. Interests," "Wanted: A Global Partner," and "Guide Globalization into a Just World Order."[6]

The world will not let America be ordinary. It will always judge the faults of American leaders more harshly than those of more unsavory regimes in nations whose history and ideology have never, in any case, promised better—that is only natural. But it will also judge them more harshly than those of other liberal democratic nations because America from the start made the role of liberal democratic exemplar part of its identity. U.S. foreign policy must somehow accommodate this fact.

In considering these expectations, it might be well to recall that the post–World War II liberal foreign policy consensus, though it seemed fractured by the Cold War and Vietnam, had nevertheless partially attained its goals. The multilateral liberal order that characterized Western international relations—centered on the United States and undergirded by its military, economic, and political power—was a genuine accomplishment based on something other than old-fashioned balance of great power logic. If that system had been merely an alliance welded together by fear of a larger menace, it should have begun to crumble into anarchic competition as soon as that menace disappeared—which indeed many predicted. It did not, but was in fact extended and strengthened during the administrations of Bush Sr. and Bill Clinton. Here was American power deeply engaged but nevertheless deliberately self-constrained, founding a system of willing alliances of remarkable resilience. John Ikenberry spent two decades exploring the nature of that order and arguing that it should be recognized for what it was and sustained by those in power, only to see it deliberately dismantled by people who, even if they understood its logic, never accepted the constraints it placed on the free use of predominant American power.[7] What Ikenberry interpreted as the virtues of hegemonic self-restraint, the Bush administration regarded as the sullying of American sovereignty, an attempt by hostile or even malevolent Lilliputians to tie down the benevolent giant and prevent it from establishing its benign imperial reign. The neoimperial program they tried to put in place of the robust liberal system received its comeuppance with shattering swiftness.

The challenge for future political leaders, surveying the wreckage wrought by hubristic zealots seduced by the singularity and seeming limitlessness of American power, is to rebuild a cooperative order capable of addressing the dangerous challenges of the twenty-first century. Indeed Ikenberry, in association with Anne-Marie Slaughter, has overseen a bipartisan endeavor known as the Princeton Project that attempts to set out clear principles and objectives to accomplish just such a rebuilding. The project's final paper, significantly titled "Forging a World of Liberty under Law," outlines a hugely ambitious plan to reform and partially refound existing international institutions to suit present times. Whether the opportunity genuinely exists for such American innovation, as it certainly did following the devastation of World War II, is of course an open question. What is interesting, however, is the project's expressed desire to beneficently use U.S. power without insisting on overwhelming predominance. A passage headed "Rethinking the Role of Force," argues:

> At their core, both liberty and law must be backed up by force. Instead of insisting on a doctrine of primacy, the United States should aim to sustain the military predominance of liberal democracies and encourage the development of military capabilities by like-minded democracies in a way that is consistent with their security interests. The predominance of liberal democracies is necessary to prevent a return to destabilizing and dangerous great power security competition; it would also augment our capacity to meet the various threats and challenges that confront us.[8]

In this paper the essential elements of the traditional American view of the world are maintained: a faith in liberal democracy as the best way of securing ordered liberty at home; a desire to see the indefinite spread of such democracies around the world; a belief that liberal democracies, being more interested in trade and economic growth than war, will not fight with one another; a distrust of competitive great power politics as dangerously destabilizing; and the belief that the prosperity and security of the United States is intimately related to that of the whole world. The proper response to the Bush years, therefore, cannot be a retreat into national isolation, but a wiser engagement that remembers the truth of the assertion that power, carelessly used, endangers the nation and its national mission. The United States must play a leadership role but will avoid the arrogant and fatal dependence on domineering power. The antinomial relationship between power and virtue must be finally overcome. If power cannot be conceived as the antithesis of virtue (in the shape of liberty and law) but rather as its essential guarantor, it must nevertheless be exercised judiciously and in concert with the power of like-minded nations.

Ikenberry and Slaughter advise updating the doctrine of deterrence for an age in which the possibility of nuclear weapons falling into terrorist hands must be taken seriously. In parallel fashion, Ian Shapiro has argued the value of a new containment doctrine that is hardheadedly realistic in its assessment of what American power can cooperatively achieve yet preserves essential democratic values. Shapiro's vision, like that of the Princeton Project, implies American engagement and leadership without resort to imperial dominance, enabling the United States, as he says, to stand up to bullies without itself becoming a bully.[9] It is a formula that encapsulates, as neatly as any, the hoped-for resolution of the dilemma of virtue and power that has bedeviled U.S. foreign policy from its beginnings.

CHAPTER 1. INTRODUCTION

1. See "President George W. Bush's Inaugural Address," January 20, 2001, available at http://www.whitehouse.gov/news/inaugural-address.html.

2. This was the lesson drawn by Robert McNamara, defense secretary of the 1960s and an architect of containment policy in Indochina. See his memoirs of the era: *In Retrospect: The Tragedy and Lessons of Vietnam*, New York, Times Books, 1995, 13; also the documentary film on McNamara by Errol Morris, *The Fog of War*, Sony Pictures, 2003.

3. Robert Endicott Osgood, *Ideals and Self-Interest in America's Foreign Relations: The Great Transformation of the Twentieth Century*, Chicago, University of Chicago Press, 1953; Henry Kissinger, *Diplomacy*, New York, Simon & Schuster, 1994, 18. Carter cited in J. Dumbrell, *The Carter Presidency: A Reevaluation*, Manchester, Manchester University Press, 1995, 2.

4. Michael Mandelbaum, *The Ideas That Conquered the World: Peace, Democracy and Free Markets in the Twenty-First Century*, New York, Public Affairs, 2002; William Appleman Williams, *The Tragedy of American Diplomacy*, New York, Delta, 1978; Michael H. Hunt, *Ideology and U.S. Foreign Policy*, New Haven, Conn., Yale University Press, 1987; Patrick Callahan, *Logics of American Foreign Policy: Theories of America's World Role*, New York, Pearson-Longman, 2004; Walter Russell Mead, *Special Providence: American Foreign Policy and How It Changed the World*, New York, Knopf, 2001. Nearly every work on U.S. foreign policy notes the salience of this myth, and some give it a central place, usually concentrating on particular aspects such as the expansive aims of "Manifest Destiny" or the frontier myth, and sometimes approaching the issue from a cultural studies perspective. See, for example, Albert K. Weinberg, *Manifest Destiny: A Study of Nationalist Expansionism in American*

History, Baltimore, Md., Johns Hopkins University Press, 1935; Frederick Merk, *Manifest Destiny and Mission in American History: A Reinterpretation,* New York, Knopf, 1963; Richard Slotkin, *The Fatal Environment: The Myth of the Frontier in the Age of Industrialisation,* New York, Atheneum, 1985; Robert W. Johannsen (ed.), *Manifest Destiny and Empire: American Antebellum Expansionism,* College Station, Texas A&M University Press, 1997; John Hellman, *American Myth and the Legacy of Vietnam,* New York, Columbia University Press, 1986; Tom Engelhardt, *The End of Victory Culture: Cold War America and the Disillusioning of a Generation,* New York, Basic Books, 1995.

5. Alexander Hamilton, James Madison, and John Jay, *The Federalist,* in *American State Papers,* Chicago, William Benton Publisher, 1982, No. 14, 62.

6. Eulogy on Henry Clay, July 6, 1852, in Don E. Fehrenbacher (ed.), *Abraham Lincoln: A Documentary Portrait through His Speeches and Writings,* Stanford, Calif., Stanford University Press, 1964, 68.

7. John Jay in *The Federalist* No. 2 hailed the common ancestry, religion, language, and principles of people in the colonies as a reason for cementing their union, but this was little more than wishful rhetoric.

8. Seymour Martin Lipset, *American Exceptionalism: A Double-Edged Sword,* New York, Norton, 1996, 19; Hartz, *Liberal Tradition.*

9. John Locke, *Second Treatise on Civil Government,* in Ian Shapiro (ed.), *Two Treatises of Government and a Letter Concerning Toleration,* New Haven, Conn., Yale University Press, Ch. V, para. 49.

10. Slavery, at the time of the Revolution, was widely argued to be an unfortunate evil inherited from colonial times, an economic necessity in a plantation culture, or both. It was an evil that would, with development, eventually be superseded. The South's continuing addiction to slavery eventually aroused the moral wrath of abolitionists in the North, whose fervent attacks produced a hysterical reaction among southerners, particularly after Nat Turner's slave rebellion in 1831. The trend then was rapidly toward justifying slavery on the grounds of natural inequality, using arguments from the Bible, Aristotle, and Edmund Burke. In 1832 Prof. Thomas R. Dew published a comprehensive defense of slavery in *Review of the Debate of the Virginia Legislature of 1831.* In the 1850s, southern apologists like George Fitzhugh (*Sociology for the South; or, the Failure of a Free Society*) began to compare the conditions of slavery favorably with the abuses and "wage slavery" of the northern factory system. See William J. Cooper, *The South and the Politics of Slavery, 1828–1856,* Baton Rouge, Louisiana State University Press, 1978; James Oakes, *The Ruling Race: A History of American Slaveholders,* New York, Knopf, 1982.

11. David Hackett Fischer, *Albion's Seed: Four British Folkways in America,* New York, Oxford University Press, 1989.

12. Mead, *Special Providence,* 44, and Ch. 7; on the existence of a singular, genuine American nation, see Michael Lind, *Next American Nation:*

The New Nationalism and the Fourth American Revolution, New York, Free Press, 1995.

13. "Address to Newly Naturalized American Citizens," Philadelphia, May 10, 1915, in James Brown Scott (ed.), *President Wilson's Foreign Policy: Messages, Addresses, Papers*, New York, Oxford University Press, 1918, 94–95.

14. Frances Milton Trollope, *Domestic Manners of the Americans*, ed. Donald Smalley, New York, Knopf, 1949 [1832], 132. Other nineteenth-century writers on America who produced often uncomplimentary portraits included Harriet Martineau; Michel Chevalier; Charles Dickens; Captain Frederick Marryat; Fanny's own son, the novelist Anthony Trollope; and, of course, most famous of all, Alexis de Tocqueville.

15. Elizabeth Cady Stanton at the Seneca Falls Convention on the social, civil, and religious condition and rights of women, paraphrased the Declaration of Independence as the Declaration of Sentiments, in which the self-evident truth was that "all men and women are created equal." King's "I Have a Dream" speech, which looked forward to a time when black people could cry "Free at last!," was, at base, an appeal for the realization of the American myth.

16. Herbert Croly, *The Promise of American Life*, New York, Capricorn Books, 1964 [1909], 3; Samuel P. Huntington, *American Politics: The Promise of Disharmony*, Cambridge, Mass., Belknap Press, 1981, 262; Abraham Lincoln, "Letter to Henry L. Pierce," April 6, 1859, in Roy P. Basler, Marion D. Pratt, and Lloyd A. Dunlap (eds.), *The Collected Works of Abraham Lincoln*, 8 vols., New Brunswick, N.J., Rutgers University Press, 1953–1955, 3, 374–376 at 376.

17. Huntington, *American Politics*, 11. Huntington argues that the force of Americans' belief in their own creed waxes and wanes but grows large during periods of "creedal passion," when the gap between ideal and reality causes such cognitive dissonance as to produce upheaval. He discerns four such periods in U.S. history: the Revolutionary, the Jacksonian, the Progressive, and the years of protest during the 1960s and 1970s; see Ch. 5.

CHAPTER 2. ORIGINS AND SIGNIFICANCE OF THE AMERICAN MYTHOLOGY

1. To say that the embedded myth acts as a structural constraint on individual historical agency is to raise the old sociological debate regarding the primacy of either structure or agency in the explanation of social action. I do not wish to engage this debate here save to say that of the three possible responses—structure determines, agency is free, or some middle ground—I adhere to the last, as the preceding paragraph should make clear. See Nicos P. Mouzelis, *Sociological Theory: What Went Wrong? Diagnosis and Remedies*, New York, Routledge, 1995.

2. Rogers M. Smith, *Civic Ideals: Conflicting Visions of Citizenship in U.S. History*, New Haven, Conn., Yale University Press, 1997.

3. Ibid., 469; Joanna Overing, "The Role of Myth: An Anthropological Perspective, or: 'The Reality of the Really Made-up,'" in Geoffrey Hosking and George Schöpflin (eds.), *Myths and Nationhood*, London, Hurst & Co., 1997, 16.

4. Thomas Heilke, "Realism, Narrative, and Happenstance: Thucydides' Tale of Brasidas," *American Political Science Review* 98 (1), 2004: 121–138 at 128. Heilke quotes from Paul Ricouer (*From Text to Action: Essays in Hermeneutics*, II, trans. K. Blamey and J. B. Thompson, Evanston, Ill., Northwestern University Press, 1991, 5): "Ultimately history cannot make a complete break with narrative, because it cannot break with action, which itself implies agents, aims, circumstances, interactions, and results both intended and unintended. But the plot is the basic narrative unity that organizes these heterogeneous ingredients into an intelligible totality" (129). See also John Milbank, *Theology and Social Theory: Beyond Secular Reason*, London, Basil Blackwell, 1990; Joshua Mitchell, *Not by Reason Alone: Religion, History and Identity in Early Modern Political Thought*, Chicago, University of Chicago Press, 1993.

5. For example, the group known during the French Revolution as the *idéologues*, which included Condorcet, Benjamin Constant, and Madame de Staël. The name came from the "ideology" of liberal oppositionist Destutt de Tracy, who wrote the multivolume *Éléments d'Idéologie* between 1801 and 1815. His notion was to transform society by replacing superstition and blind custom with only "true ideas." He was highly influential on Jefferson, who translated and published the last volume in the United States. John Adams dismissed the ideologues, including Jefferson, as people nursing the perilous illusion that utopian ideals, however beautiful, could be actually realized in the world. Indeed, Adams may have originated the word "ideology" rather than de Tracy, who is generally credited with having coined it in 1796. Adams used the concept only to condemn it in *A Defence of the Constitutions of Government of the United States of America* in 1787. On de Tracy, see Emmet Kennedy, *A Philosophe in the Age of Revolution: Destutt de Tracy and the Origins of "Ideology,"* Philadelphia, American Philosophical Society, 1978; on Adams, see Joseph John Ellis, *Passionate Sage: The Character and Legacy of John Adams*, New York, Norton, 1993.

6. Robert R. Palmer, "The Great Inversion," in Richard Herr and Harold Parker (eds.), *Ideas in History*, Durham, N.C., Duke University Press, 1965, 5.

7. Eric Hobsbawm, *Nations and Nationalism since 1780: Programme, Myth, Reality*, Cambridge, Cambridge University Press, 1990, 12. Nationalism has been regarded as a veritable scandal because political potency is allegedly accompanied by "philosophical poverty." A nation is, in a famous phrase, only an "imagined community," susceptible to socio-psychological explanation, perhaps, but not to be taken seriously as a political-philosophical category; Benedict Anderson, *Imagined Communities: Reflections on the Origin and Spread of Nationalism*, London, Verso, 1983. Nationalism as an ideology

seemed to be a prime example of false consciousness, which, like Marx's view of religion, could be explained only by being explained away. See also M. Ginsberg, *Nationalism: A Reappraisal*, Leeds, Leeds University Press, 1963; Ernest Gellner, *Nations and Nationalism*, Oxford, Basil Blackwell, 1983; E. Hobsbawm and T. Ranger (eds.), *The Invention of Tradition*, Cambridge, Cambridge University Press, 1983; A. D. Smith, *The Ethnic Origin of Nations*, Oxford, Blackwell, 1986; J. G. Kellas, *The Politics of Nationalism and Ethnicity*, London, Macmillan, 1991.

8. George Schöpflin claims that these myths are common in Central and Eastern Europe, but what is striking is that all of them play a part in America's mythological self-understanding and even then do not exhaust the store of American myth; see "The Functions of Myth and a Taxonomy of Myths," in Hosking and Schöpflin, *Myths and Nationhood*, 28–35.

9. Lincoln, "Speech on Kansas-Nebraska Act," in Don Fehrenbacher (ed.), *Selected Speeches and Writings, 1859–1865*, New York, Library of America, 1989, 315. One can overstate the argument that class consciousness has not been a potent political force in the United States—the Marxist meaning of American Exceptionalism—but to the extent that it is true, the effect of this myth must be considered significant; Charles R. Hearn, *The American Dream in the Great Depression*, Westport, Conn., Greenwood Press, 1977, 16.

10. D. Echeverria, *Mirage in the West: A History of the French Image of American Society to 1815*, Princeton, N.J., Princeton University Press, 1958, 38.

11. Famed revolutionary orator Patrick Henry had electrified a Virginian court as early as 1763 by invoking the doctrine of inalienable natural rights in a trial concerning the payment of clergy with tobacco, a practice disallowed by King George III. The assumption was also explicit in the Massachusetts Circular Letter of 1768 and in many other colonial documents; see Gerald Stourzh, *Alexander Hamilton and the Idea of Republican Government*, Stanford, Calif., Stanford University Press, 1970, 15. Stourzh notes John Adams's recollections of the argument in 1774 about whether to "recur to the Law of Nature," which he strenuously urged. Hamilton was equally enthusiastic. Stourzh shows that, to support the case that the law of nature underlay the law, the colonists could turn to even the most conservative and famous of British constitutionalists, William Blackstone; see 11–18.

12. Caroline Robbins, *The Eighteenth Century Commonwealthman*, Cambridge, Mass., Harvard University Press, 1959; Bernard Bailyn, *The Ideological Origins of the American Revolution*, Cambridge, Mass., Harvard University Press, 1967, 86–92; Gordon Wood, *The Creation of the American Republic*, Chapel Hill, University of North Carolina Press, 1969, Ch. III; Phillip S. Foner (ed.), *The Complete Writings of Thomas Paine, 1737–1809*, 2 vols., New York, Citadel Press, 1945, I, 32.

13. Richard Price, "Observations on the Importance of the American Revolution" [1785], in D. O. Thomas (ed.), *Richard Price: Political Writings*, Cambridge, Cambridge University Press, 1991, 117–118. Price was a millennialist who

held that the one thousand years preceding Christ's coming would be a time of gradual human improvement that would make the earth fit for Christ and saints. See Thomas, ibid., Introduction. This and other apocalyptic traditions served to give religious meaning to secular history; Norman Cohn, *The Pursuit of the Millennium*, New York, Harper and Row, 1961. It was significant, too, that millennialism was often associated with the medieval doctrine of "translation of empire," meaning the progressive transmission of imperial and ecclesiastical power (or Christian "civilization") from east to west since the time of Christ. Protestants in sixteenth-century Britain had designated England an "elect nation" with a special role in sacred history, and it was tempting to imagine that role passing westward as England grew more corrupt. Certainly, America's western position in relation to Europe made it a plausible candidate for the final kingdom on earth; Ernest Tuveson, *Millennium and Utopia*, Berkeley, University of California Press, 1949. Margaret C. Jacob reveals precedents for this view among Anglican "latitudinarians," including Isaac Newton, in seventeenth-century England, who interpreted the English revolution, the Restoration, and then the Glorious Revolution in terms of Divine Providence and "election." Newton and his friends believed that his science, with its emphasis on design, order, and simplicity, were incontrovertible proof of God's providential design in human and natural affairs. It is surely no accident that Newton was one of Jefferson's great heroes. Jacob, *The Newtonians and the English Revolution, 1689–1720*, Ithaca, N.Y., Cornell University Press, 1976, 137.

14. Quoted in Echeverria, *Mirage in the West*, 153.

15. Wood, *Creation*, 99–100. The title of a book by Henry Steele Commager says it all: *The Empire of Reason: How Europe Imagined and America Realized the Enlightenment*, Garden City, N.Y., Anchor Press/Doubleday, 1977.

16. Joyce Appleby, Lynn Hunt, and Margaret Jacob, *Telling the Truth about History*, New York, Norton, 1995, Ch. 3.

17. See, for example, Jacob Needleman, *The American Soul: Rediscovering the Wisdom of the Founders*, New York, Tarcher Putnam, 2002.

CHAPTER 3. FOUNDING A VIRTUOUS REPUBLIC

1. Hartz, *Liberal Tradition*. On why the Declaration of Independence asserts fundamental rights to "life, liberty and the pursuit of happiness" and not to property, see Morton White, *The Philosophy of the American Revolution*, New York, Oxford University Press, 1978, 182–220. The Straussian contribution for the most part concerns itself with an alleged "crisis" (mainly theoretical) of modern liberalism, an ideology to which they are, in the main, opposed. See Strauss, *Liberalism Ancient and Modern*, Ithaca, N.Y., Cornell University Press, 1968, and *Natural Right and History*, Chicago, University of Chicago Press, 1953. The least "Straussian" of the Straussians in interpretation is Henry Jaffa, *Crisis of the House Divided: An Interpretation of the Issues in the Lincoln-Douglas Debates*, Chicago, University of Chicago Press, 1959; *How*

to Think about the American Revolution, Durham, N.C., Carolina University Press, 1978; and *American Conservatism and the American Founding*, Durham, N.C., Carolina University Press, 1984. Opposed to Jaffa are Allan Bloom, *The Closing of the American Mind*, New York, Simon & Schuster, 1987; and Thomas Pangle, *The Spirit of Modern Republicanism: The Moral Vision of the American Founders and the Philosophy of Locke*, Chicago, Chicago University Press, 1988. The latter, in final effect, support the Hartzian thesis of America as modern, liberal-capitalist, and Lockean. See also important papers by Martin Diamond, "Ethics and Politics: The American Way" and "Democracy and the Federalist: A Reconsideration of the Framers' Intent," both reprinted in Robert H. Horwitz (ed.), *The Moral Foundations of the American Republic*, Charlottesville, University Press of Virginia, 1986.

2. The famous phrase was coined by C. B. MacPherson, *The Political Theory of Possessive Individualism: Hobbes to Locke*, Oxford, Oxford University Press, 1962.

3. Isaac Kramnick, "Republican Revisionism Revisited," *American Historical Review* 87 (3), June 1982: 629–664; Forrest E. McDonald, *Novus Ordo Seculorum: The Intellectual Origins of the Constitution*, Lawrence, University Press of Kansas, 1985; J. G. A. Pocock, "Between Gog and Magog: The Republican Thesis and the Ideologia Americana," *Journal of the History of Ideas* 48 (2), April–June 1987: 325–346; Lance Banning, "The Republican Interpretation: Retrospect and Prospect," in Milton M. Klein, Richard D. Brown, and John B. Hench (eds.), *The Republican Synthesis Revisited: Essays in Honor of George Athan Billias*, 91–118, Worcester, Mass., American Antiquarian Society, 1992; James T. Kloppenberg, "The Virtues of Liberalism: Christianity, Republicanism, and Ethics in Early American Political Discourse," *American Journal of History* 74 (1), June 1987: 9–33; Wood, *Creation*; Montesquieu, *The Spirit of the Laws*, Bk. III. In Bk. V, 3–6, Montesquieu allows that a commercial republic did not necessarily mean the abandonment of virtue since "the spirit of commerce is naturally attended with that of frugality, economy, moderation, labour, prudence, tranquility, order, and rule."

4. Donald S. Lutz, *The Origins of American Constitutionalism*, Baton Rouge, Louisiana State University Press, 1988. Payson's sermon can be found in Charles S. Hyneman and Donald S. Lutz (eds.), *American Political Writing during the Founding Era, 1760–1805*, 2 vols., Indianapolis, Ind., Liberty Press, 1983, I, 523–538.

5. Machiavelli, *Discourses*, Bk. I, vi, vii, xvii, xxxvii, lv. Montesquieu, *Spirit of the Laws*, Bk. V, 2. Wood, *Creation*, 93–97, 473–474, 507–518.

6. Terence Ball argues that the search for the true nature of early American republican thought is misguided because the nature of true republicanism was itself the subject of dispute during the founding: "A Republic—If You Can Keep It," in Terence Ball and J. G. A. Pocock (eds.), *Conceptual Change and the Constitution*, Lawrence, University Press of Kansas, 1988, 137–164. Madison quotes Montesquieu at some length in *The Federalist* No. 9 to

demonstrate that a "Confederate Republic" could solve the problem of how a republic of large extent could exist without internal corruption. McDonald notes that American republicans regarded selected doctrines of Montesquieu's as "on a par with Holy Writ"; *Novus Ordo Seculorum*, 80, 81–83. Research has shown that Montesquieu and Locke were far and away the most cited thinkers of the 1760s and 1770s, with Montesquieu pulling well ahead in the 1780s, that is, when the focus had moved from justificatory to institutional questions; see Donald S. Lutz, "The Relative Influence of European Writers on the Late Eighteenth Century American Political Thought," *American Political Science Review* LXXVIII (1984): 189–197; and Lutz, *Origins of American Constitutionalism*, 139–147. Jefferson noted that Americans had no need to search into musty records for historical precedents to their political institutions: "We appealed to those of nature, and found them engraved on our hearts." "Letter to Major John Cartwright," June 5, 1824, in Merrill D. Peterson (ed.), *The Portable Thomas Jefferson*, New York, Viking, 1977, 578.

7. David Hume, whose views of the British constitution were influential at America's Constitutional Convention, and also on Hamilton's thought, had argued that it is best to assume all public men are knaves and that good government is determined primarily by good institutions and not by the morals and manners of the people; see McDonald, *Novus Ordo Seculorum*, 210–212. McDonald provides two lists of convention delegates, the first of which constituted the Bolingbroke-Montesquieu ("Country") camp —these hoped to found the republic on virtue—and the second the Hume-Mandeville ("Court") camp—who wished it founded on new principles that enabled the channeling of self-interest; ibid., 200.

8. Wood, *Creation*, 53–54.

9. Jefferson, "Letter to Dr. Benjamin Rush," January 16, 1811, in Peterson, *Portable Thomas Jefferson*, 123. Hamilton, *The Federalist* No. 76.

10. John C. Hamilton, *Life of Alexander Hamilton*, New York, (publisher unknown), 1911, 488; Stourzh, *Alexander Hamilton*, 183.

11. On Hamilton's financial and economic reforms, see McDonald, *Novus Ordo Seculorum*, 135–142. John Locke, "Notes for an Essay on Trade," quoted in Barbara Arneil, *John Locke and America: The Defence of English Colonialism*, Oxford, Clarendon Press, 1996, 159. On Hamilton as a Machiavellian, see John Harper, *American Machiavelli: Alexander Hamilton and the Origins of U.S. Foreign Policy*, Cambridge, Cambridge University Press, 2004. A work that argues he was not is Karl-Friedrich Walling, *Republican Empire: Alexander Hamilton on War and Free Government*, Lawrence, University Press of Kansas, 1999.

12. The main problem, as the Dissenters conceived it, was how to establish a broad and stable balance between rulers and ruled that would constrain the power of rulers, who were always inclined to abuse their public trust, while yet avoiding delivering power into the hands of an undisciplined democratic mob. For the general pattern of dissenting thought, see Richard Buel Jr.,

"Democracy and the American Revolution: A Frame of Reference," *William and Mary Quarterly* XXI (April 1964): 165–190. For the tendency toward revolutionary democratization, see Elisha P. Douglas, *Rebels and Democrats: The Struggle for Equal Political Rights and Majority Rule during the American Revolution*, Chicago, Ivan R. Dee, 1989 [1955]. The American case for the representative form was most famously put, in essentially Dissenting terms, by James Madison in *The Federalist* No. 10, but see also No. 57.

13. Henry Clay, "Speech on the state of the country under Mr. Van Buren's administration," quoted in Stourzh, *Alexander Hamilton*, 97.

14. In *The Federalist* No. 55, Madison concluded:

> As there is a degree of depravity in mankind which requires a certain degree of circumspection and distrust, so there are other qualities in human nature which justify a certain portion of esteem and confidence. Republican government presupposes the existence of these qualities in a higher degree than any other form. Were the pictures which have been drawn by the political jealousy of some among us faithful likenesses of the human character, the inference would be, that there is not sufficient virtue among men for self-government; and that nothing less than the chains of despotism can restrain them from destroying and devouring one another.

> For a defense of Madison's moderate view of virtue, see Lance Benning, "Some Second Thoughts on Virtue and the Course of Revolutionary Thinking," in Ball and Pocock, *Conceptual Change*, 194–212.

15. Martin Diamond, "Ethics and Politics," 59, notes the revulsion expressed for the low bargain by Richard Hofstadter in his book *The American Political Tradition and the Men Who Made It*, New York, Knopf, 1948. One possible reason for the continued faith in virtue suggested by Pocock is that the stable balancing of interests so powerfully simulated a virtuous republic that it was easy to forget that the political edifice was in fact no longer founded in virtue; J. G. A. Pocock, *The Machiavellian Moment: Florentine Political Thought and the Atlantic Tradition*, Princeton, N.J., Princeton University Press, 2003, 522, 528–529.

16. John Adams included Locke's name in a list of English republican writers and said that reading them "will convince any candid mind that there is no good government but what is republican"; *Thoughts on Government in a Letter from a Gentleman to his Friend* (1776), reprinted in K. M. Dolbeare (ed.), *Directions in American Political Thought*, New York, Wiley, 1969, 124–128 at 124. Jacob, *Newtonians*, 38–59. Alan Craig Houston, *Algernon Sidney and the Republican Heritage in England and America*, Princeton, N.J., Princeton University Press, 1991, 166. Jefferson, "Letter to Jean Baptiste Say," February 1, 1804, in Peterson, *Portable Thomas Jefferson*, 499.

17. Michael Zuckert, *Natural Rights and the New Republicanism*, Princeton, N.J., Princeton University Press, 1994, argues that the synthesis of liberalism

and republicanism had already been achieved in the radical Whiggery of John Trenchard and Thomas Gordon, writing under the pseudonym "Cato" early in the eighteenth century. *Cato's Letters* were highly regarded in America but had been interpreted in the republican thesis as the transmitters of classical republicanism rather than liberalism. Jerome Huyler, *Locke in America: The Moral Philosophy of the Founding Era,* Lawrence, University of Kansas Press, 1995, convincingly argues the synthetic view of Cato at greater length and goes further by finding all the elements of the synthesis already prefigured in Locke's life and thought.

18. On the influence of Scottish thinkers such as Frances Hutcheson, Adam Ferguson, Thomas Reid, Dugald Stewart, David Hume, and Adam Smith, see Henry F. May, *The Enlightenment in America,* New York, Oxford University Press, 1976; White, *Philosophy of the American Revolution;* McDonald, *Novus Ordo Seculorum.*

19. A basis for this division of labor between America and Europe can be found in Locke's economic theory (who in this followed Sir Josiah Child and Charles Davenant). Arguing for a plantation economy in the Americas, at a time when it was unpopular in England because of losses sustained by investors, he argued that American agricultural produce would exchange for English manufactures to the mutual benefit of all, boosting trade and shipping and creating employment in the homeland; see Arneil, *John Locke and America,* Ch. 4.

20. McDonald, *Novus Ordo Seculorum,* 94–95, 134–135; Drew R. McCoy, *The Elusive Republic: Political Economy in Jeffersonian America,* Chapel Hill, University of North Carolina Press, 1980, 129–132. Jefferson wrote: "Dependance begets subservience and venality, suffocates the germ of virtue, and prepares fit tools for the design of ambition. This, the natural progress and consequence of the arts, has sometimes perhaps been retarded by natural circumstances." Jefferson thinks it will not happen in America as long as there is "land and labour," and it is better to "let our workshops remain in Europe"; in Peterson, *Portable Thomas Jefferson,* 217.

21. Jefferson, "Letter to John Jay," August 23, 1785; and *Notes on Virginia,* Query XIX, in Peterson, *Portable Thomas Jefferson,* 384, 217.

22. Jefferson, *Letters,* Raleigh, N.C., Alex Catalogue, May 20, 1782. The same materialistic, optimistic outlook had already been prefigured by another great American philosopher, Ben Franklin, who had written: "Be industrious and frugal and you will be rich. Be sober and temperate, and you will be healthy. Be in general virtuous, and you will be happy"; quoted in Daniel Boorstin, *The Lost World of Thomas Jefferson,* Boston, Beacon Press, 1960 [1948], fn. 34, 275.

23. Another great hero of Jefferson's was Francis Bacon, the prophet of knowledge as power and progress. On Jeffersonian pragmatism generally, see Boorstin, *Lost World,* Chs. 3 and 4. It was entirely fitting that one of Ameri-

ca's foremost pragmatist philosophers, John Dewey, should present a book called *The Living Thoughts of Thomas Jefferson*, New York, Longmans, Green, 1941. "Letter to Jean Baptiste Say," 498.

24. Paul Goodman, "The First American Party System," in William Nisbet Chambers and Walter Dean Burnham (eds.), *American Party Systems: Stages of Political Development*, New York, Oxford University Press, 1967, 56–77 at 57. Hamilton had not been happy with a Constitution that fragmented power he wished to see concentrated, though he fought for its acceptance because it seemed better than nothing. His preference was to reduce the states to nothingness or at least to extreme subservience and dependence on central government. See Henry Cabot Lodge (ed.), *The Works of Alexander Hamilton*, New York, G. P. Putnam's Sons, 1899, Vol. I, 404. Claude G. Bowers, *Jefferson and Hamilton: The Struggle for Democracy in America*, Boston, Houghton Mifflin, 1925, 29–31.

25. Croly, *Promise of American Life*, 28, 419.

26. Hartz, *Liberal Tradition*, 215–216; Clinton Rossiter, *Conservatism in America*, New York, Vintage Books, 1962, 131; generally Richard Hofstadter, *Social Darwinism and American Thought*, Boston, Beacon Press, 1955. The man who did more than anyone to popularize and Americanize Spencer's theories was William Graham Sumner; see Stow Persons (ed.), *Social Darwinism: Collected Essays of William Graham Sumner*, Englewood Cliffs, N.J., Prentice-Hall, 1963. Joyce Appleby, *Without Resolution: The Jeffersonian Tensions in American Nationalism*, Oxford, Clarendon Press, 1992, 9; "Letter to James Madison," October 28, 1785, and "Letter to James Madison," December 20, 1787, in Peterson, *Portable Thomas Jefferson*, 396–397, 432. It was this Jeffersonian-Madisonian view that informed Pocock's analysis of a freehold agrarian virtue that had constantly to adjust itself to an expansive and potentially corrupting commerce, which it could do only by itself becoming expansive, pushing the frontier of settlement ever westward; *Machiavellian Moment*, 535.

27. Jefferson, *Notes on Virginia*, Query VIII, and "To the President of the United States (James Monroe)," October 24, 1823, in Peterson, *Portable Thomas Jefferson*, 124–125, 574–575.

28. The paper was *Wallaces' Farmer*, and the writer, Uncle Henry Wallace, was a profound influence on his grandson, Henry Agard Wallace, secretary of agriculture for Franklin D. Roosevelt during the New Deal and Progressive presidential candidate in 1948; J. Samuel Walker, *Henry A. Wallace and American Foreign Policy*, Westport, Conn., Greenwood Press, 1976, 4–5, 32.

29. Ron Chernow, *Alexander Hamilton*, New York, Penguin, 2004.

30. Appleby, *Without Resolution*, 2–3. Appleby notes here, too, that Jefferson "had the unique distinction of being claimed as the founder of both major American political parties."

CHAPTER 4. PROBLEMS OF VIRTUE AND POWER

1. On the amalgamation of the civic and religious virtue in Puritanism, see Pocock, *Machiavellian Moment*, 463. Kloppenberg, in "The Virtues of Liberalism," identifies religious, republican, and liberal influences and argues that each was ambiguous in its meaning for American virtue. I believe the influences were in fact more numerous even than this.

2. The agrarian philosophy of the New Deal, despite its traditional contrast of the humanizing effect of farm labor as opposed to the dehumanizing effect of factory work, valorized commercial rather than subsistence farmers. It also had a new concern for the environmental damage done by individualistic, short-sighted "Old Americans." See Henry Agard Wallace, *New Frontiers*, New York, Reynal & Hitchcock, 1934; and the work of Franklin Roosevelt's undersecretary of agriculture, Rexford G. Tugwell, *The Battle for Democracy*, New York, Columbia University Press, 1935.

3. The Dutchman Cornelius de Pauw had argued in 1768 that the climate of the New World, over generations, would inevitably cause the physical and mental degeneration of the colonists as it allegedly had of Native American tribes and fauna. De Pauw aimed to prove the falsity of Rousseau's "noble savage" theory by demonstrating the infinite superiority of European civilization and thus to discourage the large-scale emigration to the New World that, he claimed, was sapping European strength to the point of catastrophe. Benjamin Franklin, well aware how deeply this theme had penetrated French consciousness, was tireless in his efforts to counter it, both by his own brilliant example and through tales that caused his French hosts to think that, in America, every citizen must be a philosopher. De Pauw's views, however, were further popularized (and vulgarized) by the Abbé Raynal in the 1770s and remained in wide circulation (perhaps never quite to fade from the Gallic mind); Echeverria, *Mirage in the West*, 28–36.

4. Adams, *Defence of the Constitutions of Government of the United States of America*, quoted in Stourzh, *Alexander Hamilton*, 65; Jean-Jacques Rousseau, "A Dissertation on the Origin and Foundation of the Inequality of Mankind," *Great Books of the Western World*, 38, Chicago, William Benton Publisher, 1982, 333–366; Alexis de Tocqueville, *Democracy in America*, ed. J. P. Mayer, Garden City, N.Y., Doubleday, 1969, Vol. 2, Part II, Ch. 13; Part II, Ch. 17; Part III, 615.

5. On the Jeffersonian view of virtue, see Boorstin, *Lost World*, 144–148; Boorstin, *The Americans: The National Experience*, New York, Random House, 1965. On liberalism and Protestantism, see Isaac Kramnick, "The 'Great National Discussion': The Discourse of Politicians in 1787," *William and Mary Quarterly* 3 (45), 1988: 18. Kramnick (22) sees the virtue of industriousness, and thus of economic activity, as displacing that of civic virtue and public action. Huyler, *Locke in America*, Ch. 8, argues that Americans understood virtue in *both* senses without contradiction. On Hamilton, see McDonald, *Novus Ordo Seculorum*, 141–142.

6. According to Barbara Arneil, for three centuries Amerindian society found itself, by virtue of Locke's theory, "a distorted inversion of civil society"; *Locke and America*, 44; see 27–33, Ch. 7. On a "producerist ideology" that stressed work (and the money and independence it brought) as an Enlightenment way of seeing the world that succeeded best in America, see Judith Shklar, *American Citizenship: The Quest for Inclusion*, Cambridge, Mass., Harvard University Press, 1991, 63–79; W. J. Cash, *The Mind of the South*, New York, Knopf, 1941, 60; Jefferson, "Letter to Chastellux," September 2, 1785, in Peterson, *Portable Thomas Jefferson*, 387.

7. George M. Marsden, *Jonathan Edwards: A Life*, New Haven, Conn., Yale University Press, 2003; James A. Monroe, *Hellfire Nation: The Politics of Sin in American History*, New Haven, Conn., Yale University Press, 2003.

8. Richard L. Bushman, *From Puritan to Yankee: Character and the Social Order in Connecticut, 1690–1765*, Cambridge, Mass., Harvard University Press, 1967, excerpted in Marvin Meyers and J. R. Pole, *The Meanings of American History: Interpretations of Events, Ideas, and Institutions*, Glenview, Ill., Scott, Foresman, 1971, Vol. 1, 67–73 at 73.

9. It seems curious that Clark Roof should criticize modern evangelist Rick Warren on the grounds that he equates success with the size of his church and because "we're told that [his philosophy] not only does something for you in the sense of giving your life meaning but it also makes you happy materially, religiously and spiritually. What Rick is marketing is a kind of American religious ideology that conflates growth with salvation." (Cited in Sonia Steptoe, "The Man with the Purpose," *Time*, March 29, 2004, 53.) Such a conflation has long been a tendency of American evangelicalism. See Edward McNall Burns, *The American Idea of Mission: Concepts of National Purpose and Destiny*, Westport, Conn., Greenwood Press, 1973 [1957], 30–31, and Richard Hofstadter, *Anti-Intellectualism in American Life*, New York, Knopf, 1962, 81–106. On the significance of revivalism, see T. L. Smith, *Revivalism and Social Reform: American Protestantism on the Eve of the Civil War*, New York, Harper and Row, 1957; Perry Miller, *The Life and Mind of America*, New York, Harcourt, Brace & World, 1965 (Book I, "The Evangelical Basis"); James E. Johnson, "Charles G. Finney and a Theory of Revivalism," *Church History* 38 (September 1969): 338–358. Alan Wolfe in *The Transformation of American Religion: How We Actually Live Our Faith*, New York, Free Press, 2003, argues that the tendency toward personalized, individualistic religious practices has become characteristic of all denominations, Protestant or not, in the past half century, denoting the triumph of American culture over doctrinal religion.

10. Jefferson, "Letter to Doctor Benjamin Rush," April 21, 1803, in Peterson, *Portable Thomas Jefferson*, 491–494. Jefferson produced an expurgated version of the New Testament leaving out all the supernatural elements and presenting Jesus as a moral teacher; see Stephen Prothero, *American Jesus: How the Son of God Became a National Icon*, New York, Farrar, Straus & Giroux,

2003. "Letter to Elbridge Gerry," January 26, 1799, in Peterson, *Portable Thomas Jefferson*, 479.

11. Susan Jacoby, *Freethinkers: A History of American Secularism*, New York, Metropolitan Books, 2004.

12. Wilson's view can be found in Arthur S. Link (ed.), *The Papers of Woodrow Wilson*, Princeton, N.J., Princeton University Press, 1972, 12, 474–478. See Lloyd C. Ambrosius, *Wilsonianism: Woodrow Wilson and His Legacy in American Foreign Relations*, New York, Palgrave Macmillan, 2002, 36. On Bush, see Mark Crispin Miller, *Cruel and Unusual: Bush/Cheney's New World Order*, New York, Norton, 2004; Peter Schweizer and Rochelle Schweizer, *The Bushes: Portrait of a Dynasty*, New York, Doubleday, 2004. On the influence of religion on contemporary U.S. politics and politicians, see *Time* poll of 2004; Nancy Gibbs, "The Faith Factor," *Time*, June 21, 2004, 18–23.

13. Jacob, *Newtonians*, in a passage that strikingly prefigures fundamental American beliefs, writes:

> To my mind, the most historically significant contribution of the latitudinarians lies in their ability to synthesize the operations of a market society and the workings of nature in such a way as to render the market society natural . . . Natural religion made the actions of the prosperous compatible with Christian virtue and with the very mechanism of the universe. According to their preachers, the prosperous benefited because they worked, and success in this world as well as in the next rested not on any imagined predestination but on an act of individual will. . . . So probable is the success of the virtuous that their prosperity is an even higher sign of God's providence than is the order inherent in nature. Only true industry constitutes the proper pursuit of self-interest; indeed Scripture recommends it as both just and necessary; covetousness and greed are actually antithetical to the fulfillment of desire. (51, 56)

14. Gunfighters acted in accordance with a principle of "no duty to retreat," an Americanization of the traditional English law on self-defense that said a defender had a duty to "retreat to the wall" rather than stand against or pursue an attacker. The so-called Texas rule, in contrast, maintained it was justifiable to kill an attacker. It was incorporated into American law in the Supreme Court's decision in *Brown v. United States* (1921), when Justice O. W. Holmes noted approvingly that it was well settled that "a man was not born to run away." See Richard M. Brown, *No Duty to Retreat*, New York, Oxford University Press, 1991, 39.

15. Henry Demarest Lloyd, the leading intellectual defender of American populism in the 1890s, expressed a version of this dilemma in his indictment of the "corporate caesars" of monopoly capitalism: "Liberty produces wealth, and wealth destroys liberty." (Quoted in James P. Young, *Reconsidering*

American Liberalism: The Troubled Odyssey of the Liberal Idea, Boulder, Colo., Westview Press, 1996, 141.)

16. Staughton Lynd, "The Abolitionist Critique of the United States Constitution," in Martin Duberman (ed.), *The Antislavery Vanguard,* Princeton, N.J., Princeton University Press, 1965, 209–239.

17. Phillip Shaw Paludan notes the "pervasive constitutionalism" of northerners during the Civil War era; *A Covenant with Death: The Constitution, Law, and Equality in the Civil War Era,* Urbana, University of Illinois Press, 1975, 46. This constitutionalism was fully shared by Abraham Lincoln; see John Kane, *The Politics of Moral Capital,* Cambridge, Cambridge University Press, 2001, 69–70; *The Federalist* No. 78.

18. See Jean-Jacques Rousseau, *The Social Contract,* II, 6, *Great Books of the Western World,* 38, Chicago, William Benton Publisher, 1982, 387–439. Rousseau, however, settled the problem of finding the general will not through people's rational deliberation but in the deus ex machina of a wise law-giver, thus undermining the argument of democratic legitimacy; ibid., II, 7.

CHAPTER 5. NONENTANGLEMENT: THE ECONOMIC DIMENSION

1. George Washington, "The National Interest in Diplomatic Freedom," September 17, 1796; excerpted in Norman A. Graebner (ed.), *Ideas and Diplomacy: Readings in the Intellectual Tradition of American Foreign Policy,* New York, Oxford University Press, 1964, 75.

2. William Appleman Williams, *The Tragedy of American Diplomacy,* 2nd ed., New York, Delta, 1978, 13; Melvyn P. Leffler, "National Security," in Michael J. Hogan and Thomas G. Paterson (eds.), *Explaining the History of American Foreign Relations,* Cambridge, Cambridge University Press, 1991, 211.

3. See Allister Sparks, *The Mind of South Africa,* New York, Ballantine Books, 1990.

4. The nullification crisis began when South Carolina, with the support of John C. Calhoun, declared tariff acts passed in 1828 and 1832 null and void and prohibited their enforcement within its borders. President Jackson condemned nullification theory (which asserted states' rights to determine the constitutionality of federal laws) as a threat to the Union. He passed a Force Bill empowering the president to enforce federal law while simultaneously reducing the tariffs, thus averting the first great crisis of the Union; see Richard E. Ellis, *The Union at Risk: Jacksonian Democracy, States' Rights, and the Nullification Crisis,* New York, Oxford University Press, 1987. The "Silverites" wanted to induce domestic inflation of the currency, thus arguably increasing crop prices and effectively reducing the excessive debts that burdened and often broke them. Industrialists and their political protectors wanted the dollar to remain firmly tied to the gold standard to maintain international respectability and defend the profitability of industrial trade. William Jennings Bryan became the champion of the Silverites with his famous "Cross of Gold" speech at the 1896 Democratic Convention, but he

lost the election to McKinley, and in 1900 a Republican majority passed the Gold Standard Act that pinned the currency to gold; on populism generally, see Norman Pollack, *The Populist Response to American Industrialization: Mid-Western Populist Thought*, Cambridge, Mass., Harvard University Press, 1962.

5. This school drew inspiration from Appleman Williams and included figures like Martin Sklar, Lloyd Gardner, Thomas McCormick, and Walter LaFeber. LaFeber reminisces on the work of this group and the continuing influence of its "economistic" interpretations in his preface to the 1998 edition of *The New Empire: An Interpretation of American Expansion, 1860–1898*, Ithaca, N.Y., Cornell University Press [1963]. See also his useful updating of his own work in *The Cambridge History of American Foreign Relations, Vol. II: The American Search for Opportunity, 1865–1913*, Cambridge, Cambridge University Press, 1993.

6. Benjamin Franklin Cooling, *Gray Steel and Blue Water Navy: The Formative Years of America's Military-Industrial Complex, 1881–1917*, Hamden, Conn., Archon, 1979; Kenneth J. Hagan, *This People's Navy: The Making of America's Sea Power*, New York, Free Press, 1991; David M. Potter, *People of Plenty: Economic Abundance and the American Character*, Chicago, University of Chicago Press, 1954; William H. Becker and Samuel F. Wells (eds.), *Economics and World Power: An Assessment of American Diplomacy since 1789*, New York, Columbia University Press, 1984. For the dominance of the economic motive early in the nineteenth century, see Mary W. M. Hargreaves, *The Presidency of John Quincy Adams*, Lawrence, University of Kansas Press, 1985; John H. Belohlavek, *"Let the Eagle Soar!": The Foreign Policy of Andrew Jackson*, Lincoln, University of Nebraska Press, 1985; Ernest N. Paolino, *The Foundations of American Empire: William Henry Seward and U.S. Foreign Policy*, Ithaca, N.Y., Cornell University Press, 1973.

7. LaFeber, *American Search for Opportunity*, 135.

8. The Nye Committee arraigned bankers like J. P. Morgan and manufacturers like the Du Ponts as "merchants of death" whose international dealings in armaments were the ultimate cause of American entry into the war. See Wayne S. Cole, *Senator Gerald P. Nye and American Foreign Relations*, Minneapolis, University of Minnesota Press, 1962.

9. Henry A. Wallace, *America Must Choose*, New York and Boston, Foreign Policy Association and World Peace Foundation, 1934, 8–11, 14–17; Charles A. Beard, *The Open Door at Home: A Trial Philosophy of National Interest*, New York, Macmillan, 1934; Henry A. Wallace, "Beard: The Planner," *New Republic* 81 (January 2, 1935): 225–227.

10. J. Samuel Walker, *Henry A. Wallace and American Foreign Policy*, Westport, Conn., Greenwood Press, 1973, 29.

11. Montesquieu, *Spirit of the Laws*, Bk. XX, Chs. 23, 4, 7.

12. Paine, *Common Sense*, in Harry Hayden Clark (ed.), *Thomas Paine: Representative Selections*, New York, Hill & Wang, 1944, 17.

13. *The Federalist* No. 6 repeated the arguments that Hamilton had made in a speech to the Federal Convention on June 18, 1787. On this theme generally, see Stourzh, *Alexander Hamilton*, 140–145.

14. Ralph Eldin Minger, *William Howard Taft and United States Foreign Policy: The Apprenticeship Years, 1900–1908*, Urbana, University of Illinois Press, 1975, Ch. VII, 136–137.

15. Joseph Brandes, *Herbert Hoover and Economic Diplomacy: Department of Commerce Policy, 1921–1928*, Westport, Conn., Greenwood Press, 1975 [1962]. See also Herbert Feis, *The Diplomacy of the Dollar*, Baltimore, Md., Johns Hopkins University Press, 1950, and Joan Hoff Wilson, *American Business and Foreign Policy, 1920–1933*, Lexington, University Press of Kentucky, 1971. Hoover put his own economic philosophy on record in the book *American Individualism*, Garden City, N.Y., Doubleday, Page, 1922.

16. Robert H. Ferrell, *American Diplomacy in the Great Depression: Hoover-Stimson Foreign Policy, 1929–1933*, Hamden, Conn., Archon, 1969 [1957].

CHAPTER 6. NONENTANGLEMENT: THE POLITICAL DIMENSION

1. *The Federalist* Nos. 25 and 34.

2. See Paul Goodman, "The First American Party System," in W. N. Chambers and W. D. Burnham (eds.), *American Party Systems: Stages of Political Development*, Oxford, Oxford University Press, 1967.

3. The fact that the possibility of war with Britain ended with Jay's Treaty has not prevented historians ever since from damning it, and Jay, for undue submissiveness. See Samuel Flagg Bemis, *Jay's Treaty: A Study in Commerce and Diplomacy*, 2nd ed., New Haven, Conn., Yale University Press, 1962.

4. Henry Adams, "The Inauguration," in *History of the United States during the Administration of Jefferson and Madison*, New York, Charles Scribner's Sons, 1889–1891, I, 132.

5. Arthur Bestor, "Respective Roles of Senate and President in the Making and Abrogation of Treaties: The Original Intent of the Framers Historically Reviewed," *Washington Law Review* 55 (1979): 4–135; Jack N. Rakove, "Solving a Constitutional Puzzle: The Treatymaking Clause as a Case Study," *Perspectives in American History* n.s., 1, 1984: 233–281; Frederick W. Marks III, *Independence on Trial: Foreign Affairs and the Making of the Constitution*, Baton Rouge, Louisiana State University Press, 1973.

6. This was how England interpreted the proclamation, according to the Democratic Society of Philadelphia; *Philadelphia Daily Advertiser*, April 14, 1794, cited in Claude G. Bowers, *Jefferson and Hamilton: The Struggle for Democracy in America*, Boston, Houghton Mifflin, 1925, 245.

7. "Letter to Elbridge Gerry," January 26, 1799, in Peterson, *Portable Thomas Jefferson*, 478.

8. For the concern over national weakness, see Walter LaFeber, "The Constitution and United States Foreign Policy," *Journal of American History* 74 (1987–1988): 693–717.

9. "Letter to John Jay," August 23, 1785, in Peterson, *Portable Thomas Jefferson*, 385.

10. "Letter to Elbridge Gerry," January 26, 1799, in Peterson, *Portable Thomas Jefferson*, 478.

11. "Letter to James Madison," March 24, 1793, in Peterson, *Portable Thomas Jefferson*, 467.

12. Bradford Perkins, *Prologue to War: England and the United States 1805–1812*, Berkeley, University of California Press, 1961, 428; Bradford Perkins, *The Cambridge History of American Foreign Relations: The Creation of a Republican Empire, 1776–1865*, Cambridge, Cambridge University Press, 1993, 120; Henry Adams, *History of the United States during the Second Administration of Thomas Jefferson*, New York, Charles Scribner's Sons, 1890, Vol. II, 104.

13. Cited in Reginald Horsman, "Western War Aims, 1811–1812," in Bradford Perkins (ed.), *The Causes of the War of 1812: National Honor or National Interest?*, Hinsdale, Ill., Dryden Press, 1962, 97. See this volume generally on the debate over causes of the war.

14. Donald R. Hickey, *The War of 1812: A Forgotten Conflict*, Urbana, University of Illinois Press, 1989.

15. Perkins, *Prologue to War*, 437, 435.

16. Michael H. Hunt, *Ideology and U.S. Foreign Policy*, New Haven, Conn., Yale University Press, 1987, Ch. 3.

17. John Quincy Adams, address of July 4, 1821, in Walter Lafeber (ed.), *John Quincy Adams and American Continental Empire: Letters, Papers and Speeches*, Chicago, Quadrangle Books, 1965, 44–46.

18. Croly, *Promise of American Life*, 291. On the Monroe Doctrine, see Dexter Perkins, *The Monroe Doctrine, 1823–1826*, Gloucester, Mass., P. Smith, 1965 [1927]; Armin Rappaport (ed.), *The Monroe Doctrine*, Huntington, N.Y., R. E. Krieger, 1976 [1964].

19. Robert Charles Thomas, "Andrew Jackson versus France: American Policy toward France, 1834–1836," *Tennessee Historical Quarterly* 35 (Spring 1976): 51–64; Belohlavek, *"Let the Eagle Soar!"*

20. Tocqueville, *Democracy in America*, Vol. 2, Part III, 612.

CHAPTER 7. INNOCENT VIRTUE AND THE CONQUEST OF A CONTINENT

1. Howard Jones, *Union in Peril: The Crisis over British Intervention in the Civil War*, Chapel Hill, University of North Carolina Press, 1992. Northerners were particularly upset by Britain's declaration granting belligerent status to the South in 1861. Britain could hardly do otherwise in the circumstances, but northerners took it as virtual recognition of the South's independence and a sign of British animosity. Lincoln always insisted on referring to the war as a "domestic insurrection" rather than a civil war on the grounds that the Confederate states had no legal right to secede therefore could not form a distinct entity entitled to foreign recognition.

2. Stephen Pelz, "Balance of Power," in Hogan and Paterson, *Explaining the History*, 111–140.

3. C. Vann Woodward called this era one of "free security" for the United States given that Britain's monopoly of control of the seas in defense of its own empire inadvertently served the latter and saved it from having to seriously deploy forces of its own; "The Age of Reinterpretation," *American Historical Review* 66 (1), October 1960: 1–19; Lawrence S. Kaplan, *Entangling Alliances with None: American Foreign Policy in the Age of Jefferson*, Kent, Ohio, Kent State University Press, 1987. Others have argued that other factors need consideration, including British military weakness: Kenneth Bourne, *Britain and the Balance of Power in North America, 1815–1908*, Berkeley, University of California Press, 1967; see also Wilbur Devereux Jones, *The American Problem in British Diplomacy*, Athens, University of Georgia Press, 1974.

4. American expansion from earliest times had multiple causes, one being the poor soil of New England that inspired Yankee farmers to move ever farther northwestward in the early nineteenth century, stimulating demands for canals for transportation of trade products; see, for example, Stewart H. Holbrook, *The Yankee Exodus: An Account of Migration from New England*, New York, Macmillan, 1950. On expansionism in the 1840s, see David M. Pletcher, *The Diplomacy of Annexation: Texas, Oregon, and the Mexican War*, Columbia, University of Missouri Press, 1972. Beef for miners in California in the 1850s stimulated the cattle industry, which after the Civil War went on to serve the growing appetite for American beef in the East and in England, stimulating the pushing westward of the railways; Ernest S. Osgood, *The Day of the Cattleman*, Chicago, Chicago University Press, 1957 [1929]; H. O. Brayer, "The Influence of British Capital on the Western Range-Cattle Industry," *Journal of Economic History*, Supplement IX, 1949. On poor southern farming methods that promoted expansion, see Eugene D. Genovese, "The Slave South: An Interpretation," *Science and Society* XXV (4), December 1961: 320–337.

5. Croly, *Promise of American Life*, 8.

6. He wrote: "From the time when we became an independent people it was as much a law of nature that this should become our pretension as that the Mississippi should flow to the sea." November 16, 1819, *Memoirs of John Quincy Adams*, IV, excerpted in Graebner, *Ideas and Diplomacy*, 132–133.

7. On Adams, see Paul C. Nagel, *John Quincy Adams: A Public Life, a Private Life*, Cambridge, Mass., Harvard University Press, 1999; Samuel Flagg Bemis, *John Quincy Adams and the Foundations of American Foreign Policy*, 2 vols., New York, Norton, 1973 [1949]; Hargreaves, *Presidency of John Quincy Adams*; William Earl Weeks, *John Quincy Adams and American Global Empire*, Lexington, University Press of Kentucky, 1992.

8. John H. Schroeder, *Mr. Polk's War: American Opposition and Dissent, 1846–*

1848, Madison, University of Wisconsin Press, 1973; Paul H. Bergeron, *The Presidency of James K. Polk*, Lawrence, University of Kansas Press, 1987; Pletcher, *Diplomacy of Annexation;* Frederick Merk, *Slavery and the Annexation of Texas*, New York, Knopf, 1972; Reginald Horsman, *Race and Manifest Destiny*, Cambridge, Mass., Harvard University Press, 1981. Polk quotations from Thomas R. Hietala, *Manifest Design: Anxious Aggrandizement in Late Jacksonian America*, Ithaca, N.Y., Cornell University Press, 1985, 122.

9. Robert E. May, *The Southern Dream of a Caribbean Empire: 1854–1861,* Baton Rouge, Louisiana State University Press, 1973.

10. On surviving racism, note, for example, a right-wing "revisionist" like Thomas E. Woods Jr., *The Politically Incorrect Guide to American History*, Washington, D.C., Regnery, 2004. The classic works on Manifest Destiny are Albert K. Weinberg, *Manifest Destiny: A Study of Nationalist Expansionism in American History*, Baltimore, Md., Johns Hopkins University Press, 1935; Frederick Merk, *Manifest Destiny and Mission in American History: A Reinterpretation*, Westport, Conn., Greenwood Press, 1983 [1963].

11. Thomas Jefferson, *Notes on the State of Virginia*, in Peterson, *Portable Thomas Jefferson.*

12. "Letter to Williamson Durley," October 3, 1845, in *Collected Works*, 2, 348.

13. "Message to Congress in Special Session," July 4, 1861, in *Collected Works*, 4, 427. For my more detailed account of Lincoln's reasoning, see John Kane, *The Politics of Moral Capital*, Cambridge, Cambridge University Press, 2001, Ch. 3. See also Mark E. Neely Jr., *The Last Best Hope of Earth: Abraham Lincoln and the Promise of America*, Cambridge, Mass., Harvard University Press, 1995; Paludan, *Covenant with Death;* John S. Wright, *Lincoln and the Politics of Slavery*, Reno, University of Nevada Press, 1970.

14. On the speech, see Garry Wills, "Lincoln's Greatest Speech?" *Atlantic Monthly*, September 1999, available at http://www.theatlantic.com/cgi-bin/0/issues/99sep/9909lincoln.htm; William Lee Miller, "Lincoln's Second Inaugural: The Zenith of Statecraft," *Center Magazine* 13 (July–August 1980): 53–64.

15. John P. Diggins, *The Lost Soul of American Politics*, New York, Basic Books, 1984, 296–333; Jaffa, *Crisis of the House Divided* (which argues the "Socratic" nature of Lincoln's argument in stressing a standard of right and wrong independent of and above mere popular opinion); Phillip Shaw Paludan, *"A People's Contest": The Union and Civil War, 1861–1865*, New York, Harper and Row, 1988, 378.

16. Lincoln advised that "I could not afford to hang men for votes." David A. Nichols, *Lincoln and the Indians: Civil War Policy and Politics*, Columbia, University of Missouri Press, 1978, Chs. 6–8, 13.

17. Locke's "strange doctrine" is that conquest gives the conqueror power over the lives of the conquered but no title over their possessions: *Second Treatise on Civil Government*, para. 180. For my analysis of Locke's rhetorical strategy, see John Kane, "Man the Maker versus Man the Taker: Locke's Theory of

Property as a Theory of Just Settlement," *Eighteenth Century Thought* 3, 2007: 235–253.

18. Jefferson quotation of June 14, 1817, from Stourzh, *Alexander Hamilton*, 193. Anthony F. C. Wallace, *Jefferson and the Indians: The Tragic Fate of the First Americans*, Cambridge, Mass., Harvard University Press, 2001; Tocqueville, *Democracy in America*, Vol. 1, Part II, 337.

19. The relevant cases were *Johnson and Graham's Lessee v. M'Intosh* (1823); *The Cherokee Nation v. The State of Georgia* (1831); and *Worcester v. The State of Georgia* (1832). See Arneil, *John Locke and America*, 194–197, who I follow in this account. On the legal niceties, see Joseph C. Burke, "The Cherokee Cases: A Study in Law, Politics, and Morality," *Stanford Law Review* 21 (February 1969): 500–531; and Edwin A. Miles, "After John Marshall's Decision: *Worcester v. Georgia* and the Nullification Crisis," *Journal of Southern History* 39 (November 1973): 519–544.

20. Most of the opposition to Jackson's Indian policies came, naturally enough, from Whig opponents in the Northeast, but there was the odd honorable exception in the West, like David (Davy) Crockett, congressman from Tennessee; see *Speeches on the Passage of the Bill for the Removal of the Indians*, in Louis Filler and Allen Guttmann (eds.), *The Removal of the Cherokee Nation: Manifest Destiny or National Dishonor?*, Huntington, N.Y., Krieger, 1962. On Jackson and the Indians, see Michael P. Rogin, *Fathers and Children: Andrew Jackson and the Subjugation of the American Indian*, New York, Knopf, 1975; Ronald N. Satz, *American Indian Policy in the Jacksonian Era*, Lincoln, University of Nebraska Press, 1975; Anthony F. C. Wallace, *The Long, Bitter Trail: Andrew Jackson and the Indians*, New York, Hill & Wang, 1993. A rare exception that tried to exculpate Jackson was Francis Paul Prucha, "Andrew Jackson's Indian Policy: A Reassessment," *Journal of American History* 56 (December 1969): 527–539, which was supported, hardly more convincingly, by Robert V. Remini, *Andrew Jackson and His Indian Wars*, New York, Penguin, 2001.

21. Unfortunately, the main guardian of the law, the Supreme Court, sullied its hands in 1871 by giving Congress the power to override treaties with the Indian "dependent nations" with new laws. Thus the Dawes Severalty Act of 1887 created a new era of legal dispossession by forcing Indians to switch from communal to individual ownership, enabling whites to buy thousands of acres from bankrupt Indians. Satz, *American Indian Policy*; Arneil, *John Locke and America*, 197.

22. Sherman letter to his brother Philemon, February 7, 1842, cited in Stanley P. Hirshon, *The White Tecumseh: A Biography of General William T. Sherman*, New York, Wiley, 1997, 20. Sherman famously took the same realistic attitude during the Civil War in 1864: "War is cruelty. There is no use trying to reform it; the crueler it is, the sooner it will be over" (181).

23. Weinberg, *Manifest Destiny*, 22; Charles Stewart Davies, "Popular Government," An Address Delivered on the Commemoration at Freyburg, May 19,

1825, in Joseph L. Blau (ed.), *Social Theories of Jacksonian Democracy: Representative Writings of the Period 1825–1850*, New York, Liberal Arts Press, 1954, 38–53.

24. Alexander Nemerov, *Frederic Remington and Turn-of-the-Century America*, New Haven, Conn., Yale University Press, 1995, 10.

25. Quoted in Gary Arnold and Kenneth Turan, "The Duke: 'More Than Just a Hero,'" *Washington Post*, June 13, 1979. See also Garry Wills, *John Wayne: The Politics of Celebrity*, London, Faber and Faber, 1999.

26. Frederick Jackson Turner, "The Significance of the Frontier in American History," American Historical Association, *Annual Report for the Year 1893* (Washington, 1894), 199–227.

27. Ray Allen Billington, *America's Frontier Heritage*, Albuquerque, University of New Mexico Press, 1974, 15; Merk, *Manifest Destiny*, 1963; Norman Graebner (ed.), *Manifest Destiny*, Indianapolis, Bobbs-Merrill, 1968; Richard White, *"It's Your Misfortune and None of My Own": A History of the American West*, Norman, University of Oklahoma Press, 1991; Richard Slotkin, *The Fatal Environment: The Myth of the Frontier in the Age of Industrialization, 1800–1890*, New York, Atheneum, 1985, Ch. 3, 34; Henry Nash Smith, *Virgin Land: The American West as Symbol and Myth*, Cambridge, Mass., Harvard University Press, 1950; William H. Truettner, "Ideology and Image: Justifying Westward Expansion," in W. H. Truettner (ed.), *The West as America: Reinterpreting Images of the Frontier, 1820–1920*, Washington, D.C., Smithsonian Press, 1991, 27–50.

28. Quoted in John S. Miller, *Life on the Frontier*, New York, Delacorte, 1966, 139.

29. Garry Wills, *Reagan's America: Innocents at Home*, New York, Doubleday, 1987, Ch. 41.

30. The story of *Shane*, notably, possessed two heroes: one the classical Jeffersonian agrarian settler, Starrett, and the other the lonely, drifting gunfighter, Shane; Jack Schaefer, *Shane*, Boston, Houghton Mifflin, 1954 [1949]; the movie, *Shane*, dir. George Stevens, 1953. In John Ford's film *The Man Who Shot Liberty Valance*, it is a peace-loving but courageous lawyer, James Stewart, who comes from the East to try to bring law to the West but must confront the intimidation of crazy owlhoot Valance, played by Lee Marvin (note the significance of the name Liberty). The dependence of law on the decent man of violence is affirmed by John Wayne's hidden intervention. On Hickock, see Brown, *No Duty to Retreat*, 49–60.

31. Richard White, "Outlaw Gangs and Social Bandits," in C. A. Milner (ed.), *Major Problems in the History of the American West: Documents and Essays*, Lexington, Mass., D. C. Heath, 1989, 370–384; John Dewey, "From Absolutism to Experimentalism," in Debra Morris and Ian Shapiro (eds.), *John Dewey: The Political Writings*, Cambridge, Hackett, 1993, 178.

32. Robert Wiebe, *The Search for Order: 1877–1920*, New York, Hill & Wang, 1977; Martin Sklar, *The Corporate Reconstruction of American Capitalism: 1890–1916*, New York, Cambridge University Press, 1988.

33. The Industrial Workers of the World (IWW, or Wobblies), an anarcho-syndicalist organization founded in 1905 by William Haywood, Eugene Debs, and Daniel De Leon, became the main American symbol of this threat. The correct interpretation of Progressivism has long been a controversial subject; see Richard Hofstadter, *The American Political Tradition*, New York, Knopf, 1973 [1948]; Daniel T. Rodgers, "In Search of Progressivism," *Reviews in American History* (December 1982): 113–132.

34. The disputes involved Brazil, Nicaragua, and Venezuela. See David Healy, *Drive to Hegemony: The United States and the Caribbean, 1898–1917*, Madison, University of Wisconsin Press, 1988, 32–35; LaFeber, *American Search for Opportunity*, 121–6.

CHAPTER 8. FROM IMPERIALISM TO WORLD PEACE

1. Hawaii had been under U.S. protection (from the intrigues of France and Great Britain) since 1851 and the United States had acquired rights to a naval base at Pearl Harbor in 1887. Annexation was finally agreed in 1898, and Hawaii became a territory of the United States in 1900. Cleveland's written statement to the Associated Press, January 24, 1898, *Letters of Grover Cleveland, 1850–1908*, ed. Allan Nevins, Boston, Houghton Mifflin, 1933, 491–492.

2. Raymond Carr, *Puerto Rico: A Colonial Experiment*, New York, New York University Press, 1984.

3. The United States also annexed Eastern Samoa (American Samoa) in 1899.

4. Beveridge's statement was made at a New Year's Eve 1901 address, Bryan's at an address of August 1900; quoted in Osgood, *Ideals and Self-Interest*, 87.

5. Mahan, a prophet with little honor in his own country, was avidly read in Britain and by imperialists in the rising countries of Germany and Japan, who would become bitter foes of the United States in the twentieth century. His main works were *The Influence of Sea Power upon History, 1660–1783*, Boston, Little, Brown, 1890, and *The Influence of Sea Power upon the French Revolution and Empire, 1793–1812*, Boston, Little, Brown, 1892. Of most direct relevance to the United States was *The Interest of America in Sea Power, Present and Future*, Boston, Little, Brown, 1898.

6. The first note immediately preceded a violent outbreak known as the Boxer Rebellion of Chinese wishing to overthrow the Qing dynasty who, stirred up by various foreign interventions, besieged the legations in Peking. McKinley dispatched five thousand U.S. troops, without congressional approval, to join the twenty-thousand-strong foreign army that marched to its relief. The question then became whether the foreign contingents would withdraw or stay and carve up China among them, presenting McKinley with a dilemma of whether to abandon China or get dangerously entangled with foreign powers in an election year. Hay convinced him to stay, and the powers at length departed in 1901, pledging allegiance to the Open Door principles.

Jane E. Elliott, *Some Did It for Civilization, Some Did It for Their Country: A Revised View of the Boxer War*, Hong Kong, Chinese University Press, 2002.

7. Not all imperialists were Social Darwinists, and not all Social Darwinists supported the imperialists' aims. William Graham Sumner, perhaps America's foremost prophet of Social Darwinism, condemned the outcome of the Spanish-American War in an address titled *The Conquest of the United States by Spain* (Boston, D. Estes, 1899). Sumner argued the traditional view that imperialistic expansion would bring no advantages while plunging the United States into endless problems and perils. On the anti-imperialists, see Robert L. Beisner, *Twelve against Empire: The Anti-Imperialists, 1898–1900*, New York, McGraw Hill, 1968.

8. H. L. Higginson to Lodge, February 22 and May 9, 1902; cited in Richard E. Welch Jr., *Response to Imperialism: The United States and the Philippine-American War, 1899–1902*, Chapel Hill, University of North Carolina Press, 1979, 141; Daniel B. Schirmer, *Republic or Empire: American Resistance to the Philippine War*, Cambridge, Mass., Schenkman, 1972.

9. Welch, *Response to Imperialism*, 149. Though the "Philippine Insurrection" ended with the capture of its leader, Emilio Aguinaldo, in 1902, extended outbreaks of fighting against tribal peoples on various islands continued right up to 1935; Russell Roth, *America's "Indian Wars" in the Philippines, 1899–1935*, Hanover, Mass., Christopher Publishing House, 1981; Leon Wolff, *Little Brown Brother: How the United States Purchased and Pacified the Philippine Islands at the Century's Turn*, Garden City, N.Y., Doubleday, 1961; Stuart Creighton Miller, *"Benevolent Assimilation": The American Conquest of the Philippines, 1899–1903*, New Haven, Conn., Yale University Press, 1982.

10. August 21, 1907, cited in Osgood, *Ideals and Self-Interest*, 77–78. Roosevelt was having doubts about the Philippines as early as 1901; see Roosevelt to Coudert, July 3, 1901, *The Letters of Theodore Roosevelt*, ed. Elting E. Morison, Cambridge, Mass., Harvard University Press, 1951, Vol. III, 105.

11. Theodore Roosevelt, "Grant," in *The Works of Theodore Roosevelt*, ed. Hermann Hagedorn, New York, Charles Scribner's Sons, 1923–1926, Vol. 13, 437; see also "Brotherhood and the Heroic Virtues," ibid., 463; Smith, *Virgin Land*, Chs. V and VI; Sarah Watts, *Rough Rider in the White House: Theodore Roosevelt and the Politics of Desire*, Chicago, University of Chicago Press, 2003, Chs. 1 and 2; Kathleen Dalton, *Theodore Roosevelt: A Strenuous Life*, New York, Knopf, 2002.

12. Roosevelt explained away the anomaly to anti-imperialist Carl Schurz by saying that strong, civilized nations had a duty to police the world; Watts, *Rough Rider*, 219. See generally Wallace Chessman, *Theodore Roosevelt and the Politics of Power*, Boston, Little, Brown, 1969; John Morton Blum, *The Republican Roosevelt*, 2nd ed., Cambridge, Mass., Harvard University Press, 1977; John Milton Cooper, *The Warrior and the Priest: Woodrow Wilson and Theodore Roosevelt*, Cambridge, Mass., Belknap Press of Harvard University Press, 1983; Richard H. Collin, *Theodore Roosevelt: Culture, Diplomacy, and*

Expansion: A New View of American Imperialism, Baton Rouge, Louisiana State University Press, 1985. On Roosevelt's foreign policy, see Howard K. Beale, *Theodore Roosevelt and the Rise of America to World Power,* Baltimore, Md., Johns Hopkins University Press, 1956; Frederick W. Marks III, *Velvet on Iron: The Diplomacy of Theodore Roosevelt,* Lincoln, University of Nebraska Press, 1979; Lewis L. Gould, *The Presidency of Theodore Roosevelt,* Lawrence, University of Kansas Press, 1991.

13. An International League of Peace and Freedom had been founded in Europe in 1867, and most European countries had their own peace organizations. In 1891, the Permanent International Peace Bureau was founded in Bern, Switzerland, as a central office through which peace activities of various countries could be coordinated. It was awarded the Nobel Peace Prize in 1910. Rainer Santi, *100 Years of Peacemaking: A History of the International Peace Bureau and Other International Peace Organisations and Networks,* Geneva, International Peace Bureau, 1991.

14. David S. Jordan, *Imperial Democracy,* New York, Garland Publishing, 1972 [1899], 36, and Bryan, *Speeches of William Jennings Bryan,* New York, Funk & Wagnalls, 1909, II, 222–223; both quoted in Osgood, *Ideals and Self-Interest,* 93.

15. Burton J. Hendrick (ed.), *Miscellaneous Writings of Andrew Carnegie,* Garden City, N.Y., Doubleday, 1933, Vol. II, 237; quoted in Osgood, *Ideals and Self-Interest,* 94.

16. Quotations from Minger, *William Howard Taft,* 2.

17. Letter to his brother, Charles, June 12, 1900, quoted in Minger, *William Howard Taft,* 31. See Julius W. Pratt, *America's Colonial Experiment: How the United States Gained, Governed, and Part Gave Away a Colonial Empire,* New York, Prentice Hall, 1950, 193; and Wolff, *Little Brown Brother,* 17. Taft nevertheless had a strong sense of the American national interest as his later actions as Roosevelt's secretary of war attested. Nor was he above playing power politics, as demonstrated by his 1905 signing of the Taft-Katsura Agreement, which gave Japan a free hand in Korea in return for a guarantee of safety for the Philippines.

18. Theodore Roosevelt, *An Autobiography,* New York, Charles Scribner's Sons, 1913, 389. Roosevelt had been very impressed, as had Progressive Senator Robert LaFollette, by a book by J. Allen Smith, *The Spirit of American Government,* Cambridge, Mass., Belknap Press, 1965 [1907], that labeled the Constitution as undemocratic because of its checks and balances, judicial review, and concern with protection of property. This work also became the basis of Charles A. Beard's *Economic Interpretation of the Constitution of the United States,* New York, Macmillan, 1924. See Paolo E. Coletta, *The Presidency of William Howard Taft,* Lawrence, University Press of Kansas, 1973.

19. Taft, quoted in Coletta, *Presidency of William Howard Taft,* 12, 18.

20. Taft, State of the Union Address, December 3, 1912, available at http://www.gutenberg.org/dirs/etext04/sutaf11.txt.

21. Quoted in Coletta, *Presidency of William Howard Taft*, 198.
22. The pacifically inclined Root, secretary for war under McKinley and Roosevelt, was awarded the Nobel Peace Prize in 1912. It was he who, when the Spanish-American War showed up the disorganization and corruption of the war department and the chaotic ill-preparedness of the army, began the successful modernization of both bureaucracy and military, the irony of which he himself noted. See Richard William Leopold, *Elihu Root and the Conservative Tradition*, Boston, Little, Brown, 1954.
23. Coletta, *Presidency of William Howard Taft*, Ch. 9. Roosevelt formed the Progressive Party ("Bull Moose Party") and ran on a "New Nationalism" platform that promised greater regulation of the economy and more social welfare provision, hoping to draw the votes of Progressive Democrats. But Wilson, promising a "New Freedom," was an attractive candidate who held the Democratic constituency intact while that of the Republicans split.

CHAPTER 9. WOODROW WILSON AND THE REIGN OF VIRTUE

1. "Address to Newly Naturalized American Citizens," Philadelphia, May 10, 1915, in *The Wilson Reader*, Frances Farmer (ed.), New York, Oceana Publications, 1956, 134–138.
2. Alexander DeConde, *Ethnicity, Race and American Foreign Policy: A History*, Boston, Northeastern University Press, 78–79.
3. Woodrow Wilson, *A History of the American People*, Vol. VIII, New York, Harper and Brothers (Documentary Edition), 1918, 57–58; IX, 82.
4. See Ambrosius, *Wilsonianism*, 26–27. I follow Ambrosius's account of the essence of "Wilsonianism" here but draw my own implications about the primacy of virtue that it embodies.
5. John Milton Cooper in *The Warrior and the Priest* argues the Jeffersonian roots of Wilson's belief that free individuals, given sufficient space, were self-organizing for the public good. Actually, Wilson's thought, with its emphasis on a dominant executive embodying the people's will, was a curious combination of Jeffersonian and Hamiltonian ideas.
6. Wilson's brand of Progressivism recognized problems with the American experiment but rejected at the outset the interventionist approach of other Progressives, clinging to a belief in the virtues of laissez-faire economics. The essence of his New Freedom was the removal of special privileges and artificial barriers to individual enterprise. His actions in the summer of 1916, however, took a more radically interventionist turn and persuaded many that Democrats could also be real Progressives. See Arthur S. Link, *Woodrow Wilson and the Progressive Era, 1910–1917*, New York, Harper and Row, 1954, Chs. 1, 2, 9; N. Gordon Levin Jr., *Woodrow Wilson and World Politics: America's Response to War and Revolution*, New York, Oxford University Press, 1968, 25–28; Akira Iriye, *The Cambridge History of American Foreign Relations, Vol. III, The Globalizing of America, 1913–1945*, Cambridge, Cambridge University Press, 1993, 71–72. Iriye is generally sympathetic to Wil-

son's attempt to make "cultural forces" rather than "naked power" the basis of international relations.

7. "Address at the Unveiling of the Statue of Commodore John Barry," Washington, May 16, 1914, *President Wilson's Foreign Policy: Messages, Addresses, Papers*, ed. James Brown Scott, New York, Oxford University Press, 1918, 45. On nationalism Wilson said: "The greatest nationalist is the man who wants his nation to be the greatest nation, and the greatest nation is the nation which penetrates to the heart of its duty and mission among the nations of the world." Quoted in Ambrosius, *Wilsonianism*, 28.

8. "Address to Audience in Willard Hotel," Washington, May 27, 1916; in *Wilson Reader*, 149.

9. "Address at the Unveiling," in Scott, *President Wilson's Foreign Policy*, 44–45.

10. "Address on the Conditions of Peace," Joint Session of Houses of Congress, January 8, 1918, in Scott, *President Wilson's Foreign Policy*, 354–363; "Address on the Navy," New York City, May 17, 1915, ibid., 101.

11. John Morton Blum, *Woodrow Wilson and the Politics of Morality*, Boston, Little, Brown, 1956, 87–93; Link, *Woodrow Wilson and the Progressive Era*, Chs. 4 & 5; Frederick Katz, *The Secret War in Mexico: Europe, the United States, and the Mexican Revolution*, Chicago, University of Chicago Press, 1981.

12. Link, *Woodrow Wilson and the Progressive Era*, 81–81. Link's biography in five volumes is *Wilson*, Princeton, N.J., Princeton University Press, 1947–1965.

13. Ambrosius, *Wilsonianism*, 43; "Address to Newly Naturalized American Citizens," *Wilson Reader*, 93.

14. "Princeton for the Nation's Service," *Wilson Reader*, 108–109.

15. Wilson, *History*, VIII, 121.

16. Note Eric Foner's comment that "the Constitution and national political system had failed in the difficult task of creating a nation—only the Civil War would accomplish it." *Politics and Ideology in the Age of the Civil War*, New York, Oxford University Press, 1980, 52.

17. Croly, *Promise of American Life*, 312.

18. German and Irish Americans ("hyphenate" Americans) strenuously opposed entry on the French-British side, as did Jewish and Scandinavian Americans, who disliked Russia. But the Anglo sympathies of the administration were undeniable, as was its distaste for an autocratic, militaristic Germany that some, like Elihu Root and Secretary of State Robert Lansing, came to see as a ruthless menace to world peace. On the varying influence of hyphenate Americans during this period, see Melvin Small, *Democracy and Diplomacy: The Impact of Domestic Politics on U.S. Foreign Policy, 1789–1994*, Baltimore, Md., Johns Hopkins University Press, 42–48; DeConde, *Ethnicity, Race and American Foreign Policy*, 81–98.

19. Wilson expressed the tension within the "double obligation" the nation had laid upon him: "We are relying on you, Mr. President, to keep us out of this war, but we are relying on you, Mr. President, to keep the honor of the Nation unstained." "Address Delivered at Cleveland, Ohio," January 29, 1916,

in Scott, *President Wilson's Foreign Policy*, 173. Wilson declared, while campaigning in the West in January 1916, that, in the case of hostile attack, he would not be able to defend either the Western hemisphere or the national honor without military power. There was a profound rural-urban, and South and West-East, split over preparedness, with rural members of Congress stalwartly opposed: Link, *Woodrow Wilson and the Progressive Era*, 184–186.

20. Lloyd C. Gardner, *Safe for Democracy: The Anglo-American Response to Revolution, 1913–1923*, New York, Oxford University Press, 1984, 117–121.

21. This was despite the profound shock of the infamous "Zimmerman note," a secret communication to Mexico by the German foreign secretary offering Texas, New Mexico, and Arizona in return for going to war against the United States, that Wilson released to the public.

22. A recollection by Frank Cobb of a meeting in which an agonized Wilson unburdened his soul; Ray S. Baker, *Woodrow Wilson: Life and Letters,* 8 vols., Garden City, N.Y., Doubleday, 1927–1939, VI, 506; quoted in Link, *Woodrow Wilson and the Progressive Era*, 277.

23. Quoted in Link, *Woodrow Wilson and the Progressive Era*, 282.

24. *Congressional Record*, 66 Congress, 1 Session, 58: 2339, July 10, 1919; quoted in Ambrosius, *Wilsonianism*, 152.

25. For a full account, see Thomas J. Knock, *To End All Wars: Woodrow Wilson and the Quest for a New World Order*, New York, Oxford University Press, 1992.

26. Ambrosius, *Wilsonianism*, 152. The specter of Bolshevism and its possible spread in postwar Germany was a powerful incentive for the Wilson administration, particularly for Secretary Lansing, in trying to reintegrate Germany peacefully in Europe; see Levin, *Woodrow Wilson and World Politics*.

27. From the *Congressional Records* of 1918 and 1919, quoted in Ambrosius, *Wilsonianism*, 94. Ambrosius describes how Wilson was willing to accept an accord with France provided it was later brought under the league covenant as an instance of collective security, whereas Knox, Lodge, and others wanted it as a *substitute* for the latter. Wilson failed to fully understand this, and his intransigence doomed both options. For another account of the Senate battles, see William C. Widenor, *Henry Cabot Lodge and the Search for an American Foreign Policy*, Berkeley, University of California Press, 1980.

28. The idea of a league to enforce peace was not original to Wilson (and indeed could be traced back to the Abbé de Saint-Pierre's *Le Projet de Paix Perpétuelle* of 1713 and Immanuel Kant's idea of a league of republican governments to ensure perpetual peace of the 1780s). It had been internationally mooted frequently in the early twentieth century, and Teddy Roosevelt himself had advocated such a league when he accepted his Nobel Peace Prize in 1910. During the war, the idea that the United States might join a League of Nations to guarantee a peace settlement was first suggested by Sir Edward Grey, the British foreign minister, in late 1915 when Wilson was considering

demanding a peace conference to eliminate "militarism and navalism." Wilson's friend Colonel Edward M. House, who delivered the proposal to Wilson, urged him to accept the part that he was "destined to play in this world tragedy . . . the noblest part that has ever come to a son of man." Wilson agreed. Quoted in Link, *Woodrow Wilson and the Progressive Era*, 199.

29. Robert Lansing, *The Peace Negotiations: A Personal Narrative*, Boston, Houghton Mifflin, 1921, 43.

30. Note of November 22, 1918, ibid., 44, and see 45, 85.

31. Ibid., 38–40, 52, 82, 166–167. Wilson customarily used his friend Colonel Edward M. House for diplomatic purposes rather than his secretary of state. Lansing put Wilson's distance from him down to Lansing's opposition to the political version of the league and to the fact that Lansing was a lawyer. Lansing was appalled that Wilson was willing to make the legal apparatus of the league subservient to its political structure, thus showing his lack of sympathy for the American system of government with its principle of judicial independence; see ibid., 41, 70.

32. Friedrich Nietzsche, *The Will to Power*, ed. Walter Kaufmann, New York, Vantage, 1968, 513.

33. Irwin Shaw, "Weep in Years to Come," reprinted in William E. Leuchtenburg (ed.), *The New Deal: A Documentary History*, New York, Harper and Row, 1968, 233–238.

CHAPTER 10. DISILLUSIONMENT AND HOPE

1. Robert Dallek, *The American Style of Foreign Policy*, New York, Oxford University Press, 1983, 7.

2. The different meanings of isolationism are traced by Manfred Jonas in *Isolationism in America, 1935–1941*, Ithaca, N.Y., Cornell University Press, 1966.

3. See Osgood, *Ideals and Self-Interest*, 312–313, 329.

4. The labor leader and socialist politician Eugene Debs was the most famous victim of this act. See Ray Ginger, *Eugene V. Debs: A Biography*, New York, Collier, 1962 [1949].

5. Eric Foner, *The Story of American Freedom*, London, Papermac, 2000, 177. The Klan had faded in the South in the 1890s but was reformed in 1915 as a nativist organization to combat the influence or influx of Catholics, Jews, foreigners, radicals, and labor unions. See Arnold S. Rice, *The Ku Klux Klan in American Politics*, Washington, D.C., Public Affairs Press, 1962; David M. Chalmers, *Hooded Americanism: The History of the Ku Klux Klan*, New York, New Viewpoints, 1965; Wyn Craig Wade, *The Fiery Cross: The Ku Klux Klan in America*, New York, Simon & Schuster, 1987; David H. Bennett, *The Party of Fear: From Nativist Movements to the New Right in American History*, New York, Vintage, 1990. In general, see Seymour Martin Lipset and Earl Raab, *The Politics of Unreason: Right-Wing Extremism in America, 1790–1970*, New York, Harper and Row, 1970.

6. H. L. Mencken's savage portrait of what he took, no doubt unfairly, to be the typical American closely reflected the character of this Americanism:

> He likes money and knows how to amass property, but his cultural development is but little above that of the domestic animals. He is intensely and cock-surely moral, but his morality and his self-interest are crudely identical. . . . He is violently jealous of what he conceives to be his rights, but brutally disregardful of the other fellow's. He is religious, but his religion is wholly devoid of beauty and dignity. This man, whether city or country bred, is the normal Americano—the 100 per cent Methodist, Odd Fellow, Ku Kluxer, and Know Nothing. He exists in all countries, but in America alone he rules . . . Around every one of his principal delusions—of the sacredness of democracy, of the feasibility of sumptuary law, of the incurable sinfulness of other peoples, of the menace of ideas, of the corruption lying in all the arts —there is thrown a barrier of taboos, and woe to the anarchist who seeks to break it down! . . . Anything strange is to be combated: it is of the Devil. The American mob-man cannot grasp ideas in their native nakedness. They must be dramatized and personalized for him, and provided either with white wings or forked tails.

"On Being American," *Selected Prejudices*, London, Jonathan Cape, 1932, 25.

7. Henry C. Lodge, *The Senate and the League of Nations*, New York, Scribner's Sons, 1925, 146–147; Lawrence E. Gelfand, "The Mystique of Wilsonian Statecraft," *Diplomatic History* 7 (2), 1983: 87–102 at 89.

8. The rejection of force was most clearly articulated by Harold Stearns in his book *Liberalism in America: Its Origin, Its Temporary Collapse, Its Future*, New York, Boni and Liveright, 1919. Osgood (*Ideals and Self-Interest*, 319, and generally Ch. XIII) argues that the common cynicism of writers and of muckraking journalists, who crusaded against crusading, was really "inverted idealism."

9. The Dawes Plan of 1924 rescheduled and reduced reparations payments and stabilized the German currency with the help of foreign, particularly American, loans. In 1929 the Young Plan further eased the German plight by another rescheduling of reparations payments; see Melvin Leffler, *The Elusive Quest: America's Pursuit of European Stability and French Security, 1919–1933*, Chapel Hill, University of North Carolina Press, 1979; J. Samuel Walker, *Henry A. Wallace and American Foreign Policy*, Westport, Conn., Greenwood Press, 1973, 29.

10. Joseph Brandes, *Herbert Hoover and Economic Diplomacy: Department of Commerce Policy, 1921–1928*, Westport, Conn., Greenwood Press, 1975 [1962].

11. Emily S. Rosenberg, *Spreading the American Dream*, New York, Hill & Wang, 1982; Joseph S. Nye Jr., *The Paradox of American Power: Why the World's Only Superpower Can't Go It Alone*, New York, Oxford University Press, 2002.

12. "The Doctrine of Fascism," reprinted in Michael Oakeshott (ed.), *The Social and Political Doctrines of Contemporary Europe*, Cambridge, Cambridge University Press, 1939, 164–179. In general, see Roger Griffin, *The Nature of Fascism*, London, Routledge, 1993; Zeev Sternhell, Mario Sznajder, and Maia Asheri, *The Birth of Fascist Ideology: From Cultural Rebellion to Political Revolution*, trans. David Maisel, Princeton, N.J., Princeton University Press, 1994; A. James Gregor, *The Ideology of Fascism: The Rationale of Totalitarianism*, New York, Free Press, 1969.

13. Adolf Hitler, *Mein Kampf*, London, Hutchinson, 1969; Paul Brooker, *The Faces of Fraternalism: Nazi Germany, Fascist Italy, and Imperial Japan*, Oxford, Clarendon Press, 1991; William Ebenstein, *The Nazi State*, New York, Octagon Books, 1975 [1943]; Alan Bullock, *Hitler: A Study in Tyranny*, rev. ed., Harmondsworth, Penguin, 1962; Hannah Arendt, *The Origins of Totalitarianism*, New York, Harcourt Brace Jovanovich, 1973.

CHAPTER 11. AMERICAN ISOLATION

1. The economic motive is stressed by Michael A. Barnhart, *Japan Prepares for Total War: The Search for Economic Security, 1919–1941*, Ithaca, N.Y., Cornell University Press, 1988.

2. See Carl Crow (ed.), *Japan's Dream of World Empire: The Tanaka Memorial*, New York, Harper and Brothers, 1942.

3. Akira Iriye, *Pacific Estrangement: Japanese and American Expansion, 1897–1911*, Cambridge, Mass., Harvard University Press, 1972. Japan demanded confirmation of its railway and mining claims in Shantung Province; special concessions in Manchuria; Sino-Japanese control of the Han-Yeh-P'ing mining base in central China; access to harbors, bays, and islands along the Chinese coast; and control, through advisers, of Chinese financial, political, and police affairs. U.S. troops were in Siberia for complicated strategic reasons relating to Russia's withdrawal from the war, a rescue mission for a regiment of Czechs, and a desire to thwart Japanese intentions in the area, but mostly because President Wilson had succumbed to intense pressure from his allies to intervene in revolutionary Russia. The entire deployment turned into a major fiasco that embittered relations between not just the United States and Japan but the United States and the new Bolshevik Russian government. See Frederick Calhoun, *Power and Principle: Armed Intervention in Wilsonian Foreign Policy*, Kent, Ohio, Kent State University Press, 1986, 193–210.

4. Dorothy Jones, *Code of Peace: Ethics and Security in the World of the Warlord States*, Chicago, University of Chicago Press, 1991, 41–44.

5. *Bushido* means "Way of the Warrior" and formerly pertained exclusively to the samurai class. In the mid-nineteenth century Bushido was made the ethical basis of the whole of Japanese society, with the emperor replacing the feudal lord (*daimyo*) as the supreme object of loyalty and sacrifice. This adoption obviously placed severe limits on the spread of individualism

of a Western kind, and indeed Japanese purists always emphasized social solidarity and loyalty above all else. Generally, see Edwin O. Reischauer and Albert M. Craig, *Japan: Tradition and Transformation*, Boston, Houghton Mifflin, 1989; Thomas M. Huber, *The Revolutionary Origins of Modern Japan*, Stanford, Calif., Stanford University Press, 1981.

6. Secretary of State Henry Lewis Stimson wrote: "To liken the aggressive policy now being pushed by Japan under the name of the 'Monroe Doctrine in Asia' to that defensive bulwark of local independence and self-government among the South American republics which was provided by the announcement in 1823 of the American doctrine, should be fantastic enough to be seen through by any impartial observer." *The Far Eastern Crisis: Recollections and Observations*, New York, H. Fertig, 1974 [1936], 236.

7. For a highly critical view of Stimson's foreign policy at this period, see Armin Rappaport, *Henry L. Stimson and Japan, 1931–1933*, Chicago, Chicago University Press, 1963. In general on this period, see Christopher G. Thorne, *The Limits of Foreign Policy: The West, the League, and the Far-Eastern Crisis of 1931–1933*, New York, Putnam, 1973; Ferrell, *American Diplomacy*. Quotations from Elting E. Morison, *Turmoil and Tradition: A Study of the Life and Times of Henry L. Stimson*, Boston, Houghton Mifflin, 1960, 445, 448; Stimson, *Far Eastern Crisis*, 252; 189; 12–13.

8. Stimson, *Far Eastern Crisis*, 153, 155. Stimson goes on to argue it was this same spirit that had turned "our colonial adventure in the Philippines into a farsighted attempt to train Oriental people in the art of self-government according to the American model."

9. Ibid., 55–56.

10. Ibid., 80.

11. Ibid., 56–57; 76.

12. Ibid., 135.

13. Ibid., 95. Unfortunately, the beneficial force was quickly undercut by the skeptical attitude expressed by the British that greatly encouraged the Japanese.

14. Ibid., 152.

15. Morison, *Turmoil and Tradition*, 449, 468, and see Ch. 32 on the doubts and discussions surrounding the decision to use the bomb. One of the calculations made was of the number of lives, Japanese and American, that would be saved by a swift end to the war. The documentary film *Fog of War* dramatizes the fact that the casualties caused by the atomic bombs were relatively slight compared with the results of the fire-bombing campaign pursued against Japanese cities under the command of General Curtis LeMay. In the film, Robert McNamara states that he and LeMay undoubtedly would have been tried as war criminals had the Japanese won the war and expresses rhetorical doubt as to whether it was right or wrong to take one hundred thousand civilian lives in a single night over Tokyo. Walter Russell Mead (*Special Providence*, Ch. 7) describes such action as an example of the "Jack-

sonian" mode of U.S. foreign policy that, when forced to defend American interests or honor, will always bring maximal force uncompromisingly to bear, making the United States the most dangerous nation on earth. This may be so, and certainly LeMay was always the most hawkish of hawks, then and after. But on the historical record America appears hardly less restrained than other nations in the prosecution of war, merely better armed (it was an Englishman, Air Marshal Arthur "Bomber" Harris, who initiated the policy of saturation "terror bombing" by the Allies, not the Americans). To label overwhelming force an American "tradition" obscures the interesting question of how Americans squared such devastating action with their tender mythological conscience, and the answer is always original innocence (America did not start the war) and necessity (stopping evil, minimizing casualties through swift termination of the conflict). It is when either or both of these reasons fail (as for example in the Philippines, Vietnam, and Iraq) that America suffers heartache.

16. Joseph C. Grew, "The 'Green Light' Telegram," reprinted in Leuchtenburg, *New Deal*, 251–254 at 253. Grew still wished to preserve the peace and hoped the mere show of force would compel Japan to come to its senses. He kept a record of his mental struggles in a diary, published as *Ten Years in Japan: A Contemporary Record Drawn from the Diaries and Private and Official Papers of Joseph C. Grew*, New York, Arno Press, 1972 [1944].

17. Reinhold Niebuhr, *Moral Man and Immoral Society: A Study in Ethics and Politics*, New York, Scribner's Sons, 1932; *Christianity and Power Politics*, New York, Scribner's Sons, 1940. Niebuhr was immensely influential among liberal Cold War Warriors. In 1947, in association with Eleanor Roosevelt, Hubert Humphrey, and Walter Reuther, he established Americans for Democratic Action to combat Left-liberal communist sympathizers like Henry Wallace and, once Wallace was defeated, to oppose forces on the right. Niebuhr was concerned to stand up positively to the communist challenge without falling into the Right's automatic and dangerous presumption of moral infallibility. Only thus, he reasoned, could idealism be prevented from falling into the kind of moral fanaticism that characterized both communism and, at home, the attitudes that led to McCarthyism. See Peter Beinart, *The Good Fight: Why Liberals—and Only Liberals—Can Win the War on Terror and Make America Great Again*, New York, HarperCollins, 2006.

18. Arnold A. Offner, *American Appeasement: United States Foreign Policy and Germany, 1933–1938*, Cambridge, Mass., Belknap Press of Harvard University Press, 1969.

19. Ibid., 189.

20. The Japanese, who had been hoping for an alliance with Germany against the Soviet Union, were equally shocked by this unexpected development.

21. On the pacifists, see Lawrence S. Wittner, *Rebels against War: The American Peace Movement, 1933–1983*, rev. ed., Philadelphia, Temple University Press, 1984. America First challenged Roosevelt's efforts to intervene in the

international conflict, but the movement was dissolved after Pearl Harbor; see Wayne S. Cole, *America First: The Battle against Intervention, 1940–1941,* New York, Octagon Books, 1971 [1953]; Ruth Sarles, *A Story of America First: The Men and Women Who Opposed U.S. Intervention in World War II,* ed. Bill Kauffman, Westport, Conn., Praeger, 2003; Justus D. Doenecke (ed.), *In Danger Undaunted: The Anti-interventionist Movement of 1940–1941 As Revealed in the Papers of the America First Committee,* Stanford, Calif., Hoover Institution Press, 1990. On the Committee to Defend America, see Mark Chadwin, *The Hawks of World War II,* Chapel Hill, University of North Carolina Press, 1968.

22. The sum of Roosevelt's measures on the Atlantic front were repealing the arms embargo on belligerents in order to allow sales of armaments (though only on a "cash and carry" basis); striking up a close and continuing relationship with British Prime Minister Winston Churchill; transferring aged warships to Britain under long leases and then, as Britain approached bankruptcy, establishing "lend-lease" arrangements to continue the supply of arms; secretly arranging joint U.S.-British staff talks; forwarding collaboration between Britons and Americans on the German U-boat menace, eventually authorizing U.S. naval ships to attack German submarines; and sending U.S. marines to occupy Iceland. On the general course of Roosevelt's foreign policy, see Robert Dallek, *Franklin D. Roosevelt and American Foreign Policy, 1932–1945,* New York, Oxford University Press, 1979; on the wartime period particularly, see the collection edited by Warren F. Kimball, *Franklin D. Roosevelt and the World Crisis, 1937–1945,* Lexington, Mass., Heath, 1973. A considerable revisionist history accuses Roosevelt, perhaps in cahoots with Churchill, of deliberately precipitating the United States into war by not using alleged foreknowledge of the Japanese sneak attack; see, for example, Bruce M. Russett, *No Clear and Present Danger: A Skeptical View of the United States Entry into World War II,* New York, Harper and Row, 1972. A thorough reading of the Roosevelt-Churchill letters just before Pearl Harbor seems to indicate the falsity of this thesis; Warren F. Kimball (ed.), *Churchill & Roosevelt: The Complete Correspondence,* 3 vols., Princeton, N.J., Princeton University Press, 1984.

23. Robert A. Taft, "Shall the President Make War without the Approval of Congress?" in Nancy Schoonmaker and Doris F. Reid (eds.), *We Testify,* New York, Smith & Durrell, 1941, 215–229.

CHAPTER 12. AMERICAN VIRTUE AND THE SOVIET CHALLENGE

1. Melvyn P. Leffler, "The American Conception of National Security and the Beginnings of the Cold War, 1945–1948," *American Historical Review* 89 (2), April 1984: 346–381 at 347–356.

2. Thomas J. McCormick, *America's Half-Century: United States Foreign Policy in the Cold War and After,* 2nd ed., Baltimore, Md., Johns Hopkins University Press, 1995, 48.

3. See, for example, Nicholas J. Spykman, *America's Strategy in World Politics*, New York, Harcourt Brace, 1942.

4. Hans J. Morgenthau, "The Escape from Power in the Modern World," in R. M. McIver et al. (eds.), *Conflicts of Power in Modern Culture*, New York, Harpers, 1947; *Scientific Man vs. Power Politics*, Chicago, University of Chicago Press, 1946, 101; *In Defense of the National Interest: A Critical Examination of American Foreign Policy*, New York, Knopf, 1951, 13, 131. Another important early work not cited is *Politics among Nations: The Struggle for Power and Peace*, New York, Knopf, 1948.

5. See, for example, *The Purpose of American Politics*, New York, Knopf, 1960.

6. From the public papers of Harry S. Truman, quoted in David McCullough, *Truman*, New York, Simon & Schuster, 1992, 429.

7. Quoted in Morison, *Turmoil and Tradition*, 638.

8. Dean Acheson, *Present at the Creation: My Years in the State Department*, New York, Norton, 1969, 3–4.

9. For the different aims and motivations of the main parties, see, for example, Herbert Feis, *Churchill, Roosevelt, Stalin: The War They Waged and the Peace They Sought*, Princeton, N.J., Princeton University Press, 1957; Martin J. Sherwin, *A World Destroyed: Hiroshima and Its Legacies*, 3rd ed., Stanford, Calif., Stanford University Press, 2003 [1975]; Gaddis Smith, *American Diplomacy during the Second World War, 1941–1945*, 2nd ed., New York, Knopf, 1985; Wm. Roger Louis, *Imperialism at Bay, 1941–1945: The United States and the Decolonization of the British Empire*, Oxford, Clarendon Press, 1977.

10. Richard N. Gardner, *Sterling-Dollar Diplomacy*, expanded ed., New York, McGraw-Hill, 1969, 40–68.

11. Roosevelt, impatient with Chiang Kai-shek's inaction in China, suggested in the fall of 1944 that General Joseph Stilwell be placed in command of all Chinese forces, nationalist and communist. Chiang was furious, seeing this as getting in the way of his plans to crush the communists when the war ended. He demanded Stilwell be recalled and thus forfeited any significant role in the liberation of China. Roosevelt turned consequently to the Soviets, who had claims on Manchuria, to participate in the war against Japan. See Barbara W. Tuchman, *Stilwell and the American Experience in China, 1911–1945*, New York, Grove Press, 2001 [1971].

12. Josef Stalin, "New Five Year Plan for Russia," address delivered over Radio Moscow, February 9, 1946, quoted in Lee Edwards, *The Conservative Revolution: The Movement That Remade America*, New York, Free Press, 1999, 6–7.

13. John Kane, "The End of Morality? Theory, Practice and the 'Realistic Outlook' of Karl Marx," *NOMOS XXXVII: Theory and Practice*, New York, New York University Press, 1995, 403–439.

14. See Melvyn P. Leffler, *A Preponderance of Power: National Security, the Truman Administration, and the Cold War*, Stanford, Calif., Stanford University Press, 1992, which portrays Soviet policies as mainly reactive, and John Lewis Gaddis, *We Now Know: Rethinking Cold War History*, New York, Oxford

University Press, 1997, which puts most of the burden on Stalin's policies
and personality. Vladislav Zubok and Constantine Pleshakov, *Inside the
Kremlin's Cold War: From Stalin to Khrushchev*, Cambridge, Mass., Harvard
University Press, 1996, argue that Stalin wished to avoid confrontation and
would have sought accommodation with the West had it been possible.

15. Leffler, *A Preponderance of Power*. With regard to communist ideology, faith
in the party was meant to be all-consuming. Central Committee member
Grigori Pyatakov noted in 1928 that Lenin averred that a true Bolshevik
submerged his own personality in the collectivity of the party, fused with it,
"so there was no particle left inside him which did not belong to the Party";
quoted by Robert Conquest, *The Great Terror: A Reassessment*, London,
Hutchinson, 1990, 113. Stalin understood the indispensability of ideology to
the legitimacy of his rule thoroughly enough to impose his own version
of it in 1938 with the publication of his *A History of the CPSU: Short Course*.
One-time Marxist philosopher Leszek Kolakowski, who had lived under
communist rule, related how inculcation of faith in the party caused half-
starved people to deny even the evidence of their own senses: "Truth, they
knew, was a Party matter, and therefore lies became true even if they contradicted the plain facts of experience"; *Main Currents of Marxism, Vol. III,
The Breakdown*, Oxford, Clarendon Press, 1978, 97.

16. For a general history, see E. H. Carr, *The Russian Revolution: From Lenin to
Stalin*, New York, Free Press, 1979.

17. Read was the founder of the libertarian Foundation for Economic Education
(FEE) in 1946; "Notes from FEE," April 15, 1954, quoted in Sara Diamond,
*Roads to Dominion, Right-Wing Movements and Political Power in the United
States*, New York, Guilford Press, 1995, 27. Dulles made his comment in a
radio address on Wilson in December 1948; in Farmer, *Wilson Reader*,
256–261.

18. Stalin officially dissolved the Comintern in 1943 to allay fears of his allies
the United States and Great Britain about communist subversion. He
set up the Communist Information Bureau (Cominform) in 1947 as a re-
placement means of control. This was dissolved in 1956, as divisions between Russia and China, among other things, broke up the international
movement.

19. Joan Hoff, *Ideology and Economics: U.S. Relations with the Soviet Union,
1918–1933*, Columbia, University of Missouri Press, 1974.

20. Dulles introduced the idea of "massive retaliation" for any aggressive Soviet
move. See the critical biography by Richard Goold-Adams, *John Foster
Dulles: A Reappraisal*, New York, Appleton-Century-Crofts, 1962. A useful
collection is Richard H. Immerman (ed.), *John Foster Dulles and the Diplomacy of the Cold War*, Princeton, N.J., Princeton University Press, 1990;
and see Richard H. Immerman, *John Foster Dulles: Piety, Pragmatism, and
Power in U.S. Foreign Policy*, Wilmington, Del., Scholarly Resources, 1999.
A classic study of the period is John Lewis Gaddis, *Strategies of Containment:*

A Critical Appraisal of Postwar American National Security Policy, Fairlawn, N.J., Oxford University Press, 1982.

21. In general, see William T. Lee and Richard F. Staar, *Soviet Military Policy since World War II,* Stanford, Calif., Hoover Institution Press, 1986; William E. Griffith, *The Sino-Soviet Rift,* Cambridge, Mass., MIT Press, 1964; Alfred D. Low, *Sino-Soviet Confrontation since Mao Zedong: Dispute, Detente, or Conflict?* New York, Columbia University Press, 1987.

22. Frances Fukuyama's famous book, *The End of History and the Last Man,* London, Hamish Hamilton, 1992, was a theoretical argument that the fall of communism represented the "inevitable" triumph of liberal capitalism.

CHAPTER 13. ANTICOMMUNISM AND AMERICAN VIRTUE

1. The propaganda activities of Marvin Liebman and various organizations of the China lobby in the 1950s and 1960s, to prevent the international recognition of Communist China, provides an illustration of such influence. Ross Y. Koen, *The China Lobby in American Politics,* New York, Harper and Row, 1974; Stanley D. Bachrack, *The Committee of One Million: "China Lobby" Politics, 1953–1971,* New York, Columbia University Press, 1976.

2. Woodrow Wilson's personal secretary, Joseph Tumulty, argued in a memo to Lansing that Bolshevism must be treated like a new form of contagious disease, to be dealt with by the Public Health Service. See Gardner, *Safe for Democracy,* 261.

3. In the 1960s FBI Director J. Edgar Hoover updated the metaphor by arguing that "the Communists are today spraying the world with ideological and propaganda missiles to create a deadly radioactive cloud of Marxism-Leninism." Communist gunners trained in "atheistic perversity," he said, had their sights on the clergy, "hoping to shatter, immobilize, and confuse this powerful form of idealism, morality, and civic virtue"; article in *Christianity Today,* October 24, 1960, cited in Diamond, *Roads to Dominion,* 101. Richard Hofstadter analyzes the way that "the paranoid style" begins from plausible facts and then moves to implausible conspiracy theories to "explain" them. Such interpretations are reinforced whenever genuinely secret deals of governments, which always occur, are revealed. *The Paranoid Style in American Politics and Other Essays,* New York, Vintage Books, 1967.

4. "Is It Well with These States?" in Stephen Vincent Benét, *Burning City: New Poems,* New York, Farrar & Rinehart, 1936, 32–35. On the feeling within America and reaction to Roosevelt, see William E. Leuchtenburg, *Franklin D. Roosevelt and the New Deal,* New York, Harper and Row, 1963, Ch. 1.

5. This intellectual movement included names like Frances Charles Montague, T. H. Green, John Hobson, Leonard Hobhouse, and Émile Chartier (known as Alain). See J. G. Merquior, *Liberalism Old and New,* Boston, Twayne Publishers, 1991, 99–126.

6. David Green, *Shaping Political Consciousness,* Ithaca, Cornell University Press, 1987, 119–134, 175. By liberal, Taft meant he was open to reasonable

change, tolerant of individual freedom, and willing to entertain any proposal, but always with the proviso that stability was paramount and that what was on offer was really better than what existed; see Edwards, *The Conservative Revolution*, 9. Rejecting the "liberal" label nevertheless remained problematic for libertarian conservatives who adhered to the "classical liberal" philosophies of Friedrich von Hayek and Ludwig von Mises. Clinton Rossiter, *Conservatism in America*, New York, Knopf, 1955, 12, 15; Theodore J. Lowi, *The End of Liberalism: The Second Republic of the United States*, New York, Norton, 1979, 42–43.

7. In 1940, the anti–New Deal Church League of America published an article titled "Communism's Iron Grip on the U.S.A." This argued that communism was a more dangerous "alien force" than fascism or Nazism because it was "linked inseparably" with the kind of "liberalism" purveyed by the administration in Washington since 1932, adding greatly to the strength of the "subversive stem"; cited in Diamond, *Roads to Dominion*, 102. See also Harvey Klehr and John Earl Haynes, *The American Communist Movement*, New York, Twayne Publishers, 1992.

8. Numerous studies exist of the left-wing surge during this period. See, for example: Fraser M. Ottanelli, *The Communist Party of the United States: From the Depression to World War II*, New Brunswick, N.J., Rutgers University Press, 1991; Judy Kutalas, *The Long War: The Intellectual People's Front and Anti-Stalinism, 1930–1940*, Durham, N.C., Duke University Press, 1995; Michael Denning, *The Cultural Front: The Laboring of American Culture in the Twentieth Century*, New York, Verso, 1998; Patricia Sullivan, *Days of Hope: Race and Democracy in the New Deal Era*, Chapel Hill, University of North Carolina Press, 1996.

9. Diamond, *Roads to Dominion*, 21–23; Alan Brinkley, *Voices of Protest: Huey Long, Father Coughlin and the Great Depression*, New York, Knopf, 1982; Morris Schonbach, *Native American Fascism during the 1930s and 1940: A Study of Its Roots, Its Growth and Its Decline*, New York, Garland Publishing, 1985; David H. Bennett, *The Party of Fear: From Nativist Movements to the New Right in American History*, New York, Vintage, 1990; Glen Jeansonne, *Gerald L. K. Smith: Minister of Hate*, New Haven, Conn., Yale University Press, 1988.

10. One of the leading anticommunist organizations of the 1950s, the American Security Council (ASC), for example, had among its original incorporators General Robert E. Wood and publisher William Regnery, both formerly of America First; Harry Jung of the anti-Semitic American Vigilante Intelligence Federation; and John Trevor of the American Coalition of Patriotic Societies, a pro-Nazi organization. The ASC was a private organization, formed by ex-FBI agents in 1955, that gathered more than a million files on "subversive" citizens. Unconstrained by government regulations on confidentiality, it was free to make these available to large businesses. It also undertook Cold War public education exercises and organized annual Na-

tional Military-Industrial Conferences aimed at influencing military and political leaders and ultimately U.S. Cold War policy. Diamond, *Roads to Dominion*, 46–47; Russ Bellant, *Old Nazis, the New Right, and the Republican Party*, Boston, South End Press, 31–33.

11. The Wagner Act (National Labor Relations Act [1935]) has been described as the most important piece of labor legislation in the United States in the twentieth century. Its aim was to eliminate employers' interference with workers' autonomous organization into unions: Jerold S. Auerbach, *Labor and Liberty: The La Follette Committee and the New Deal*, Indianapolis, Bobbs-Merrill, 1966, 210–213. The Supreme Court also moved in 1937 from its usual habit of censoring economic legislation to protecting democratic rights to free thought and expression, thus replacing freedom of contract with civil liberties as the foundation of freedom in America: Henry J. Abraham, *Freedom and the Court: Civil Rights and Liberties in the United States*, New York, Oxford University Press, 1988, 7–25.

12. Martin Dies, *The Trojan Horse in America*, New York, Arno Press, 1977 [1940]; William Gellerman, *Martin Dies*, New York, Da Capo Press, 1972 [1944]; August Raymond Ogden, *The Dies Committee: A Study of the Special House Committee for the Investigation of Un-American Activities, 1938–1944*, Westport, Conn., Greenwood Press, 1984 [1945]; see also Kenneth O'Reilly, *Hoover and the Un-Americans: The FBI, HUAC, and the Red Menace*, Philadelphia, Temple University Press, 1983. McCarran was a populist from Nevada who rode Roosevelt's coattails to Congress in 1932 but promptly turned into one of his most resolute enemies. He combined rural America's resentment of big-city elites, nativist fear of all minorities, and traditional republican suspicion of encroaching big government. During the 1940s McCarran's anticommunism grew more extreme and shaded into anti-Semitism. He fought a series of legislative battles on behalf of xenophobic Americans to prevent the entry of European war refugees, some of them survivors of the death camps, into the United States. See the voluminous biography by Michael J. Ybarra, *Washington Gone Crazy: Senator Pat McCarran and the Great American Communist Hunt*, Hanover, N.H., Steerforth Press, 2004.

13. J. Ronald Oakley, *God's Country: America in the Fifties*, New York, Dembner Books, 1988, 51. The Smith Act, passed in June 1940, required annual registration of aliens and strengthened the government's powers of deportation. It made it a criminal offense to teach, advertise, or organize in pursuit of the overthrow of the U.S. government. On Soviet spies, see Allen Weinstein and Alexander Vassilev, *The Haunted Wood: Soviet Espionage in America*, New York, Random House, 1999; Christopher Andrew and Vasili Mitrokhin, *The Sword and the Shield: The Mitrokhin Archive and the Secret History of the KGB*, New York, Basic Books, 1999; James Earl Haynes and Harvey Klehr, *Venona: Decoding Soviet Espionage in America*, New Haven, Conn., Yale University Press, 1999.

14. The libertarians had gained intellectual ballast from the 1944 work of Friedrich A. von Hayek, particularly his *Road to Serfdom* (University of Chicago Press), which argued that any kind of state or economic planning suppressed individual enterprise and led down the road to totalitarian "collectivism." Moral-traditionalists for their part gained stimulus from Russell Kirk's book, *The Conservative Mind from Burke to Santayana* (Chicago, H. Regnery, 1953) which, though it accepted private property as the foundation of human freedom, defined conservatism in terms of the established moral order and existing hierarchies rather than in terms of individual against state. It was significant that compromise with the moral-traditionalists opened the way for the New Right to accommodate the nascent Christian evangelical Right in the 1970s.

15. The term "New Right" was first used as self-description by conservatives in the 1970s. On its political progress, see Alan Crawford, *Thunder on the Right: The "New Right" and the Politics of Resentment,* New York, Pantheon, 1980; Jerome L. Himmelstein, *To the Right: The Transformation of American Conservatism,* Berkeley, University of California Press, 1990, 29–62, 97–197; Diamond, *Roads to Dominion,* Ch. 9. Buckley was a key figure in the fusionist movement by virtue of his book *God and Man at Yale: The Superstitions of Academic Freedom* (Chicago, Regnery, 1951), his organization of student conservative movements, and his founding of the *National Review* in 1955. See generally Diamond, *Roads to Dominion,* Ch. 1, whose analysis of the rise of the postwar Right I largely follow here. Goldwater was an almost perfect representative of fusionist conservatism, combining temporization with civil rights with emphasis on a strong military and anti–New Deal economics. He was politically damaged when accused of "extremism" by virtue of his association with the John Birch Society, which he refused to renounce, though even this reflected the importance of anticommunism to the movement. See David Reinhard, *The Republican Right since 1945,* Lexington, University Press of Kentucky, 1983; William A. Rusher, *The Rise of the Right,* New York, William Morrow, 1984.

16. The importance of Cold War anticommunism in explaining the development of party politics in modern America is the theme of John Kenneth White's *Still Seeing Red: How the Cold War Shapes the New American Politics,* Boulder, Colo., Westview Press, 1997.

17. After the 1960s and 1970s, as Left-liberals increased the range of their concerns for the dispossessed and underprivileged to include women, gays, Indians, Hispanics, and so on, the conservative movement took up a general position against federal intervention on behalf of all "minorities." William Rusher's book *The Making of a New Majority Party* (New York, Sheed and Ward, 1975) made the general case here on behalf of "producers" who could coalesce in opposition to liberal talkers in the media, universities, schools, and bureaucracies.

18. The Liberty Lobby was founded by Willis Carto in 1958 to unify mass-based

far-Right groups. It emphasized racism, anticommunism, and anti-Semitic conspiracy theories and grew to significance during the 1960s after failure and factionalism destroyed groups supportive of George Wallace. In the 1970s it got heavily into Holocaust revisionism: Frank P. Mints, *The Liberty Lobby and the American Right: Race, Conspiracy, and Culture,* Westport, Conn., Greenwood Press, 1985.

19. James T. Patterson, *Mr. Republican: A Biography of Robert A. Taft,* Boston, Houghton Mifflin, 1972, 371; Herbert S. Parmet, *Eisenhower and the American Crusades,* New York, Macmillan, 1972, 298–303.

20. William F. Buckley Jr., "Veni, Vidi, Victus," *National Review,* March 17, 1972, 258; cited in Diamond, *Roads to Dominion,* 120.

21. And even Reagan was eventually seen by his own administration as too "sentimental" because of his belief in Mikhail Gorbachev and his consequent hopes for nuclear disarmament; see Chapter 16.

22. Quotations from Edwards, *The Conservative Revolution,* 12, 36.

23. This was the combined result of the advance of the conservative New Right in the Republican Party after 1960 and the leftward movement of the Democrats after Vietnam.

24. The GI Bill of Rights (actually the Servicemen's Readjustment Act 1944) promised benefits to World War II veterans delivered via the Veterans Administration. It provided grants for school and college, low-interest mortgage and small-business loans, job training, hiring privileges, and unemployment payments. These benefits were later extended to anyone who had served in the armed forces.

CHAPTER 14. COLD WAR IRONIES

1. On this crucial period generally, see Gabriel Kolko, *The Politics of War: The World and United States Foreign Policy, 1943–1945,* New York, Pantheon Books, 1990 [1968]; Deborah Welch Larson, *Origins of Containment: A Psychological Explanation,* Princeton, N.J., Princeton University Press, 1985; John Lewis Gaddis, *The United States and Origins of the Cold War, 1941–1947,* New York, Columbia University Press, 1972, and his revision, *We Now Know: Rethinking Cold War History,* New York, Oxford University Press, 1997. For a good descriptive account of Truman's relations with Stalin and Churchill at Potsdam, see David McCullough, *Truman,* New York, Simon & Schuster, 1992, Ch. 10.

2. The era was kicked off in February 1950 when McCarthy waved a piece of paper during a speech in which he claimed to know the names of 205 communists in the State Department. A special subcommittee of the Foreign Relations Committee was set up to hold hearings that were expected to defuse McCarthy's charges, but the attention only magnified the man by giving him center stage. In the fall of 1953, McCarthy, in the course of investigating an alleged subversive in the military, intemperately declared witness Brigadier General Ralph Zwicker, a highly decorated war veteran,

as "not fit" to wear the uniform. McCarthy's performance in the televised Army-McCarthy hearings that ensued destroyed his popular image and led to a censure vote in the Senate in which even McCarthy's former supporters deserted him. See Thomas C. Reeves, *The Life and Times of Joe McCarthy*, Briarcliff Manor, N.Y., Stein and Day, 1982; Robert Griffith, *The Politics of Fear: Joseph R. McCarthy and the Senate*, Amherst, University of Massachusetts Press, 1987.

3. For a useful critical summary, see Lloyd Gardner's "'Long Essay' on Cold War History," a review of Gaddis's *We Now Know*, available at http://www .h-net.org/~diplo/essays/PDF/Gardner_LongEssay.pdf.

4. Henry Kissinger, "Legacy of Defeat," *Courier-Mail*, April 29, 2000, 26.

5. U.S. Department of State, *Foreign Relations of the United States*, 1946, 6: 698–708. Kennan presented his article under the pseudonym "X": "The Sources of Soviet Conduct," *Foreign Affairs* 25 (July 1947): 566–582 at 582.

6. Wilson D. Miscamble, "The Evolution of an Internationalist: Harry S. Truman and American Foreign Policy," *Australian Journal of Politics and History* 23 (August 1977): 270. For Truman's private comments, see Robert H. Ferrell (ed.), *Off the Record: The Private Papers of Harry S. Truman*, New York, Penguin, 1980, 44, 56–57, 98, 99, 101–102; Robert H. Ferrell (ed.), *Dear Bess: The Letters from Harry to Bess Truman, 1910–1959*, New York, Norton, 1983, 101–102, 238, 307, 388, 419, 471, 474, 551.

7. Kennan would claim all his life that the "X" article had been misinterpreted and that he had never recommended that the United States should automatically resist Soviet expansionism in any part of the world it might occur; see his *Memoirs: 1925–1950*, London, Hutchinson, 1968, 354–367.

8. See Melvyn P. Leffler, "The American Conception of National Security and the Beginnings of the Cold War, 1945–1948," *American Historical Review* 89 (2), April 1984: 346–381 at 368; Dean Acheson, *Present at the Creation: My Years in the State Department*, New York, Norton, 1969, 489.

9. Michael J. Hogan, *The Marshall Plan: America, Britain, and the Reconstruction of Western Europe, 1947–1952*, Cambridge, Cambridge University Press, 1987. NATO negotiations were finally concluded in April 1949, though the administration was hardly more enthusiastic about them than were most members of Congress. See Lawrence Kaplan, *NATO and the United States: The Enduring Alliance*, Boston, Twayne Publishers, 1988, 16–30.

10. Roger G. Miller, *To Save a City: The Berlin Airlift, 1948–1949*, College Station, Texas A&M University Press, 2000.

11. Warren I. Cohen, *The Chinese Connection: Roger S. Greene, Thomas W. Lamont, George E. Sokolsky and American–East Asian Relations*, New York, Columbia University Press, 1978; Dorothy Borg and Waldo Heinrichs (eds.), *Uncertain Years: Chinese-American Relations, 1947–1950*, New York, Columbia University Press, 1980; Robert P. Newman, *Owen Lattimore and the "Loss" of China*, Berkeley, University of California Press, 1992. Despite failure to find any convincing evidence, and despite Lattimore's spirited defense, he was

hounded for two decades by the FBI, Justice Department, and McCarran Committee. After his death in May 1989, the whole affair was briefly revived in an exchange of articles and letters in the *New York Times*, with conservatives like William F. Buckley Jr. still insisting that Lattimore was a conscious agent of the communist conspiracy. See particularly *New York Times* articles by Tom Wicker, "Lesson of Lattimore," June 9, 1989, A31; "Smearing the Dead," July 11, A19; "Heresy and Disloyalty," July 25, 1989, A23.

12. Hiss's first trial ended in a hung jury, but his next in January 1950 for perjury produced a conviction, thanks to evidence advanced by Congressman Richard M. Nixon that proved Hiss had lied about passing documents. G. Edward White, *Alger Hiss's Looking-glass Wars: The Covert Life of a Soviet Spy*, Oxford, Oxford University Press, 2004; Patrick Swan (ed.), *Alger Hiss, Whittaker Chambers, and the Schism in the American Soul*, Wilmington, Del., ISI Books, 2003.

13. Ironically, the Korean War provided a huge economic boost to Japan that stimulated industrial recovery and cemented the American-Japanese alliance. Howard Schonberger, "U.S. Policy in Post-War Japan: The Retreat from Liberalism," *Science and Society* 46 (1), 1982, 39–59; William S. Borden, *The Pacific Alliance: United States Foreign Economic Policy and Japanese Trade Recovery, 1947–1955*, Madison, University of Wisconsin Press, 1984; Michael Schaller, *The American Occupation of Japan: The Origins of the Cold War in Asia*, New York, Oxford University Press, 1985.

14. Harry S. Truman, *Memoirs, Vol. II: Years of Trial and Hope*, Garden City, N.Y., Doubleday, 1956, 332–337; Robert J. Donovan, *Tumultuous Years: The Presidency of Harry S. Truman, 1949–1953*, New York, Norton, 1977, 197–199; McCullough, *Truman*, 775–783.

15. One large "revisionist" history has emphasized the internal, civil war dimensions of the conflict that the Americans did not appreciate or understand: see Bruce Cumings, *The Origins of the Korean War*, 2 vols., Princeton, N.J., Princeton University Press, 1981, 1990; another has insisted on the international, Cold War aspects: William Stueck, *The Korean War: An International History*, Princeton, N.J., Princeton University Press, 1995, and *Rethinking the Korean War: A New Diplomatic and Strategic History*, Princeton, N.J., Princeton University Press, 2002. The debate can easily be overstated, however, for Cumings portrays quite plainly the Cold War aspects of the war's origin (see *Origins, Vol. I: Liberation and the Emergence of Separate Regimes*, Ch. 12), and Stueck's concern is to mesh internal and external factors to provide for a full explanation.

16. Allen S. Whiting, *China Crosses the Yalu: The Decision to Enter the Korean War*, Stanford, Calif., Stanford University Press, 1968; Rosemary Foot, *The Wrong War: American Policy and the Dimensions of the Korean Conflict, 1950–1953*, Ithaca, N.Y., Cornell University Press, 1985, and *A Substitute for Victory: Politics of Peacemaking at the Korean Armistice Talks*, Ithaca, N.Y., Cornell University Press, 1990.

17. Quoted in Parmet, *Eisenhower and the American Crusades*, 298.

18. Stueck, *Rethinking the Korean War*, 215–216.

19. Truman is chided for bypassing Congress by Gary R. Hess, *Presidential Decisions for War: Korea, Vietnam and the Persian Gulf*, Baltimore, Md., Johns Hopkins University Press, 2001, 225; Parmet, *Eisenhower and the American Crusades*, 312–313.

20. The Tenth Amendment states: "The powers not delegated to the United States by the Constitution, nor prohibited by it in the States, are reserved to the States respectively or the people." Holman's reference point was an old 1920 Supreme Court judgment by Oliver Wendell Holmes, in *Missouri v. Holland*, that upheld the state of Missouri's obligation to comply with a U.S. treaty with Britain designed to protect migrant birds from extinction. Arthur A. Dean, "The Bricker Amendment and the Authority over Foreign Affairs," *Foreign Affairs* (October 1953): 1–19.

21. Lyndon Johnson's 1964 Civil Rights Act was the most far-reaching civil rights bill in U.S. history. It forbade discrimination in public accommodations and threatened to withhold federal funds from communities that maintained segregated schools. The Voting Rights Act of 1965 eradicated the tactics used in the South to disenfranchise black voters and permitted blacks to attain political office in record numbers.

22. Quoted in Parmet, *Eisenhower and the American Crusades*, 308.

23. L. Henkin, "The Universal Declaration and the U.S. Constitution," *PS: Political Science and Politics* 31 (3), 1998: 512–515.

24. Richard J. Barnet, *Intervention and Revolution*, New York, New American Library, 1972; Joseph B. Smith, *Portrait of a Cold Warrior*, New York, Putnam, 1976; Melvin Gurtov, *The U.S. against the Third World: Antinationalism and Intervention*, New York, Praeger, 1974.

25. Cumings, *Origins of the Korean War*, Vol. II, 441; Suki Kim, "Korea's New Wave," *New York Times*, May 10, 2003.

26. Cumings, *Origins of the Korean War*, Vol. II, 443.

27. Arthur Schlesinger, *The Imperial Presidency*, London, Andre Deutsch, 1974.

28. G. John Ikenberry, *Liberal Order and Imperial Ambition*, Cambridge, Polity Press, 2006. Ikenberry noted, "The United States has frequently sought to reshape the world precisely so it does not need to manage it" (157).

CHAPTER 15. VIETNAM: VIRTUE STAINED, POWER HUMBLED

1. Henry Kissinger, *Diplomacy*, New York, Simon & Schuster, 1994, 809.

2. It is no doubt rather disingenuous of Kissinger to call Vietnam a national tragedy, a description suggestive of an impersonal fate over which the actors involved have little real control, and thus an attenuation of individual responsibility that Kissinger might welcome. On the anniversary of Vietnam, see Kissinger, "Legacy of Defeat," *Courier-Mail*, April 29, 2000, 26. On the U.S. foreign policy dilemma generally, see Kissinger, *Does America Need a Foreign Policy?* New York, Simon & Schuster, 2001.

3. On the history of the "doctrine of credibility," see Jonathon Schell, *The Time of Illusion*, New York, Knopf, 1975.

4. For an excellent account that argues that the Americans misunderstood Diem and his motives, see Philip E. Catton, *Diem's Final Failure: Prelude to America's War in Vietnam*, Lawrence, University Press of Kansas, 2002.

5. See, for example, Paul Kennedy, *The Rise and Fall of the Great Powers*, New York, Random House, 1987, 405; Herbert Parmet, *JFK: The Presidency of John F. Kennedy*, Harmondsworth, Penguin, 1984, 333–336; Noam Chomsky, "Vain Hopes, False Dreams," *Z*, October 1992; John Ranelagh, *The Agency: The Rise and Decline of the CIA*, New York, Touchstone, 1987, 420. The last depicts Kennedy as an arrogant and committed Cold Warrior who ignored the advice of a CIA allegedly skeptical on prospects in Vietnam.

6. *Pentagon Papers, as Published by the New York Times*, New York, Bantam, 1971, 211–212. For the news conference of October 31, see Harold W. Chase and Allen H. Lerman (eds.), *Kennedy and the Press: The News Conferences*, New York, Thomas Y. Crowell, 1965, 508. Secretary of Defense Robert McNamara and General Maxwell Taylor had already reported the feasibility of this, probably at Kennedy's guidance, on October 2; *Documents on American Foreign Relations 1963*, Council on Foreign Relations, New York, Harper and Row, 1964, 296. A conference in Honolulu on the eve of Kennedy's killing apparently agreed to speed up withdrawal and reduce aid; see Peter Scott, "Vietnamization and the Drama of the Pentagon Papers," *Pentagon Papers: The Defense Department History of United States Decisionmaking in Vietnam*, Senate Gravel edn., Vol. 5, Boston, Beacon Press, 1971–1972, 224.

7. A. J. Langguth, *Our Vietnam: The War, 1954–1975*, New York, Simon & Schuster, 208–209; Howard Jones, *Death of a Generation*, New York, Oxford University Press, 2003, Ch. 10; Kenneth O'Donnell and Dave Powers, *Johnny, We Hardly Knew Ye*, Boston, Little, Brown, 1970, 13–18, 383.

8. Theodore C. Sorensen and Arthur Schlesinger Jr. reflecting on the Iraq conflict in their article "What Would J.F.K. Have Done?" *New York Times*, Op-Ed, December 4, 2005; Richard Parker, *John Kenneth Galbraith: His Life, His Politics, His Economics*, New York, Farrar, Straus and Giroux, 2005, 354–355, 357–359, 362–377, 389–392, 404–405, 409–410. By mid-1963 Galbraith was convinced that Kennedy was preparing to further defy his advisers by moving toward a new era of peaceful entente with the Cold War enemy in Moscow; see Parker, *John Kenneth Galbraith*, 405–406.

9. *Pentagon Papers, NYT*, 205. Johnson's own directive, NSAM 273, issued four days after the assassination, explicitly confirmed the withdrawal policy of NSAM 263, though it toughened up Kennedy's language with respect to the Viet Cong, who were now not a nationalist insurgency but "an externally directed and supported communist conspiracy." *Pentagon Papers, NYT*, 233. On this issue, see the memoirs of adviser to both Kennedy and Johnson, Richard Goodwin, *Remembering America*, New York, Harper and Row, 1988,

373, where he claims that the Johnson administration's insistence on policy continuity was purely for public consumption.

10. Chomsky, "Vain Hopes, False Dreams"; Jim Garrison, *On the Trail of the Assassins: My Investigation and Prosecution of the Murder of President Kennedy*, New York, Sheridan Square Press, 1988; Oliver Stone, director, *JFK*, Warner Brothers, 1991. There are more than three hundred assassination plot books in the John F. Kennedy Library in Boston.

11. Arthur M. Schlesinger Jr., *A Thousand Days: John F. Kennedy in the White House*, New York, Houghton Mifflin, 1965.

12. John F. Kennedy, Inaugural Address, January 20, 1961, available at http://www.bartleby.com/124/pres56.html; on the missile crisis, see James G. Blight and David A. Welsh, *On the Brink: Americans and Soviets Reexamine the Cuban Missile Crisis*, New York, Hill & Wang, 1989.

13. Diane Kunz argues, on the contrary, that JFK was a mediocre president whose death did not alter the course of history in Vietnam though his survival might have weakened civil rights policy: "Camelot Continued: What If John F. Kennedy Had Lived?" in Niall Ferguson (ed.), *Virtual History: Alternatives and Counterfactuals*, New York, Basic Books, 1997, 368–392.

14. According to Henry Kissinger, Nixon would spend hours ruminating on the ruthless tactics and gimmicks he believed had made the Kennedys so formidable; Henry Kissinger, *The Years of Upheaval*, Boston, Little, Brown, 1982. For just some Kennedy-debunking books see Thomas Reeves, *A Question of Character: A Life of John F. Kennedy*, London, Bloomsbury, 1991; Richard Reeves, *President Kennedy*, New York, Simon & Schuster, 1993; Seymour Hersh, *The Dark Side of Camelot*, New York, HarperCollins, 1998; Thomas G. Paterson (ed.), *Kennedy's Quest for Victory: American Foreign Policy, 1961–1963*, New York, Oxford University Press, 1989; Taylor Branch, *Pillar of Fire: America in the King Years*, New York, Simon & Schuster, 1998.

15. The Senate Gravel edition of the *Pentagon Papers* states that "the policy of phase out and withdrawal and all the plans and programs oriented to it" ended "de jure" in March 1964; "Phased Withdrawal of U.S. Forces, 1962–1964," Vol. 2, 160–200 at 196.

16. Michael H. Hunt, *Lyndon Johnson's War: America's Cold War Crusade in Vietnam, 1945–1968*, New York, Hill & Wang, 1996, 79, 103; Michael Beschloss (ed.), *Taking Charge: The Johnson White House Tapes*, New York, Simon & Schuster, 1997; *New York Times*, March 18, 1997, 12.

17. Johnson could not solve the problem by asking Congress for a tax increase in 1966, since he had used up his political capital the previous year persuading Congress to grant a tax cut. See Geoffrey Hodgson, *All Things to All Men: The False Promise of the Modern American Presidency*, London, Wiedenfield and Nicolson, 1980, 48. See also Richard E. Neustadt, *Presidential Power and the Modern Presidents: The Politics of Leadership from Roosevelt to Reagan*, New York, Free Press, 1990, 210–211.

18. Brian VanDeMark, *Into the Quagmire: Lyndon Johnson and the Escalation of*

the Vietnam War, New York, Oxford University Press, 1988; Doris Kearns, *Lyndon Johnson and the American Dream*, New York, Knopf, 1976.

19. Schlesinger, *Imperial Presidency*, 380–88; Theodore H. White, *Breach of Faith: The Fall of Richard Nixon*, New York, Atheneum, 1975.

20. See Kane, *Politics of Moral Capital*, Chs. 7–10.

21. Edward Doyle and Stephen Weiss (eds.), *A Collision of Cultures*, The Vietnam Experience series, Boston, Boston Publishing, 1984, 127–128; Hackworth quoted in John Kipner, "Report on Brutal Vietnam Campaign Stirs Memories," *New York Times*, December 28, 2003. The brutal exploits of Tiger Force were published in a series of articles in the *Toledo Blade*, October 22, 2003. On the general campaign of 1967, see Jonathon Schell, *The Military Half: An Account of the Destruction of Quang Mei and Quang Tin*, New York, Vintage, 1968. Many books deal with American atrocities: Edward S. Herman, *Atrocities in Vietnam: Myths and Realities*, Philadelphia, Pilgrim Press, 1970; Philip Caputo, *A Rumor of War*, New York, Holt, Rinehart and Winston, 1977; Michael Herr, *Dispatches*, London, Picador, 1978; Peter Goldman and Tony Fuller, *Charlie Company: What Vietnam Did to Us*, New York, Morrow, 1983; Joseph Goldstein, Burke Marshall, and Jack Schwartz, *The My Lai Massacre and Its Cover-Up*, New York, Free Press, 1976. A Vietnam vet responding to the Abu Ghraib photos told *Time* (May 24, 2004, 30): "I knew guys with dried ears and penises hanging from their dog tags. What these guys did in Iraq was bad, and they ought to burn for it, but it's not the worst thing we've done in war."

22. Draper in Richard M. Pfeffer (ed.), *No More Vietnams? The War and the Future of American Foreign Policy*, New York, Harper and Row, 1968, 28–29; Paul M. Kattenburg, *The Vietnam Trauma in American Foreign Policy, 1945–75*, New Brunswick, Transaction Books, 1982, 316–317.

23. April 22, 1971. Full speech available at http://www.democracynow.org/article .pl?sid=04/02/20/1535232 (accessed September 10, 2007).

24. Hans J. Morgenthau, *Vietnam and the United States*, Washington, D.C., Public Affairs Press, 1965, 19–20. W. D. Ehrhart similarly wrote, "[America] can't deal with . . . the vision of the United States as a source of evil in the world, every bit as malignant as that arch villain, the Soviet Union." *In the Shadow of Vietnam: Essays, 1977–1991*, Jefferson, N.C., McFarland, 1991, 60.

25. Nixon, "Address to the Nation on Vietnam," May 14, 1969, quoted in Richard A. Melanson, *American Foreign Policy since the Vietnam War: The Search for Consensus from Nixon to Clinton*, Armonk, N.Y., M. E. Sharpe, 2000, 53–54.

26. Ibid., 56; Kissinger, *Diplomacy*, 683–684; Jeffrey Kimball, *Nixon's Vietnam War*, Lawrence, University Press of Kansas, 1998; Larry Berman, *No Peace, No Honor: Nixon, Kissinger, and Betrayal in Vietnam*, New York, Free Press, 2001.

27. Kane, *Politics of Moral Capital*, 218–222.

CHAPTER 16. PUTTING HUMPTY TOGETHER AGAIN

1. McNamara, *In Retrospect*, 13.

2. Melanson, *American Foreign Policy*; Kissinger, *Does America Need a Foreign Policy?*.

3. Robert S. Litwak, *Détente and the Nixon Doctrine: American Foreign Policy and the Pursuit of Stability, 1969–1976*, Cambridge, Cambridge University Press, 1984, 126.

4. Melanson, *American Foreign Policy* 76–79.

5. Erwin C. Hargrove, *Jimmy Carter as President: Leadership and the Politics of the Public Good*, Baton Rouge, Louisiana State University Press, 1988; Jimmy Carter, "Address to the Nation on Energy and National Goals," July 15, 1979, *Public Papers of Presidents of the United States: Jimmy Carter, 1977–1981*, Washington, D.C., Government Printing Office, 1978–1983, 1236.

6. Jimmy Carter, *Keeping Faith: Memoirs of a President*, Toronto, Bantam, 1982, 143. In his views on the increasing complexity of the world and America's failure to appreciate it, Carter was influenced by the critique presented by David Rockefeller's Trilateral Commission.

7. Jerel A. Rosati, "Jimmy Carter: A Man before His Time?," *Presidential Studies Quarterly* 23 (3), 1993: 459–476 at 465–467; Rosati, *The Carter Administration's Quest for Global Community: Beliefs and Their Impact on Behavior*, Columbia, University of South Carolina Press, 1987; Gaddis Smith, *Morality, Reason, and Power: American Diplomacy in the Carter Years*, New York, Hill & Wang, 1986; U.S. House of Representatives, Committee on Foreign Affairs, *Human Rights in the World Community: A Call for U.S. Leadership*, 93rd Cong., 1st sess., Washington, D.C., Government Printing Office, 1974.

8. Louis Henkin, "The Universal Declaration and the U.S. Constitution," *PS: Political Science and Politics* 31 (3), 1998: 512–515 at 512; Louis Henkin and John Lawrence Hargrove (eds.), *Human Rights: An Agenda for the Next Century*, Washington, D.C., American Society of International Law, 1994; John Kane, "American Values or Human Rights? U.S. Foreign Policy and the Fractured Myth of Virtuous Power," *Presidential Studies Quarterly* 33 (4), (December): 772–800; Michael Ignatieff, "No Exceptions?" *Legal Affairs*, May/June 2002: 59–61; D. P. Forsythe, "Human Rights Fifty Years after the Universal Declaration," *PS: Political Science and Politics* 31 (3), 1998: 507–511.

9. Betty Glad, *Jimmy Carter in Search of the Great White House*, New York, Norton, 1980, 316.

10. Rosati, "Jimmy Carter," 464; Hargrove, *Jimmy Carter as President*, 168. The general academic debate over the coherence or otherwise of the Carter administration's foreign policy perspective is summarized in Rosati, *The Carter Administration's Quest*, Ch. 1; Zbigniew Brzezinski, "The New Dimensions of Human Rights," *Ethics and International Affairs* 10, 1996: 165–174 at 166.

11. Daniel Yankelovitch and L. Kaagan, "Assertive America," *Foreign Affairs* 59, 1981: 696–713 at 696; see also Hargrove, *Jimmy Carter as President*, 191. For

Soviet penetration of the Third World, see for example Christopher Stevens, *The Soviet Union and Black Africa*, London, Macmillan, 1976; Robert H. Donaldson (ed.), *The Soviet Union in the Third World: Successes and Failures*, Boulder, Colo., Westview Press, 1981; Carol R. Saivetz (ed.), *The Soviet Union in the Third World*, Boulder, Colo., Westview Press, 1989.

12. Quoted in Melanson, *American Foreign Policy*, 108–110.

13. Cyrus Vance, *Hard Choices*, New York, Simon & Schuster, 1983, 394; Zbigniew Brzezinski, *Power and Principle: Memoirs of the National Security Adviser, 1977–1981*, London, Wiedenfield and Nicolson, 1983, 459–460; Rosati, "Jimmy Carter," fn. 49, 476; Dumbrell, *The Carter Presidency*, 198.

14. The State Department, for example, in which Carter set up his Bureau of Human Rights and Humanitarian Affairs, saw its role as safeguarding *national*, not human, interests; see R. J. Vincent, *Human Rights and International Relations*, Cambridge, Cambridge University Press, 135. Also Congressional Research Service for the Subcommittee on International Organizations, House Committee on International Relations, *Human Rights Conditions in Selected Countries and the US Response*, July 1978, 246–351; Dumbrell, *The Carter Presidency*, 179–180; A. Glenn Mower, *Human Rights and American Foreign Policy*, New York, Greenwood, 1987, Ch. 2; Brzezinski, "New Dimensions," 166

15. All citations from Dumbrell, *The Carter Presidency*, 192.

16. Jeane J. Kirkpatrick, "Dictatorships and Double Standards," *Commentary* (November 1979): 34–45. This article was included in a later book, *Dictatorships and Double Standards: Rationalism and Reason in Politics*, New York, Simon & Schuster, 1982.

17. M. E. Galey, "The Universal Declaration of Human Rights: The Role of Congress," *PS: Political Science and Politics* 31 (3), 1998: 524–529 at 526.

18. Samuel P. Huntington, "The Defense Policy of the Reagan Administration, 1981–1982," in Fred I. Greenstein (ed.), *The Reagan Presidency: An Early Assessment*, Baltimore, Md., Johns Hopkins University Press, 1982. There has been an extensive debate over Reagan's rhetoric, for example over how far he was himself an author of it, whether it was unreservedly conservative, whether it relied on emotion more than factual analysis, and so on. Robert C. Rowland and John M. Jones, "'Until Next Week': The Saturday Radio Addresses of Ronald Reagan," *Presidential Studies Quarterly* 32 (1), 2002: 84–111, give a useful summary and provide their own interpretive analysis of Reagan's radio addresses. On foreign policy, which is my main focus here, they argue that Reagan's talks were much more heavily ideological than on domestic policy and aimed at tapping into basic American values such as freedom, peace, the value of the free market, and so on. I would add that Reagan's *actions* also had strong rhetorical import, particularly in Grenada and Libya. Reagan quote in Gary C. Woodward, "Reagan as Roosevelt: The Elasticity of Pseudo-populist Appeals," *Central States Speech Journal* 34, 1983: 44–58 at 54.

19. Ronald Reagan, Second Inaugural Address, January 21, 1985, available at http://www.bartleby.com/124/pres62.html.

20. Quoted in Melanson, *American Foreign Policy,* 150.

21. Reagan, "Address before a Joint Session of Congress on the State of the Union," February 6, 1985, quoted in ibid., 155–156. This attitude was buoyed by a July 1980 report of the so-called Committee of Santa Fe that rejected Carterism as naive and declared that America was involved in World War III against communism in Latin America; ibid., 157–158.

22. Ibid., Ch. 4; Robert W. Tucker, "Reagan's Foreign Policy," *Foreign Affairs, American and the World, 1988/89,* 68 (1), 1989: 1–27 at 16. U.S. troops had been sent into Lebanon to maintain order after an Israeli invasion aimed at crushing bases of the Palestinian Liberation Organization and creating a buffer zone on Israel's northern border. Though the invasion had Secretary of State Al Haig's approval (the Israelis acting as U.S. surrogates against Soviet-supported Syria), Reagan was appalled, even more so when the Israelis failed to prevent their Lebanese Christian allies from slaughtering Palestinians in refugee camps. See Raymond L. Garthoff, *Détente and Confrontation: American-Soviet Relations from Nixon to Reagan,* Washington, D.C., Brookings Institution, 1985, 1062ff.

23. Tucker remarked that "what was striking about the policy implementing the Reagan Doctrine was the caution and moderation that marked it"; "Reagan's Foreign Policy," 14.

24. Ibid., 22–24.

25. Michael R. Beschloss and Strobe Talbott, *At the Highest Levels: The Inside Story of the End of the Cold War,* Boston, Little, Brown, 1993, Ch. 1.

26. Kissinger put the matter thus: "In the post–World War II period, America had been fortunate to have never had to choose between its moral convictions and its strategic analysis. All of its key decisions had been readily justified as both promoting democracy and resisting aggression"; *Diplomacy,* 667.

27. Bush had been ambassador to the United Nations under Nixon and Ford, and a representative to China and head of the CIA under Ford. As Reagan's vice president, he had been all but invisible; George H. W. Bush and Brent Scowcroft, *A World Transformed,* New York, Knopf, 1998, 35; C. V. Crabb and K. Mulcahy, "The Elitist Presidency: George Bush and the Management of Operation Desert Storm," in R. E. Waterman (ed.), *The Presidency Reconsidered,* Itasca, Ill., D. E. Peacock, 1993, 275–330 at 281; "Remarks at the Aspen Institute Symposium," Aspen, Colo., August 2, 1990, quoted in Melanson, *American Foreign Policy,* 212–213.

28. Stanley Cloud, "Exorcising an Old Demon," *Time* 137 (10), March 11, 1991, 52–53 at 52.

29. Bush was right that expulsion, not invasion, was all he had been legally sanctioned to perform and confessed himself bitter about the "sniping, carping, bitching, [and] predictable editorial complaints" (quoted in Bob

Woodward, *Shadow: Five Presidents and the Legacy of Watergate*, New York, Simon & Schuster, 1999, 188). The fault lay, however, with the expectations he himself had generated.

30. Beschloss and Talbott, *At the Highest Levels*, 255.

31. James Mann, *Rise of the Vulcans: The History of Bush's War Cabinet*, New York, Viking, 2004, 199, 209–213.

32. Bush, "Remarks at Texas A&M University," December 15, 1992, and "Remarks at the United States Military Academy in West Point," January 5, 1993, cited in Melanson, *American Foreign Policy*, 218–219; Caspar Weinberger, *Fighting for Peace*, New York, Warner Books, 1990, 433–445.

33. Mann, *Rise of the Vulcans*, 221–223.

34. David Rieff, *At the Point of a Gun: Democratic Dreams and Armed Intervention*, New York, Simon & Schuster, 2005. Cases like Bosnia and Rwanda made Rieff himself an interventionist in the 1990s, but he took a turn against "utopianism" after George W. Bush's invasion of Iraq in 2003.

CHAPTER 17. OFFENDED INNOCENCE, RIGHTEOUS WRATH

1. Mann, *Rise of the Vulcans*, 273–274. Mann notes that whenever the conservatives felt offended by Powell and Armitage, they accused them of having been "captured" by the State Department's bureaucracy. For the influence of the military on foreign policy, see Dana Priest, *The Mission: Waging War and Keeping Peace with America's Military*, New York, Norton, 2003.

2. Thomas H. Henriksen, *Clinton's Foreign Policy in Somalia, Bosnia, Haiti and North Korea*, Stanford University, Hoover Institution, 1996, 4–5.

3. William G. Hyland, *Clinton's World: Remaking American Foreign Policy*, New York, Praeger, 1999.

4. For the Clinton administration's dilatoriness on human rights crises, see memoirs of a participant, John Shattuck, *Freedom on Fire: Human Rights Wars and America's Response*, Cambridge, Mass., Harvard University Press, 2003; and Samantha Power, *A Problem from Hell: America and the Age of Genocide*, New York, Basic Books, 2002. For Clinton's foreign policy generally, see David Halberstam, *War in a Time of Peace: Bush, Clinton and the Generals*, New York, Scribner, 2001.

5. Michael Cox, "The Necessary Partnership? The Clinton Presidency and Post-Soviet Russia," *International Affairs* 70 (4) (October 1994), 635–658; Melanson, *American Foreign Policy*, 269–270.

6. Martin Walker, *Clinton: The President They Deserve*, London, Vintage, 1997, 285–289.

7. John Stremlau, "Clinton's Dollar Diplomacy," *Foreign Policy* 97, 1994/1995: 18; Melanson, *American Foreign Policy*, 272.

8. There was a 1994 Mexican devaluation that sparked a banking crisis, inducing Clinton to organize an $18 billion bailout; a 1997 run on the currency of Thailand that rapidly spread financial crisis throughout the countries of Southeast Asia and turned the "Asian tigers" into mewling kittens; and a

1998 default by Russia on its domestic bonds that for some reason caused U.S. stock markets to plummet.

9. Clinton was rather unfairly castigated by James McGregor Burns and Georgia Sorenson in *Dead Center: Clinton-Gore Leadership and the Perils of Moderation*, New York, Charles Scribner's, 1999, for what they interpreted as a lack of "heroic" leadership in foreign policy.

10. The Bush policy before September 11 seemed nicely to illustrate Kissinger's observation that U.S. foreign policy is increasingly driven by domestic politics in a post–Cold War world where the United States is the sole superpower: "When pressure on foreign countries appears free of risk, there is increasing scope for legislating domestic American preferences as objectives of foreign policy." *Does America Need a Foreign Policy?*, 252.

11. In February 2002, Bush made a live television broadcast from Beijing's Qinghua University in which he proclaimed that America was proof of the possibility of a free and tolerant society. He argued against religious persecution in China, dwelling heavily on the religious underpinnings to the theme of America as the exemplary nation. M. Allen and P. P. Pan, "Bush Touts U.S. Values to Chinese." *Washington Post*, February 22, 2002, A01.

12. Woodward, *Plan of Attack*, New York, Simon & Schuster, 2004. Richard A. Clarke claims that Rumsfeld, Wolfowitz, and the president were all pressing to make a connection with Saddam; *Against All Enemies: Inside the White House's War on Terror—What Really Happened*, New York, Free Press, 2004; on Wolfowitz's attitude, see Mann, *Rise of the Vulcans*, 300–301. Cheney's obsession with Iraq is evidenced in Woodward's *Plan of Attack* and also Paul O'Neill's memories of his time as treasury secretary; see Ron Suskind, *The Price of Loyalty: George W. Bush, the White House, and the Education of Paul O'Neill*, New York, Simon & Schuster, 2004.

13. See, for example, Bob Woodward, *State of Denial: Bush at War Part III*, New York, Simon & Schuster, 2006; Michael Isikoff and David Corn, *Hubris: The Inside Story of Spin, Scandal and the Selling of the Iraq War*, New York, Crown, 2006; Ron Suskind, *The One Percent Doctrine: Deep Inside America's Pursuit of its Enemies Since 9/11*, New York, Simon & Schuster, 2006; Michael R. Gordon and Bernard E. Trainor, *Cobra II: The Inside Story of the Invasion and Occupation of Iraq*, New York, Pantheon, 2006; L. Paul Bremer and Malcolm McConnell, *My Year in Iraq: The Struggle to Build a Future of Hope*, New York, Simon & Schuster, 2006.

14. Kristol quoted in Maureen Dowd, "Junior Gets a Spanking," *New York Times*, August 18, 2002, Op-Ed; Safire, "Of Turks and Kurds," *New York Times*, August 26, 2002, Op-Ed; Bayh, "Excerpts from the Debate in the Senate on Using Force against Iraq," *New York Times*, October 9, 2002; John Lewis Gaddis, "Grand Strategy in the Second Term," *Foreign Affairs* 84 (January/February 2005): 2–15.

15. William Kristol and Robert Kagan (eds.), *Present Dangers: Crisis and Opportu-*

nity in American Foreign and Defense Policy, San Francisco, Encounter Books, 2000. Michael Lind describes the neoconservatives thus:

> Most neoconservative defence intellectuals have their roots on the left, not the right. They are products of the largely Jewish-American Trotskyist movement of the 1930s and 1940s, which morphed into anti-communist liberalism between the 1950s and 1970s and finally into a kind of militaristic and imperial right with no precedents in American culture or political history. Their admiration for the Israeli Likud party's tactics, including preventive warfare such as Israel's 1981 raid on Iraq's Osirak nuclear reactor, is mixed with odd bursts of ideological enthusiasm for "democracy." They call their revolutionary ideology "Wilsonianism" (after President Woodrow Wilson), but it is really Trotsky's theory of the permanent revolution mingled with the far-right Likud strain of Zionism. Genuine American Wilsonians believe in self-determination for people such as the Palestinians.

"The Weird Men behind George W. Bush's War," *New Statesmen (UK),* April 7, 2003. Stafan Halper and Jonathon Clarke ("Reagan, Iraq, and Neoconservatism: An Exchange," *The American Spectator,* June 2004: 30–33) describe the neocons as "Wilsonians with guns." See also Halper and Clarke, *America Alone: The Neo-Conservatives and Global Order,* Cambridge, Cambridge University Press, 2004. Souder quoted in David Brooks, "Portrait of a Republican," *New York Times,* August 28, 2004, Op-Ed.

16. There were rare exceptional opponents: Robert C. Byrd, "Congress Must Resist the Rush to War," *New York Times,* October 10, 2002, Op-Ed.

17. Kenneth M. Pollack, *The Threatening Storm: The Case for Invading Iraq,* New York, Random House, 2002; Jack F. Matlock Jr., "'The Threatening Storm' Warns That an Attack on Iraq Is Dangerous and Necessary," *New York Times,* October 20, 2002, Section 7, 11.

18. Colin Powell's chief of staff, Lawrence Wilkerson, later blamed all the administration's failures on what he called the "Rumsfeld-Cheney cabal," whose secrecy, arrogance, and skewing of policy was unchallenged by a president who "is not versed in international relations, and not too much interested in them, either." Brian Knowlton, "Former Powell Aide Says Bush Policy Is Run by a 'Cabal,'" *New York Times,* October 21, 2005.

19. Thomas E. Ricks, *Fiasco: The American Military Adventure in Iraq,* New York, Penguin Press, 2006; Peter Baker, "Embittered Insiders Turn on Bush," *Washington Post,* November 19, 2006. Adelman was an administrator under Reagan and a member of Donald Rumsfeld's Defense Policy Board who had predicted a "cakewalk" in Iraq. Other notable neocons who recanted were Richard Perle and David Frum; see David Rose, "Neo Culpa," *Vanity Fair,* November 3, 2006, available at http://www.vanityfair.com/politics/features/2006/12/neocons200612; George Packer, *The Assassins' Gate: America in Iraq,* New York, Farrar, Straus and Giroux, 2005.

20. For a stinging critique on the oil issue, see Antonia Juhasz, *The Bush Agenda: Invading the World, One Economy at a Time,* New York, Regan Books, HarperCollins, 2006; Niall Ferguson, *Colossus: The Price of America's Empire,* New York, Penguin, 2004. Ferguson describes the seven characteristic phases of U.S. engagement as (1) impressive initial military success, (2) a flawed assessment of indigenous sentiment, (3) a strategy of limited war and gradual escalation of forces, (4) domestic disillusionment in the face of protracted and nasty conflict, (5) premature democratization, (6) the ascendancy of domestic economic considerations, and (7) ultimate withdrawal.

21. David Stout, "Bush Expresses 'Deep Disgust' over Abuse of Iraqi Prisoners," *New York Times,* April 30, 2004.

22. For an exhaustive catalogue of abuses and incidents, see Mark Danner, *Torture and Truth: America, Abu Ghraib, and the War on Terror,* New York, New York Review of Books, 2004.

23. January 18, 2005, "Rice Tells Senators 'The Time for Diplomacy Is Now,'" distributed by the Bureau of International Information Programs, U.S. Department of State; Information Resource Center, Office of Public Affairs, U.S. Consulate General, Sydney.

24. The case for reasserting diplomacy was vigorously pressed by Dennis Ross in *Statecraft: And How to Restore America's Standing in the World,* New York, Farrar, Straus & Giroux, 2007.

EPILOGUE

1. Samuel Hynes, "D-Day in History and in Memory," *New York Times,* June 6, 2004, Op-Ed.

2. Melvyn P. Leffler, "Think Again: Bush's Foreign Policy," *Foreign Policy,* September/October 2004, available at http://www.foreignpolicy.com.

3. Francis Fukuyama, *America at the Crossroads: Democracy, Power, and the Neoconservative Legacy,* New Haven, Conn., Yale University Press, 2007.

4. Robert Kagan, *Of Paradise and Power: America and Europe in the New World Order,* New York, Knopf, 2003. The historical reversal between Wilson and Clemenceau seems quite genuine, however, if President Jacques Chirac can lecture Britain and the United States that, while it is still possible to organize the world on the basis of the logic of power, history has taught that this is unstable and sooner or later leads to crisis or conflict. "We have another choice. That of an order based on respect for international law and the empowerment of the world's new poles by fully and wholly involving them in the decision-making mechanisms." Quoted in Patrick E. Tyler, "Chirac Offers Cooperation and Criticism to U.S. and Britain," *New York Times,* November 18, 2004.

5. Thomas L. Friedman, "Read My Ears," *New York Times,* January 27, 2005, Op-Ed. For an interesting account of one disappointed European, see Emmanuel Todd, *After the Empire: The Breakdown of the American Order,* trans. C. Jon Delogu, New York, Columbia University Press, 2003.

6. Alexander T. J. Lennon (ed.), *What Does the World Want from America? International Perspectives on U.S. Foreign Policy,* Cambridge, Mass., MIT Press, 2003.

7. Ikenberry, *Liberal Order.*

8. G. John Ikenberry and Anne-Marie Slaughter, Princeton Project on National Security, final report, *Forging a World of Liberty Under Law: U.S. National Security in the 21st Century,* Princeton, N.J., Woodrow Wilson School of Public and International Affairs, 2006 (available at http://www.wws.princeton.edu/ppns/report/FinalReport.pdf).

9. Ian Shapiro, *Containment: Rebuilding a Strategy against Global Terror,* Princeton, N.J., Princeton University Press, 2007.

Acheson, Dean, 206–207, 243, 249, 305, 371, 378

Adams, John, 26, 53, 76, 83, 84, 340–341, 345, 348

Adams, John Quincy, 6, 90, 91, 93–94, 102–103, 126, 352, 354

Addams, Jane, 154

Aguinaldo, Emilio, 131, 360

Ambrosius, Lloyd, 151, 350, 362–364

American Civil War, 98, 106–110, 152, 354, 363

American Founding, 4, 26–27, 32–49, 342–347

American identity, 5, 26, 64, 145, 327, 334; Anglo-Saxon Protestant origins of, 6, 9, 51, 56–58, 342, 348; "liberal creed" in relation to, 6–7, 11; and parochial versus transcendent nationalism, 12–13, 21–22, 26, 28–30, 39, 64, 82, 95, 279; particularist versus universalist versions of, 10, 59, 64, 78, 95, 145, 216

American imperialism: and age of formal imperialism, 74, 79, 106, 124–135, 143; versus American anti-imperialism, 28, 97, 104, 124, 136, 150; associated with American values, 258, 314, 318, 331–332; and cultural imperialism, 172, 285; and economic imperialism, 67, 71–73, 77–78; incompetence of, 322, 390; and "nonimperialistic imperialism," 77, 140

American mythology: and American exceptionalism, 6, 27, 285, 292, 338; and American mission, 3–6, 13, 18–19, 25–30, 49, 57–58, 106–107, 114, 120; Christian influence on, 6, 51, 55–58; Dissenting influence on, 24, 34–35; and doctrines of liberty and equality, 9, 11, 23, 49, 50–52, 64, 105, 275; economic version of, 67, 74–75, 77–79, 124; and the European Enlightenment, 3, 12, 20–21, 23–26, 49, 53, 114, 342; frontier version of, 115–119; and ideology, 19–21; origins of, 3–7, 18–31; and the problem of virtue and power, 2–3, 12–14, 28–30, 330–332, 336; radical Whig influence on, 24, 39–40

American Revolution, 21, 23–26, 34, 37, 82, 85, 99, 147

American Security Council, 374–375

American "traditions," 19

Annan, Kofi, 324

Appleby, Joyce, 49, 342, 347

Ascriptivism, 19

Barlow, Joel, 26

Battle of Santiago, 126

Beard, Charles, 73, 74, 361
Benét, Stephen Vincent, 224
Beveridge, Albert, J., 71, 128, 131, 132, 162, 359
Bierce, Ambrose, 106
Blackstone, William, 111, 341
Blaine, James G., 125
Bonney, William, 118
Boone, Daniel, 117
Boorstin, Daniel, 54, 346, 348
Borah, William, 158, 163, 174–176, 190
Bretton Woods, 79, 209, 236, 244, 259
Brezhnev, Leonid, 219
Briand, Aristide, 176
Brown, John, 108
Brown, Richard M., 118, 350
Brown, Ron, 306, 309
Bryan, William Jennings, 126, 131, 141, 150, 151, 154, 359; and the American mission, 128, 136; and the defeat of agrarian populism, 121, 351–352
Buckley Jr., William F., 231, 235, 376, 379
Buntline, Ned, 118
Bush, George H. W., 296–302, 304, 305, 308, 309, 334, 386, 387; and American global leadership, 298–300; pragmatic foreign policy of, 296–297; and the virtue-power dilemma, 297
Bush, George W., 79, 221, 290, 305, 311–329, 388; and Christian mission, 58; and the virtue-power dilemma, 1–2, 332–335
Bushman, Richard M., 56

Caesar, 163
Calhoun, John, 141
Calhoun, John C., 90, 351
Calvinism, 10, 52, 53, 54, 55–56
Carnegie, Andrew, 137, 141
Carnegie Endowment for International Peace, 246
Carnegie Steel Company, 70
Carter, James (Jimmy), 115–116, 219, 235, 283–289, 291, 298, 299, 385; and "Carterism," 304, 306, 386; human rights strategy of, 284–289, 291, 305–306, 328; views on U.S. foreign policy of, 2, 277, 283

Carter Doctrine, 288
Chamberlain, Neville, 195
Chang Kai-shek, 194, 244–246, 248, 371
Chinese Revolution, 245
Churchill, Winston, 207, 208, 370, 371, 377
Church League of America, 374
Clay, Henry, 4, 40, 113, 145; "American system" of, 70–71, 78; and the Missouri compromise, 108; and the War of 1812, 90–92
Clark, Tom, 228
Clemenceau, Georges, 160, 169, 390
Cleveland, Grover, 71, 125, 126, 131, 146, 359, 363
Clinton, William J., 2, 79, 301–302, 304–311, 320, 326, 334, 387–388; foreign policy of, 307, 387; geoeconomic strategy of, 308–309, and human rights, 306, 387; and the virtue-power dilemma, 310–311
Cold War, 79, 210, 215, 224, 238–241, 267, 284; and American mythology, 241; causes of, 212, 241, 371–372, 378; consequences of end of, 295–298, 307–309, 388; and domestic anti-communism, 235, 236–237, 376; effect on United Nations of, 251–253; great power logic of, 289; Jimmy Carter's view of, 277, 284, 286; and the Korean War, 247, 249, 251, 252, 258, 379; militarization of, 259; Ronald Reagan's role in ending, 295–296; and U.S. containment policy, 218–219, 241, 251, 288; and the virtue-power dilemma, 15–17, 212, 220–221, 272, 292, 313, 334
Communist International (Comintern), 194, 195, 215, 216, 372
Condorcet, Marquis de, 20, 25, 44, 340
Confederation of the United States of America, 35, 254
Congress of Industrial Organizations, 227
Constitution of the United States, 3, 27, 37, 38, 89; Alexander Hamilton's views on, 38, 347; and the approval of treaties, 85; and the Bricker Amendment proposal, 253–255; checking and balancing of powers in, 40; and the "end"

of republicanism, 37; and "pervasive constitutionalism," 351; power of adding new territories in, 105, 107, 127; as the reign of virtue, 61–63; separation of church and state in, 57; and slavery, 107–109; Theodore Roosevelt's views on, 139, 361; Thomas Jefferson's flouting of, 101; William Howard Taft's views on, 139; Woodrow Wilson's views on, 146–147, 363
Coolidge, Calvin, 172, 176
Cooper, J. Fenimore, 117
Coughlin, Charles E., 228, 374
Creel, George, 177
Crèvecoeur, St John, 25, 52
Crimean War, 98
Croly, Herbert, 11, 46, 94; and American myth of an empty land, 100, 111; views on the righteous use of force of, 153
Cummings, E. E., 170

Darwinian sociology, 10
Davies, Charles Stewart, 115
Dawes Plan of 1924, 366
Dawes Severalty Act [1887], 387
Declaration of Independence, 11, 23, 27, 42, 59, 76, 94, 339, 342; relationship to U.S. Constitution of, 61, 62, 107
De Tracy, Destutt, 340
Dewey, George, 126
Dewey, John, 119, 347, 358
Dewey, Thomas, 236
Díaz, Adolfo, 141
Dies, Martin, 229, 230, 275
Dies Committee, 229
"Dollar Diplomacy." See Taft, William Howard
Douglas, Steven, 108
Dulles, John Foster, 214, 218, 250, 263, 372

Earp, Wyatt, 118
Edwards, Jonathan, 55
Eisenhower, Dwight (Ike), 218, 235, 263, 267; effects of McCarthyism on, 239; and the Eisenhower Doctrine, 256; opposition to Bricker Amendment of, 254; rejection of unilateralism by, 165; role of in ending the Korean War, 250–

253; warning of "military-industrial complex" by, 259
Emerson, Ralph Waldo, 113
Everett, Edward, 113

Fascism, 15, 75, 217, 227, 374; in America, 228; ideology and appeal of, 177–181
Federalist Party, 35, 40, 45, 49, 62, 66, 70, 76, 89, 92; British sympathies of, 83–86; and War of 1812, 91; and westward expansion, 99
Finney, Charles Grandison, 56
Fitzgerald, F. Scott, 170
Five Power Treaty, 174
Foner, Eric, 168, 363
Ford, Gerald, 235, 277, 282, 283, 386
Ford, Henry, 173, 216
Ford, John, 358
Four Power Treaty, 174, 175
Franco, Francisco, 195
Franco-Prussian War of 1870, 98
Franklin, Benjamin, 23, 25, 52, 346, 348
Frontier thesis. See Turner, Frederick Jackson

Gardner, Lloyd C., 352, 378
General Electric Company, 70
George, David Lloyd, 155
George III, 24, 341
GI Bill of Rights (Serviceman's Readjustment Act [1944]), 237, 377
Godkin, E. L., 131
Goldwater, Barry, 231, 268, 376
Gorbachev, Mikhail, 219, 295, 296, 377
Great Depression, 15, 73–74, 116, 224; conservatives blamed for, 225, 229; and the demise of economic internationalism, 78, 166; and failure of liberal democracy, 181, 224; and fascism, 177; and myth of individual responsibility, 9; and the New Deal, 225–227, 237
Great War. See World War I
Greeley, Horace, 114
Grew, Joseph C., 201, 369

Hamilton, Alexander, 41, 69, 149, 338, 341, 344, 345, 347, 348, 353, 357; attitude to work of, 54; contest with Jefferson

Hamilton, Alexander (*continued*)
of, 45–49; and military defense, 81–82; and nonentanglement doctrine, 66; view of judiciary of, 62; views on commerce and war of, 76, vision for America of, 7, 8, 37–39
Hardin, John Wesley, 118
Harding, Warren G., 163, 167, 174, 176
Harriman, Averell, 238, 305
Harris, Arthur ("Bomber"), 369
Harrison, Benjamin, 125
Hartz, Louis, 6, 7, 11, 33, 343
Harvey, George, 167
Hay, John, 130, 187, 359
Hearst, William Randolph, 168, 175
Heilke, Thomas, 20, 340
Hickock, James Butler, 118, 358
Hideyoshi, 183
Hiss, Alger, 230, 245, 246, 379
Hitler, Adolf, 166, 192, 195, 208, 217, 218, 235, 297, 298; attack on Soviet Union by, 197–198, 217; British and French appeasement of, 196; and "Hitlerism," 225; Nazi ideology of, 179–180; wartime strategy of, 196
Hobsbawm, Eric, 340, 341
Hofstadter, Richard, 345, 373
Holmes, Oliver Wendell, 106, 246, 350, 380
Hoover, Herbert, 79, 217, 283, 309; "American system" or "economic diplomacy" of, 78, 172, 353; anti-war stance of, 197; and the failure of economic diplomacy, 177; Latin American anti-interventionism of, 194; opposition to the New Deal of, 225; and the redefining of liberalism, 226; and the threat of Japan, 186–187
House UnAmerican Activities Committee (HUAC). *See* Dies Committee
Houston, Alan Craig, 42
Huerta, Victoriana, 150
Hughes, Charles, 167, 174, 175
Hull, Cordell, 192–194, 208
Huntington, Samuel, 11, 339

Innocent virtue, 2, 12, 13, 14–15, 17, 32, 51, 98–122; ascendancy of in Wilson's

foreign policy, 144, 155, 157, 163, 167; balance of power politics undermines, 201, 221; Christian origin of idea of, 51, 55–57; and conquest of the Indians, 111–115; and the Democratic Party, 279; dogmatic anti-communism compromises, 223, 256; incompatibility of with martial virtue and war, 60, 106, 120; and hypocrisy, 105; imperialism a danger to, 124, 129, 132, 143; as innocence offended after *11 September 2001*, 311, 313; isolationism as a means of preserving, 67; Kennedy assassination and, 264, 267; national pride and, 82, 95–97, 199; "One Hundred Percent Americanism" a perversion of, 169; and the peace movement, 136; Reagan's reassurance of, 292; rule of law identified with, 119, 137; and transcendent nationalism, 29; Vietnam War causes loss of, 264, 272, 275–276, 279, 303; and the virtue-power dilemma, 63, 64–65, 137, 305, 331–332; and World War II, 204–205; as wrathful righteousness for conservatives, 234, 322–323, 326–327
International Monetary Fund, 79, 209
Isolationism, 2, 3, 15, 129, 195, 236; and America First, 241; and "arrogant indifference," 253; compromised by economic entanglement, 13, 67–75; distinguished from nonentanglement, 162; effectual end of policy of, 197; Japanese version of, 182; misleadingness of, 166; spirit of survives policy, 15, 234; undermined by conservative anti-communism, 233, 304; unilateralism leads to, 165, 207; universalistic aims of, 64; Wilson repudiates, 158

Jackson, Andrew, 52, 145; and American nationalism, 95; defeat of British and Indians by, 91; foreign policy of, 95–97; Indian removal policies of, 113, 357; invasion of Florida by, 101; and the nullification crisis of *1832–1833*, 351; and virtue of democracy, 27, 49
Jay, John, 88, 338, 353
Jay's Treaty of *1794*, 69, 84, 353

Jefferson, Thomas, 6, 25, 26, 39, 41–49,
52, 108, 145, 154, 283; admiration for
Isaac Newton of, 342; and the agrarian
ideal of virtue, 8, 41–49, 68, 348; and
the appeal to nature, 344; and the Declaration of Independence, 11, 23, 76;
desire for West Florida of, 101; effect
of 1812 War on, 91; and the "empire of
liberty," 47; failure of economic embargo policy of, 82, 89–92; as father of
American political parties, 347; fear of
contamination of virtue of, 4, 42, 44,
47; and the "Indian problem," 111–114,
120; influence of Destutt de Tracy on,
340; and innocent virtue, 51, 55–57; and
internal expansion policy, 99–100; and
the Jeffersonian Republicans, 45, 66,
72; and Jeffersonian thought, 12, 41–49,
53–55; on Jesus as moral teacher, 51,
349; as keeper of the American mythology, 48–49; and the nonentanglement
doctrine, 66–67, 86–87; opinion of
Hamilton of, 37; popular influence of,
27, 48–49; pragmatism of, 45, 346;
purchase of Louisiana Territory by, 92,
101, 106; and the quarrel with Hamiltonian Federalists, 45, 83–86; republican
anti-militarism of, 88–89; and slavery,
107; and the threat of manufacturing
to virtue, 43–44, 346
John Birch Society, 168, 233, 376
Johnson, Hiram, 158, 175
Johnson, Lyndon B., 231, 235, 268, 269–
271, 280, 292; and the Civil Rights
Act [1964], 380; and the congressional
"blank check" after Tonkin incident,
318; and the controversy over John F.
Kennedy's Vietnam commitment,
264–266, 381–382; and the Vietnam
"quagmire," 269–271
Jordan, David Starr, 131, 136
Jung, Harry, 374

Kaiser Wilhelm II, 123, 135
Kellogg, Frank, 176
Kellogg-Briand Pact (Pact of Paris [1928]),
176, 186, 188, 190, 191, 216
Kennan, George, 241, 243, 247, 378

Kennedy, John F., 235, 276; significance
of assassination of, 12, 262–270,
381–382
King, Martin Luther, Jr., 11, 267, 268
Kissinger, Henry, 241, 290, 305, 380;
détente policy of, 271; foreign policy
"style" of, 282–283; on moralism of
U.S. foreign policy, 261; on Nixon, 382;
and "Vietnamization" policy, 276–277;
views on foreign policy of, 386, 388
Knox, Philander, 140–142, 158, 159, 163, 364
Ku Klux Klan, 8, 168, 171, 228, 365

LaFeber, Walter, 73, 352
LaFollette, Robert, 154, 361
Lansing, Robert, 157, 160, 161, 164, 363,
364, 365, 373
League of Nations, 14, 15, 144, 149, 152, 153,
249; American failure to support, 154–
158, 171, 207, 208; and American fear
of "entangling alliances," 158, 161–162,
252; American people's attitude toward,
169; Article 10 controversy of, 160–162;
Covenant of, 158, 159, 170, 188, 364;
Henry Stimson's regrets concerning,
187, 190; and the Japanese invasion of
Manchuria crisis, 182, 186, 192; Japan
resigns from, 191; origin of idea of,
364; Senate battle over, 158–163, 189;
and the United Nations Organization,
209, 251–252; and the virtue-power
dilemma, 158, 164, 170. See also
Wilson, Woodrow
Lee, Richard Henry, 76
Lee, Robert E., 10
Leffler, Melvyn, 68, 212, 332
Lewis, Sinclair, 170
Liberalism: and American mythology, 6–
7, 21; anti-communist version of, 389;
conservative challenge to, 239; economic version of, 49, 70; and fascism,
181; Hitler's view of, 180; ideological
content of, 19; in Japan, 185; of the Left,
232, 306; New Deal redefinition of,
225–226, 374; and republicanism, 33,
37, 50, 345–346; Straussian "crisis" of,
342; "structural" version of, 260; and
virtue, 43, 51–52, 54, 348

Liliuokalani, Queen, 125
Lincoln, Abraham, 106–111, 145, 291, 354, 356; and American mythology, 4, 11, 22, 52; and constitutionalism, 351
Lindbergh, Charles, 196
Link, Arthur, 150
Locke, John, 42, 344, 345, 346; and American liberalism, 6, 7, 33, 41; economic theory of, 346; Jefferson's reverence for, 44; and the theory of peaceful settlement, 111–114, 349, 356; views on riches and power of, 38
Lodge, Henry Cabot, 131, 132, 165, 166, 169, 170, 174, 364; animosity between Woodrow Wilson and, 162; and the "irreconcilable" senators, 158; role in defeating William H. Taft's arbitration treaties, 142; role in the Washington Treaties of 1921, 175
Lowi, Theodore, 266

MacArthur, Arthur, 138
MacArthur, Douglas, 249, 250
Machiavelli, Niccolò, 34, 76, 202
Madison, James, 35, 46, 93, 108; and American mission, 3; influence of Dissenting thought on, 345; as Jefferson's secretary of state, 101; on the separation of church and state, 57; "solution" to the problem of manufacturing and virtue, 43, 48; views on frontier expansion of, 117, 347; views on Montesquieu of, 35, 343; views on virtue of, 354; and the virtue-power dichotomy, 39–41
Mahan, Alfred Thayer, 129–131, 133, 200, 202, 359
Marshall, George, 243, 305
Marshall, John, 112–114
Marshall Plan, 79, 234, 244, 247
Marvin, Lee, 358
Masaryk, Jan, 244
McCarran, Pat, 230, 375
McCarran Committee, 379
McCarthy, Joseph, 246, 265; fall of, 377–378; and "McCarthyism," 168, 230, 235, 239, 270, 369
McCormick, Thomas, J., 201, 352
McKinley, William, 138, 144, 150, 352, 362;

annexure of Hawaii and the Philippines by, 127; and the Boxer rebellion, 359; and the Cuban revolution, 126; defeat of William Jennings Bryan by, 121; defense of imperialism by, 106; economic goals of, 127–128; and the "Imperial presidency," 73, 259
McKinley Tariff Act [1890], 74
Mexican Revolution, 151
Mexican War of 1846, 12, 103–104, 108
Monroe, James, 44, 47, 89, 91, 96, 347, 349; and the "era of good feelings," 93; purchase of Florida by, 101
Monroe Doctrine, 82, 92, 93–95, 99, 103, 142, 201, 354; and Japan's "Monroe Doctrine for Asia," 186, 368; Theodore Roosevelt's corollary to, 134, 140, 150
Montesquieu, Charles de Secondat, 24, 36, 50, 79, 112; influence of in American Revolution, 343–344; John Adams' criticism of, 53; and the origins of economic internationalism, 75–76, 79; views on republican virtue, 34–35, 343
Morgan, J. P., 70, 352
Mussolini, Benito, 178–180

Napoleon, 90, 92, 100, 101
Napoleon III, 99
New Deal, 209, 244, 246, 347; agrarian philosophy of, 348; conservative anticommunist reaction to, 221, 223–226, 229–232, 235, 237, 374, 376; relation of Communist Party and cultural front to, 226–227, 228–229; and the Universal Declaration of Human Rights, 256
New Right, 231, 234, 365, 376, 377
Niebuhr, Reinhold, 192, 369
Nietzsche, Friedrich, 163, 365
Nine Power Treaty, 174, 188
Nixon, Richard, 235, 250, 269, 271, 305, 326, 379, 386; Carter rejects foreign policy of, 283; and détente policy, 271, 281–282; devaluation of the dollar by, 280; envy of Kennedy of, 268, 382; and the Nixon Doctrine, 281, 293; "Vietnamization" policy of, 276–277;

and virtue-power dilemma, 276; and the Watergate scandal, 271

Non-Intercourse Act [1809], 90

North Atlantic Treaty Organization (NATO), 230, 233, 234, 244, 259, 307, 308, 378

Nye, Gerald P., 73, 196, 352, 366

"One Hundred Percent Americanism," 168

Open Door Policy, 174, 207, 359; coercive consequences of, 72; Japanese threat to in China, 186; Japan's resentment of, 184–185; John Hay's proposal for, 130; public enthusiasm for, 130–131; Stimson's appreciation of, 187; Taft's attempt to realize in China, 141

Overing, Joanna, 340

Paine, Tom, 24–26, 34, 75, 76, 87, 341, 352

Paley, William, 111

Palmer, Robert, 20

Perry, Commodore Matthew, 73, 182

Platt Amendment, 127, 194

Pocock, J. G. A., 41, 343, 345, 347, 348

Polk, James, 102–105, 108, 127, 270, 355, 356

Pope, John, 110

Powell Doctrine (Weinberger-Powell Doctrine), 300, 301, 303, 319

Power: American hegemony of, 16, 79, 201, 202, 247, 259, 292, 299, 327, 332, 344; American suspicion of, 2, 12–14, 32, 39–40, 137; America's rise to, 120–122; balancing of in the American political system, 34–36; and "conquest" of the West, 110–119; conservative views of, 233–235, 253; corrupting influence of, 61–63; credibility of American, 15, 262, 269, 297, 306, 331, 381; crisis of faith in America's use of, 240–241, 266, 269, 271–276, 278–281; danger of centralization of, 36, 45, 73, 87, 97, 98; of the executive, 33, 62, 88, 95, 133–134, 139, 146, 259, 304, 318, 362; fascism's view of, 177–179; Hamilton's attitude toward, 37–39; and law, 60–62, 118–119, 137–140; Henry Stimson's attitude toward,

187; international balancing of, 123, 133–134, 159, 161, 169, 175, 201, 256, 271; Madison and the abuse of, 39–40; military, fear of, 13, 60, 88–89, 204, 279, 303, 310; military, problem of use of, 278, 300, 302, 332; and patriotic pride, 29–30, 65, 82, 90, 201; problem of virtue and, 2, 12, 14–15, 50, 60–61, 122, 133, 158, 170, 177, 266, 269; realist views of, 192, 202–203; Theodore Roosevelt's attitude toward, 124, 133–134, 139; Truman's attitude toward, 241–243, 248; unilateralist versus multilateralist use of, 207; virtuous use of, 182, 199, 204–205, 207–210, 220, 237, 239, 242, 253, 259; Woodrow Wilson's attitude toward, 77, 144, 148, 150, 157, 162–164

Price, Richard, 24, 25, 341

Progressive Movement, 19, 74, 121–122, 134, 139, 163, 347, 361

Progressive ("Bull Moose") Party, 362

Read, Leonard, 215

Reagan, Ronald, 1, 235, 267, 289–296, 377, 386, 389; and American mythology, 293; and the "evil empire," 219; foreign policy actions of, 293–294, 386; foreign policy views of, 289–291; human rights policy of, 291; and the Iran-Contra scandal, 295; Jeane Kirkpatrick's influence on, 289–291; and the Reagan Doctrine, 293–294, 386; rhetoric of, 385; role of in ending the Cold War, 295–296; Strategic Defense ("Star Wars") Initiative of, 295, 308

Regnery, William, 374

Remington, Frederic, 115, 133

Republicanism, 32, 49, 50, 158, 343; American views of, 33; ideological content of, 19; and liberalism (see Liberalism); and virtue, 13, 34–35, 37, 41, 49–53, 115

Republican Party (Jeffersonian). See Jefferson, Thomas

Republican Party (GOP), 111, 118, 138, 209, 286, 307, 325, 362; birth of, 108; China lobby and, 245; and Cold War blame, 241; and colonization of the

Republican Party (GOP) (continued)
Philippines, 132; and the congressional victory of 1946, 236; conservative ascendancy in, 279, 304; "fusion conservatism" and the New Right in, 231–232, 234, 376; Henry Cabot Lodge and, 162; and human rights policy, 290; the "irreconcilable" senators in (see League of Nations); isolationist temptations of, 237; and the Korean War, 250; "machismo" foreign policy style of, 236, 304; moderate (liberal) wing of, 209, 235, 279; neoconservative influence in, 16, 234, 316, 317, 320, 389; Right wing of, 218, 229, 231, 266, 279, 282, 296, 304; Robert A. Taft as leader of, 226; "rollback" policy of, 218, 235, 250, 292–293; "Southern Strategy" of, 231, 233; Theodore Roosevelt's relationship with, 133, 138, 143; and the Truman Doctrine, 243; victory in 1896 of, 121; and the virtue-power dilemma, 279
Robeson, Paul, 227
Roosevelt, Eleanor, 256, 369
Roosevelt, Franklin D., 73, 191, 202, 246, 292, 347, 348, 375; agrarian sympathies of, 51; and America First, 369–370; and assistance to Britain at war, 197, 370; and the Atlantic Charter, 207–208; and the beginning of the Cold War, 218, 238; and Chang Kai-shek, 371; Good Neighbor Policy of, 194; on investing U.S. power, 199; and the New Deal, 221, 223–230, 373; and the new realism, 202; and Pat McCarran, 375; policy toward Japan of, 198; recognizes Soviet Union, 194; rejection of unilateralism by, 165; and relations with Stalin and Churchill, 208, 371; and the Soviet alliance, 217; and the United Nations, 208–210; weak foreign policy of, 79, 193
Roosevelt, Theodore, 114, 138, 139, 146, 149, 184, 189; agrarian sympathies of, 51; attitude toward Constitution of (see Constitution of the United States); disappointment in Philippine adventure of, 133; expansion of Monroe Doctrine by (see Monroe Doctrine); and fear of corruption of virtue, 133; influence of Mahan on, 131; and mythology of masculine power, 119, 124, 133–134; participation of in Cuban War, 126; racism of, 10, 145; "realism" of, 14; rejection of "Dollar Diplomacy" by, 125; role of in Great Power politics, 134–135, 184; wins the Nobel Peace Prize, 135, 360
Root, Elihu, 141, 158, 362, 363
Rosenberg, Ethel, 230
Rosenberg, Julius, 230
Rousseau, Jean-Jacques, 12, 50–53, 62, 348, 351
Russian Revolution, 152, 155, 372

Schaefer, Jack, 358
Schöpflin, George, 341
Schurz, Carl, 131, 360
Seward, William H., 73, 104
Sherman, William T., 114, 357
Singer Company, 70
Sino-Japanese war of 1894–1895, 130
Sino-Japanese war of 1937, 195
Sklar, Martin, 352
Slotkin, Richard, 338, 358
Smith, Adam, 42, 74, 346
Smith, Rogers, 19
Soviet Union (Union of Soviet Socialist Republics), 172, 200–223, 252, 255, 271, 282, 286, 294, 307, 369, 383; and American hypocrisy, 233; collapse of, 219–220, 295–296, 332; and "competitive coexistence," 214–219; and the Cuban missile crisis, 267; and détente, 219, 271, 282; effects of Great Depression on U.S. relations with, 214–217; "expansive imperialism" of, 206–207; exploitation of U.S. racism by, 254–255; and foundation of NATO, 230; and the global balance of power, 256–257; Gorbachev's reform of, 295; Hitler's attack on, 197; ideological challenge of, 168, 181, 200–202, 211–214; invasion of Afghanistan by, 287–288, 385; invasion of Czechoslovakia by, 219; and Middle Eastern politics, 281, 284; and New Deal liberalism (see New Deal); and

Korea, 247–251; and nonaggression pact with Nazi Germany, 196, 217, 369; and the Sino-Soviet split, 269; and "socialism in one country," 214; and Spanish Civil War, 195; spying on U.S. by, 230, 375, 379; and start of Cold War, 218, 238–239, 371; and Strategic Arms Limitation Talks (SALT), 282; universalism of, 28, 181; and the U.N. Security Council, 249, 251–252; U.S. Cold War responses to, 241–247; U.S. containment of (*see* Cold War); U.S. recognition of, 194; U.S. wartime alliance with, 217, 232, 238

Spanish-American War of *1898*, 8, 129, 135, 136, 360, 362

Stalin, Josef, 172, 213, 230, 242, 371, 374; becomes "Uncle Joe," 217; and Berlin blockade, 245; breaks promise on Poland, 238; creates Cominform, 244; death of, 250; and the Korean War, 248, 251; meets with Truman, 238–239; and the nonaggression pact with Hitler, 196, 217; opposition to the Marshall Plan, 244; Popular Front proposal of, 227; ruthless image of, 218; and "socialism in one country," 214; and start of Cold War, 210, 372; at wartime meetings of "Big Three," 208, 377

Standard Oil Company, 70

Stanton, Elizabeth Cady, 11, 339

Stewart, James, 358

Stimson, Henry L., 186–191, 193, 368; on the exemplary justice of the Open Door policy, 191; and the Japanese crisis, 186–187; on the Monroe Doctrine, 368; recommends dropping atomic bomb on Japan, 191; on the "reign of law rather than power," 187; on the spirit of Christianity, 205; and the virtue-power dilemma, 187–191

Taft, Robert A., 198, 236, 317; as a "liberal conservative," 226, 373–374; and the foreign policy consequences of conservative anti-communism, 233–234

Taft, William Howard, 124–125, 132, 138–143, 150, 226; belief in world peace through international arbitration, 141–142; defeated by Senate, 142–143; "Dollar Diplomacy" of, 77, 125, 140–141; as Governor-General of the Philippines, 133; on primacy of rule of law, 139; sense of U.S. national interest of, 361; traditional view of American mission of, 138

Tocqueville, Alexis de, 53, 96, 112, 339

Treaty of Versailles, 157, 158, 170, 193, 196

Trevor, John, 374

Trollope, Fanny, 9, 339

Trotsky, Leon, 314, 389

Truman, Harry, 191, 202, 208, 235, 241–252, 267, 270, 378; assumes responsibility for balance of power with Truman Doctrine, 243, 256; Jeffersonian faith of, 241–242; and Korean War, 247–250; and the "loss" of China, 245–246; and McCarthyism, 230, 231, 239; and the militarization of U.S. foreign policy, 251; and National Security Council document NSC-68, 247; political use of anti-communism by, 244; rejection of unilateralism, 165, 207; relations with Stalin of, 238, 377; and the start of the Cold War, 256; use of United Nations, 249, 380; willingness to use U.S. power to underwrite international order, 199, 203; wins presidential election of *1948*, 236

Truman Doctrine, 231, 243, 256, 257

Tugwell, Rexford, G., 348

Turgot, A.-R.-J., 25

Turner, Frederick Jackson, 116, 119, 338, 358

Twain, Mark, 131, 134

Tydings-McDuffie Act [1934], 193

United Nations Organization, 237, 259, 300; and American virtue, 251–256; anti-Americanism in, 277; conservative hostility toward, 16, 162, 254–256, 299, 321; founding of, 209; George H. W. Bush's masterful use of, 298, 386; and human rights as cause for intervention, 306, 310; and the Iraq War, 310, 315, 324, 325; Jeane Kirkpatrick's disdain

United Nations Organization (*continued*) for, 290; and the Soviet Union, 210; tested by "police action" in Korea, 247–248; undermining effects of Cold War on, 221, 240, 243; and the Universal Declaration of Human Rights, 254–256; and virtuous American power, 221

United States foreign policy: and economic nationalism versus liberal internationalism, 3, 70, 78, 80, 177, 208, 217, 228; and hypocrisy, 2, 9, 10, 28, 94, 97, 105, 233, 255, 285, 286, 324, 328; and isolationism (*see* Isolationism); and the Monroe Doctrine (*see* Monroe Doctrine); and multilateralism, 15, 30, 165, 207, 259, 280, 282, 290, 293; and the Open Door Policy (*see* Open Door Policy); and Powell Doctrine (*see* Powell Doctrine); and racism, 3, 10, 19, 104, 105, 120, 129, 146, 168, 180, 196, 227, 228, 232, 233, 255, 272, 356, 377; and realism versus idealism, 2–3, 14, 29–30, 63, 129, 160, 167, 170, 173, 181, 190–193, 202–203, 274–276, 279–281, 283, 290, 332; and self-interest versus selflessness, 65, 76, 129, 131, 137, 143–144, 148, 157, 188; traditions of, 3; and unilateralism, 15, 30, 165, 207, 300

Vattel, Emeric de, 111

Vietnam War, 17, 203, 261–277, 324; bitter lesson of, 286; causes loss of public trust, 280–281; and the "credibility" of American power, 262, 269; effect of on American exceptionalist mission, 261, 269; effect of on rhetoric of "American values," 256, 258, 285, 287, 312; effects of McCarthyism on, 270; effects of on virtue-power dilemma, 2, 15, 17, 262, 271–272, 275–276, 279–280, 303, 331; and the "falling domino" theory, 263; Hans Morgenthau's warning on, 274, 383; "humbling lesson" of, 1, 278, 337; and the Iraq War compared, 318, 320–322, 324; and Nixon's "peace with honor" promise, 271, 275; origins of U.S. involvement in, 263–264; prefig-

ured in the Philippine war, 124, 132; produces uncertainty about U.S. use of military power, 16, 278, 288, 293, 303–304; question of American atrocities in, 272–274, 383; Reagan's "noble cause" view of, 292; shatters the "liberal consensus" on foreign policy, 209, 280; and Tonkin Gulf "incident," 270; "Vietnamization" of, 276; and the "Vietnam syndrome," 274, 279, 297, 300, 306

Villard, Oswald Garrison, 170; and *The Nation*, 170, 173

Virtue: American conceptions of, 12–13, 32–34, 41–42, 50–60; and the American frontier, 60, 100, 111, 115, 117–119, 124, 133, 347; civic (republican) form of, 19, 32–50, 89, 348; and equality, 34, 46–47, 50, 51–52, 105, 110; fear of corruption of, 13–14, 23, 24, 32, 33, 40, 42–44, 47–48, 49, 55, 61, 129–130, 133, 211, 217, 223, 239, 293, 303, 373; identified with the rule of law, 40, 61–63, 119, 137, 138, 147, 163–164, 177, 187, 190; of industry or hard work, 8, 34, 42, 44–45, 51–52, 54–55, 58, 348, 349, 350; and innocence (or "clean hands") (*see* Innocent Virtue); and liberty, 3–6, 12, 13, 25, 33–36, 40, 50, 51–52, 106, 147–148, 153; and martial virtue, 13, 59, 60, 119, 120, 122, 132, 143, 181, 262; and missionary spirit, 57–58; and power (*see* Power: problem of virtue and); and simplicity, 52–53; and success, 52

Voltaire, 23, 24

Wagner Act (National Labor Relations Act [1935]), 229, 375

Wallace, George, 231, 377

Wallace, Henry A., 73–75, 171, 347, 348, 369

Washington, George, 26, 35, 83, 87, 145, 192; and executive agreements, 254; and neutrality policy, 86; and the nonentanglement doctrine, 66–67, 86, 149

Washington Treaties of 1921, 173, 175, 186, 187, 190

Wayne, John, 115, 116, 118, 304, 358

Weinberg, Albert, 115, 337, 357
Weinberger, Caspar, 293, 300
Welch, Richard, 132, 160
Whitman, Walt, 224
Williams, William Appleman, 67, 201, 352
Wilson, Edmund, 170
Wilson, Woodrow, 1, 14, 141, 143–164, 166, 172, 173, 194, 199, 215, 267; agrarian sympathies of, 51; and the "American dream," 9; and the American exemplary mission, 145, 148, 157; and the Article 10 "mutual guaranty" controversy, 159–162; Carter compared to, 283; Clemenceau and, 160, 390; and the failure of neutrality policy, 154; Fourteen Points of, 157, 169, 207, 211; and the idea of a League of Nations, 157, 169, 207, 211, 364–365; and innocent virtue, 64; intervenes in revolutionary Russia, 367; Japanese dissatisfaction with, 185; Lenin mocks anti-imperialism of, 211; on the moral dangers of war, 156, 167–168, 364; naiveté of, 151; New Diplomacy of, 159; Nixon's rhetoric on, 276; organic metaphor of civil society of, 153; popular disillusionment with, 163–164, 169–171; and power as a necessary evil, 204; preserves the nonentanglement doctrine, 163; Progressivism of, 362; promises a New Freedom, 362; racist views of, 10; Reagan compared to, 293; rejection of isolationism by, 149; and religious dimension of American mission, 58; Secretary of State Lansing's view of, 160, 365; on selfishness and selflessness in foreign policy, 77, 125, 144, 148–149, 157; and the Senate battle over the Treaty of Versailles, 158, 163, 170, 364; and the Soviet challenge, 158, 168, 222, 364, 373; Truman's response to, 241; views on American nationalism of, 145–148, 363; views on Theodore Roosevelt of, 134; and the virtue-power dilemma, 144, 163–164, 363–364
"Wilsonianism," 3, 362; as "bourgeois sentimentalism," 211; of Condoleezza Rice, 328; Fukuyama advocates "realistic" form of, 332; Kissinger's definition of, 261; neoconservative brand of, 317, 389; Nixon blames Vietnam War on, 271; postwar hopes of realization of, 203
Wood, Gordon, 26, 33, 39, 41
Wood, Robert E., 196, 374
World War I, 12, 96, 138, 223, 269
World War II, 12, 15, 17, 79, 86, 162, 217, 298; American attitude to power and virtue changed by, 206–207, 220, 236–237, 261, 272, 299, 303, 304, 331; collective security fear, conditions persist after, 252; crushing of German and Japanese might in, 278; effect of on U.S. anti-communism, 232; defeat of Japanese in, 247; friendship with Soviet Union during, 238; G. H. W. Bush draws imagery from, 297–298; G.I. Bill for veterans of, 377; interpreting Soviet intentions after, 212; Kissinger's view of foreign policy options after, 386; liberal foreign policy consensus after, 334; memorial of, 330; militarization of U.S. after, 280; opportunity to create new world order after, 335; and the Powell Doctrine, 303; Stalin blames "monopoly capitalism" for, 210